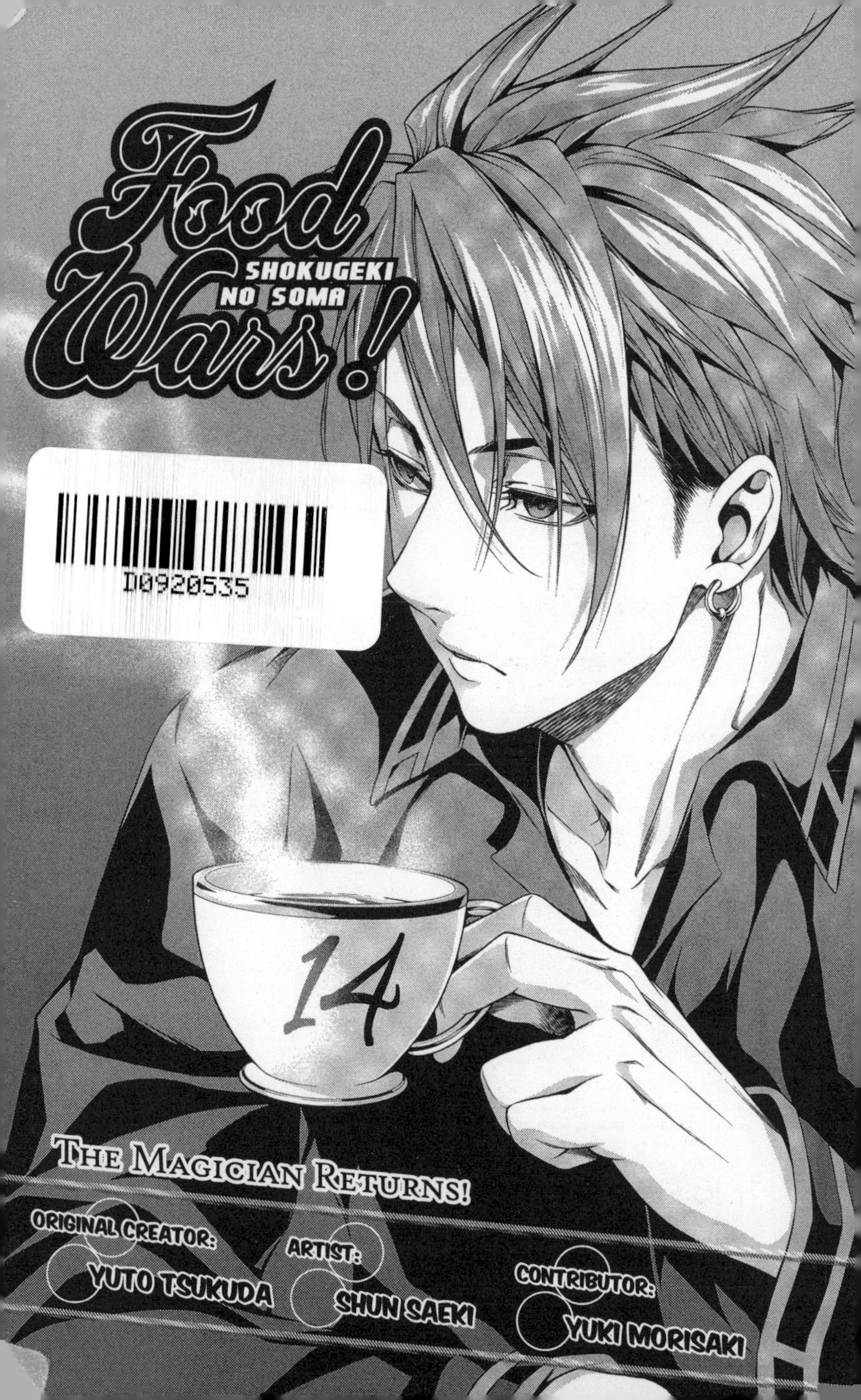
Food Wars!
SHOKUGEKI NO SOMA
14
THE MAGICIAN RETURNS!
ORIGINAL CREATOR: YUTO TSUKUDA
ARTIST: SHUN SAEKI
CONTRIBUTOR: YUKI MORISAKI

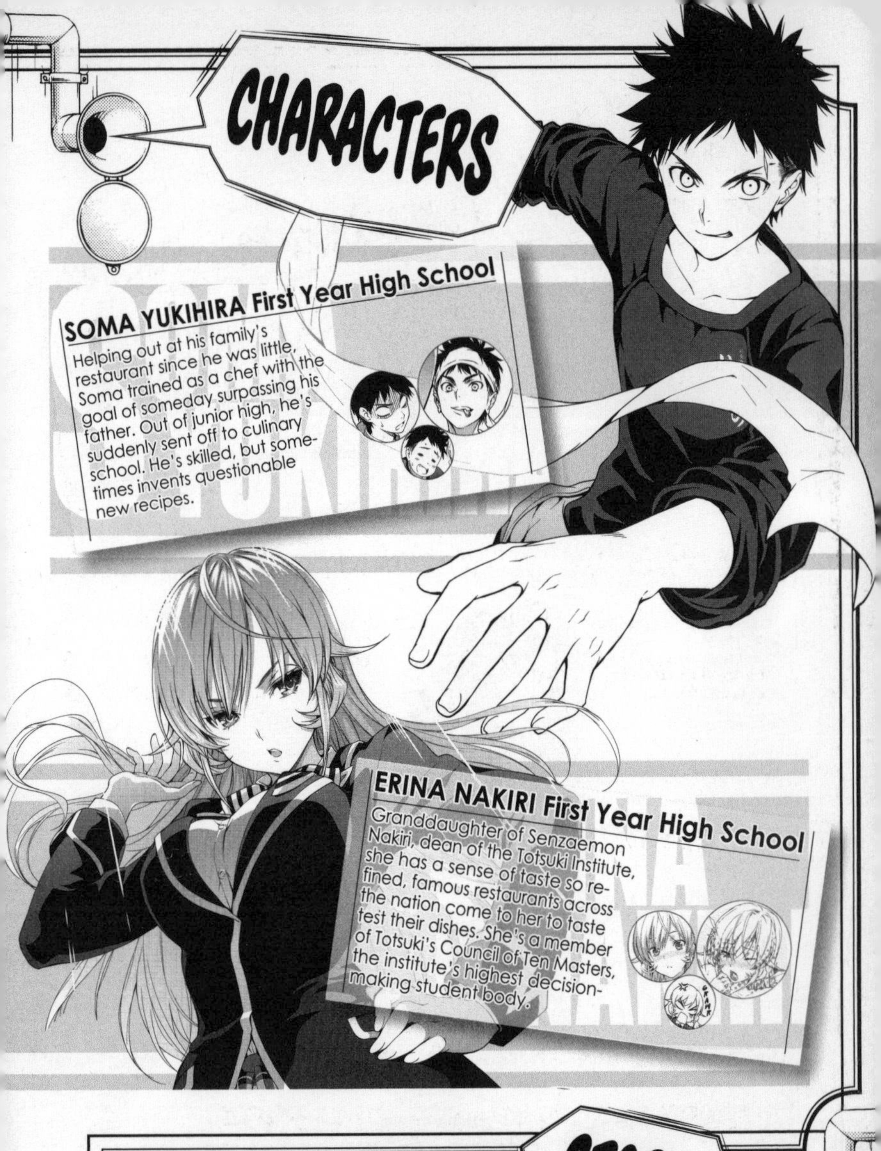
CHARACTERS
SOMA YUKIHIRA First Year High School
Helping out at his family's restaurant since he was little, Soma trained as a chef with the goal of someday surpassing his father. Out of junior high, he's suddenly sent off to culinary school. He's skilled, but sometimes invents questionable new recipes.
ERINA NAKIRI First Year High School
Granddaughter of Senzaemon Nakiri, dean of the Totsuki Institute, she has a sense of taste so refined, famous restaurants across the nation come to her to taste test their dishes. She's a member of Totsuki's Council of Ten Masters, the institute's highest decision-making student body.

## STORY

Soma grew up helping to cook at his family's restaurant, Yukihira. But one day his father enrolled him in Japan's premier culinary school, the Totsuki Institute. Having met other students as skilled as he is and with similar goals, Soma has grown a little as a chef.

With Akira Hayama declared winner of the Fall Classic, everyone takes a step back to reflect upon the long competition and what they learned from it. But after only a monthlong break, all first-year students are tossed into their next trial—the stagiaire challenge! To pass, they must achieve a visible accomplishment. After passing the first trial, Soma moves on to his second location—the new restaurant being opened by Chef Shinomiya himself!

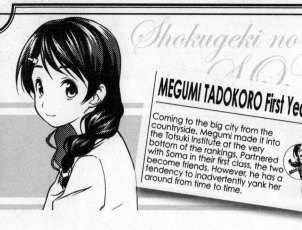

*Shokugeki no SOMA*

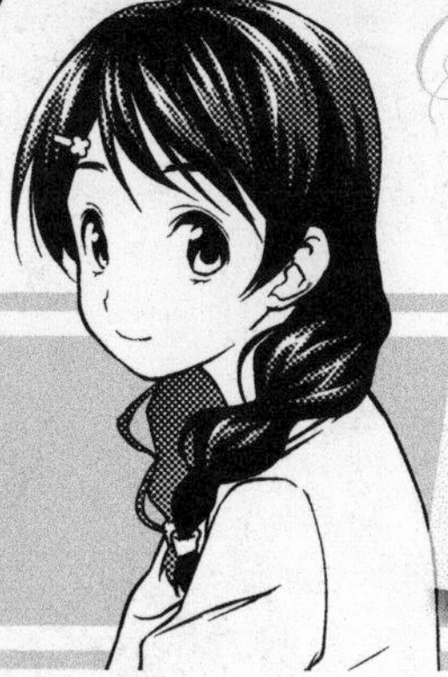

## MEGUMI TADOKORO First Year High School

Coming to the big city from the countryside, Megumi made it into the Totsuki Institute at the very bottom of the rankings. Partnered with Soma in their first class, the two become friends. However, he has a tendency to inadvertently yank her around from time to time.

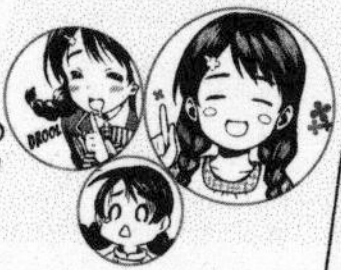

## SHUN IBUSAKI First Year High School

A resident of Polaris Dormitory, he doesn't talk much. With a talent for smoking foods, his dishes are first-class.

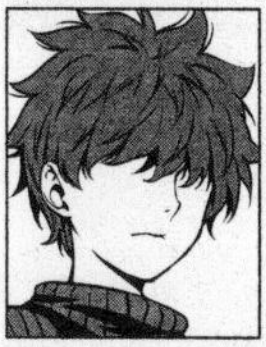

## YUKI YOSHINO First Year High School

A resident of Polaris Dormitory, she raises game animals on campus. Bright and cheerful, she is the energetic one of the Polaris bunch.

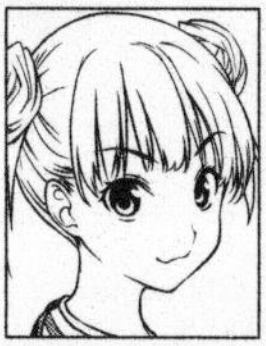

## TAKUMI ALDINI First Year High School

Working at his family's trattoria in Italy from a young age, he transferred into the Totsuki Institute in junior high. Isami is his younger twin brother

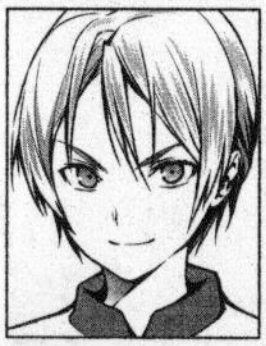

## AKIRA HAYAMA First Year High School

A master of spices and the winner of the Fall Classic, Hayama grew up as an orphan in a Southeast Asian slum, where Jun Shiomi found and adopted him.

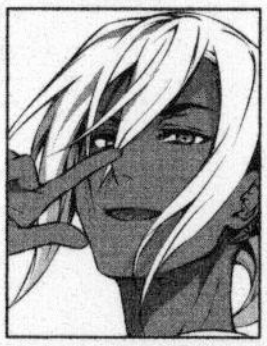

## RYO KUROKIBA First Year High School

Alice's aide, he specializes in powerful, savory seafood dishes. His personality changes drastically when he puts on his bandanna.

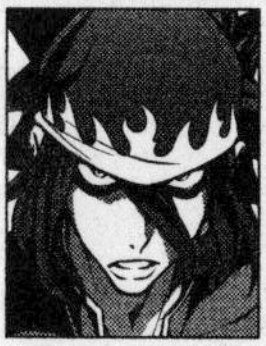

## KOJIRO SHINOMIYA

A Totsuki Institute graduate, Shinomiya is an exceptional cook who was once the first seat. Currently, he is working on opening a branch of his restaurant, Shino's, in Tokyo.

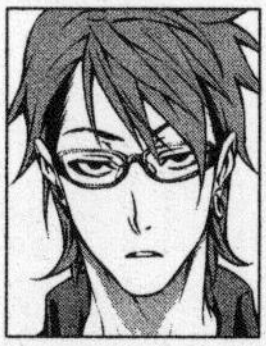

Food Wars! SHOKUGEKI NO SOMA 14

# Table of Contents

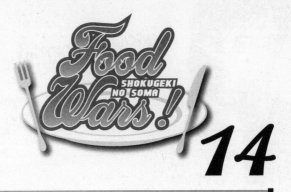

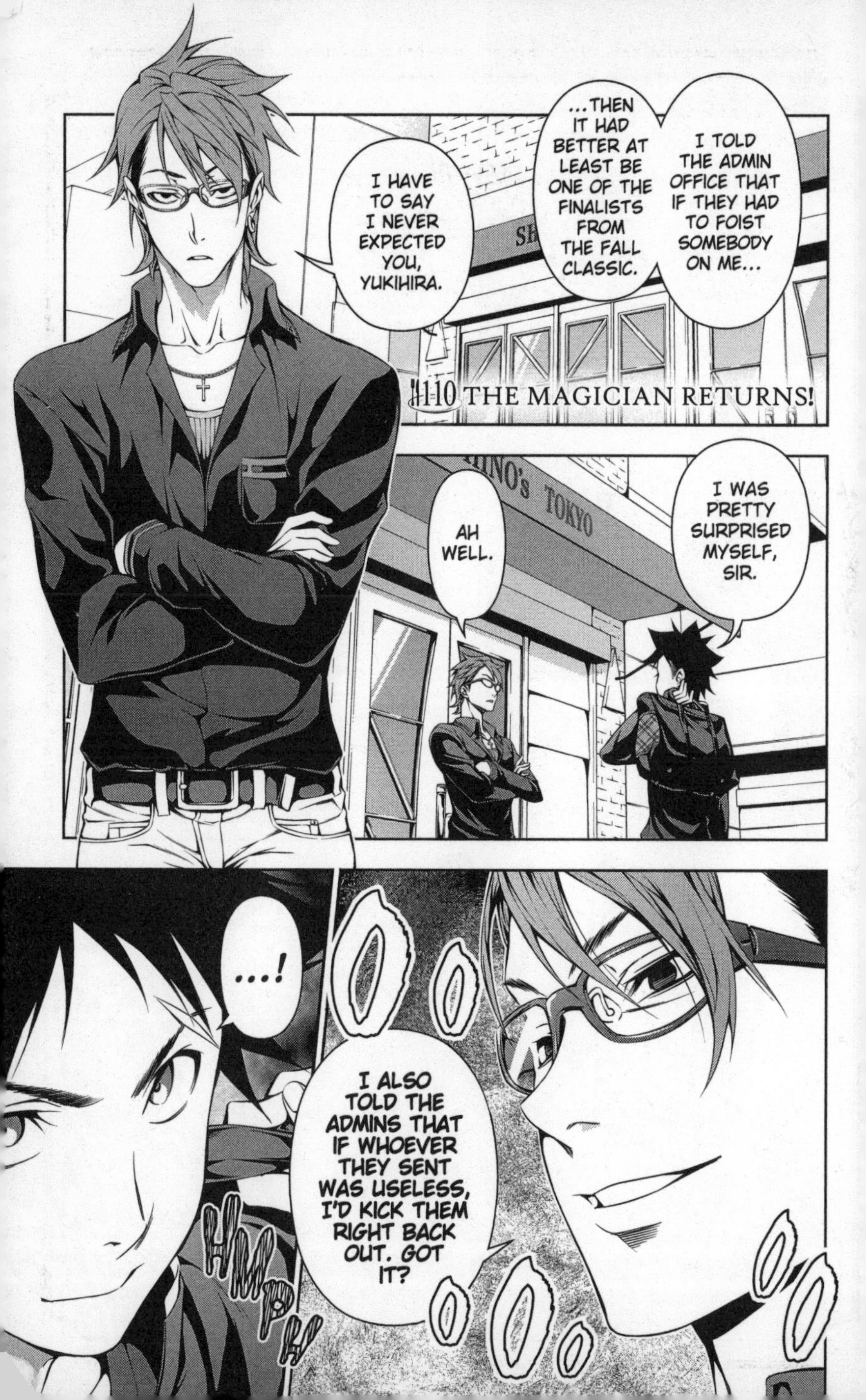

I TOLD THE ADMIN OFFICE THAT IF THEY HAD TO FOIST SOMEBODY ON ME...
...THEN IT HAD BETTER AT LEAST BE ONE OF THE FINALISTS FROM THE FALL CLASSIC.
I HAVE TO SAY I NEVER EXPECTED YOU, YUKIHIRA.
#110 THE MAGICIAN RETURNS!
I WAS PRETTY SURPRISED MYSELF, SIR.
AH WELL.
I ALSO TOLD THE ADMINS THAT IF WHOEVER THEY SENT WAS USELESS, I'D KICK THEM RIGHT BACK OUT. GOT IT?
...!
HMPH!

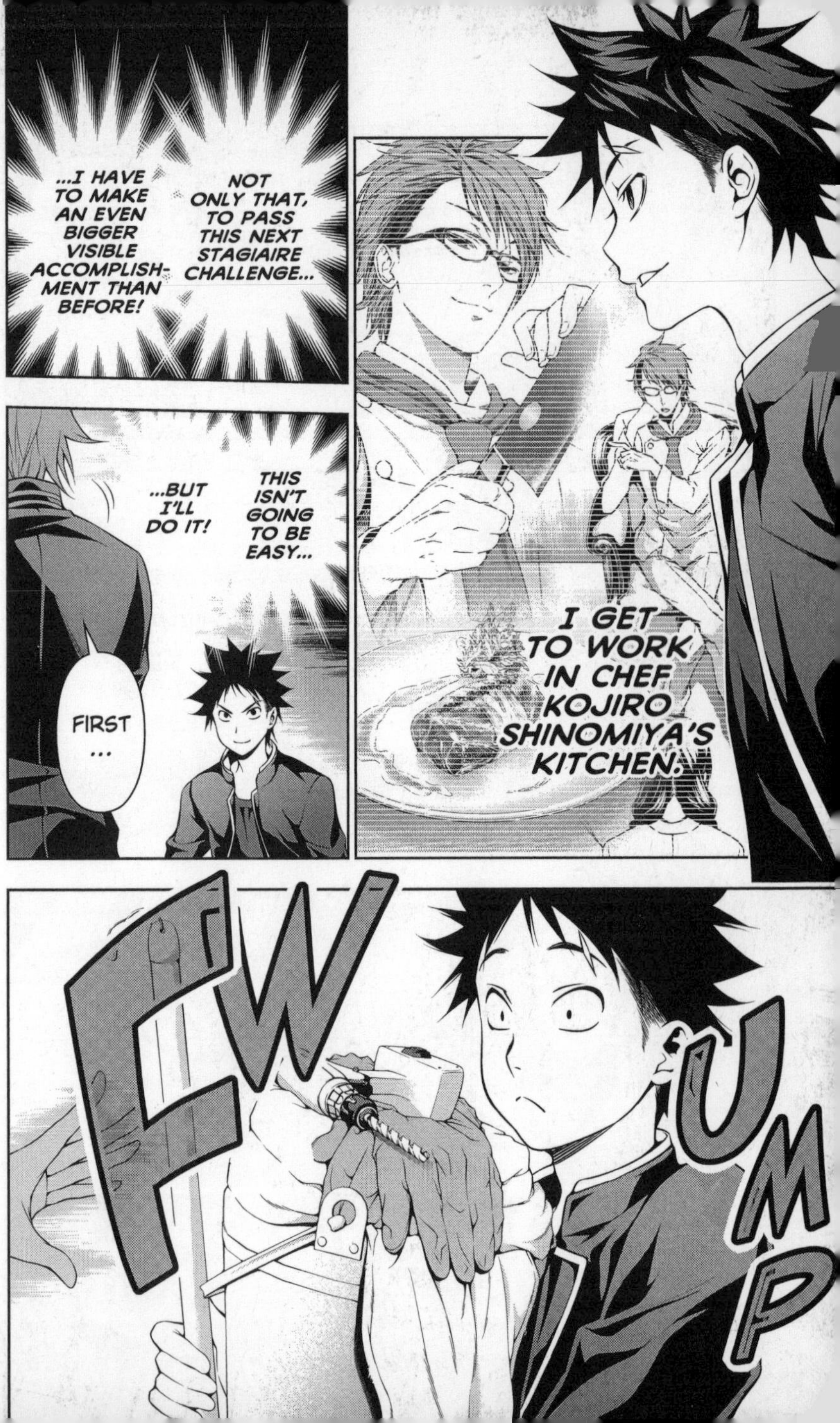
I GET TO WORK IN CHEF KOJIRO SHINOMIYA'S KITCHEN.
NOT ONLY THAT, TO PASS THIS NEXT STAGIAIRE CHALLENGE...
...I HAVE TO MAKE AN EVEN BIGGER VISIBLE ACCOMPLISHMENT THAN BEFORE!
THIS ISN'T GOING TO BE EASY...
...BUT I'LL DO IT!
FIRST...
FWUMP

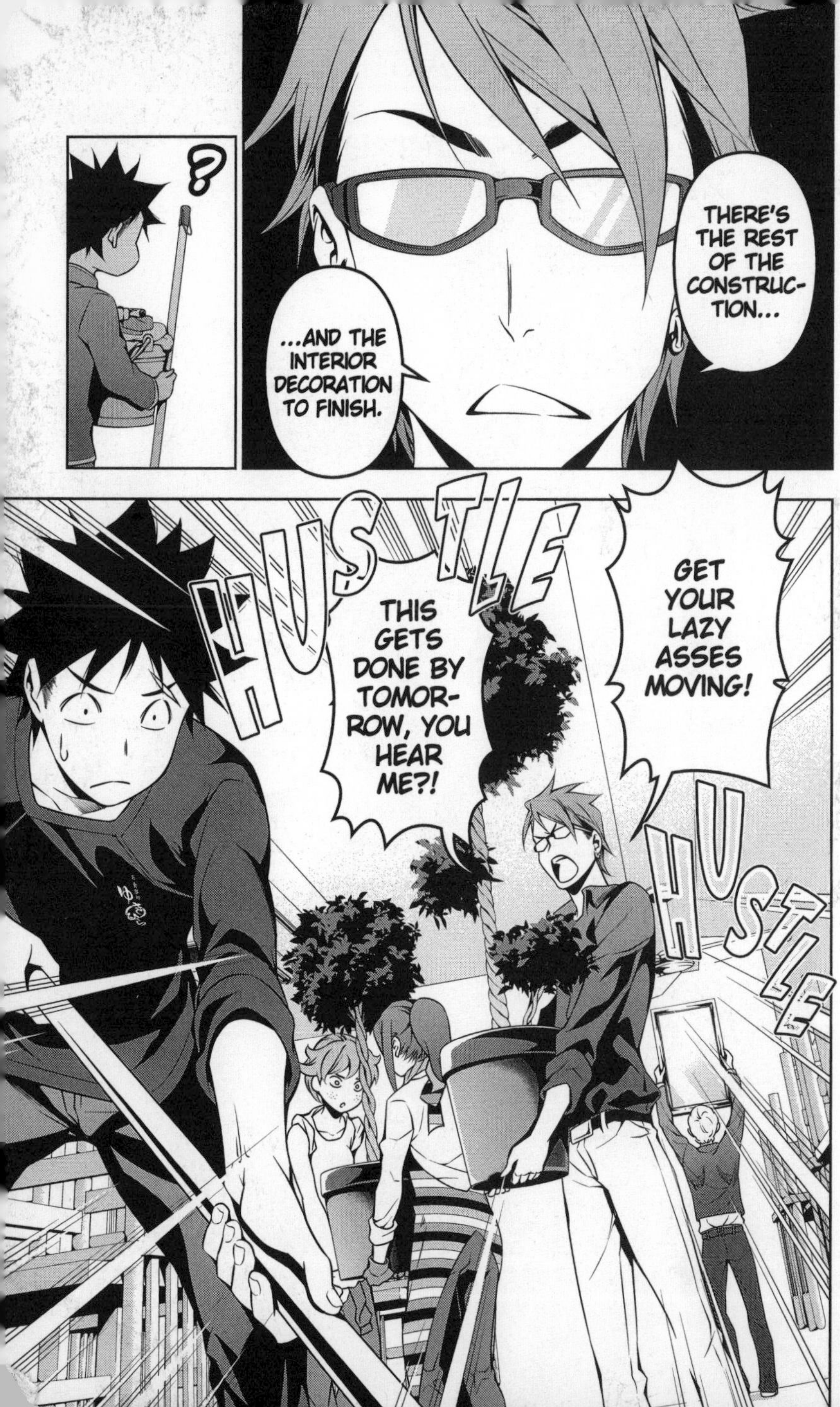

THERE'S THE REST OF THE CONSTRUCTION...
...AND THE INTERIOR DECORATION TO FINISH.
?
GET YOUR LAZY ASSES MOVING!
HUSTLE
THIS GETS DONE BY TOMORROW, YOU HEAR ME?!
HUSTLE

# 110 THE MAGICIAN RETURNS!

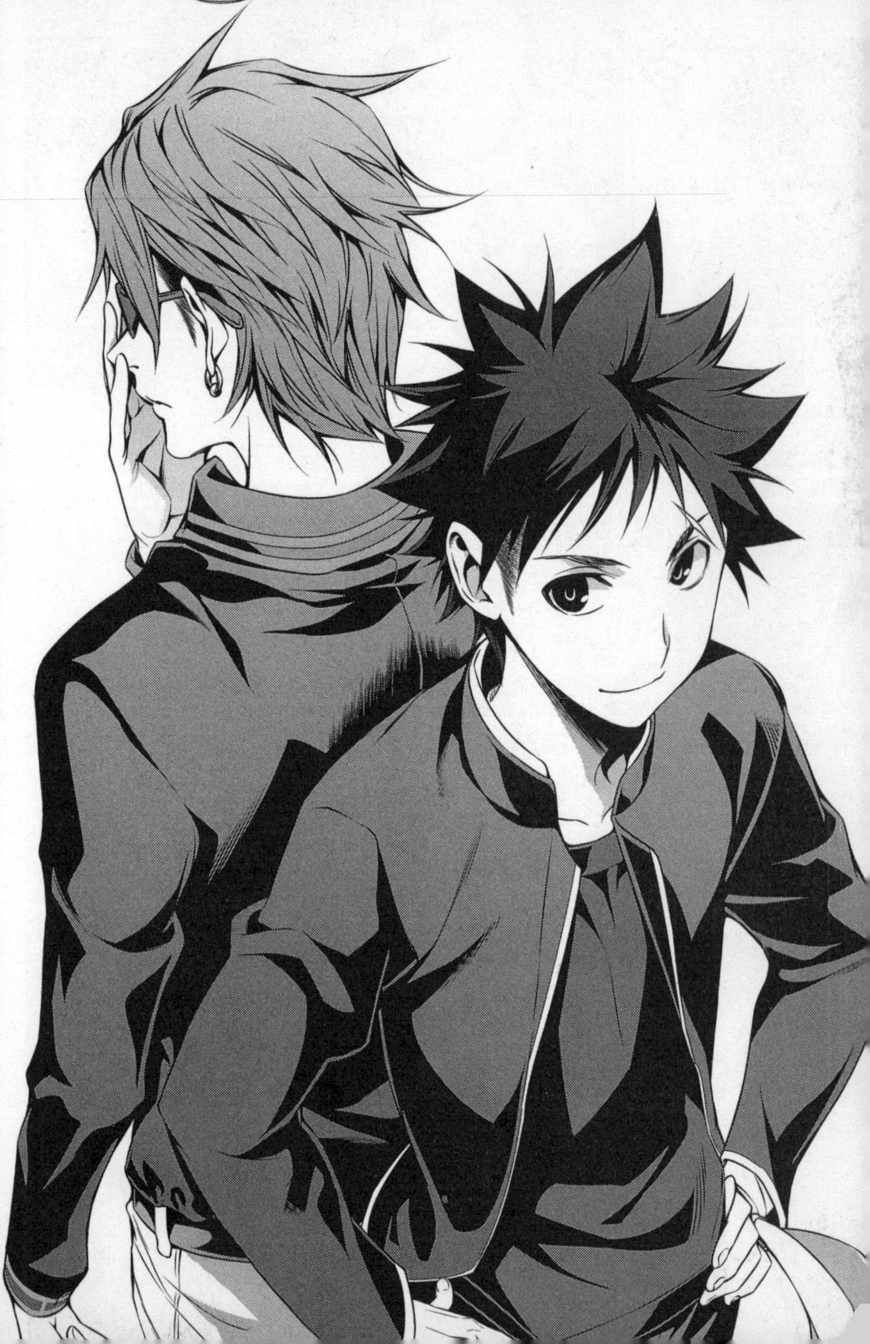

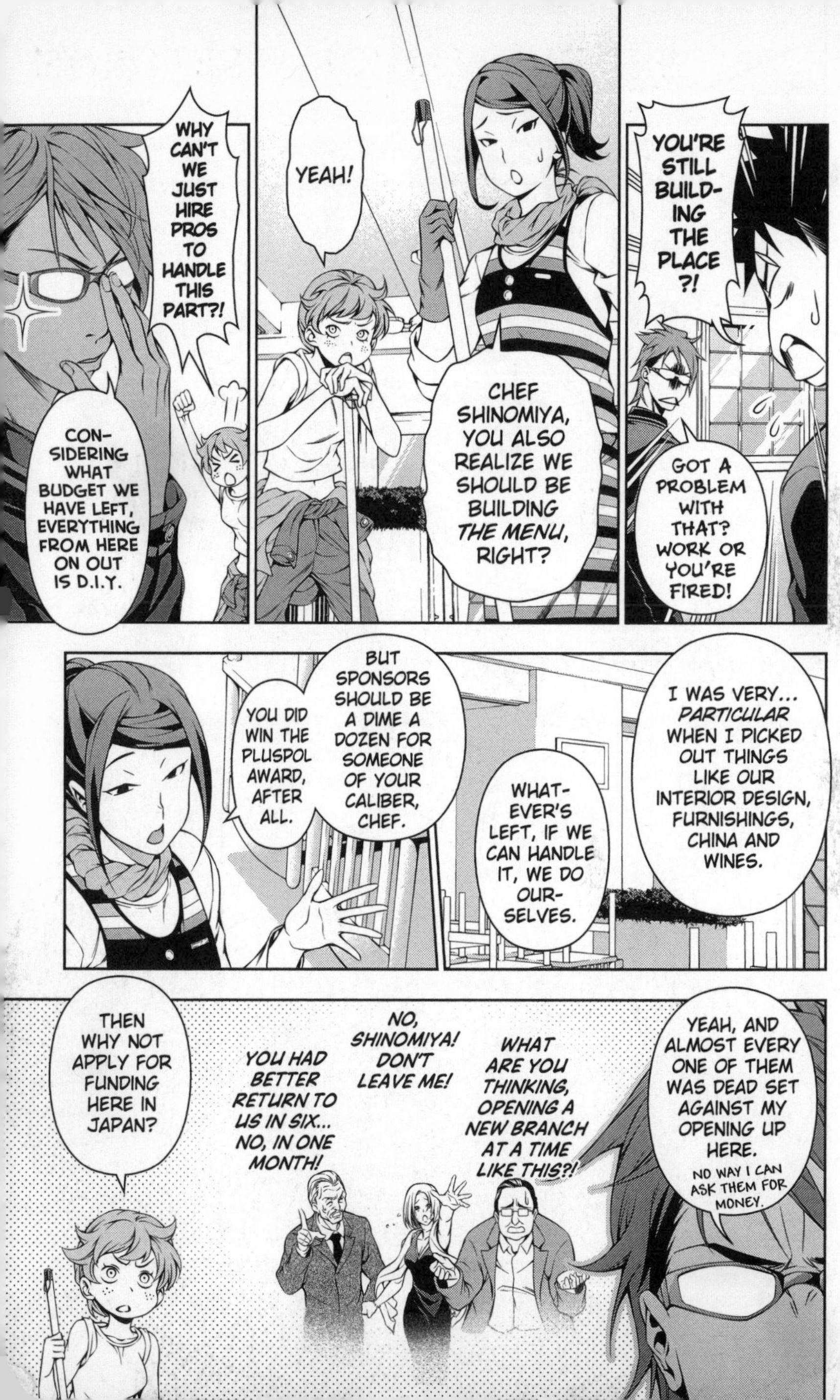
YOU'RE STILL BUILDING THE PLACE?!
GOT A PROBLEM WITH THAT? WORK OR YOU'RE FIRED!
YEAH!
CHEF SHINOMIYA, YOU ALSO REALIZE WE SHOULD BE BUILDING THE MENU, RIGHT?
WHY CAN'T WE JUST HIRE PROS TO HANDLE THIS PART?!
CONSIDERING WHAT BUDGET WE HAVE LEFT, EVERYTHING FROM HERE ON OUT IS D.I.Y.
I WAS VERY... PARTICULAR WHEN I PICKED OUT THINGS LIKE OUR INTERIOR DESIGN, FURNISHINGS, CHINA AND WINES.
WHATEVER'S LEFT, IF WE CAN HANDLE IT, WE DO OURSELVES.
BUT SPONSORS SHOULD BE A DIME A DOZEN FOR SOMEONE OF YOUR CALIBER, CHEF.
YOU DID WIN THE PLUSPOL AWARD, AFTER ALL.
YEAH, AND ALMOST EVERY ONE OF THEM WAS DEAD SET AGAINST MY OPENING UP HERE.
NO WAY I CAN ASK THEM FOR MONEY.
WHAT ARE YOU THINKING, OPENING A NEW BRANCH AT A TIME LIKE THIS?!
NO, SHINOMIYA! DON'T LEAVE ME!
YOU HAD BETTER RETURN TO US IN SIX... NO, IN ONE MONTH!
THEN WHY NOT APPLY FOR FUNDING HERE IN JAPAN?

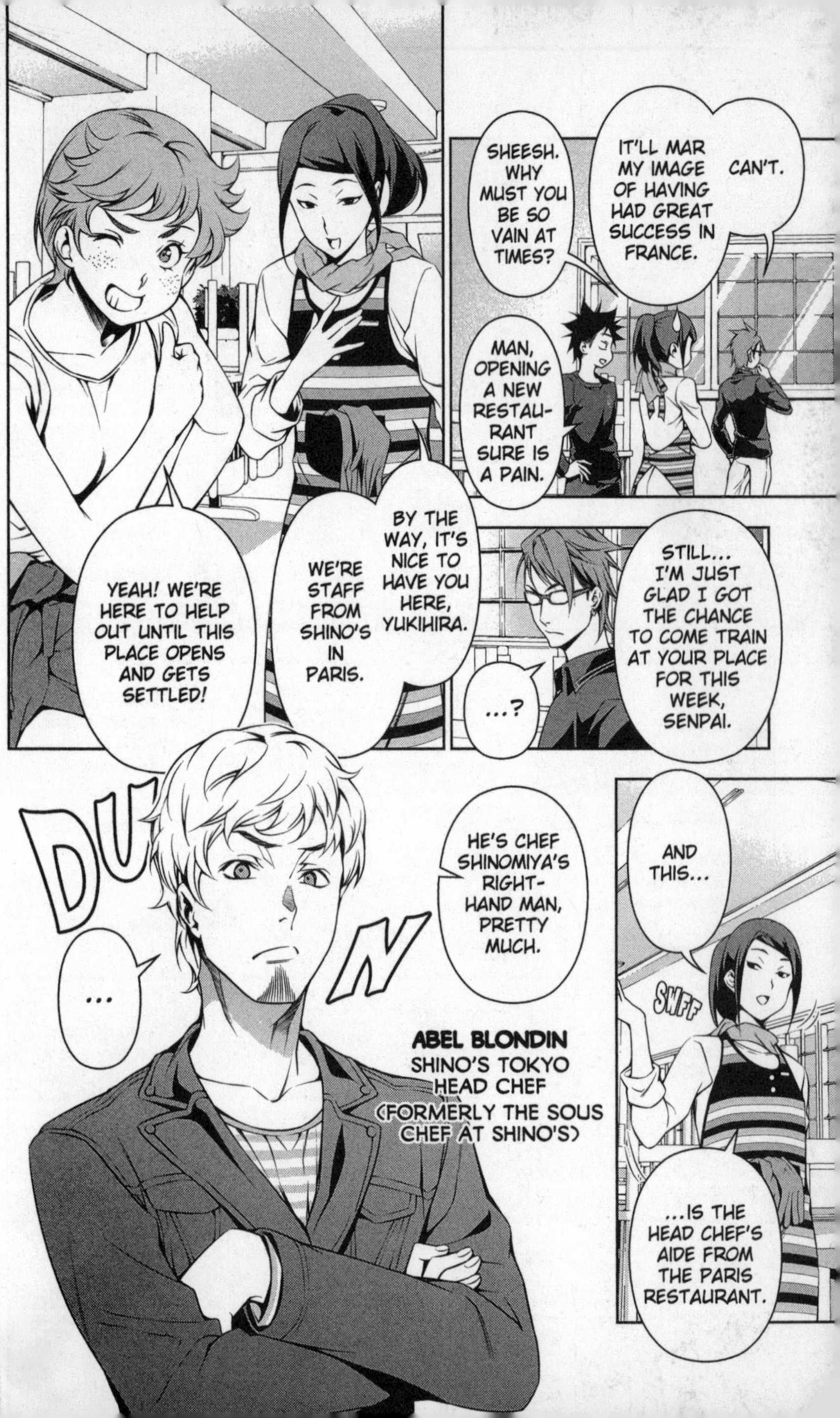
CAN'T.
IT'LL MAR MY IMAGE OF HAVING HAD GREAT SUCCESS IN FRANCE.
SHEESH. WHY MUST YOU BE SO VAIN AT TIMES?
MAN, OPENING A NEW RESTAURANT SURE IS A PAIN.
STILL... I'M JUST GLAD I GOT THE CHANCE TO COME TRAIN AT YOUR PLACE FOR THIS WEEK, SENPAI.
...?
BY THE WAY, IT'S NICE TO HAVE YOU HERE, YUKIHIRA.
WE'RE STAFF FROM SHINO'S IN PARIS.
YEAH! WE'RE HERE TO HELP OUT UNTIL THIS PLACE OPENS AND GETS SETTLED!
AND THIS...
SHFF
...IS THE HEAD CHEF'S AIDE FROM THE PARIS RESTAURANT.
HE'S CHEF SHINOMIYA'S RIGHT-HAND MAN, PRETTY MUCH.
DUN
...
ABEL BLONDIN
SHINO'S TOKYO HEAD CHEF
(FORMERLY THE SOUS CHEF AT SHINO'S)

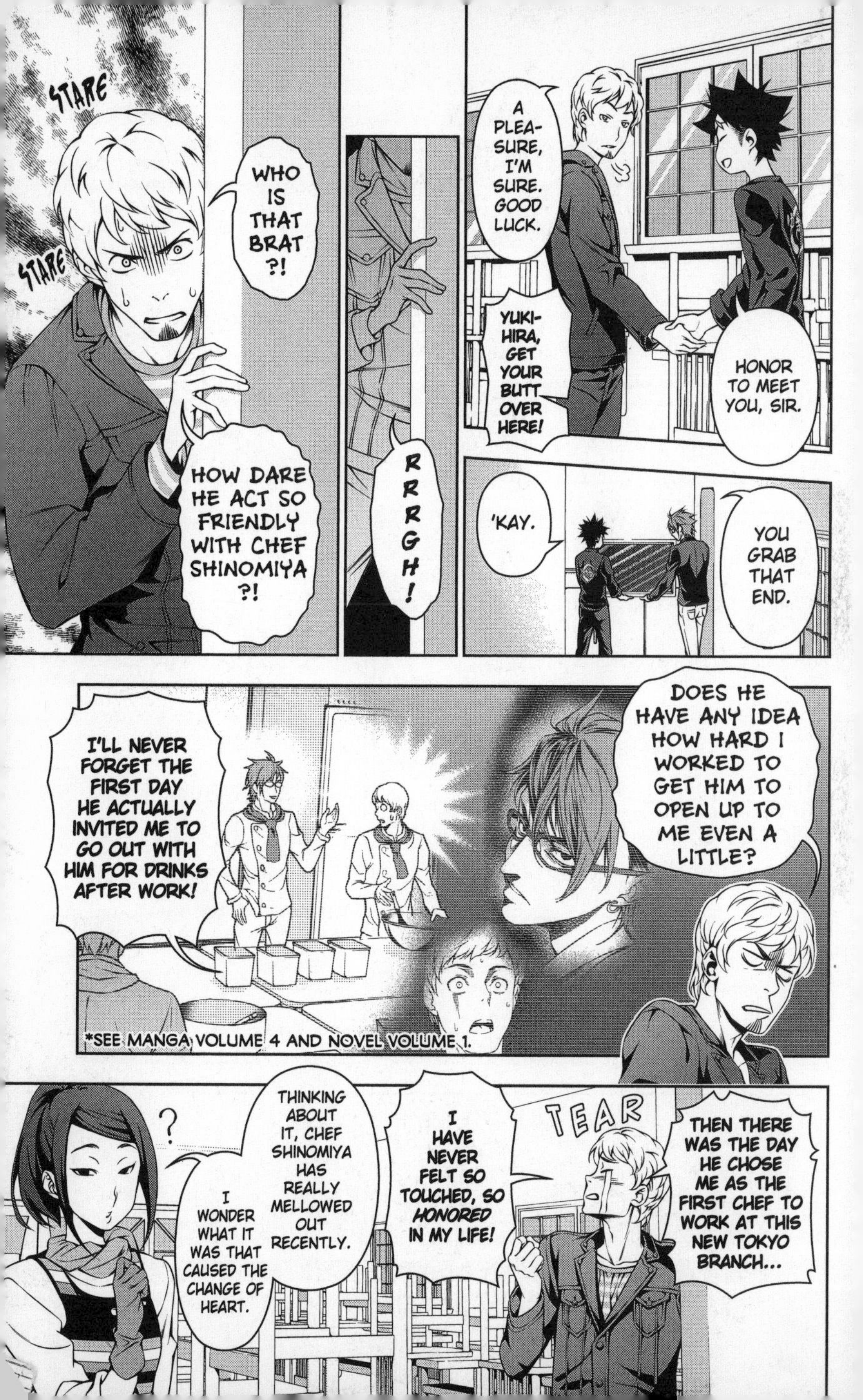
HONOR TO MEET YOU, SIR.
A PLEASURE, I'M SURE. GOOD LUCK.
YUKIHIRA, GET YOUR BUTT OVER HERE!
YOU GRAB THAT END.
'KAY.
RRRGH!
STARE
STARE
WHO IS THAT BRAT?!
HOW DARE HE ACT SO FRIENDLY WITH CHEF SHINOMIYA?!
DOES HE HAVE ANY IDEA HOW HARD I WORKED TO GET HIM TO OPEN UP TO ME EVEN A LITTLE?
I'LL NEVER FORGET THE FIRST DAY HE ACTUALLY INVITED ME TO GO OUT WITH HIM FOR DRINKS AFTER WORK!
*SEE MANGA VOLUME 4 AND NOVEL VOLUME 1.
THEN THERE WAS THE DAY HE CHOSE ME AS THE FIRST CHEF TO WORK AT THIS NEW TOKYO BRANCH...
TEAR
I HAVE NEVER FELT SO TOUCHED, SO *HONORED* IN MY LIFE!
THINKING ABOUT IT, CHEF SHINOMIYA HAS REALLY MELLOWED OUT RECENTLY.
I WONDER WHAT IT WAS THAT CAUSED THE CHANGE OF HEART.
?

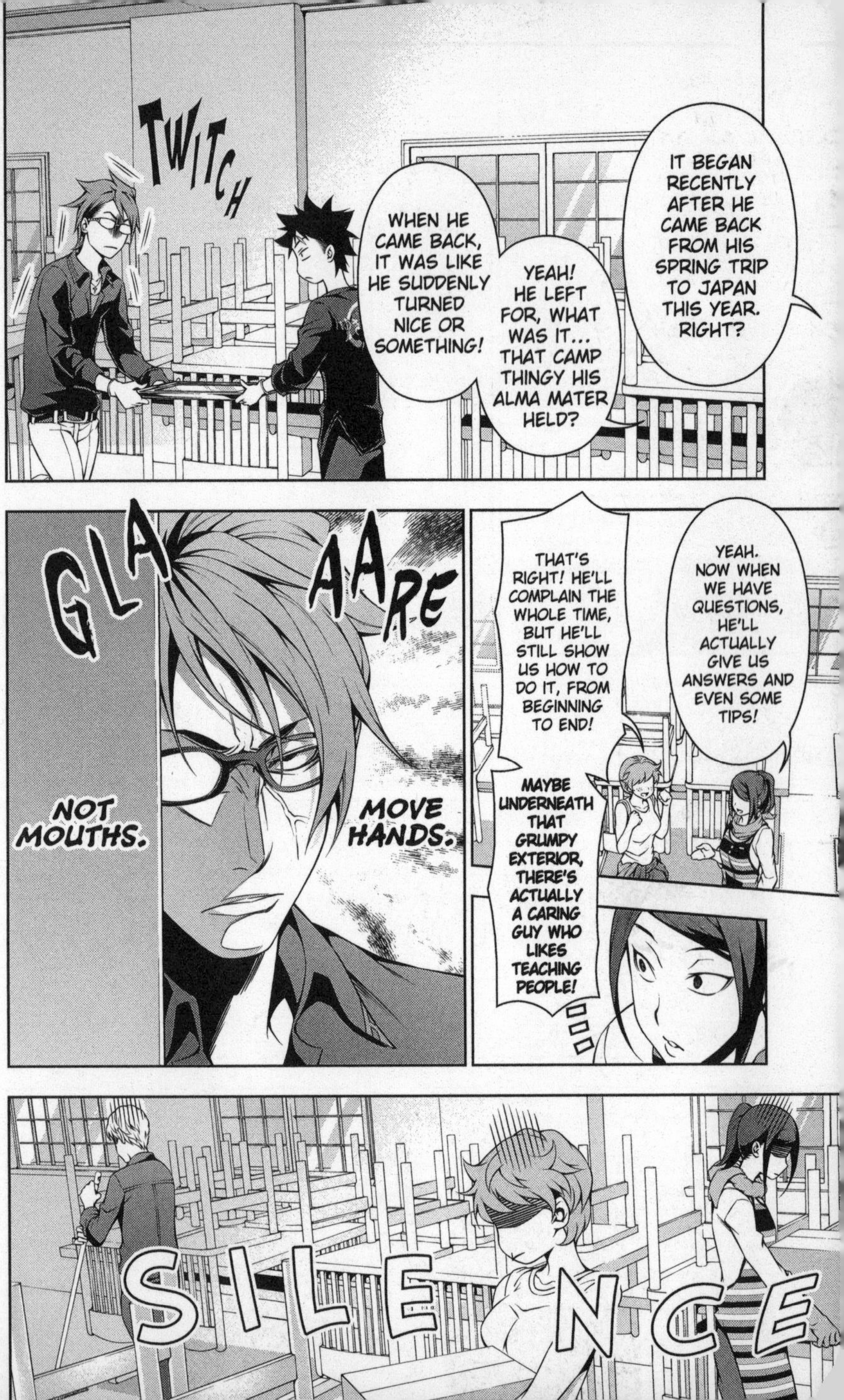
IT BEGAN RECENTLY AFTER HE CAME BACK FROM HIS SPRING TRIP TO JAPAN THIS YEAR. RIGHT?
YEAH! HE LEFT FOR, WHAT WAS IT... THAT CAMP THINGY HIS ALMA MATER HELD?
WHEN HE CAME BACK, IT WAS LIKE HE SUDDENLY TURNED NICE OR SOMETHING!
TWITCH
YEAH. NOW WHEN WE HAVE QUESTIONS, HE'LL ACTUALLY GIVE US ANSWERS AND EVEN SOME TIPS!
THAT'S RIGHT! HE'LL COMPLAIN THE WHOLE TIME, BUT HE'LL STILL SHOW US HOW TO DO IT, FROM BEGINNING TO END!
MAYBE UNDERNEATH THAT GRUMPY EXTERIOR, THERE'S ACTUALLY A CARING GUY WHO LIKES TEACHING PEOPLE!
GLAAARE
MOVE HANDS.
NOT MOUTHS.
SILENCE

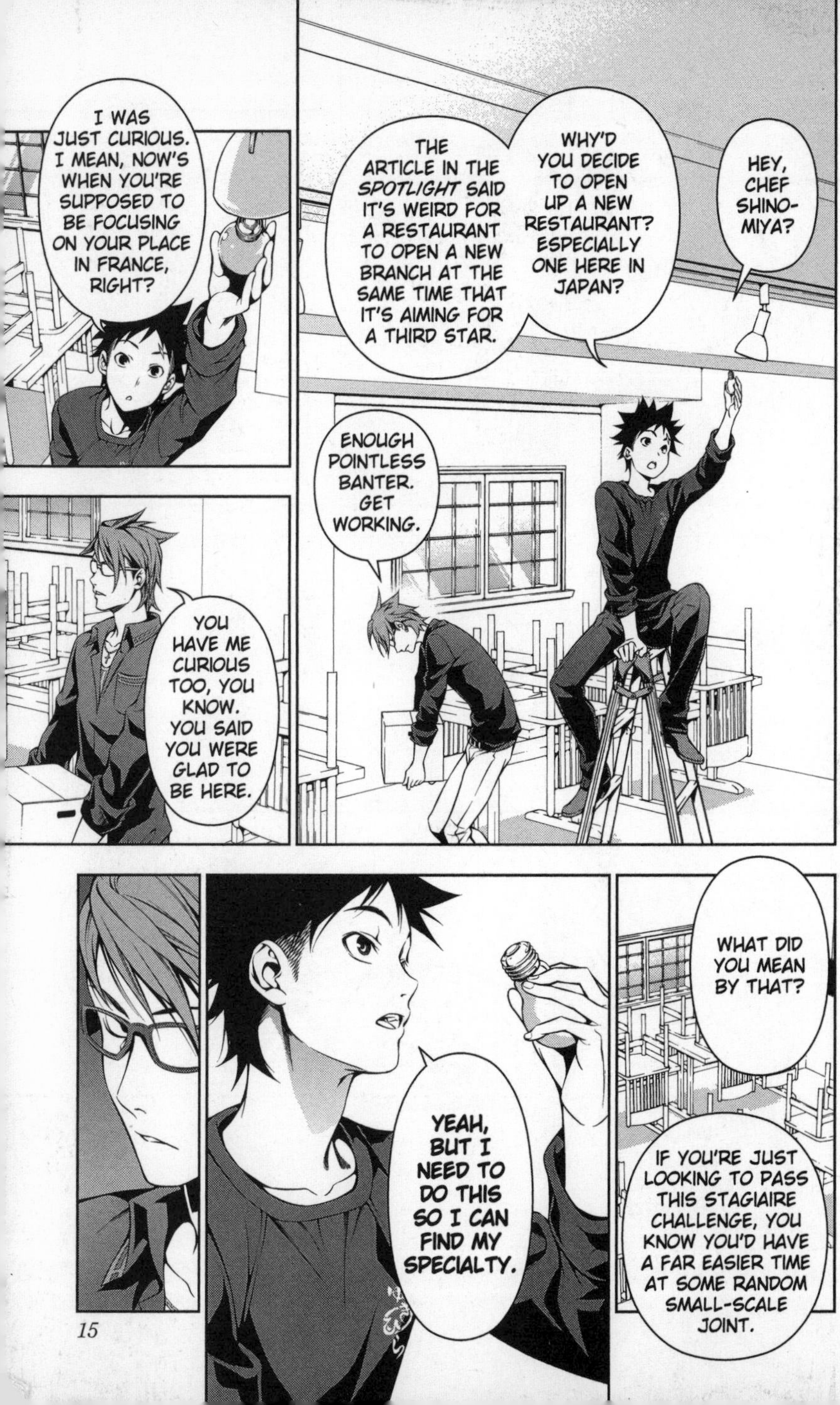
HEY, CHEF SHINOMIYA?
WHY'D YOU DECIDE TO OPEN UP A NEW RESTAURANT? ESPECIALLY ONE HERE IN JAPAN?
THE ARTICLE IN THE *SPOTLIGHT* SAID IT'S WEIRD FOR A RESTAURANT TO OPEN A NEW BRANCH AT THE SAME TIME THAT IT'S AIMING FOR A THIRD STAR.
ENOUGH POINTLESS BANTER. GET WORKING.
I WAS JUST CURIOUS. I MEAN, NOW'S WHEN YOU'RE SUPPOSED TO BE FOCUSING ON YOUR PLACE IN FRANCE, RIGHT?
YOU HAVE ME CURIOUS TOO, YOU KNOW. YOU SAID YOU WERE GLAD TO BE HERE.
WHAT DID YOU MEAN BY THAT?
IF YOU'RE JUST LOOKING TO PASS THIS STAGIAIRE CHALLENGE, YOU KNOW YOU'D HAVE A FAR EASIER TIME AT SOME RANDOM SMALL-SCALE JOINT.
YEAH, BUT I NEED TO DO THIS SO I CAN FIND MY SPECIALTY.

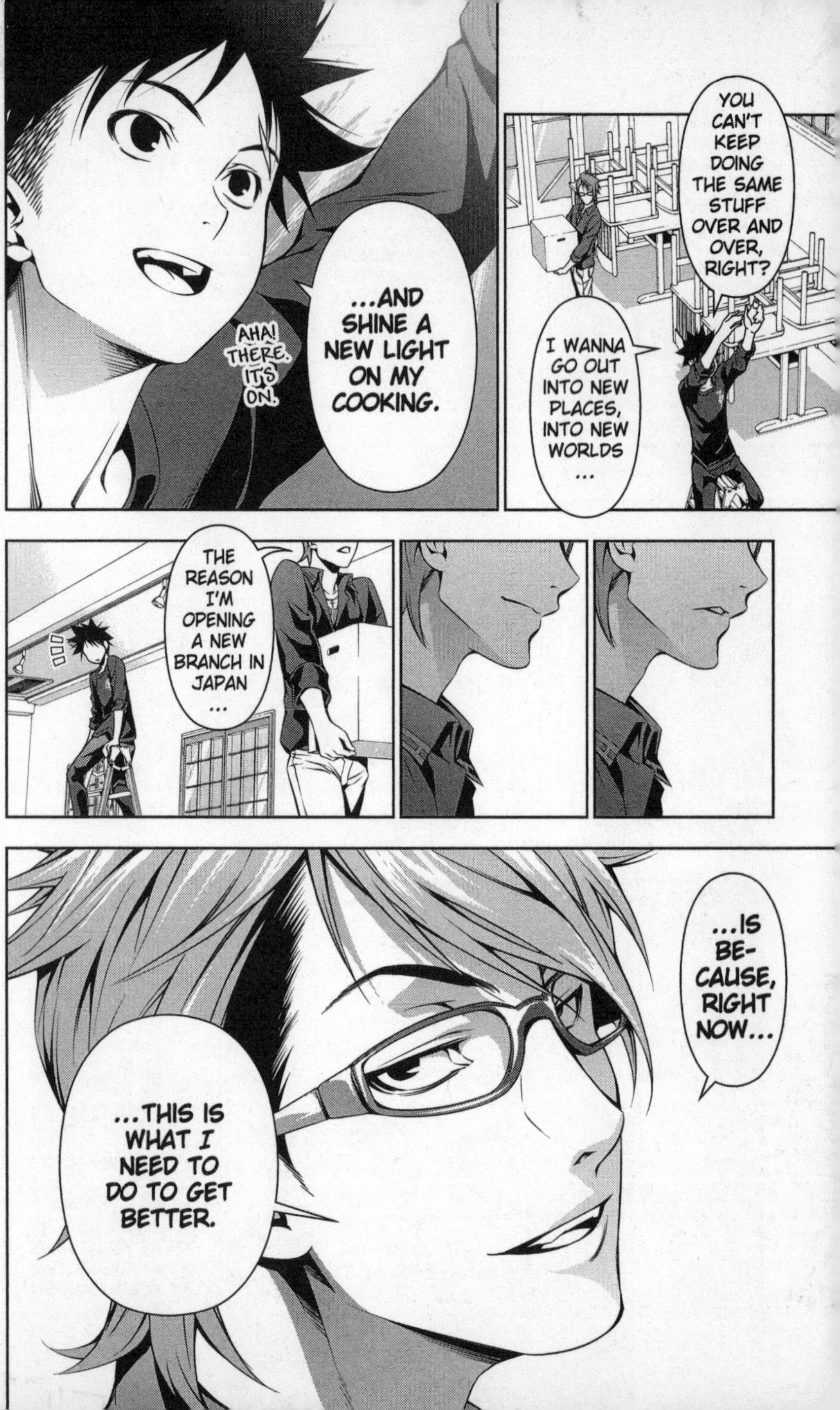
YOU CAN'T KEEP DOING THE SAME STUFF OVER AND OVER, RIGHT?
I WANNA GO OUT INTO NEW PLACES, INTO NEW WORLDS...
...AND SHINE A NEW LIGHT ON MY COOKING.
AHA! THERE. IT'S ON.
THE REASON I'M OPENING A NEW BRANCH IN JAPAN...
...IS BE-CAUSE, RIGHT NOW...
...THIS IS WHAT I NEED TO DO TO GET BETTER.

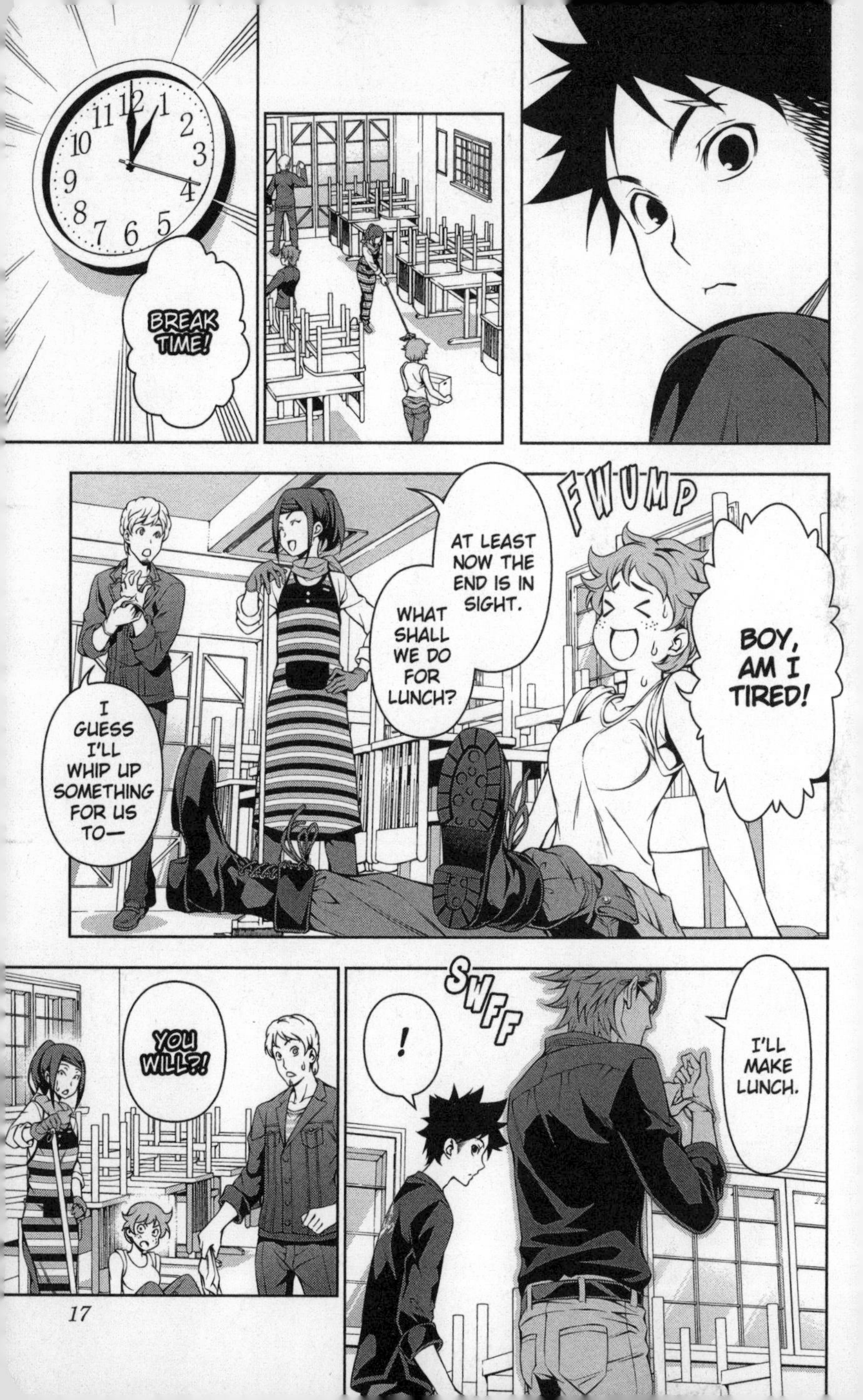
BREAK TIME!
FWUMP
BOY, AM I TIRED!
AT LEAST NOW THE END IS IN SIGHT.
WHAT SHALL WE DO FOR LUNCH?
I GUESS I'LL WHIP UP SOMETHING FOR US TO—
SWFF
I'LL MAKE LUNCH.
!
YOU WILL?!

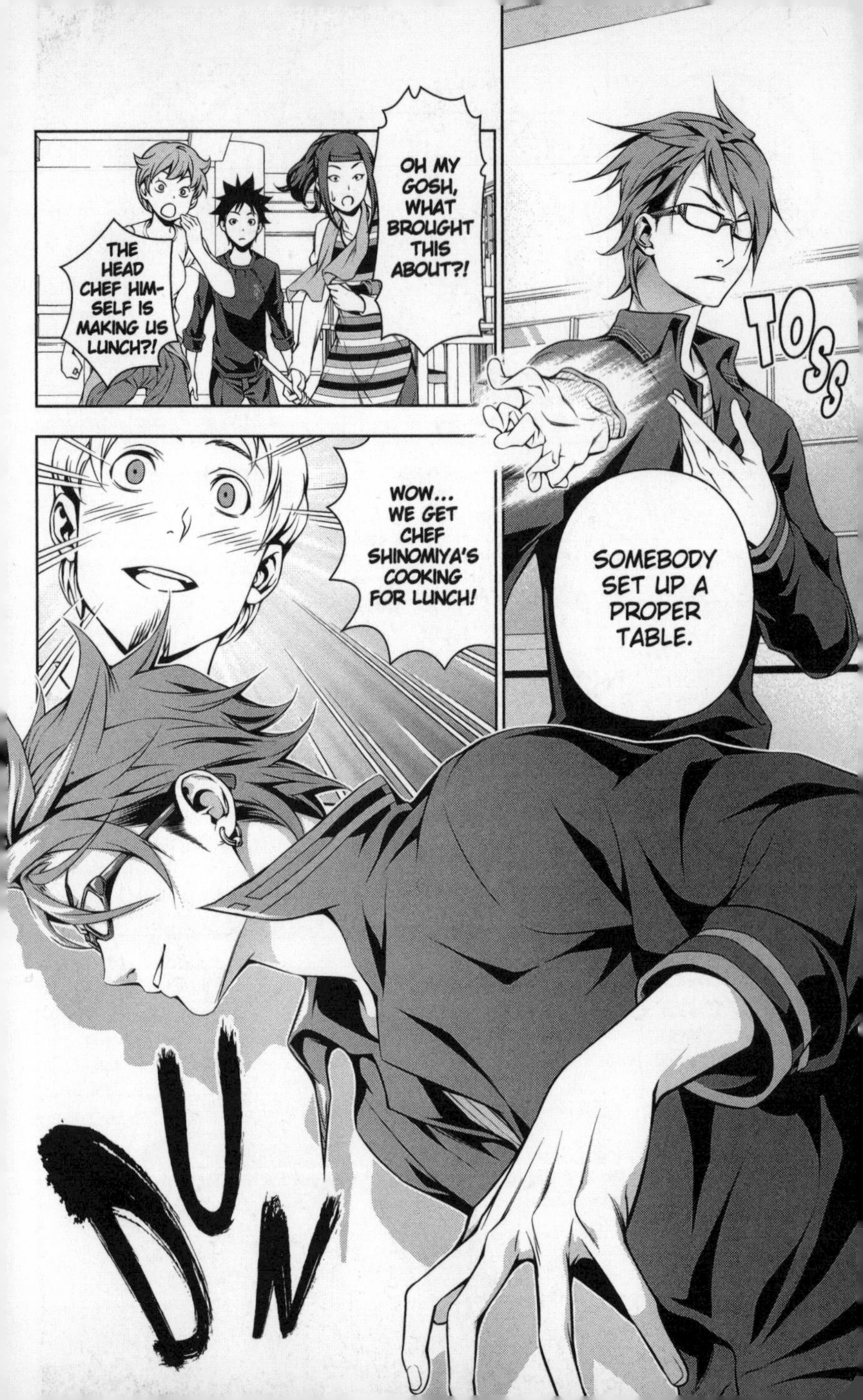
TOSS
SOMEBODY SET UP A PROPER TABLE.
OH MY GOSH, WHAT BROUGHT THIS ABOUT?!
THE HEAD CHEF HIM-SELF IS MAKING US LUNCH?!
WOW... WE GET CHEF SHINOMIYA'S COOKING FOR LUNCH!
DUN

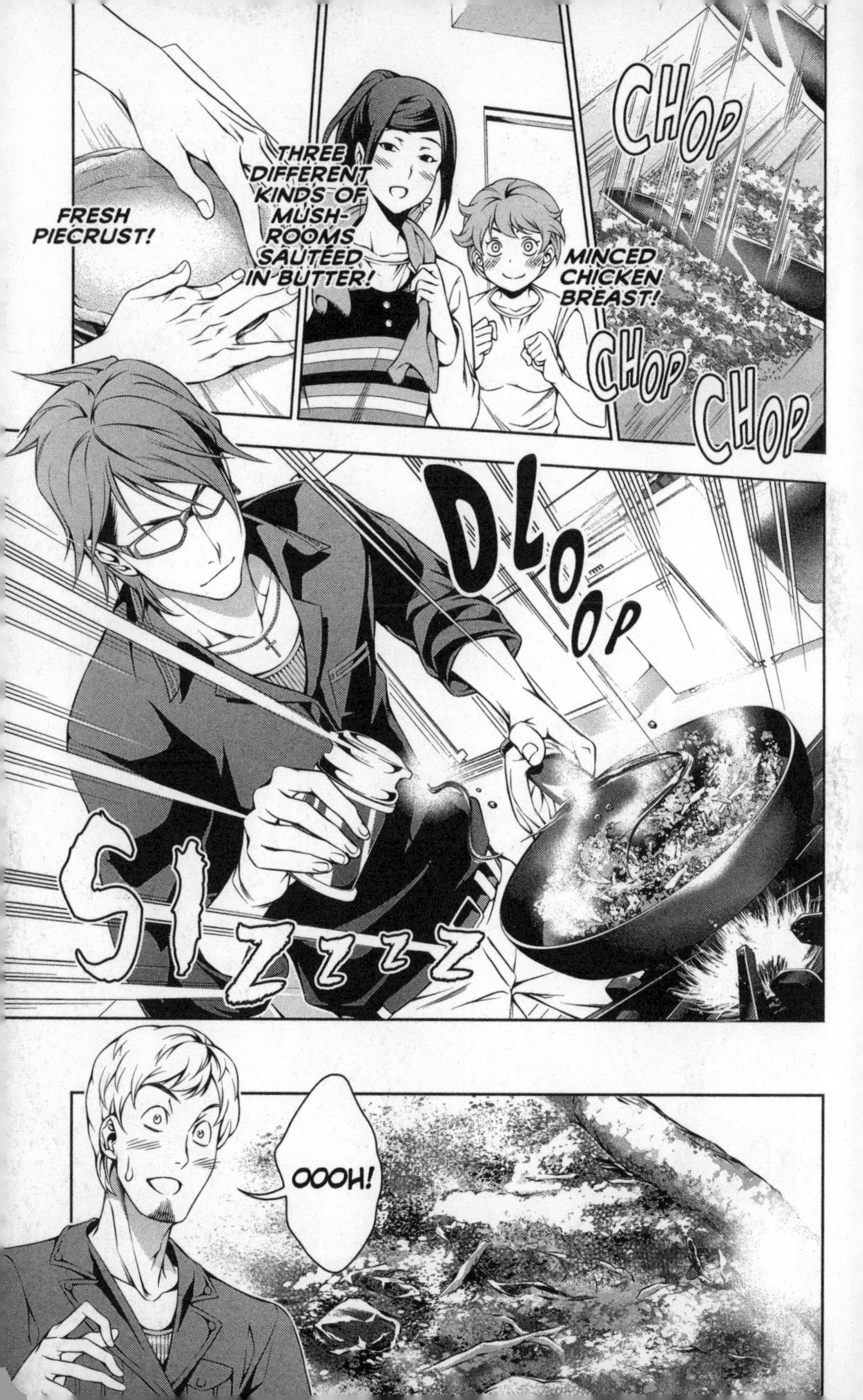
CHOP
MINCED CHICKEN BREAST!
THREE DIFFERENT KINDS OF MUSH-ROOMS SAUTÉED IN BUTTER!
FRESH PIECRUST!
CHOP CHOP
DLOOP
SIZZZZZ
OOOH!

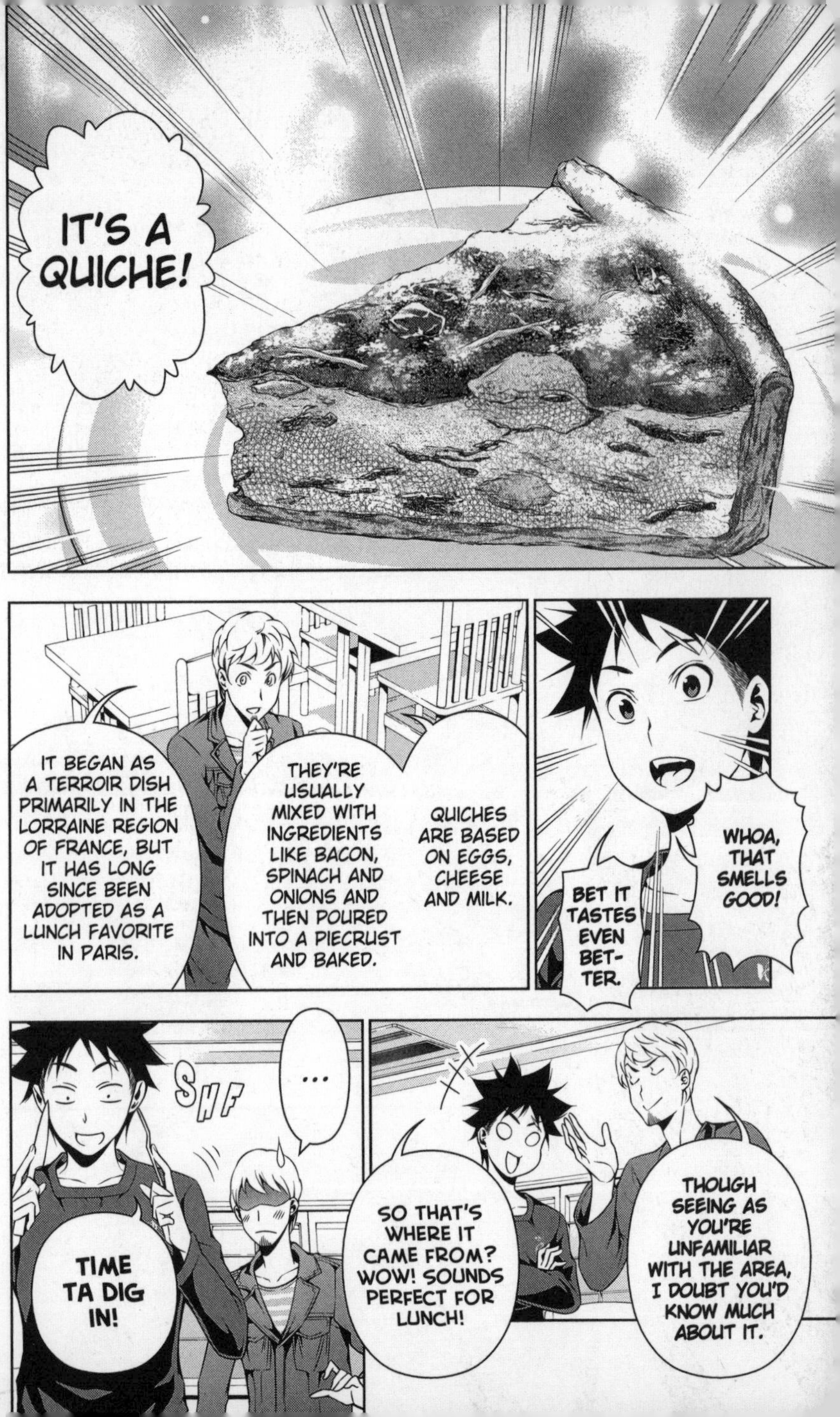
IT'S A QUICHE!
WHOA, THAT SMELLS GOOD!
BET IT TASTES EVEN BET-TER.
QUICHES ARE BASED ON EGGS, CHEESE AND MILK.
THEY'RE USUALLY MIXED WITH INGREDIENTS LIKE BACON, SPINACH AND ONIONS AND THEN POURED INTO A PIECRUST AND BAKED.
IT BEGAN AS A TERROIR DISH PRIMARILY IN THE LORRAINE REGION OF FRANCE, BUT IT HAS LONG SINCE BEEN ADOPTED AS A LUNCH FAVORITE IN PARIS.
THOUGH SEEING AS YOU'RE UNFAMILIAR WITH THE AREA, I DOUBT YOU'D KNOW MUCH ABOUT IT.
SO THAT'S WHERE IT CAME FROM? WOW! SOUNDS PERFECT FOR LUNCH!
...
SHF
TIME TA DIG IN!

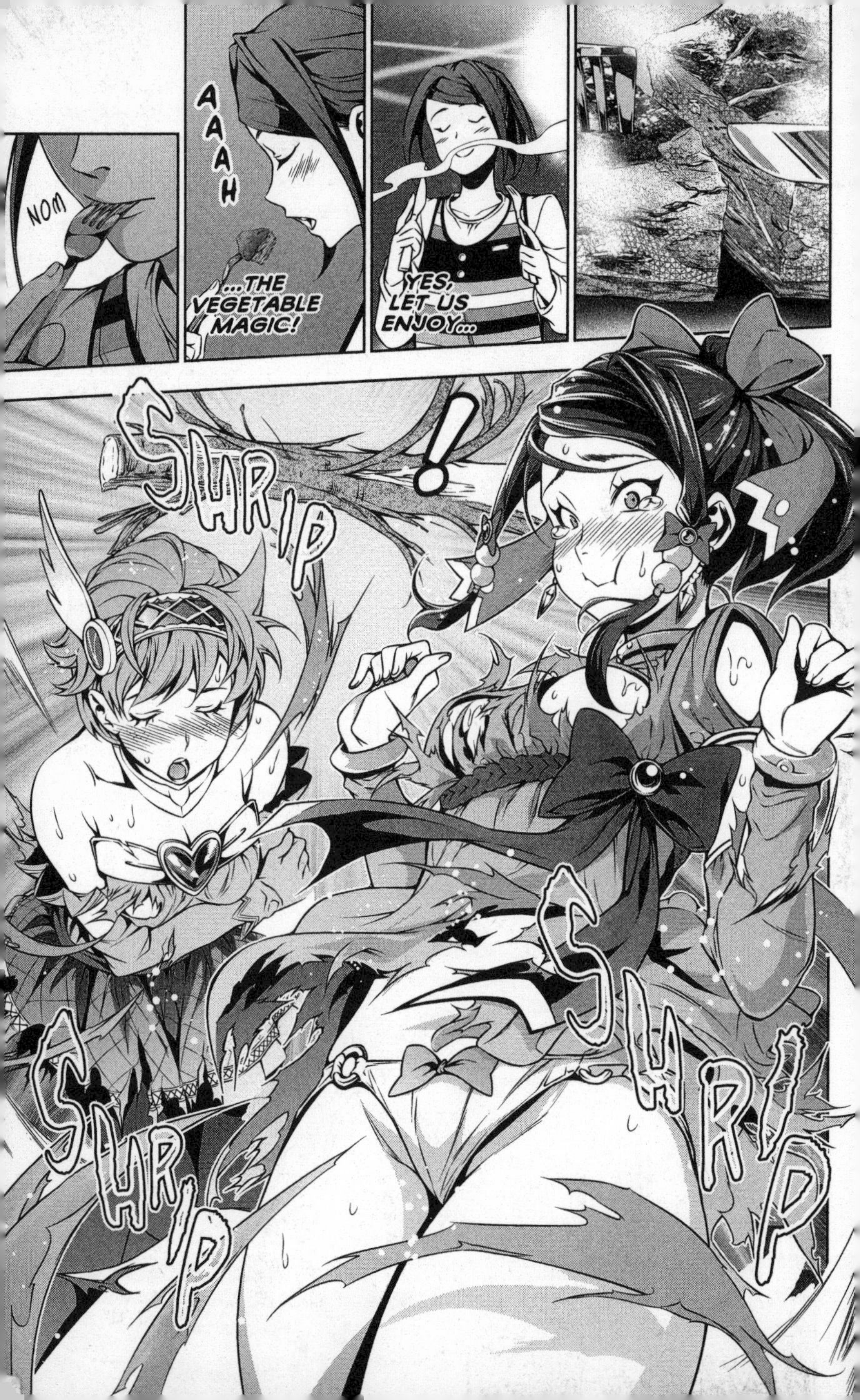
YES, LET US ENJOY...
AAAAH
...THE VEGETABLE MAGIC!
NOM
!
SHRIP
SHRIP
SHRIP

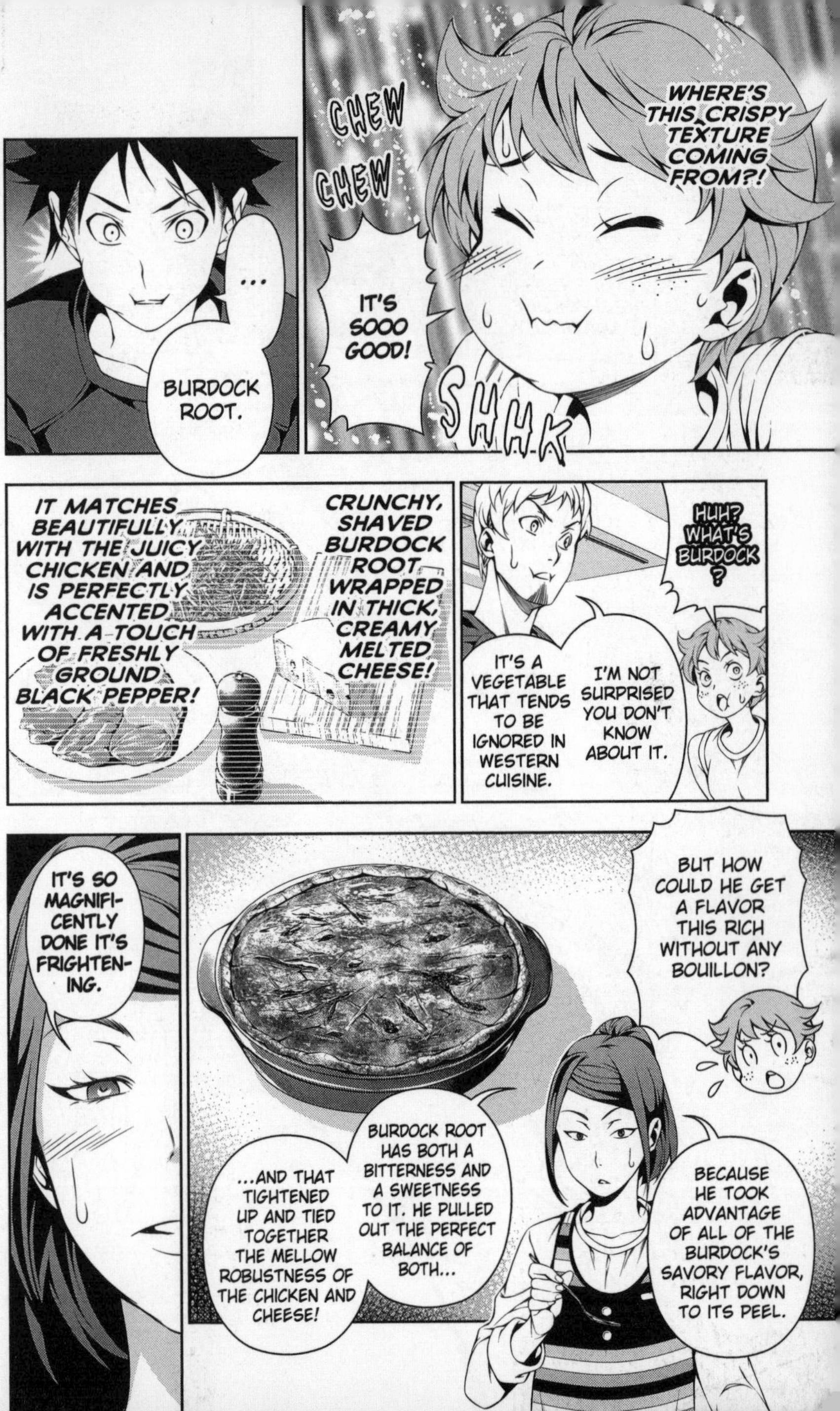
CHEW
CHEW
WHERE'S THIS CRISPY TEXTURE COMING FROM?!
IT'S SOOO GOOD!
SHHK
...
BURDOCK ROOT.
HUH? WHAT'S BURDOCK?
I'M NOT SURPRISED YOU DON'T KNOW ABOUT IT.
IT'S A VEGETABLE THAT TENDS TO BE IGNORED IN WESTERN CUISINE.
CRUNCHY, SHAVED BURDOCK ROOT WRAPPED IN THICK, CREAMY MELTED CHEESE!
IT MATCHES BEAUTIFULLY WITH THE JUICY CHICKEN AND IS PERFECTLY ACCENTED WITH A TOUCH OF FRESHLY GROUND BLACK PEPPER!
BUT HOW COULD HE GET A FLAVOR THIS RICH WITHOUT ANY BOUILLON?
BECAUSE HE TOOK ADVANTAGE OF ALL OF THE BURDOCK'S SAVORY FLAVOR, RIGHT DOWN TO ITS PEEL.
BURDOCK ROOT HAS BOTH A BITTERNESS AND A SWEETNESS TO IT. HE PULLED OUT THE PERFECT BALANCE OF BOTH...
...AND THAT TIGHTENED UP AND TIED TOGETHER THE MELLOW ROBUSTNESS OF THE CHICKEN AND CHEESE!
IT'S SO MAGNIFI-CENTLY DONE IT'S FRIGHTEN-ING.

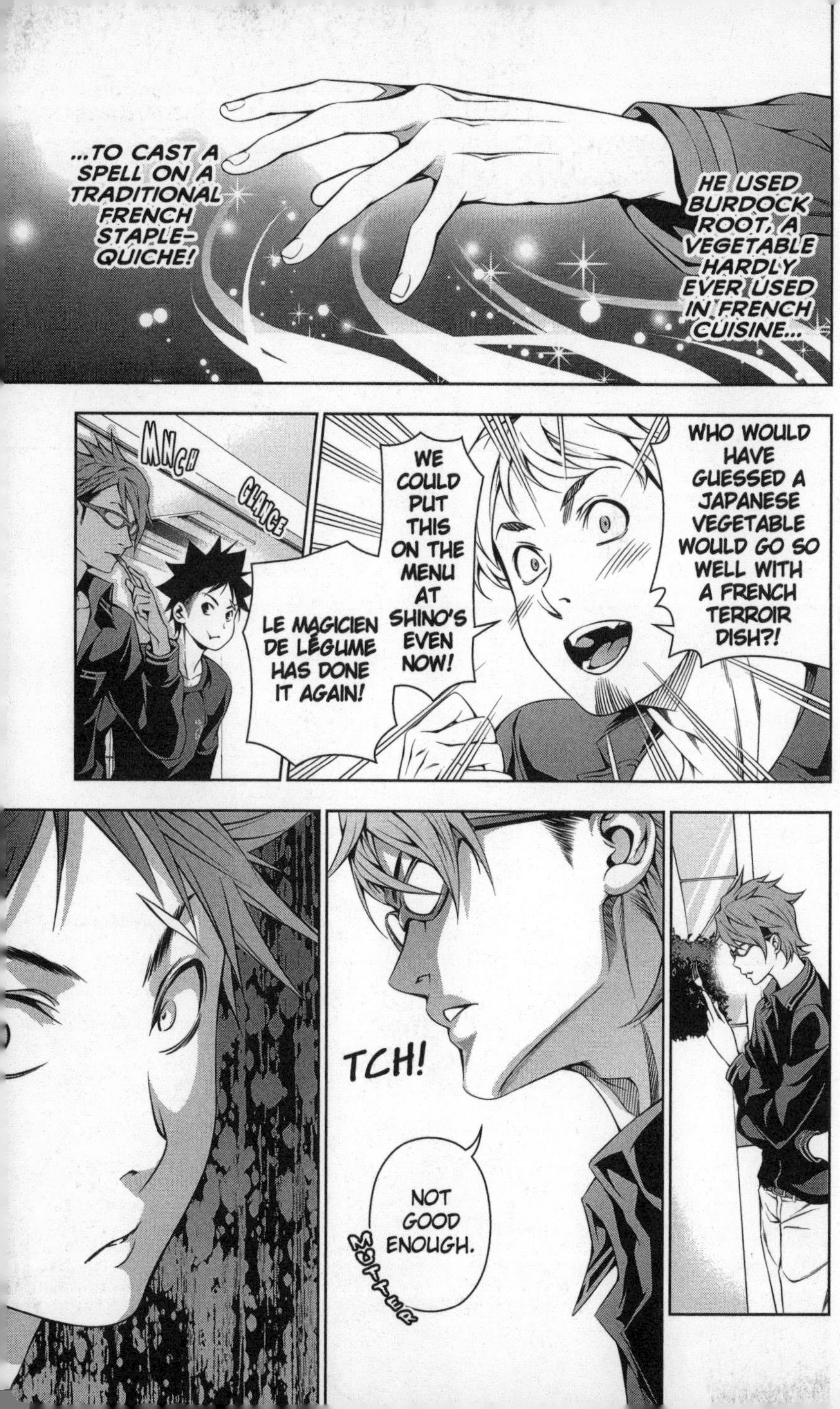
HE USED BURDOCK ROOT, A VEGETABLE HARDLY EVER USED IN FRENCH CUISINE...
...TO CAST A SPELL ON A TRADITIONAL FRENCH STAPLE- QUICHE!
WHO WOULD HAVE GUESSED A JAPANESE VEGETABLE WOULD GO SO WELL WITH A FRENCH TERROIR DISH?!
WE COULD PUT THIS ON THE MENU AT SHINO'S EVEN NOW!
LE MAGICIEN DE LÉGUME HAS DONE IT AGAIN!
MNCH
GLANCE
TCH!
NOT GOOD ENOUGH.

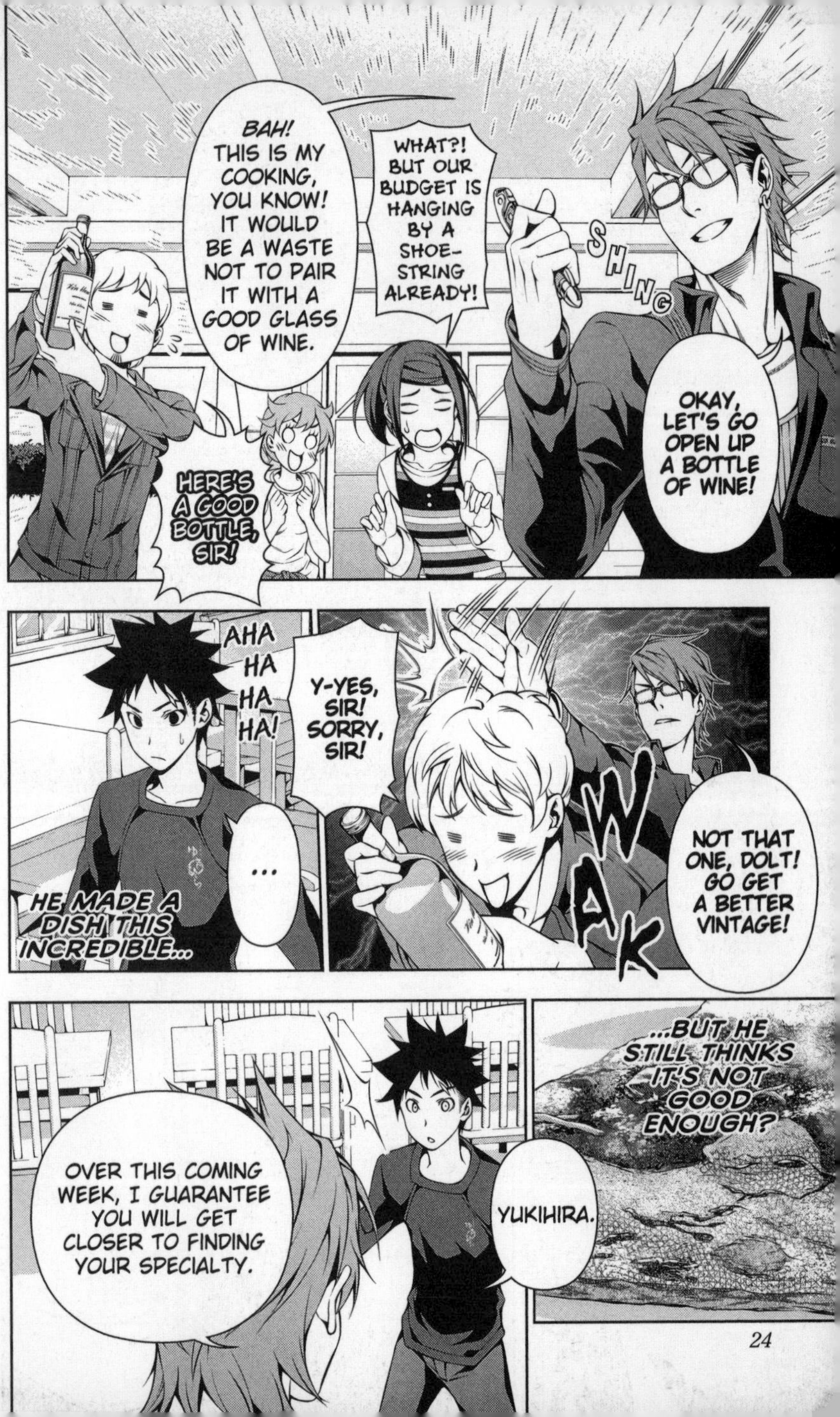
SHING
WHAT?! BUT OUR BUDGET IS HANGING BY A SHOE-STRING ALREADY!
BAH! THIS IS MY COOKING, YOU KNOW! IT WOULD BE A WASTE NOT TO PAIR IT WITH A GOOD GLASS OF WINE.
OKAY, LET'S GO OPEN UP A BOTTLE OF WINE!
HERE'S A GOOD BOTTLE, SIR!
WAK
NOT THAT ONE, DOLT! GO GET A BETTER VINTAGE!
Y-YES, SIR! SORRY, SIR!
AHA HA HA HA!
...
HE MADE A DISH THIS INCREDIBLE...
...BUT HE STILL THINKS IT'S NOT GOOD ENOUGH?
YUKIHIRA.
OVER THIS COMING WEEK, I GUARANTEE YOU WILL GET CLOSER TO FINDING YOUR SPECIALTY.

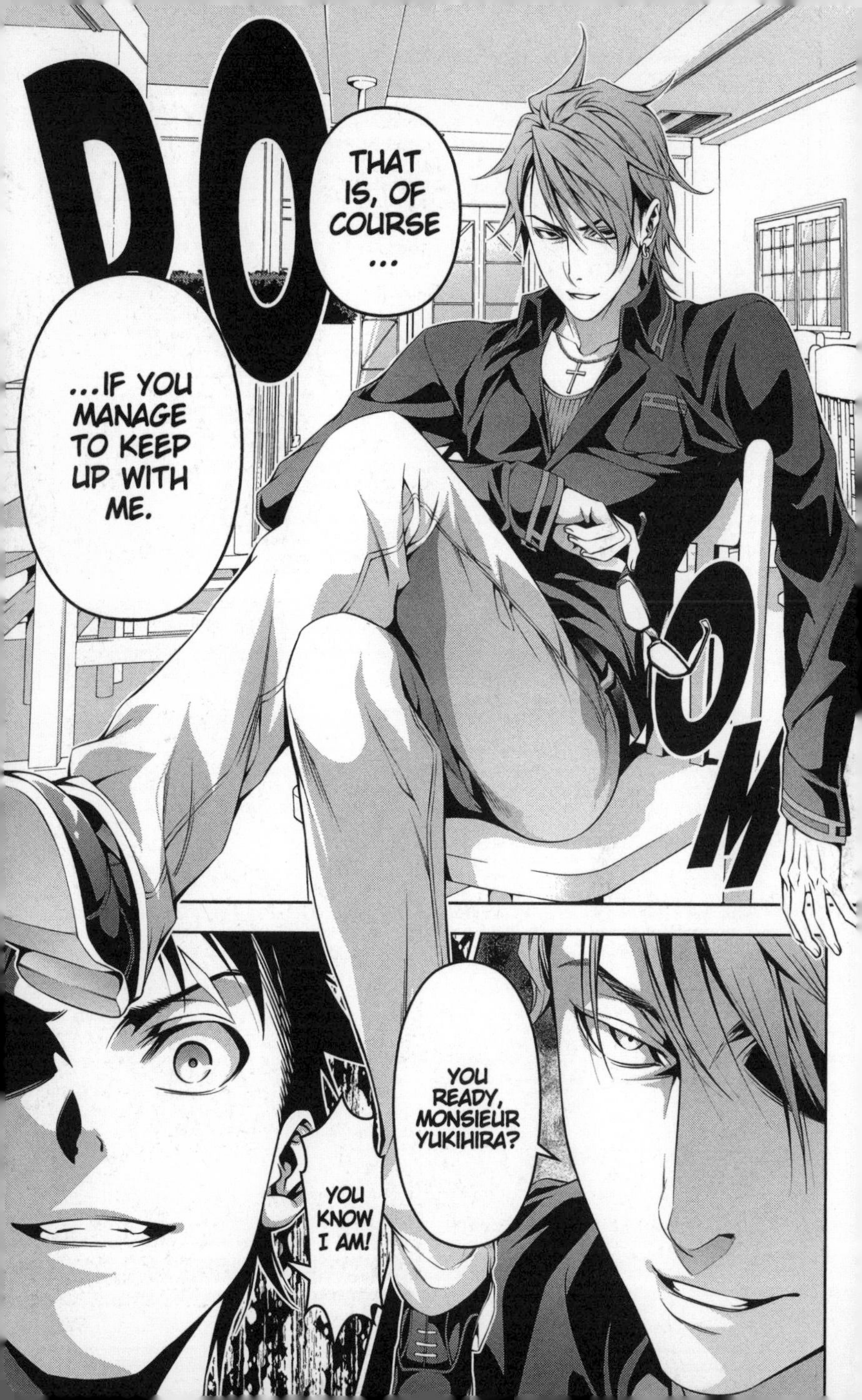
DOOM
THAT IS, OF COURSE ...
...IF YOU MANAGE TO KEEP UP WITH ME.
YOU READY, MONSIEUR YUKIHIRA?
YOU KNOW I AM!

ARTIST: YUTO TSUKUDA RECIPE BY: YUKI MORISAKI

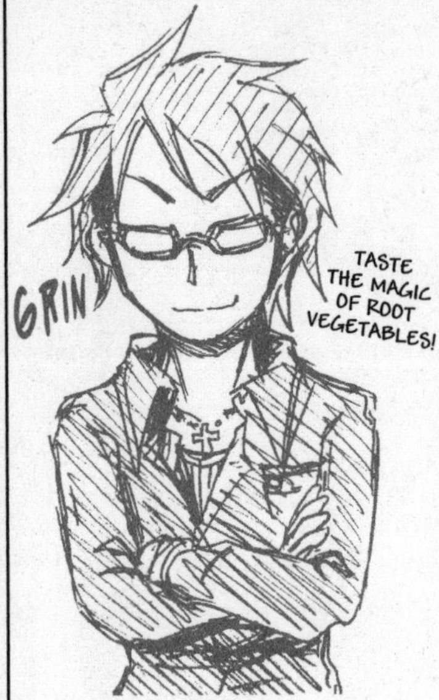
GRIN
TASTE THE MAGIC OF ROOT VEGETABLES!

VOLUME 14 SPECIAL SUPPLEMENT!

PRACTICAL RECIPE #1

# CHEF SHINOMIYA'S SPECIAL BURDOCK ROOT QUICHE

## INGREDIENTS
(USE 7" PIE PAN)

- 2 STORE-BOUGHT FROZEN PIECRUSTS (WITHOUT TIN)
- 1 BURDOCK ROOT
- 150 GRAMS GROUND CHICKEN
- 100 GRAMS MIX OF MAITAKE MUSHROOMS, SHIMEJI MUSHROOMS AND BUTTON MUSHROOMS
- 1 TABLESPOON SOY SAUCE
- 2 TABLESPOONS BUTTER

★ THE BATTER (FILLING)

- 2 EGGS
- 200 CC PURE SOY MILK
- 1 TABLESPOON WHITE MISO PASTE
- BLACK PEPPER

MOZZARELLA CHEESE, BLACK PEPPER

1. DEFROST THE FROZEN PIECRUSTS. USING A ROLLING PIN, ROLL THE DOUGH OUT UNTIL IT IS SLIGHTLY LARGER IN DIAMETER THAN THE PIE PAN. PLACE THE DOUGH IN THE PIE PAN AND FIRMLY PRESS IT INTO THE BOTTOM EDGES ALL THE WAY AROUND. SMOOTH THE DOUGH UP THE SIDE OF THE PAN AND USE THE ROLLING PIN TO LIGHTLY PRESS IT ONTO THE TOP LIP OF THE PAN, TRIMMING ANY EXCESS DOUGH OFF THE EDGES. USE A FORK TO POKE A FEW HOLES IN THE DOUGH ALONG THE BOTTOM AND THEN PLACE IN THE REFRIGERATOR TO CHILL.

2. WASH THE BURDOCK ROOT THOROUGHLY WITH A VEGETABLE BRUSH, AND USE A PEELER TO SHAVE THE ROOT INTO SHORT, THIN STRIPS. FINELY DICE THE MUSHROOMS.

3. MELT THE BUTTER IN A FRYING PAN AND ADD THE GROUND CHICKEN. ONCE LIGHTLY BROWNED, ADD THE BURDOCK ROOT FROM (2) AND STIR-FRY TOGETHER.

4. ONCE THE BURDOCK ROOT STRIPS GROW TRANSLUCENT, ADD THE MUSHROOMS AND CONTINUE STIR-FRYING UNTIL THEY ARE TENDER. THEN ADD THE SOY SAUCE AND STIR-FRY UNTIL ALL THE LIQUID IS ABSORBED. POUR INTO A BOWL, COVER AND PUT IN THE REFRIGERATOR TO CHILL.

5. PUT ALL THE INGREDIENTS FOR THE BATTER IN A BOWL AND MIX THOROUGHLY.

6. POUR (4) INTO THE PIECRUST FROM (1) AND SPREAD EVENLY. POUR THE BATTER FROM (5) OVER TOP AND THEN TOP WITH LOTS OF CHEESE. BAKE AT 375°F FOR APPROXIMATELY 30 MINUTES OR UNTIL THE SURFACE IS A DEEP GOLDEN BROWN. SPRINKLE WITH BLACK PEPPER, AND DONE!

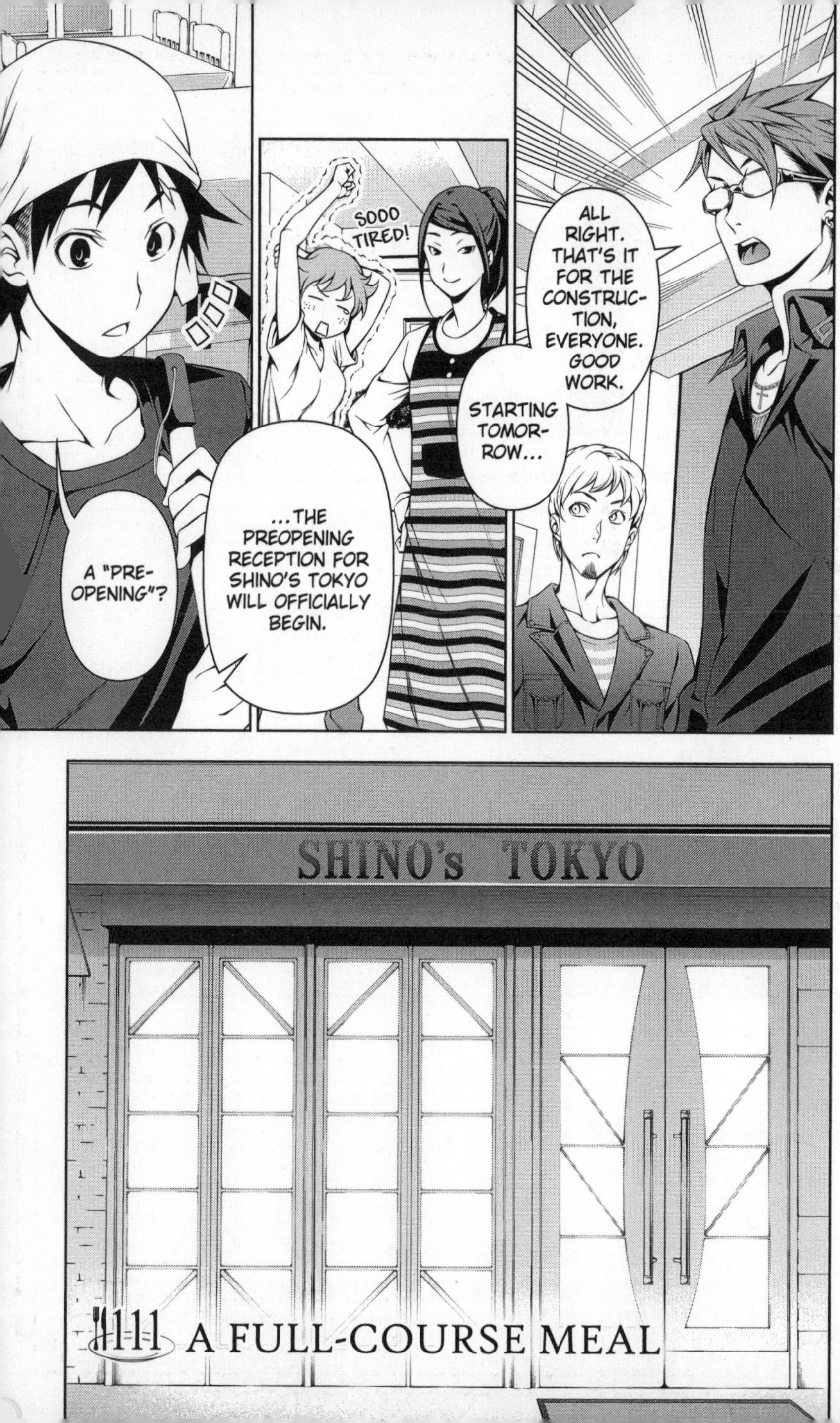
ALL RIGHT. THAT'S IT FOR THE CONSTRUCTION, EVERYONE. GOOD WORK.
STARTING TOMORROW...
SOOO TIRED!
...THE PREOPENING RECEPTION FOR SHINO'S TOKYO WILL OFFICIALLY BEGIN.
A "PRE-OPENING"?
SHINO's TOKYO
111 A FULL-COURSE MEAL

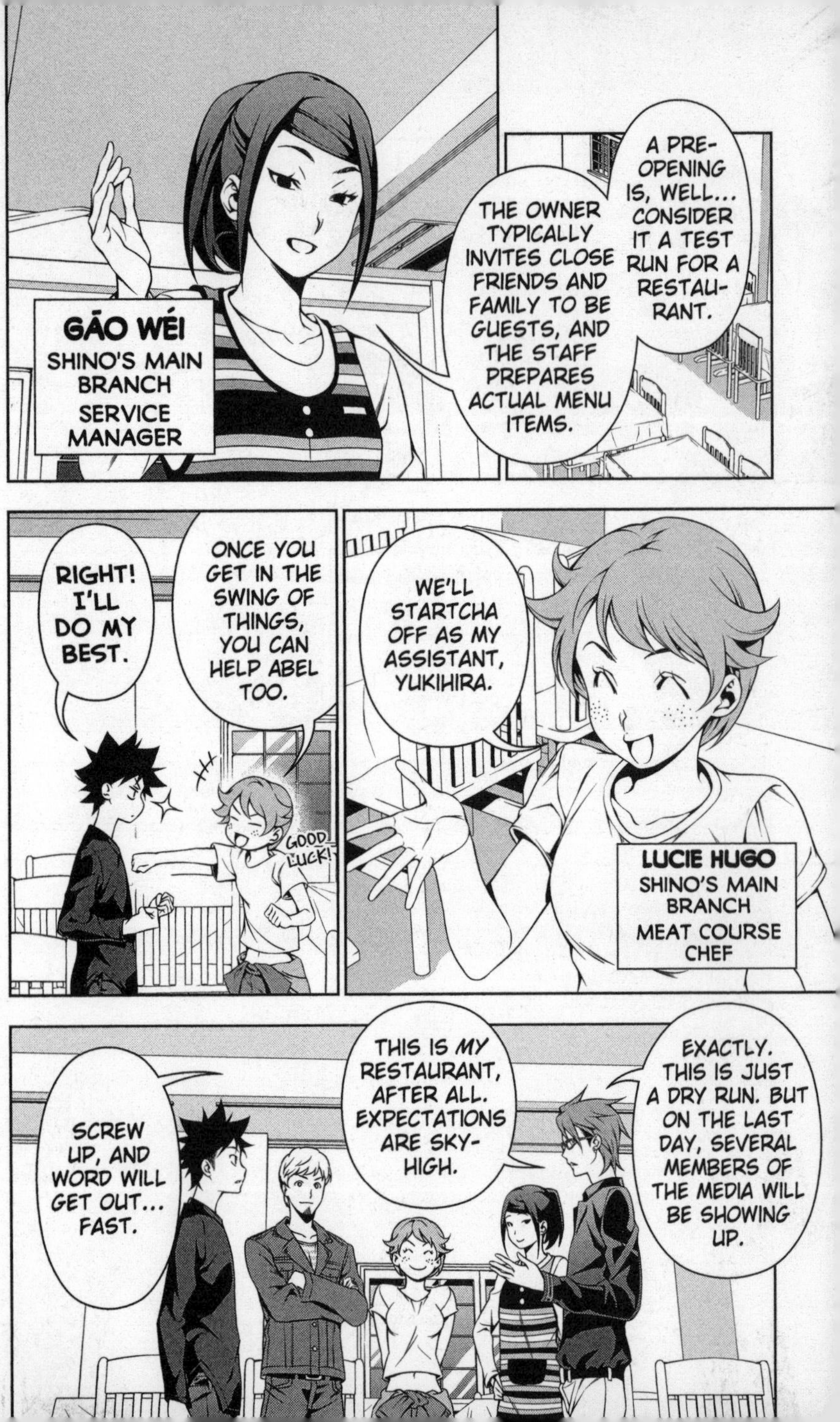
A PRE-OPENING IS, WELL... CONSIDER IT A TEST RUN FOR A RESTAURANT.
THE OWNER TYPICALLY INVITES CLOSE FRIENDS AND FAMILY TO BE GUESTS, AND THE STAFF PREPARES ACTUAL MENU ITEMS.
GĀO WÉI
SHINO'S MAIN BRANCH SERVICE MANAGER
WE'LL STARTCHA OFF AS MY ASSISTANT, YUKIHIRA.
LUCIE HUGO
SHINO'S MAIN BRANCH MEAT COURSE CHEF
ONCE YOU GET IN THE SWING OF THINGS, YOU CAN HELP ABEL TOO.
GOOD LUCK!
RIGHT! I'LL DO MY BEST.
EXACTLY. THIS IS JUST A DRY RUN. BUT ON THE LAST DAY, SEVERAL MEMBERS OF THE MEDIA WILL BE SHOWING UP.
THIS IS *MY* RESTAURANT, AFTER ALL. EXPECTATIONS ARE SKY-HIGH.
SCREW UP, AND WORD WILL GET OUT... FAST.

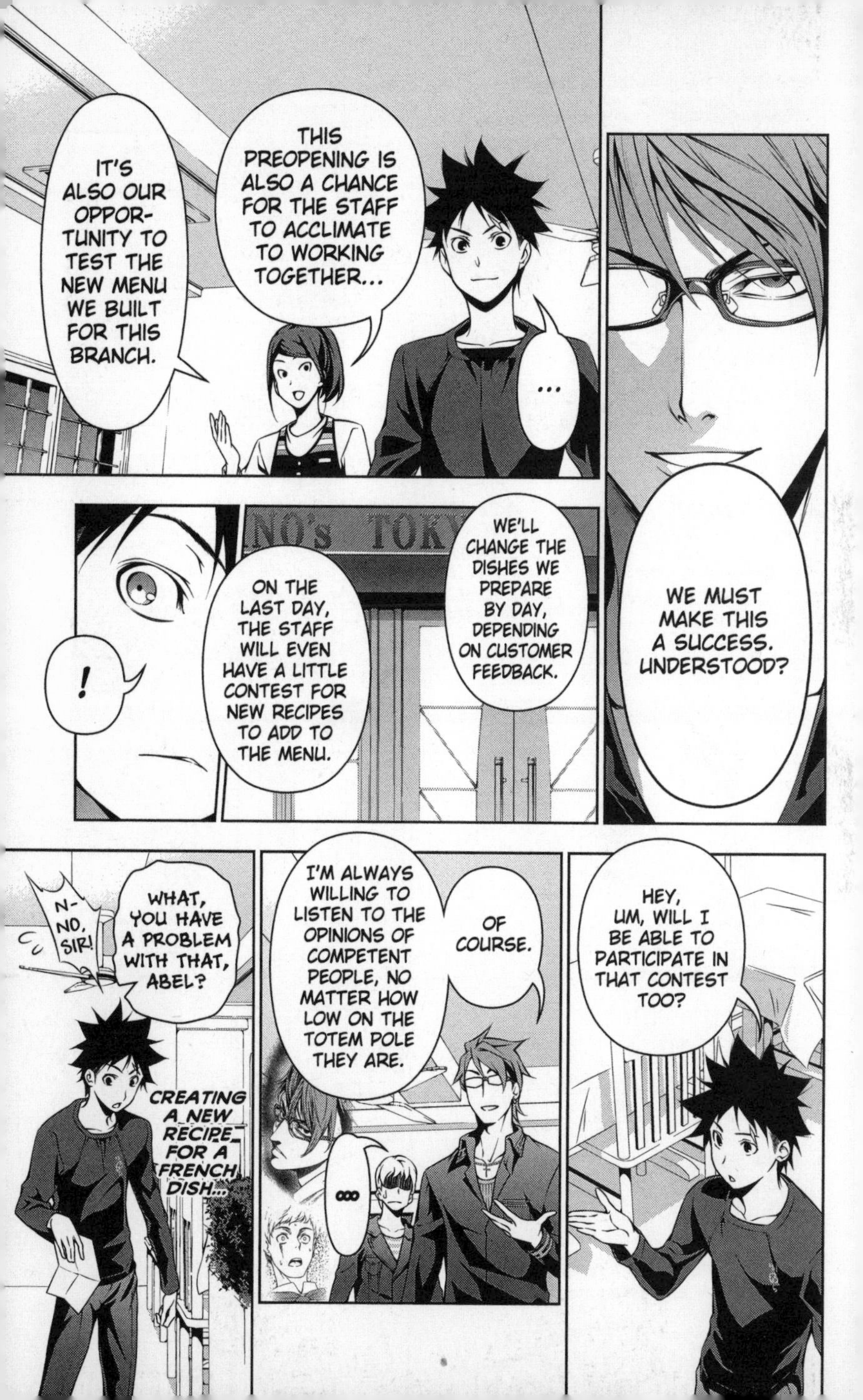
WE MUST MAKE THIS A SUCCESS. UNDERSTOOD?
THIS PREOPENING IS ALSO A CHANCE FOR THE STAFF TO ACCLIMATE TO WORKING TOGETHER...
IT'S ALSO OUR OPPOR-TUNITY TO TEST THE NEW MENU WE BUILT FOR THIS BRANCH.
...
WE'LL CHANGE THE DISHES WE PREPARE BY DAY, DEPENDING ON CUSTOMER FEEDBACK.
ON THE LAST DAY, THE STAFF WILL EVEN HAVE A LITTLE CONTEST FOR NEW RECIPES TO ADD TO THE MENU.
!
HEY, UM, WILL I BE ABLE TO PARTICIPATE IN THAT CONTEST TOO?
OF COURSE.
I'M ALWAYS WILLING TO LISTEN TO THE OPINIONS OF COMPETENT PEOPLE, NO MATTER HOW LOW ON THE TOTEM POLE THEY ARE.
...
WHAT, YOU HAVE A PROBLEM WITH THAT, ABEL?
N-NO, SIR!
CREATING A NEW RECIPE FOR A FRENCH DISH...

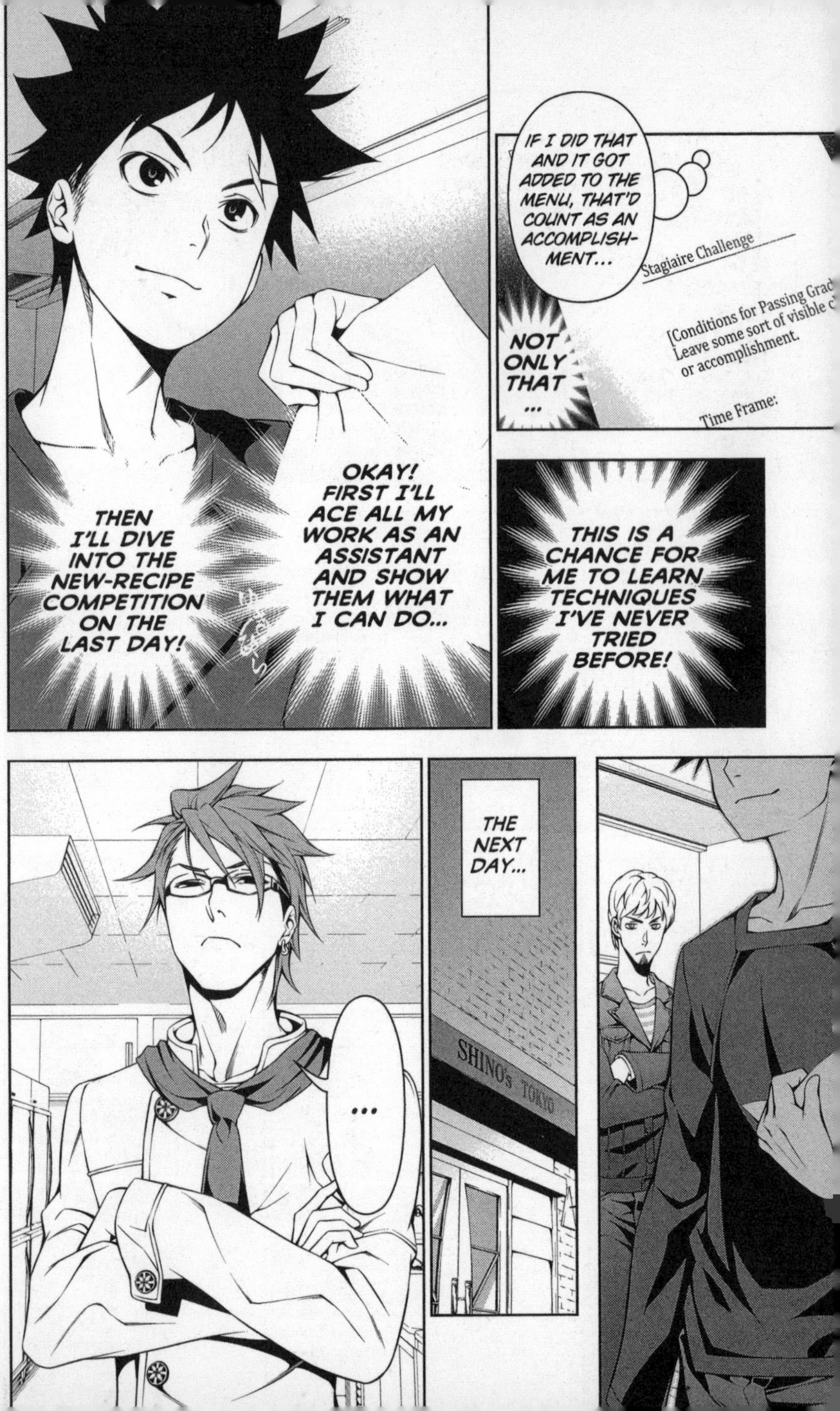
IF I DID THAT AND IT GOT ADDED TO THE MENU, THAT'D COUNT AS AN ACCOMPLISHMENT...
Stagiaire Challenge
[Conditions for Passing Grad
Leave some sort of visible c
or accomplishment.
Time Frame:
NOT ONLY THAT...
THIS IS A CHANCE FOR ME TO LEARN TECHNIQUES I'VE NEVER TRIED BEFORE!
OKAY! FIRST I'LL ACE ALL MY WORK AS AN ASSISTANT AND SHOW THEM WHAT I CAN DO...
THEN I'LL DIVE INTO THE NEW-RECIPE COMPETITION ON THE LAST DAY!
SHINO's TOKYO
THE NEXT DAY...
...

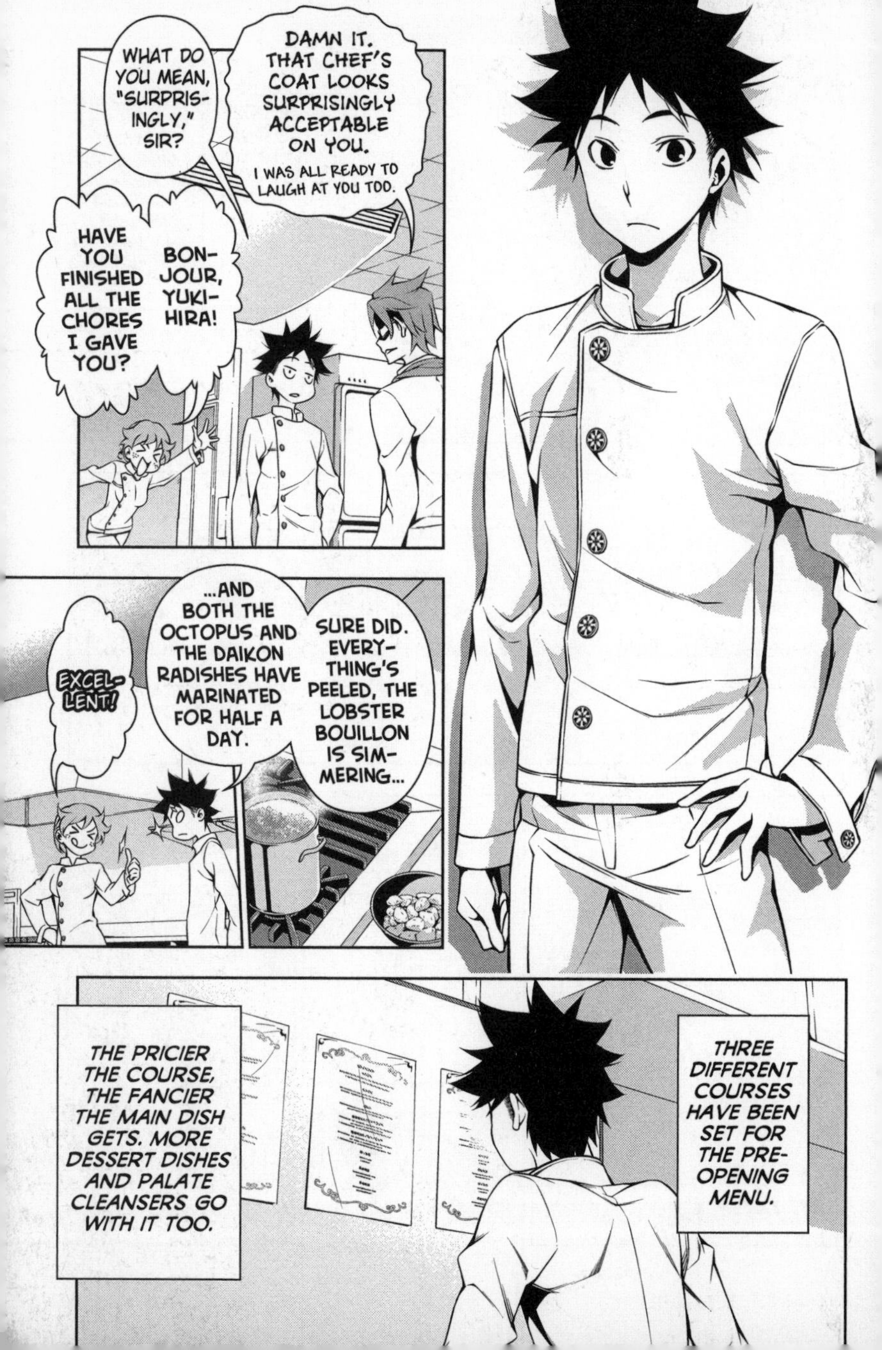
DAMN IT. THAT CHEF'S COAT LOOKS SURPRISINGLY ACCEPTABLE ON YOU.
I WAS ALL READY TO LAUGH AT YOU TOO.
WHAT DO YOU MEAN, "SURPRISINGLY," SIR?
BONJOUR, YUKIHIRA!
HAVE YOU FINISHED ALL THE CHORES I GAVE YOU?
SURE DID. EVERYTHING'S PEELED, THE LOBSTER BOUILLON IS SIMMERING...
...AND BOTH THE OCTOPUS AND THE DAIKON RADISHES HAVE MARINATED FOR HALF A DAY.
EXCELLENT!
THREE DIFFERENT COURSES HAVE BEEN SET FOR THE PRE-OPENING MENU.
THE PRICIER THE COURSE, THE FANCIER THE MAIN DISH GETS. MORE DESSERT DISHES AND PALATE CLEANSERS GO WITH IT TOO.

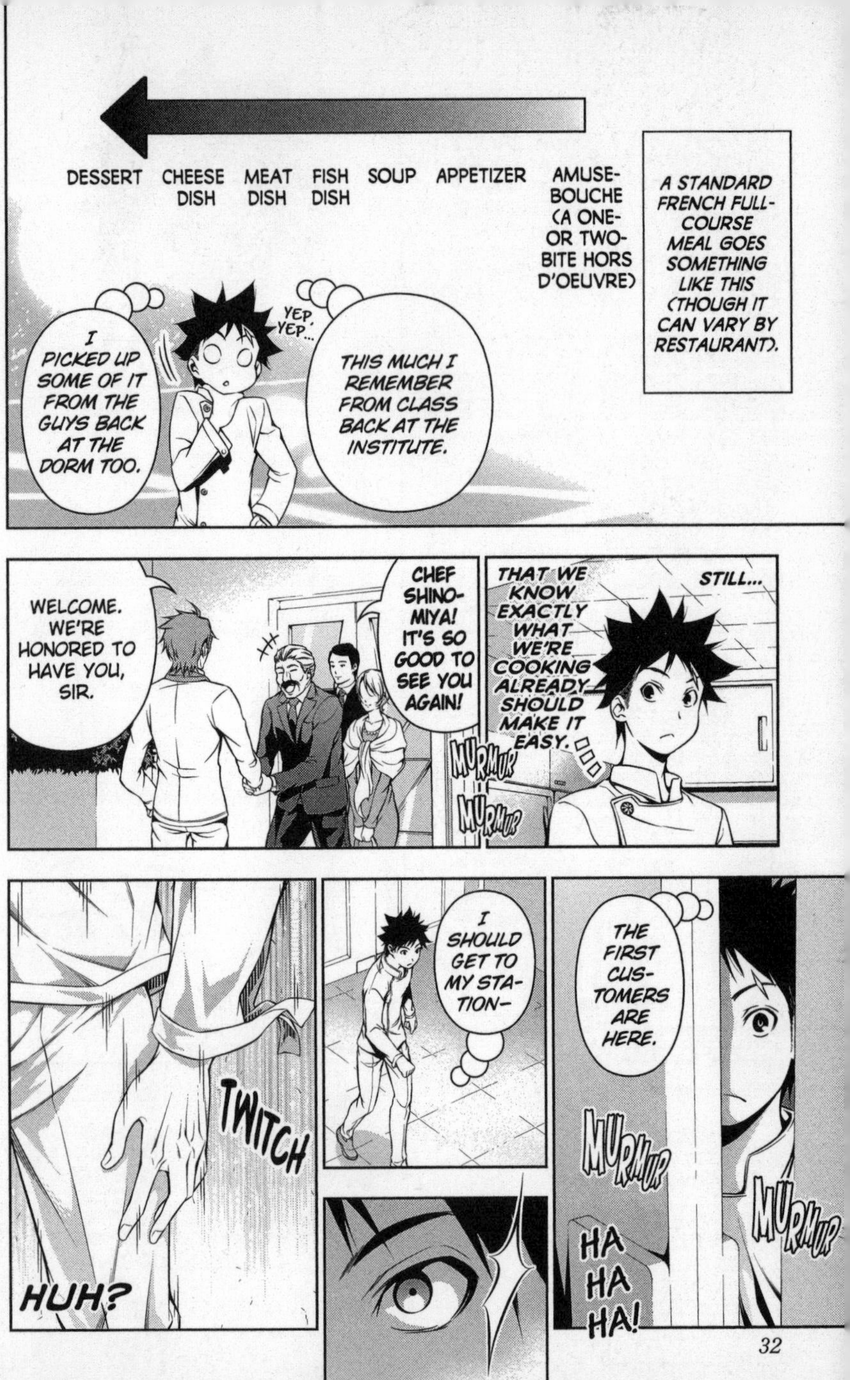
A STANDARD FRENCH FULL-COURSE MEAL GOES SOMETHING LIKE THIS (THOUGH IT CAN VARY BY RESTAURANT).
AMUSE-BOUCHE (A ONE- OR TWO-BITE HORS D'OEUVRE)
APPETIZER
SOUP
FISH DISH
MEAT DISH
CHEESE DISH
DESSERT
THIS MUCH I REMEMBER FROM CLASS BACK AT THE INSTITUTE.
YEP, YEP...
I PICKED UP SOME OF IT FROM THE GUYS BACK AT THE DORM TOO.
STILL...
THAT WE KNOW EXACTLY WHAT WE'RE COOKING ALREADY SHOULD MAKE IT EASY.
MURMUR
MURMUR
CHEF SHINO-MIYA! IT'S SO GOOD TO SEE YOU AGAIN!
WELCOME. WE'RE HONORED TO HAVE YOU, SIR.
THE FIRST CUS-TOMERS ARE HERE.
MURMUR
MURMUR
HA HA HA HA!
I SHOULD GET TO MY STA-TION—
TWITCH
HUH?

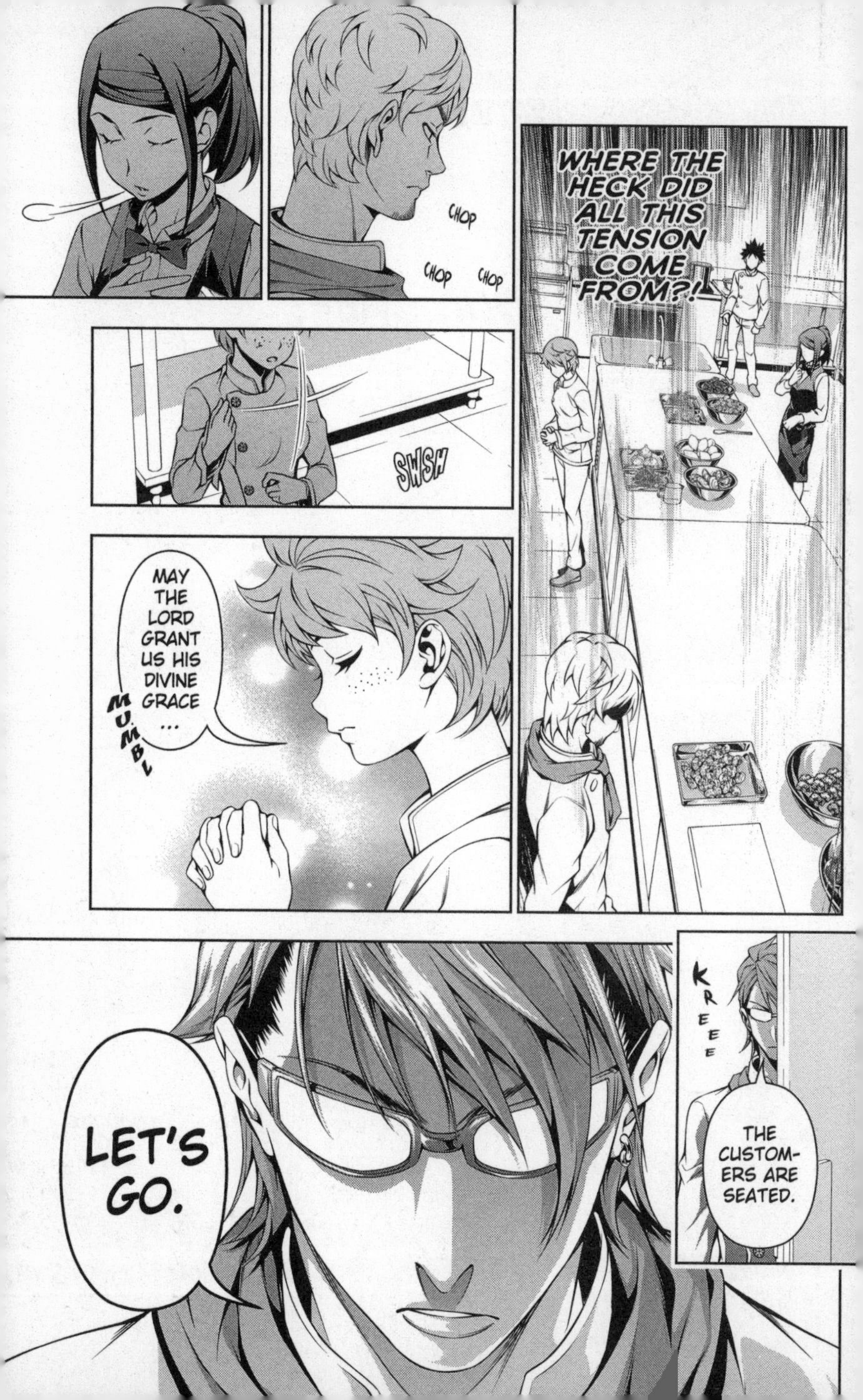
WHERE THE HECK DID ALL THIS TENSION COME FROM?!
CHOP CHOP CHOP
SWSH
MAY THE LORD GRANT US HIS DIVINE GRACE...
MUMBL
KREEE
THE CUSTOM-ERS ARE SEATED.
LET'S GO.

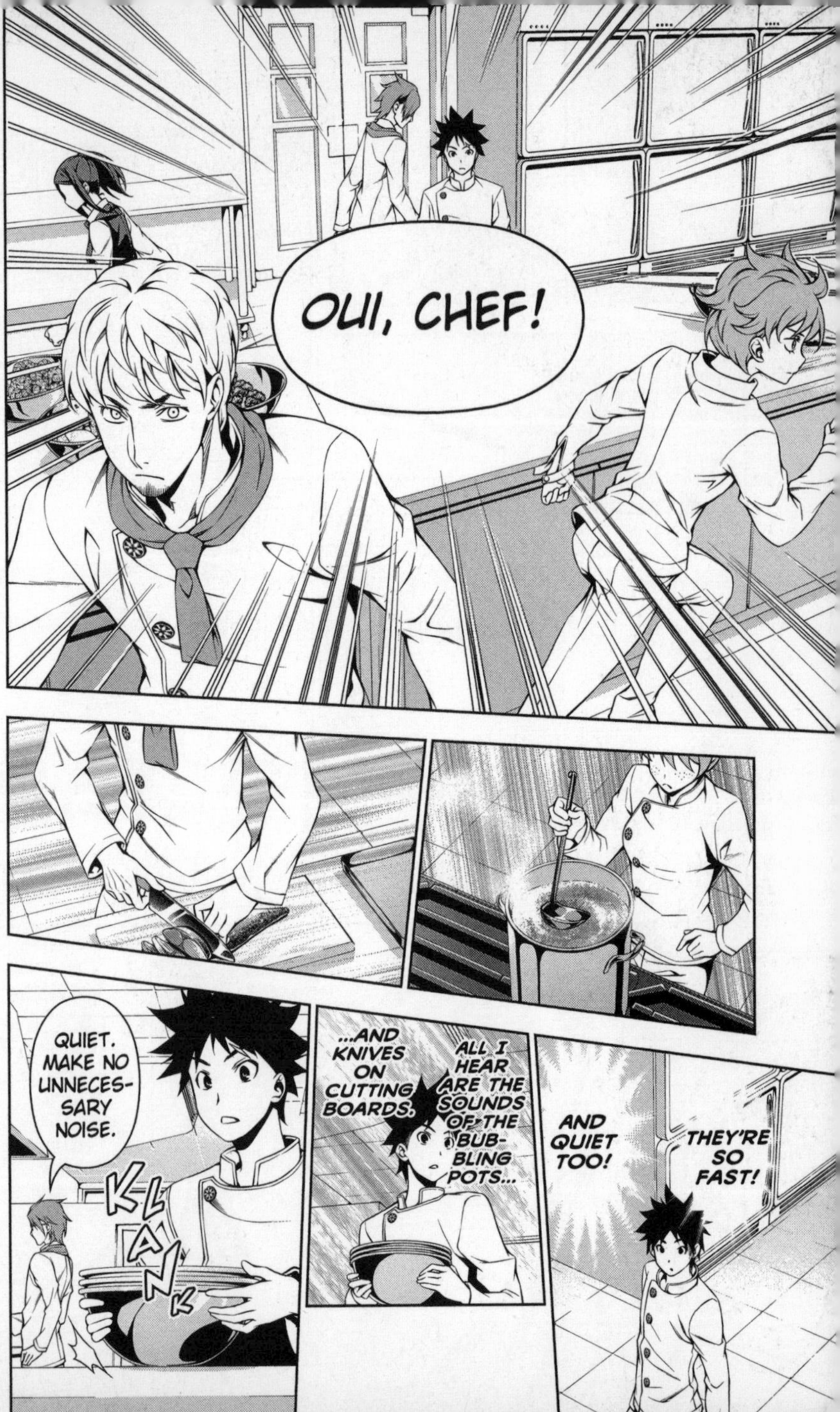
OUI, CHEF!
THEY'RE SO FAST!
AND QUIET TOO!
ALL I HEAR ARE THE SOUNDS OF THE BUB-BLING POTS...
...AND KNIVES ON CUTTING BOARDS.
QUIET. MAKE NO UNNECES-SARY NOISE.
KLANK

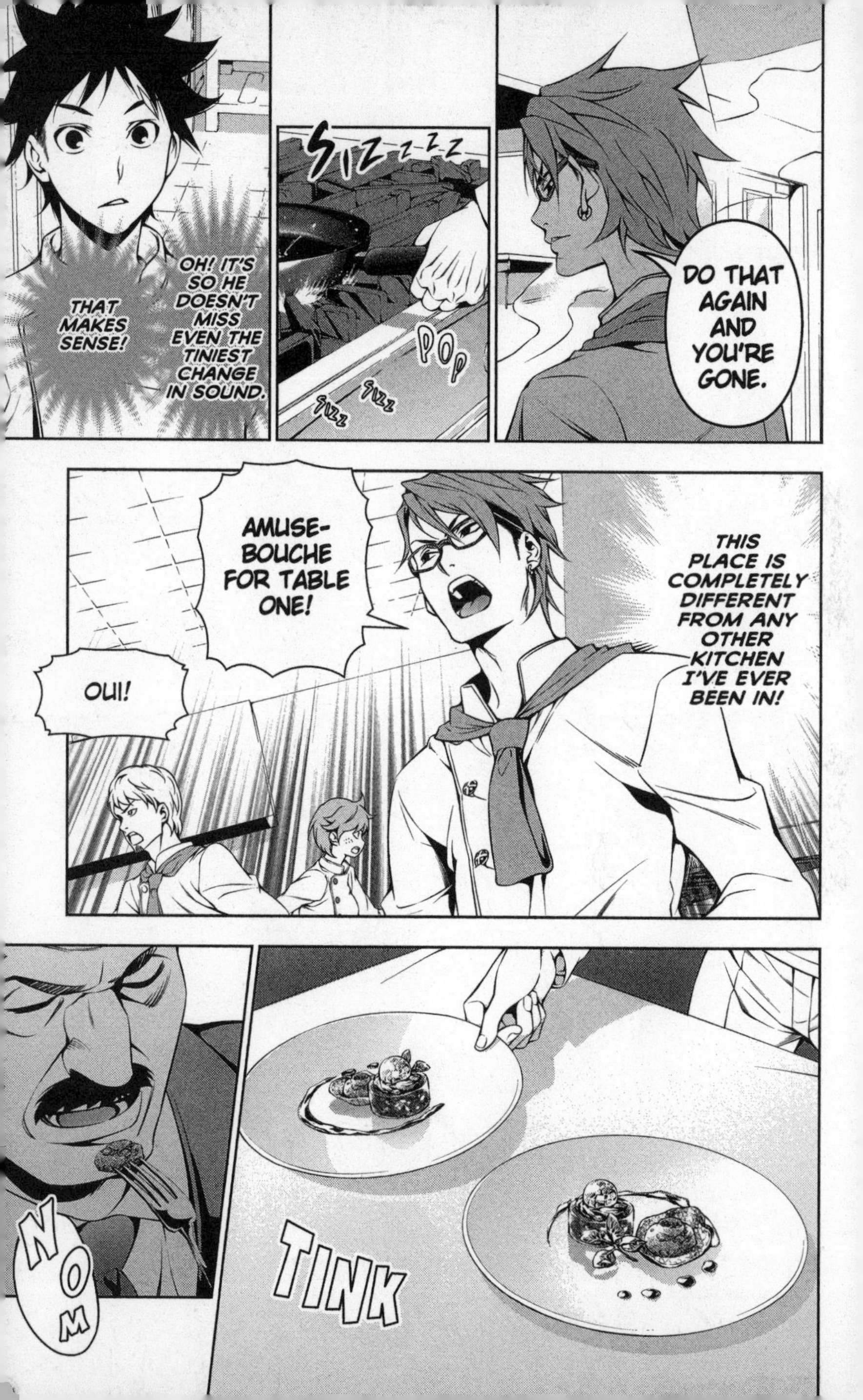
DO THAT AGAIN AND YOU'RE GONE.
SIZZZZZ
POP
SIZZ
SIZZ
OH! IT'S SO HE DOESN'T MISS EVEN THE TINIEST CHANGE IN SOUND.
THAT MAKES SENSE!
THIS PLACE IS COMPLETELY DIFFERENT FROM ANY OTHER KITCHEN I'VE EVER BEEN IN!
AMUSE-BOUCHE FOR TABLE ONE!
OUI!
TINK
NOM

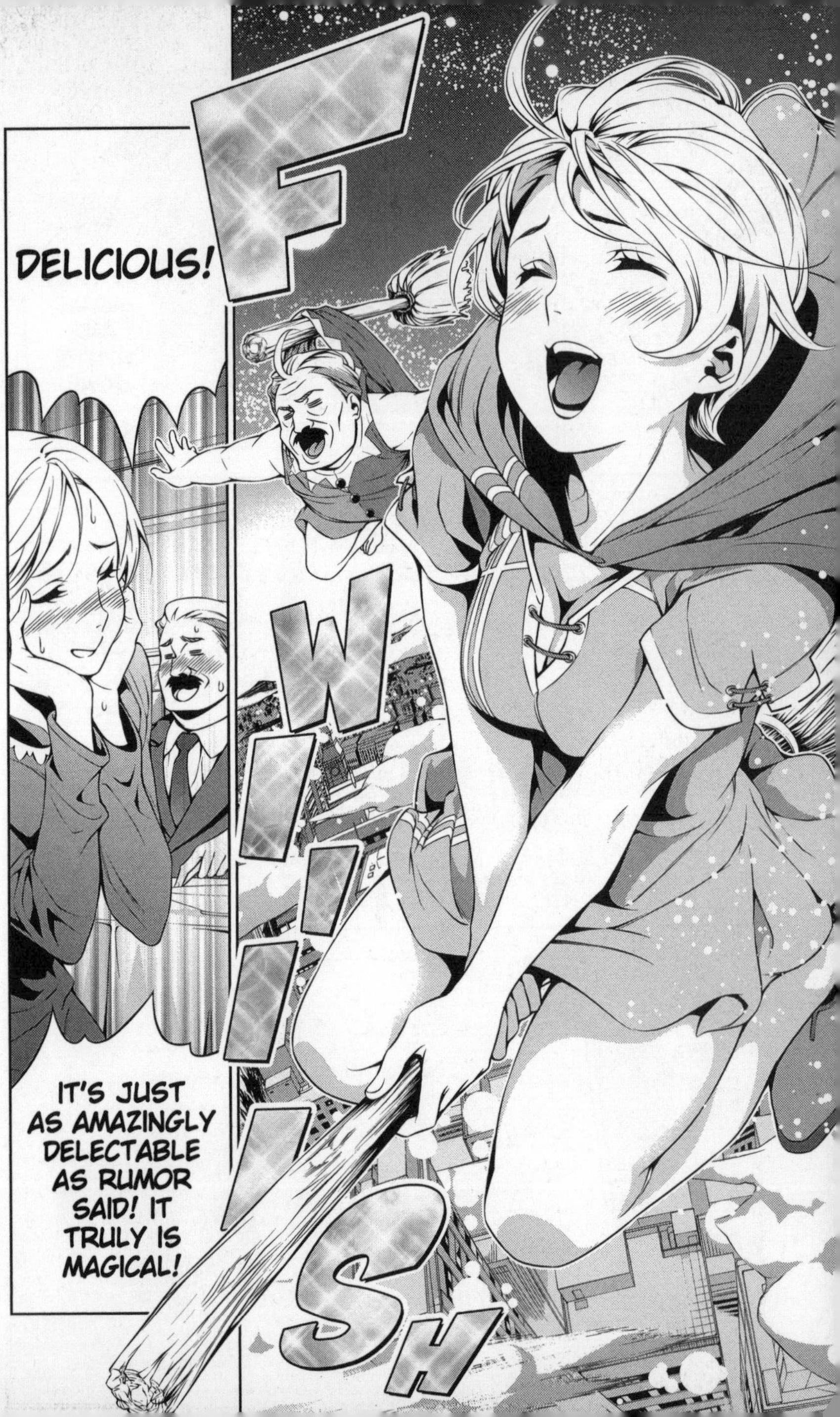
FWIIIISH
DELICIOUS!
IT'S JUST AS AMAZINGLY DELECTABLE AS RUMOR SAID! IT TRULY IS MAGICAL!

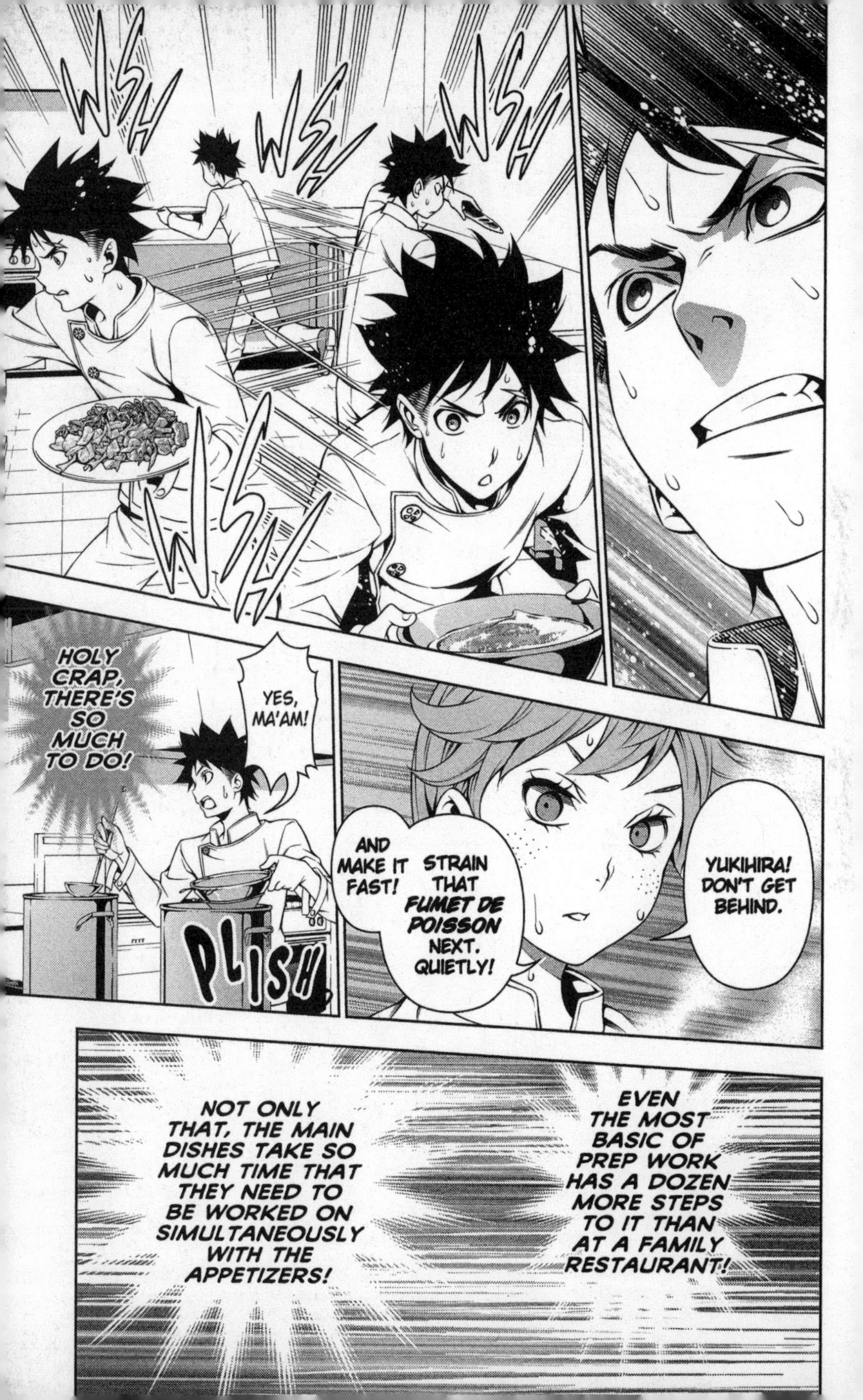
WSH
WSH
WSH
WSH
YUKIHIRA! DON'T GET BEHIND.
STRAIN THAT *FUMET DE POISSON* NEXT. QUIETLY!
AND MAKE IT FAST!
YES, MA'AM!
HOLY CRAP, THERE'S SO MUCH TO DO!
PLISH
EVEN THE MOST BASIC OF PREP WORK HAS A DOZEN MORE STEPS TO IT THAN AT A FAMILY RESTAURANT!
NOT ONLY THAT, THE MAIN DISHES TAKE SO MUCH TIME THAT THEY NEED TO BE WORKED ON SIMULTANEOUSLY WITH THE APPETIZERS!

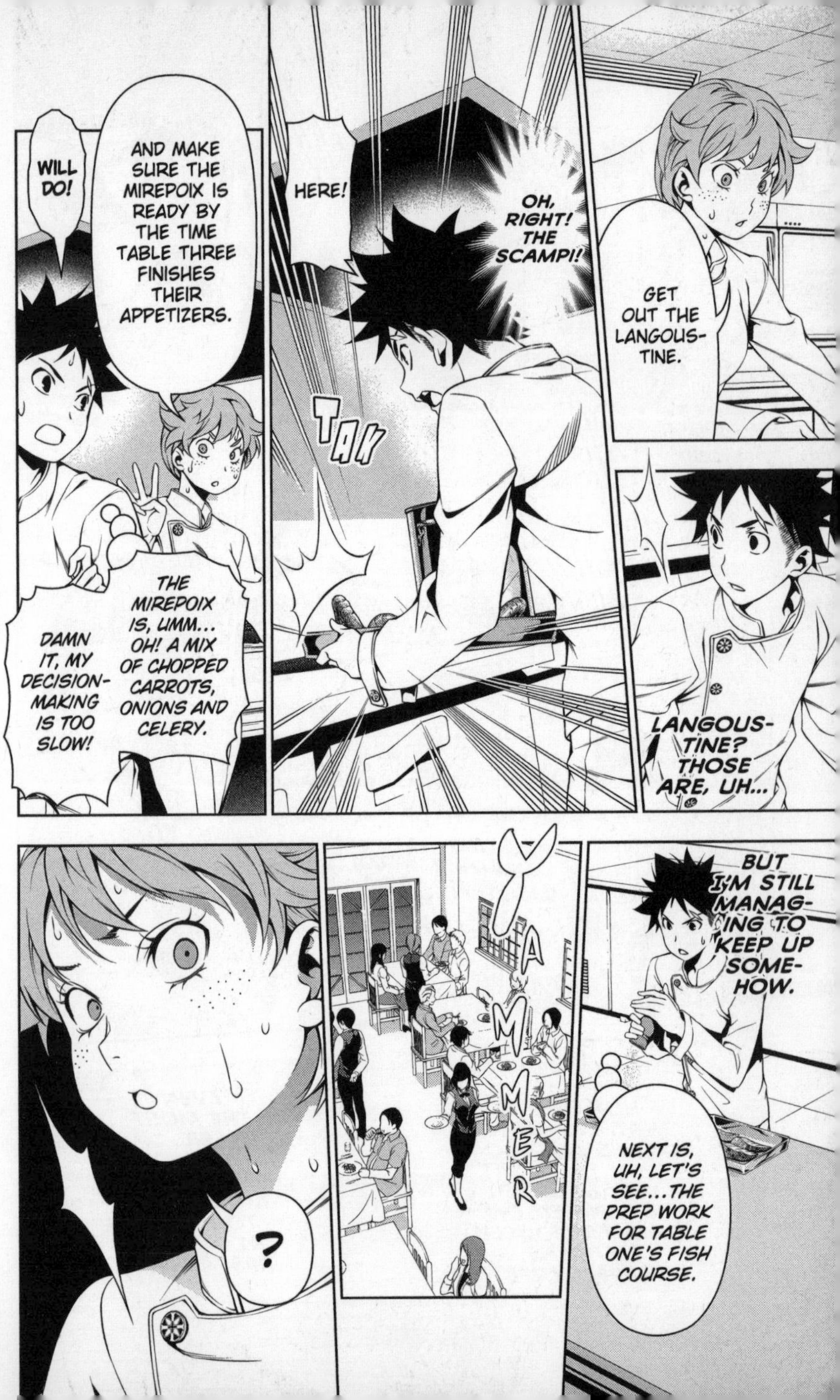
....
GET OUT THE LANGOUS-TINE.
LANGOUS-TINE? THOSE ARE, UH...
OH, RIGHT! THE SCAMPI!
HERE!
TAK
AND MAKE SURE THE MIREPOIX IS READY BY THE TIME TABLE THREE FINISHES THEIR APPETIZERS.
WILL DO!
THE MIREPOIX IS, UMM... OH! A MIX OF CHOPPED CARROTS, ONIONS AND CELERY.
DAMN IT, MY DECISION-MAKING IS TOO SLOW!
BUT I'M STILL MANAG-ING TO KEEP UP SOME-HOW.
NEXT IS, UH, LET'S SEE...THE PREP WORK FOR TABLE ONE'S FISH COURSE.
YAMMER
?

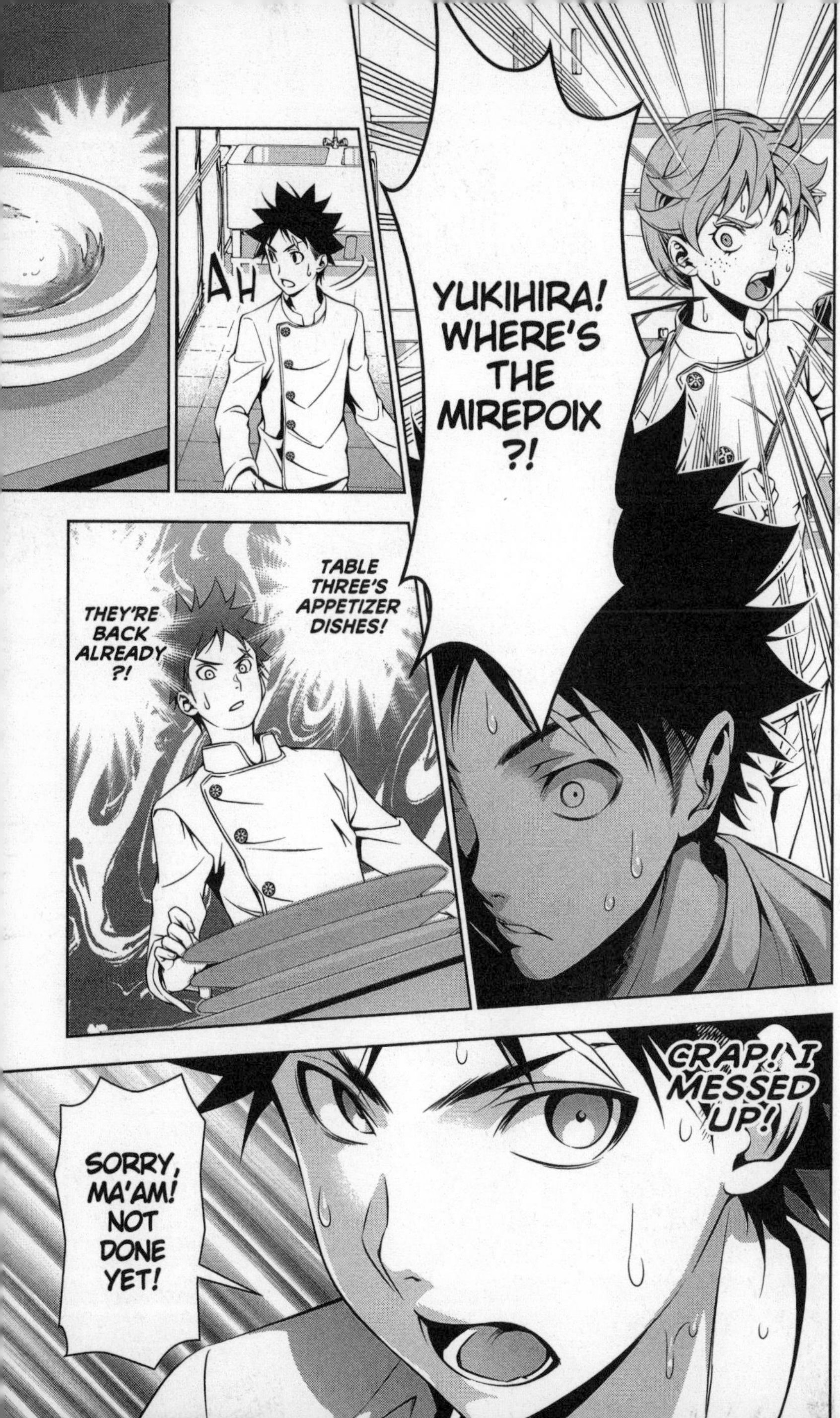

YUKIHIRA! WHERE'S THE MIREPOIX ?!
AH
TABLE THREE'S APPETIZER DISHES!
THEY'RE BACK ALREADY ?!
CRAP! I MESSED UP!
SORRY, MA'AM! NOT DONE YET!

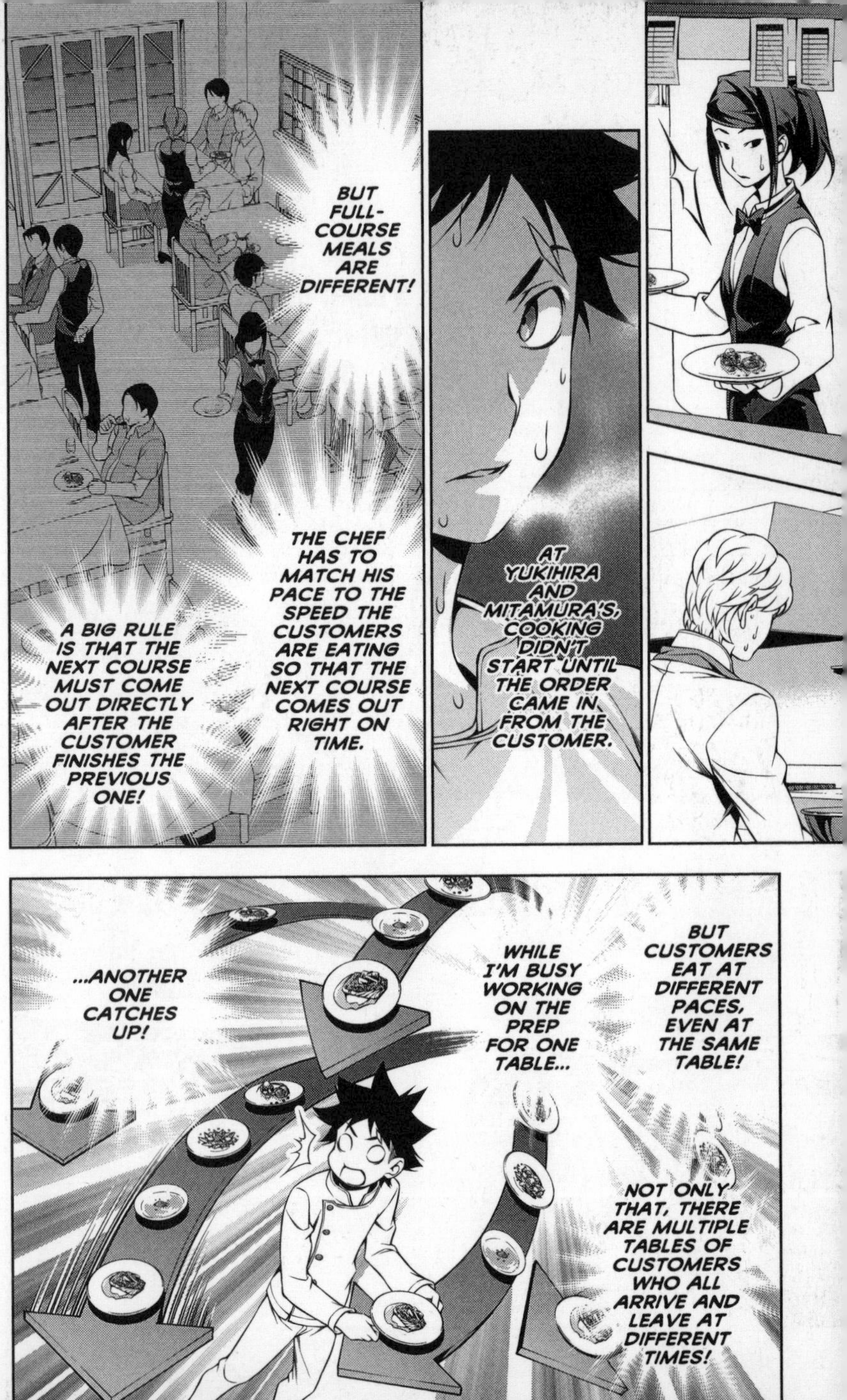
AT YUKIHIRA AND MITAMURA'S, COOKING DIDN'T START UNTIL THE ORDER CAME IN FROM THE CUSTOMER.
BUT FULL-COURSE MEALS ARE DIFFERENT!
THE CHEF HAS TO MATCH HIS PACE TO THE SPEED THE CUSTOMERS ARE EATING SO THAT THE NEXT COURSE COMES OUT RIGHT ON TIME.
A BIG RULE IS THAT THE NEXT COURSE MUST COME OUT DIRECTLY AFTER THE CUSTOMER FINISHES THE PREVIOUS ONE!
BUT CUSTOMERS EAT AT DIFFERENT PACES, EVEN AT THE SAME TABLE!
WHILE I'M BUSY WORKING ON THE PREP FOR ONE TABLE...
...ANOTHER ONE CATCHES UP!
NOT ONLY THAT, THERE ARE MULTIPLE TABLES OF CUSTOMERS WHO ALL ARRIVE AND LEAVE AT DIFFERENT TIMES!

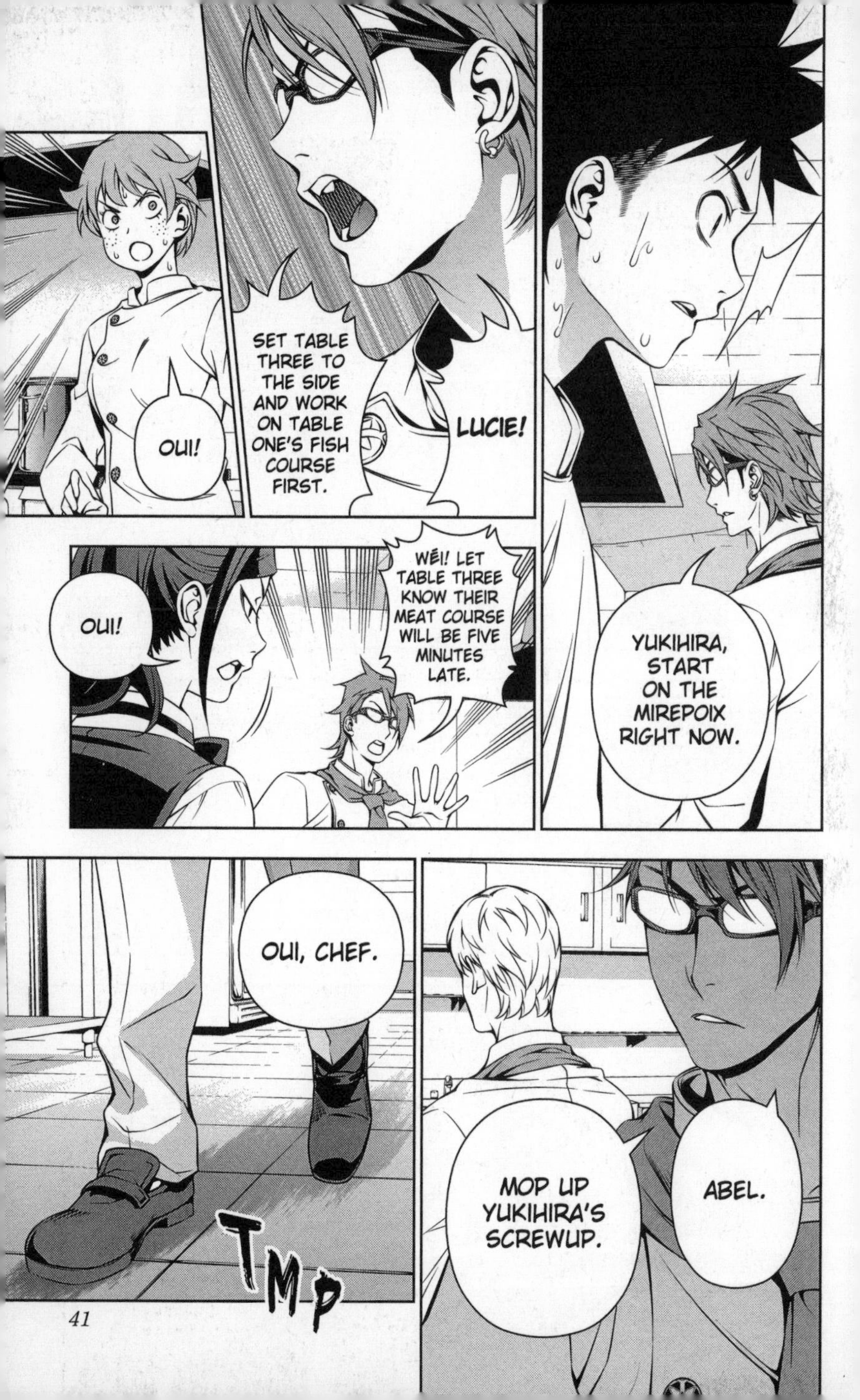
YUKIHIRA, START ON THE MIREPOIX RIGHT NOW.
LUCIE!
SET TABLE THREE TO THE SIDE AND WORK ON TABLE ONE'S FISH COURSE FIRST.
OUI!
WÊI! LET TABLE THREE KNOW THEIR MEAT COURSE WILL BE FIVE MINUTES LATE.
OUI!
ABEL.
MOP UP YUKIHIRA'S SCREWUP.
OUI, CHEF.
TMP

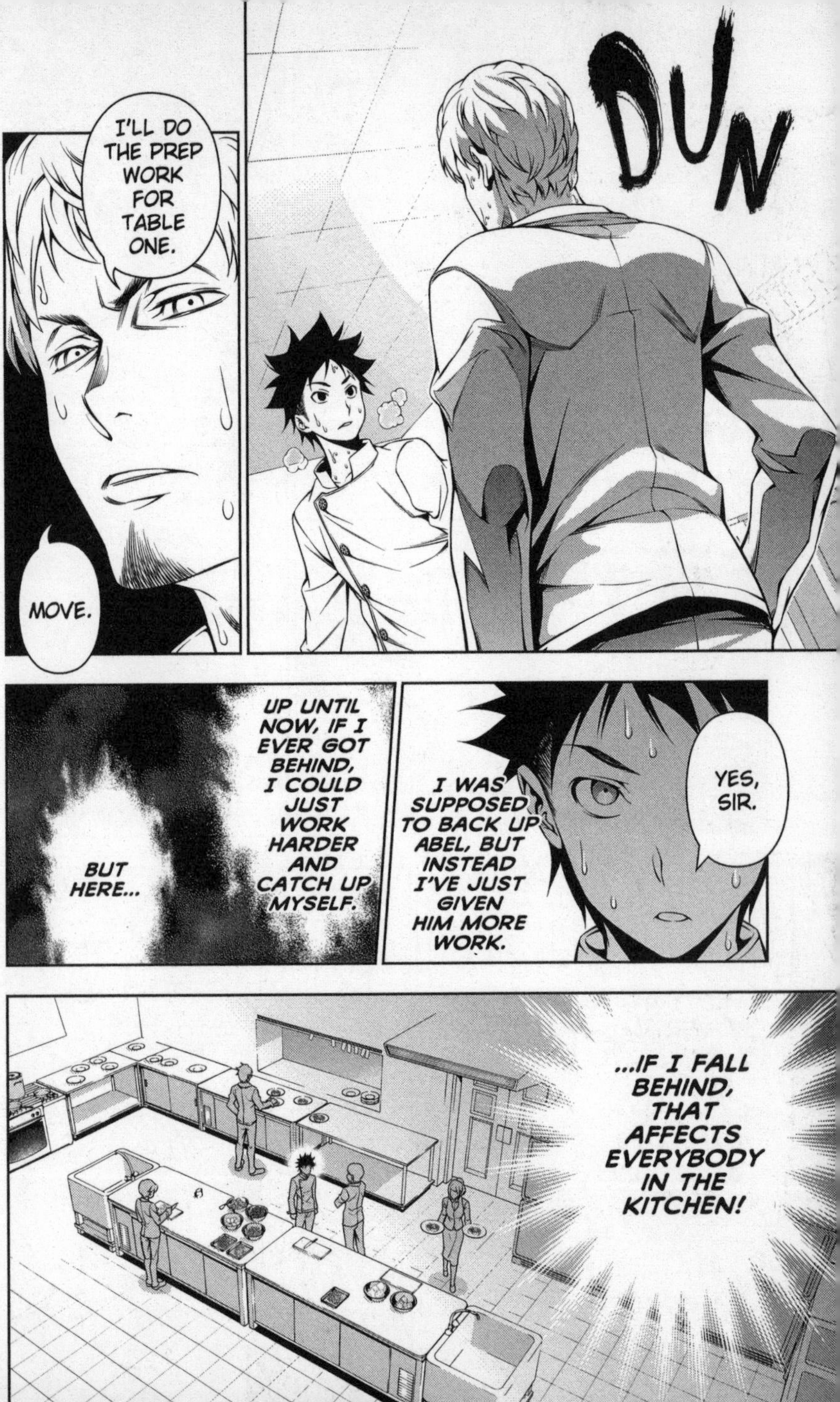
DUN
I'LL DO THE PREP WORK FOR TABLE ONE.
MOVE.
YES, SIR.
I WAS SUPPOSED TO BACK UP ABEL, BUT INSTEAD I'VE JUST GIVEN HIM MORE WORK.
UP UNTIL NOW, IF I EVER GOT BEHIND, I COULD JUST WORK HARDER AND CATCH UP MYSELF.
BUT HERE...
...IF I FALL BEHIND, THAT AFFECTS EVERYBODY IN THE KITCHEN!

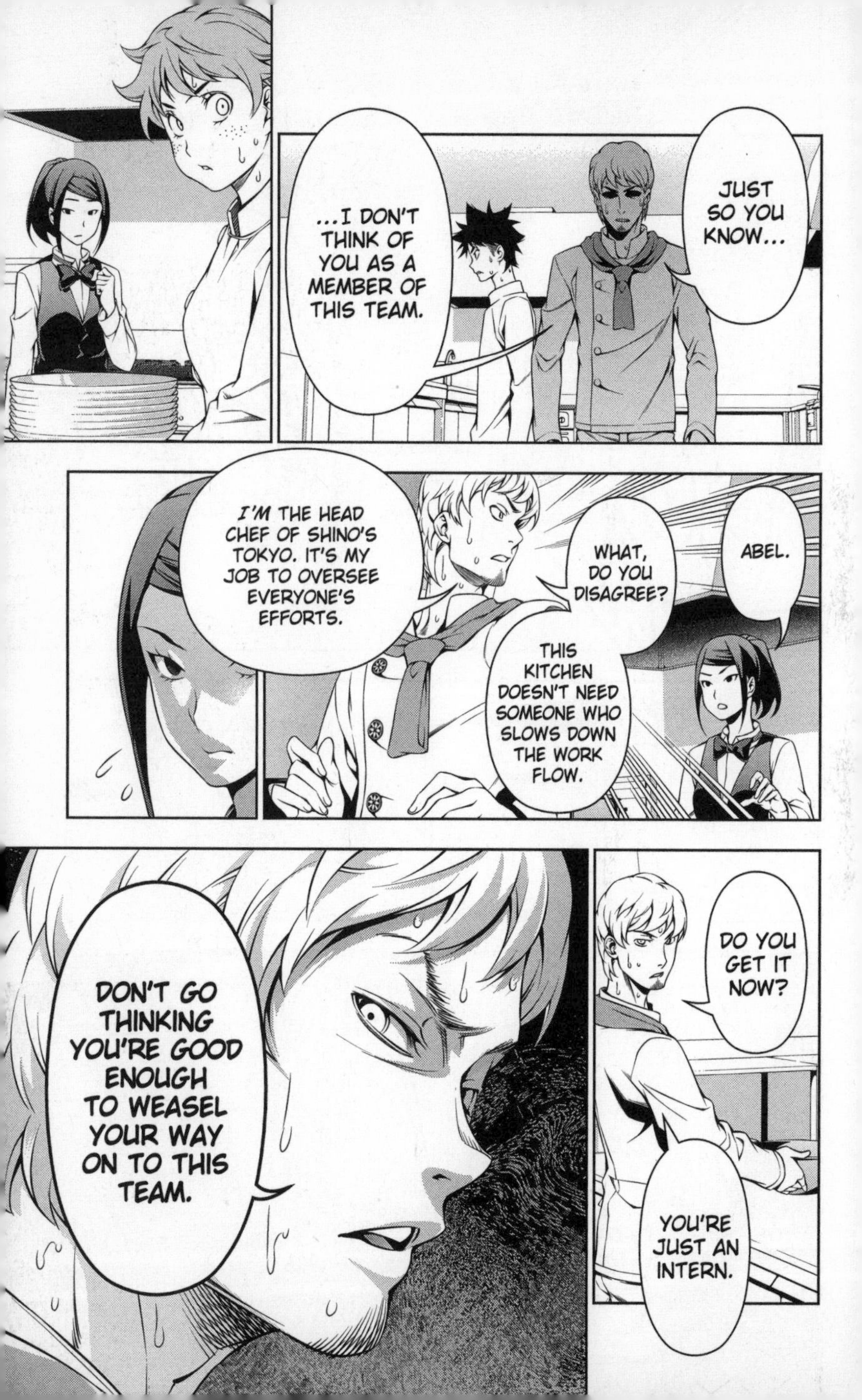
JUST SO YOU KNOW...
...I DON'T THINK OF YOU AS A MEMBER OF THIS TEAM.
ABEL.
WHAT, DO YOU DISAGREE?
THIS KITCHEN DOESN'T NEED SOMEONE WHO SLOWS DOWN THE WORK FLOW.
*I'M* THE HEAD CHEF OF SHINO'S TOKYO. IT'S MY JOB TO OVERSEE EVERYONE'S EFFORTS.
DO YOU GET IT NOW?
YOU'RE JUST AN INTERN.
DON'T GO THINKING YOU'RE GOOD ENOUGH TO WEASEL YOUR WAY ON TO THIS TEAM.

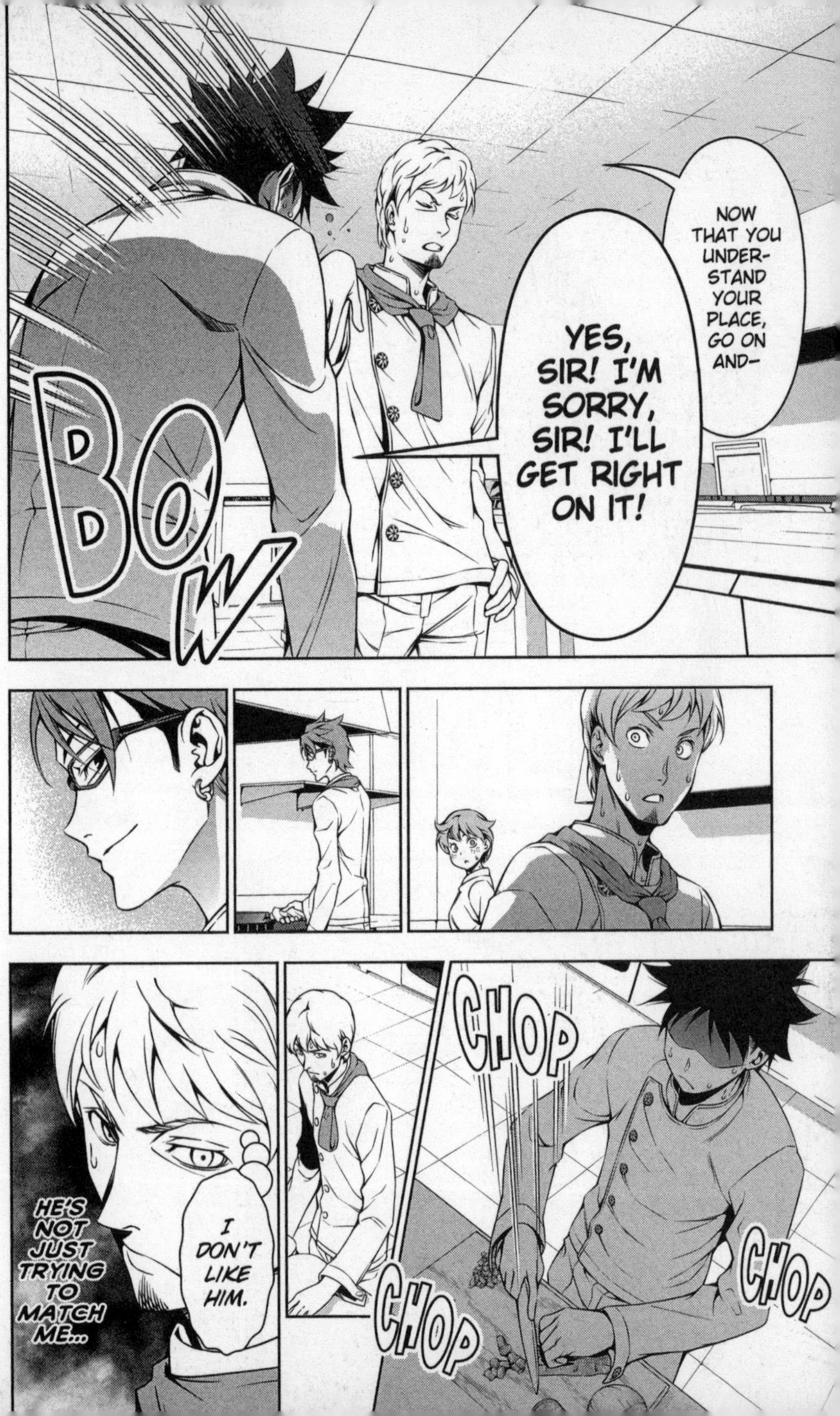
NOW THAT YOU UNDER-STAND YOUR PLACE, GO ON AND—
YES, SIR! I'M SORRY, SIR! I'LL GET RIGHT ON IT!
BOW
CHOP
CHOP
CHOP
I DON'T LIKE HIM.
HE'S NOT JUST TRYING TO MATCH ME...

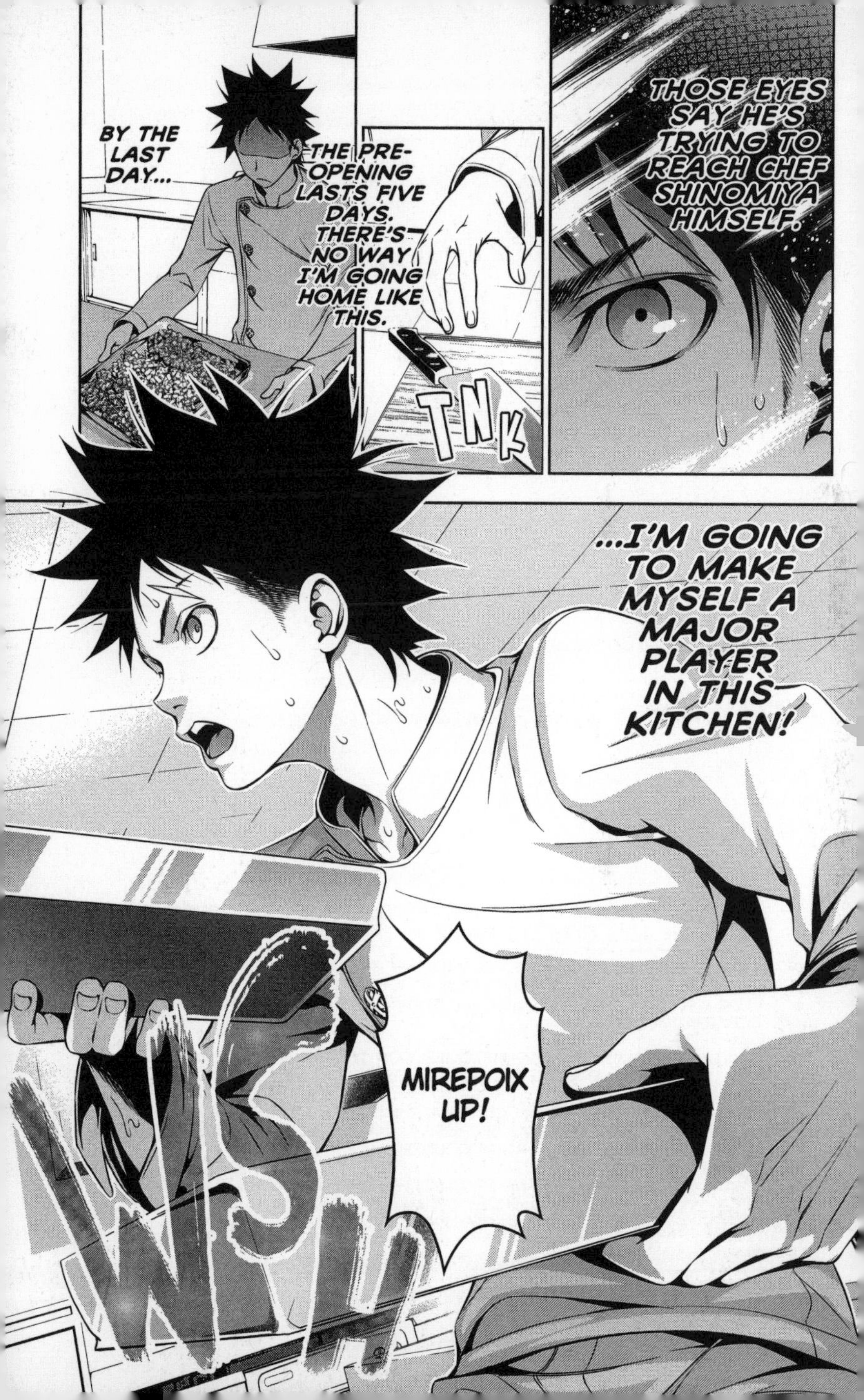
THOSE EYES SAY HE'S TRYING TO REACH CHEF SHINOMIYA HIMSELF.
THE PRE-OPENING LASTS FIVE DAYS. THERE'S NO WAY I'M GOING HOME LIKE THIS.
TNK
BY THE LAST DAY...
...I'M GOING TO MAKE MYSELF A MAJOR PLAYER IN THIS KITCHEN!
MIREPOIX UP!
WSH

## SHOKUGEKI COLUMN

### HOW SHINO'S GOT ITS NAME

I HAVE BEEN ASKED MANY TIMES WHY CHEF SHINOMIYA'S RESTAURANT, SHINO'S, HAS AN ENGLISH NAME (THE APOSTROPHE) WHEN IT'S ACTUALLY LOCATED IN FRANCE. THE REASON FOR THIS COMES FROM A QUIRK IN CHARACTER SETUP.

KOJIRO SHINOMIYA IS MODELED LOOSELY ON SEVERAL PRESENT-DAY, REAL-LIFE JAPANESE CHEFS. ONE OF THOSE CHEFS OPENED RESTAURANTS IN FRANCE AND DELIBERATELY CHOSE TO GIVE THEM ENGLISH OR JAPANESE NAMES THAT WOULD BE DIFFICULT FOR THE LOCALS TO PRONOUNCE OR REMEMBER. I EXPECT IT WAS BECAUSE HE WANTED TO EMPHASIZE THE FACT THAT HE CAME FROM A FOREIGN COUNTRY.

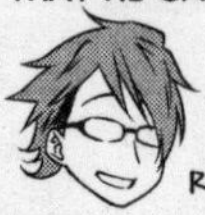

USING THE NAME OF THAT CHEF'S FIRST FOREIGN RESTAURANT AS A BASE, I CHOSE THE ENGLISH NAME "SHINO'S" FOR CHEF SHINOMIYA'S RESTAURANT.

REMEMBER IT

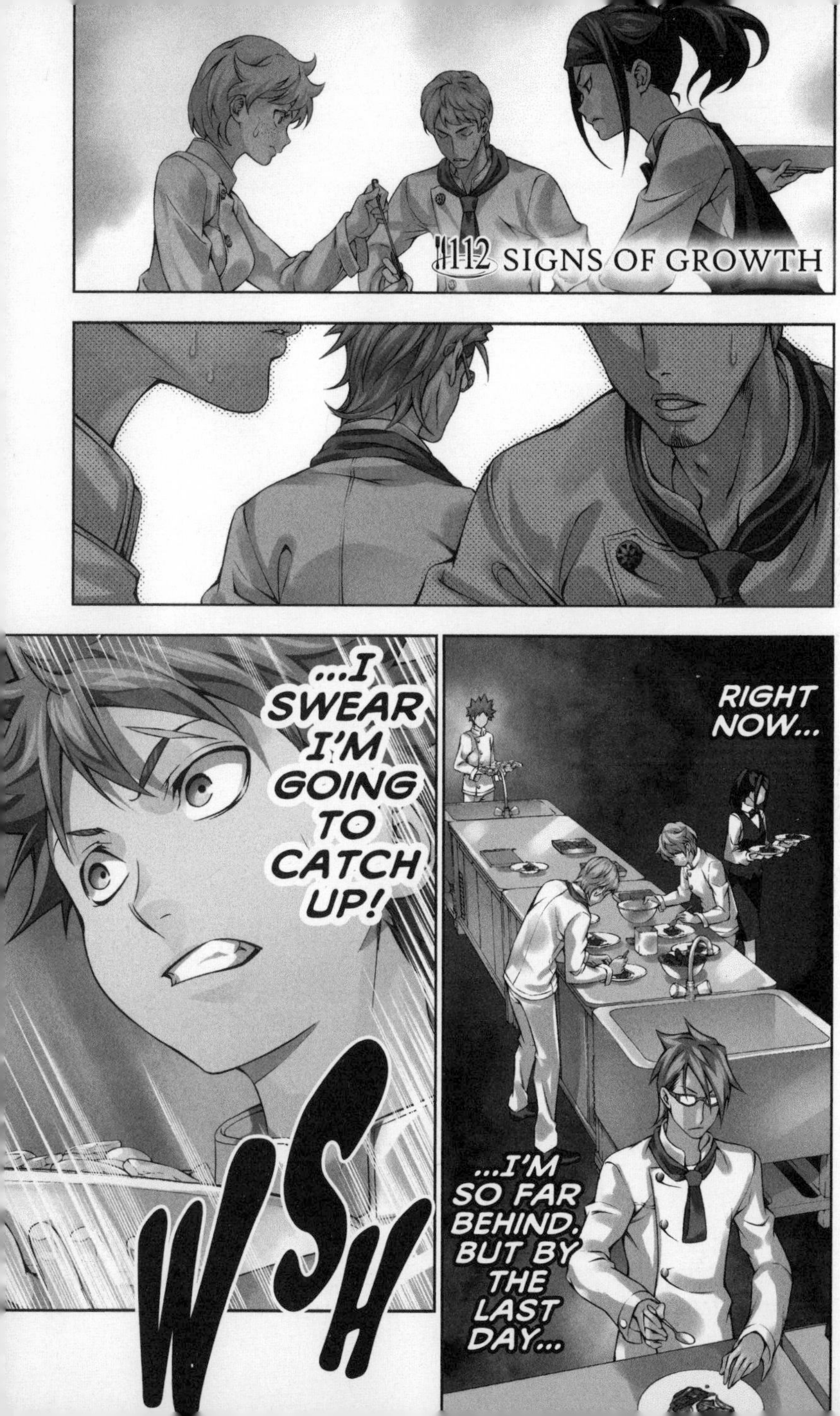
112 SIGNS OF GROWTH
RIGHT NOW...
...I'M SO FAR BEHIND, BUT BY THE LAST DAY...
...I SWEAR I'M GOING TO CATCH UP!
WSH

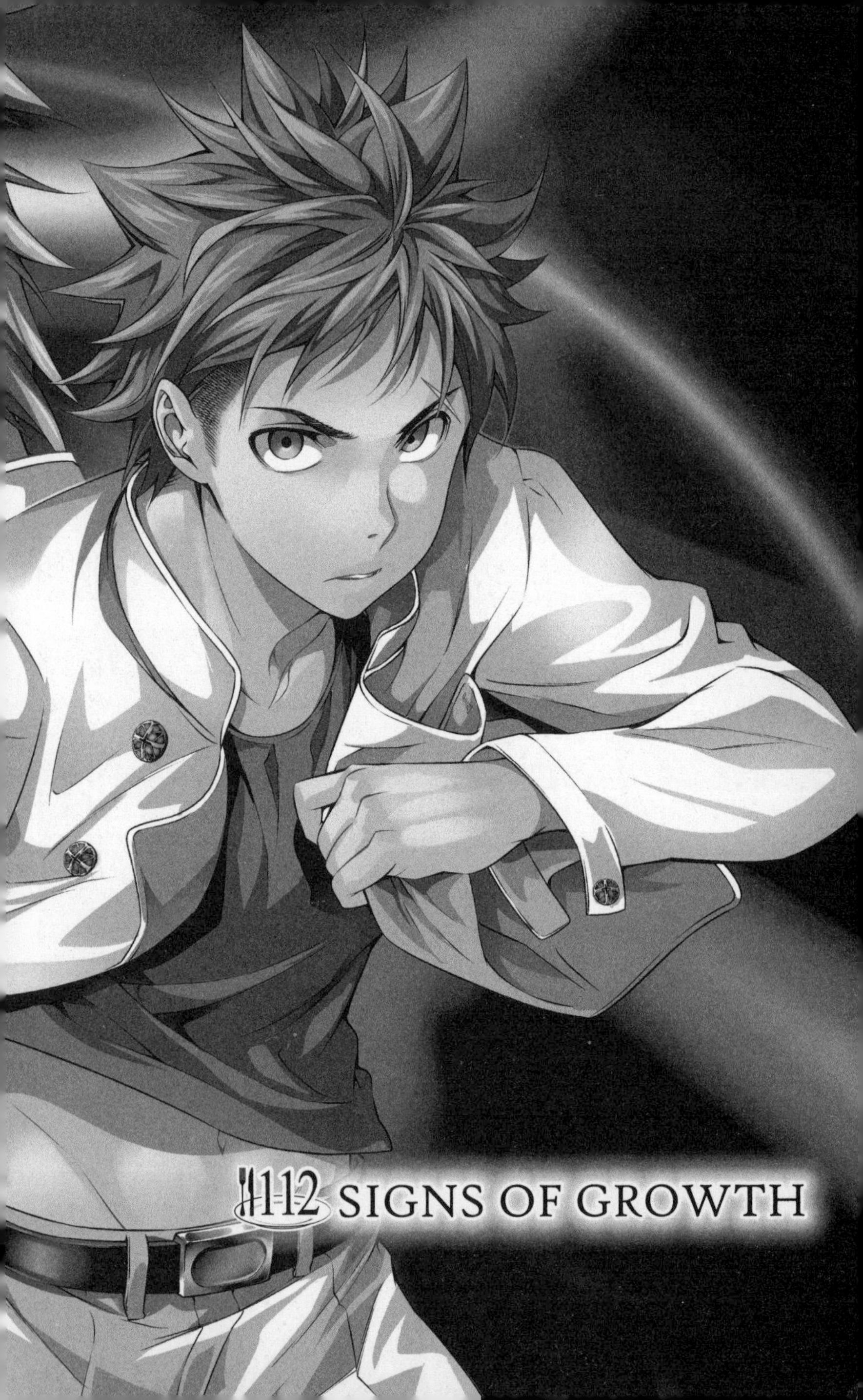
112 SIGNS OF GROWTH

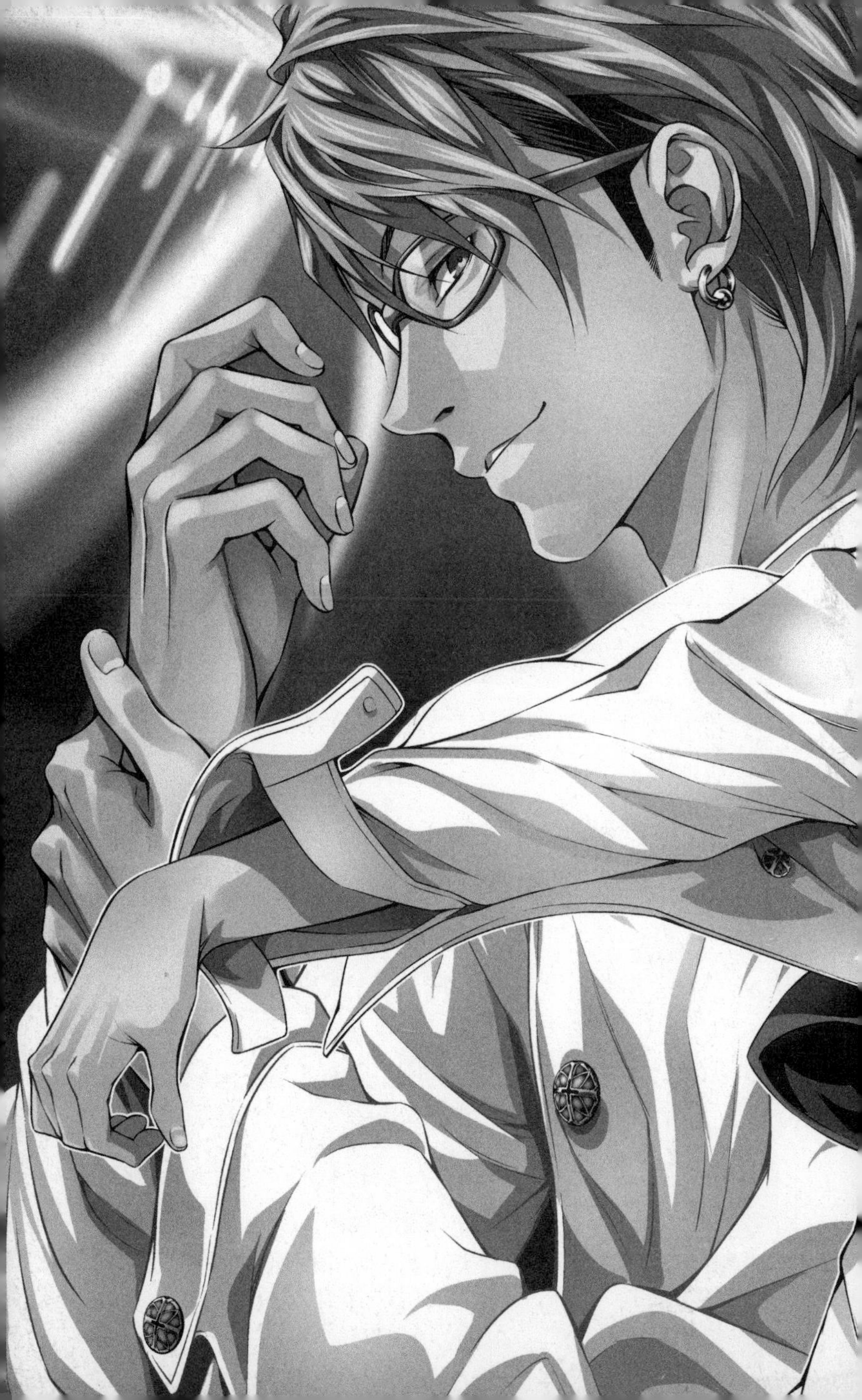

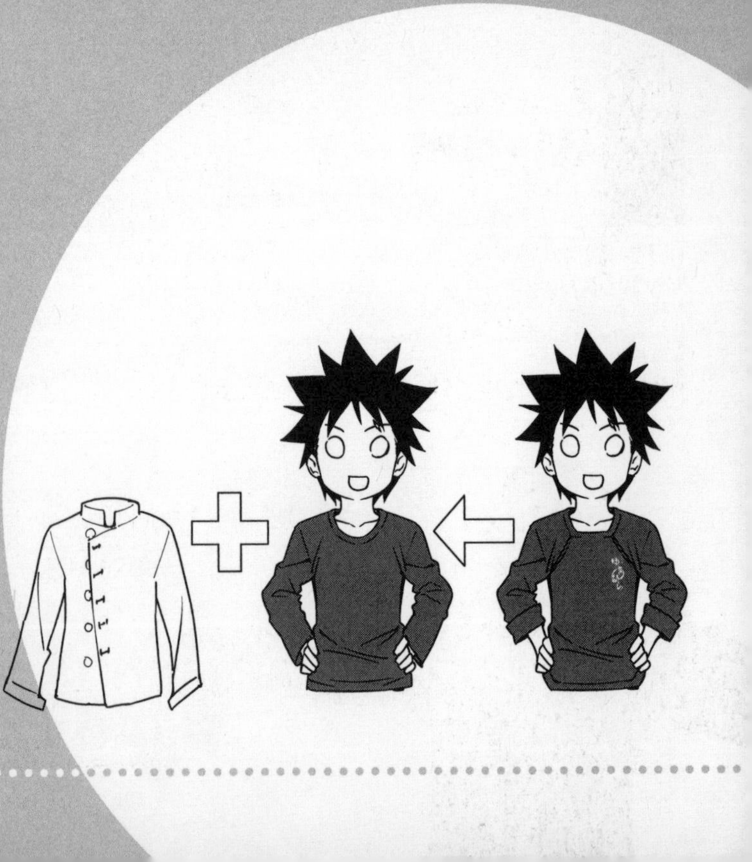

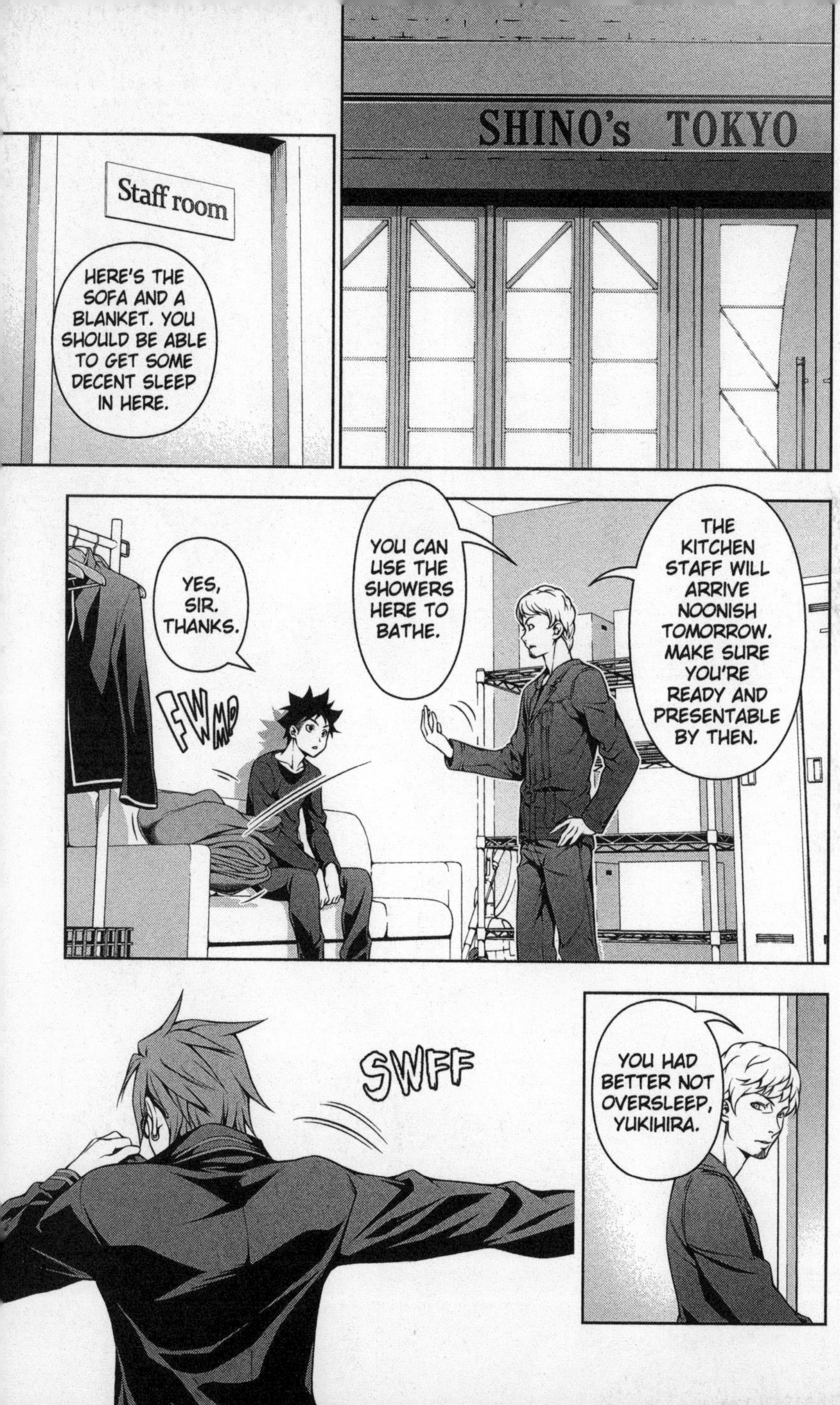
SHINO's TOKYO
Staff room
HERE'S THE SOFA AND A BLANKET. YOU SHOULD BE ABLE TO GET SOME DECENT SLEEP IN HERE.
THE KITCHEN STAFF WILL ARRIVE NOONISH TOMORROW. MAKE SURE YOU'RE READY AND PRESENTABLE BY THEN.
YOU CAN USE THE SHOWERS HERE TO BATHE.
YES, SIR. THANKS.
FWMP
YOU HAD BETTER NOT OVERSLEEP, YUKIHIRA.
SWFF

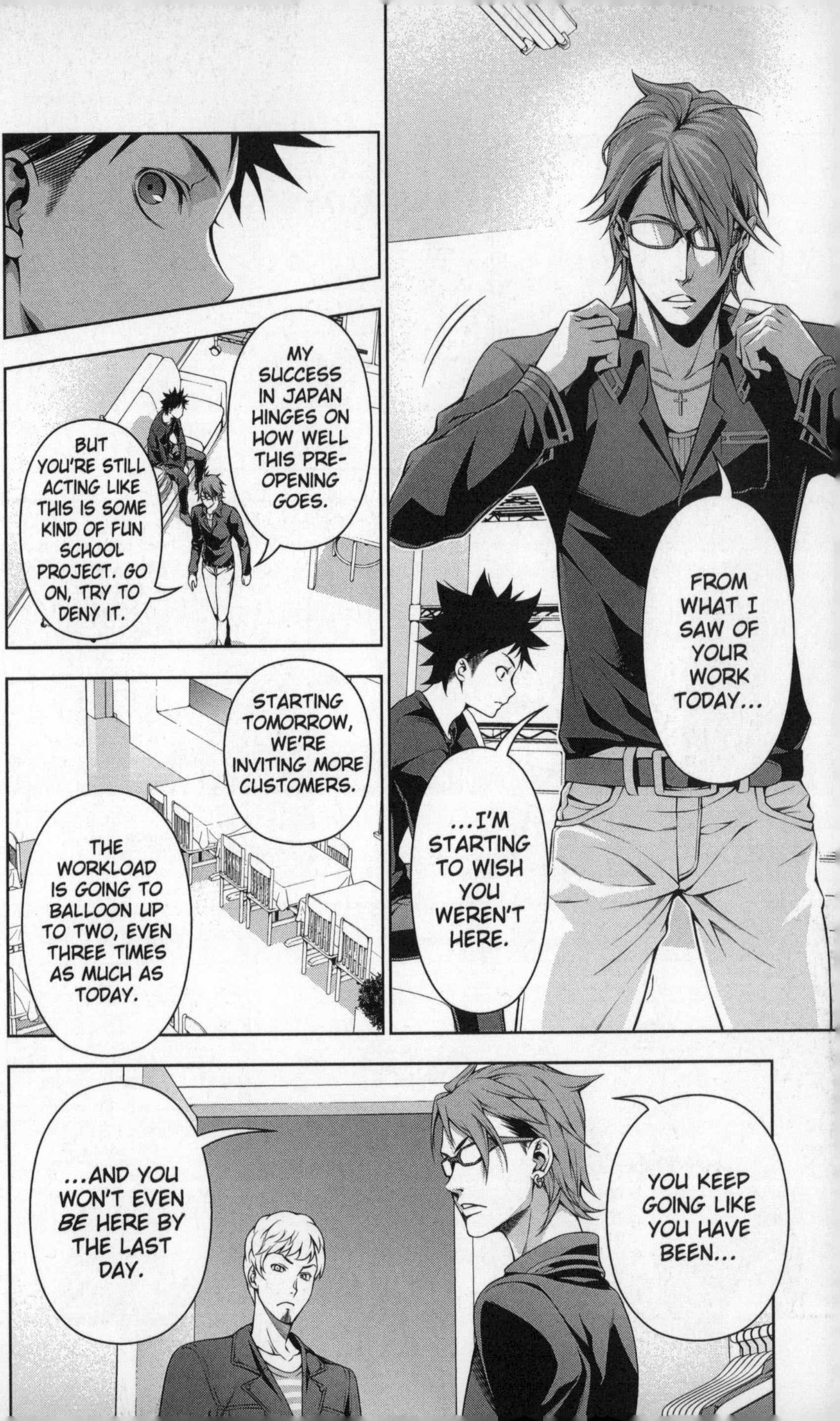
FROM WHAT I SAW OF YOUR WORK TODAY...
...I'M STARTING TO WISH YOU WEREN'T HERE.
MY SUCCESS IN JAPAN HINGES ON HOW WELL THIS PRE-OPENING GOES.
BUT YOU'RE STILL ACTING LIKE THIS IS SOME KIND OF FUN SCHOOL PROJECT. GO ON, TRY TO DENY IT.
STARTING TOMORROW, WE'RE INVITING MORE CUSTOMERS.
THE WORKLOAD IS GOING TO BALLOON UP TO TWO, EVEN THREE TIMES AS MUCH AS TODAY.
YOU KEEP GOING LIKE YOU HAVE BEEN...
...AND YOU WON'T EVEN *BE* HERE BY THE LAST DAY.

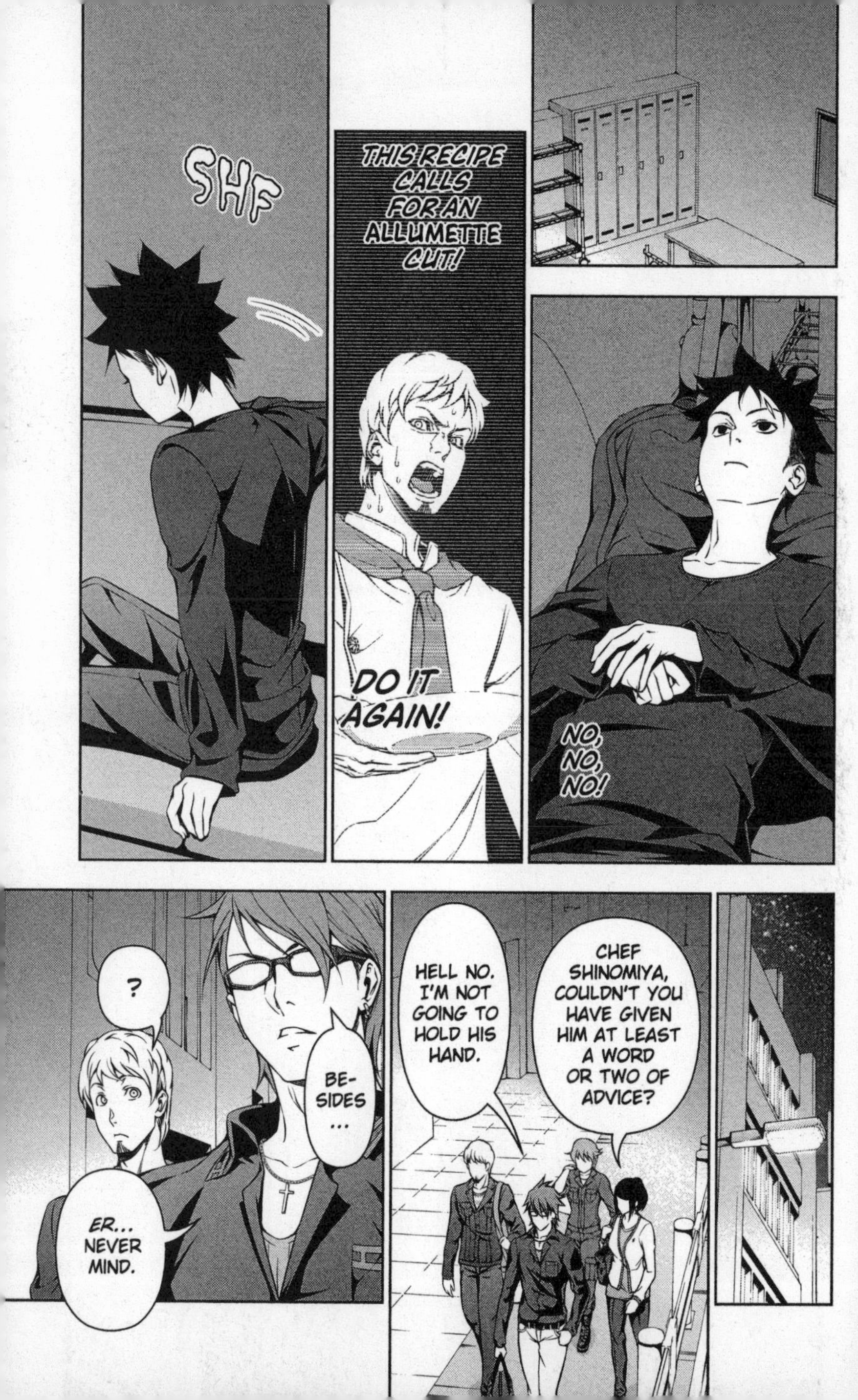
NO, NO, NO!
THIS RECIPE CALLS FOR AN ALLUMETTE CUT!
DO IT AGAIN!
SHF
CHEF SHINOMIYA, COULDN'T YOU HAVE GIVEN HIM AT LEAST A WORD OR TWO OF ADVICE?
HELL NO. I'M NOT GOING TO HOLD HIS HAND.
BE-SIDES...
?
ER... NEVER MIND.

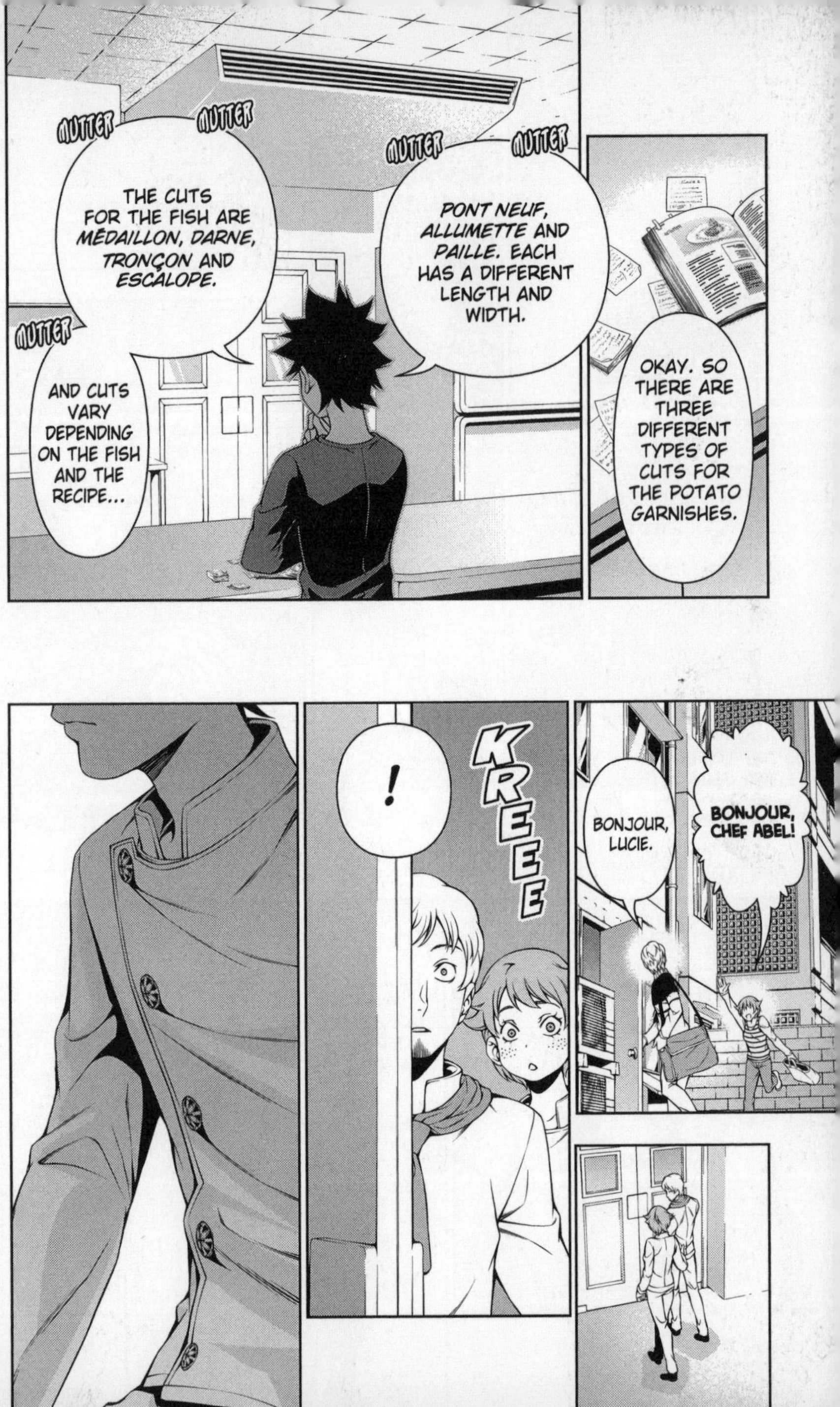
OKAY. SO THERE ARE THREE DIFFERENT TYPES OF CUTS FOR THE POTATO GARNISHES.
MUTTER
MUTTER
PONT NEUF, ALLUMETTE AND PAILLE. EACH HAS A DIFFERENT LENGTH AND WIDTH.
MUTTER
MUTTER
THE CUTS FOR THE FISH ARE MÉDAILLON, DARNE, TRONÇON AND ESCALOPE.
MUTTER
AND CUTS VARY DEPENDING ON THE FISH AND THE RECIPE...
BONJOUR, CHEF ABEL!
BONJOUR, LUCIE.
KREEE
!

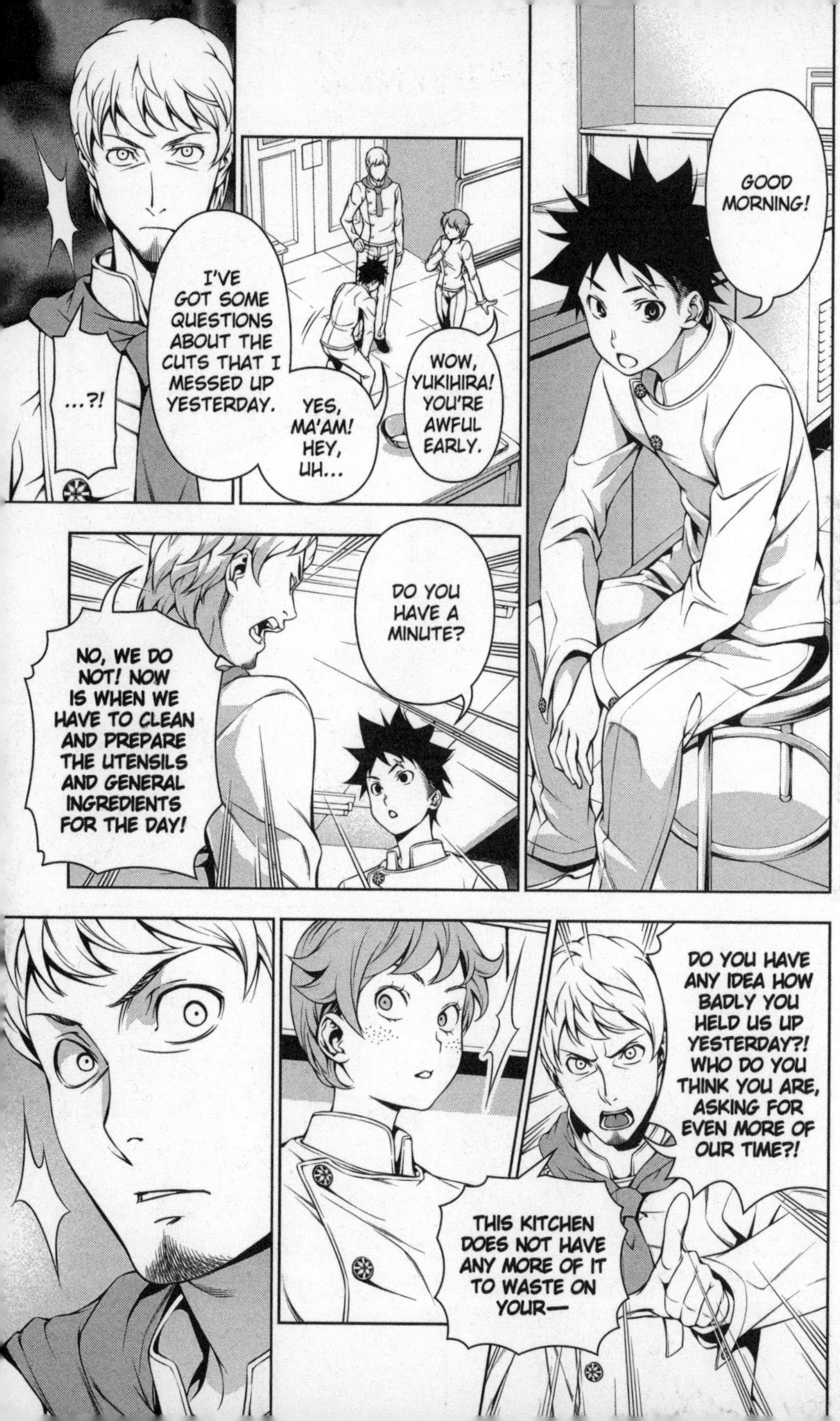
GOOD MORNING!
WOW, YUKIHIRA! YOU'RE AWFUL EARLY.
YES, MA'AM! HEY, UH...
I'VE GOT SOME QUESTIONS ABOUT THE CUTS THAT I MESSED UP YESTERDAY.
...?!
DO YOU HAVE A MINUTE?
NO, WE DO NOT! NOW IS WHEN WE HAVE TO CLEAN AND PREPARE THE UTENSILS AND GENERAL INGREDIENTS FOR THE DAY!
DO YOU HAVE ANY IDEA HOW BADLY YOU HELD US UP YESTERDAY?! WHO DO YOU THINK YOU ARE, ASKING FOR EVEN MORE OF OUR TIME?!
THIS KITCHEN DOES NOT HAVE ANY MORE OF IT TO WASTE ON YOUR—

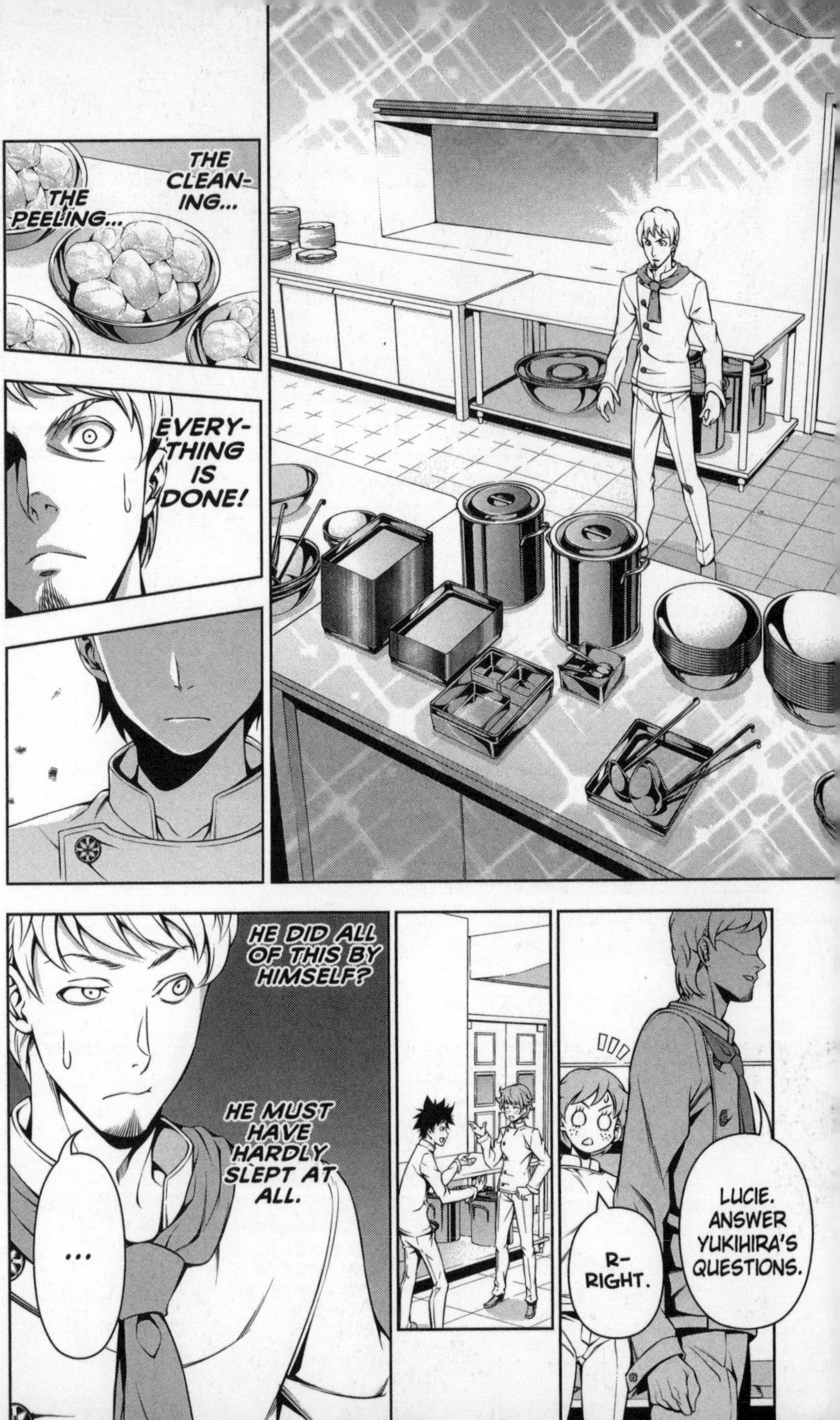
THE CLEANING...
THE PEELING...
EVERYTHING IS DONE!
LUCIE. ANSWER YUKIHIRA'S QUESTIONS.
R-RIGHT.
HE DID ALL OF THIS BY HIMSELF?
HE MUST HAVE HARDLY SLEPT AT ALL.
...

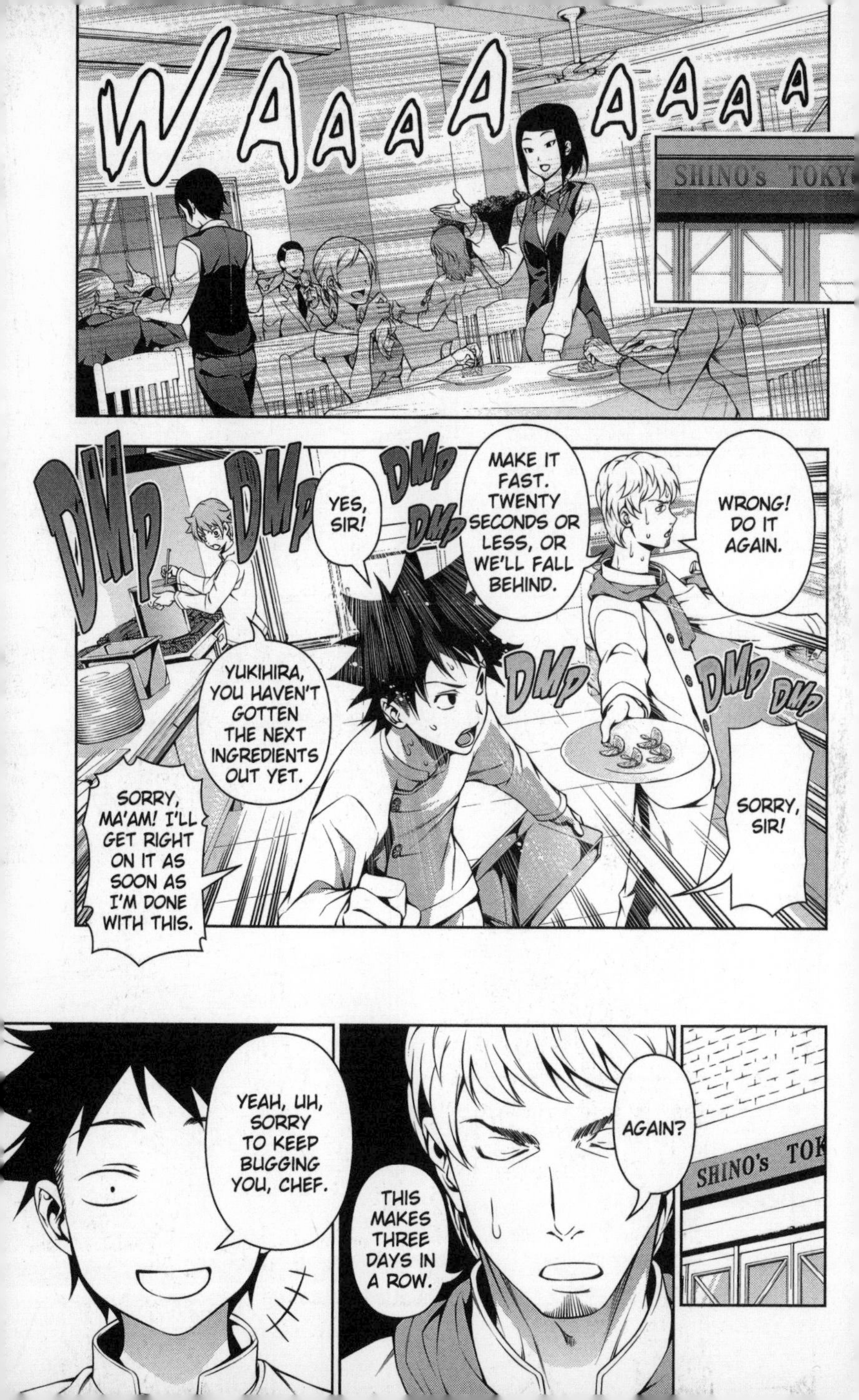
WAAAAAAAA
SHINO's
WRONG! DO IT AGAIN.
SORRY, SIR!
DMP DMP
MAKE IT FAST. TWENTY SECONDS OR LESS, OR WE'LL FALL BEHIND.
YES, SIR!
DMP DMP
YUKIHIRA, YOU HAVEN'T GOTTEN THE NEXT INGREDIENTS OUT YET.
SORRY, MA'AM! I'LL GET RIGHT ON IT AS SOON AS I'M DONE WITH THIS.
DMP DMP
SHINO's
AGAIN?
THIS MAKES THREE DAYS IN A ROW.
YEAH, UH, SORRY TO KEEP BUGGING YOU, CHEF.

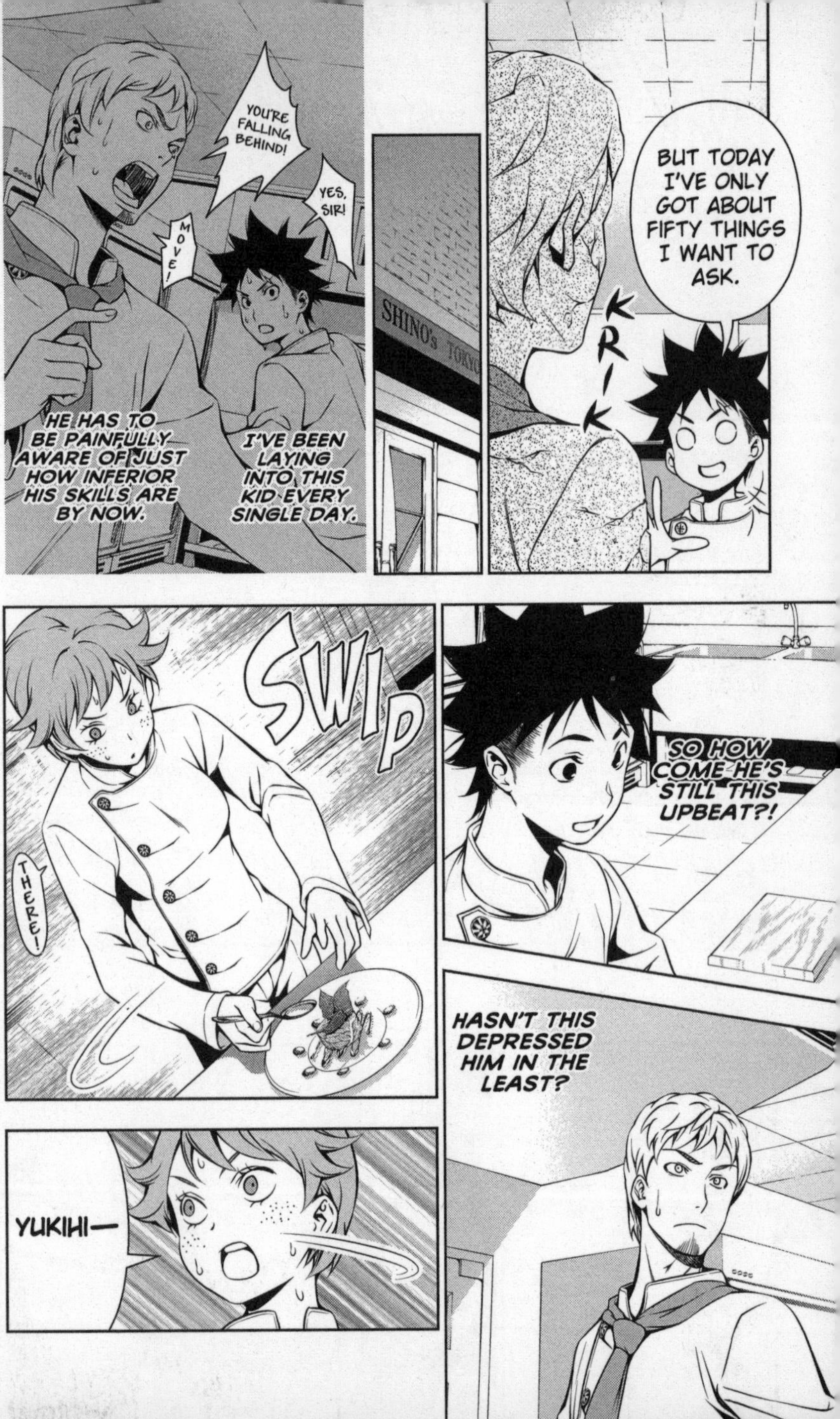
BUT TODAY I'VE ONLY GOT ABOUT FIFTY THINGS I WANT TO ASK.
KRIK
SHINO's TOKYO
YOU'RE FALLING BEHIND!
MOVE!
YES, SIR!
I'VE BEEN LAYING INTO THIS KID EVERY SINGLE DAY.
HE HAS TO BE PAINFULLY AWARE OF JUST HOW INFERIOR HIS SKILLS ARE BY NOW.
SO HOW COME HE'S STILL THIS UPBEAT?!
SWIP
THERE!
HASN'T THIS DEPRESSED HIM IN THE LEAST?
YUKIHI—

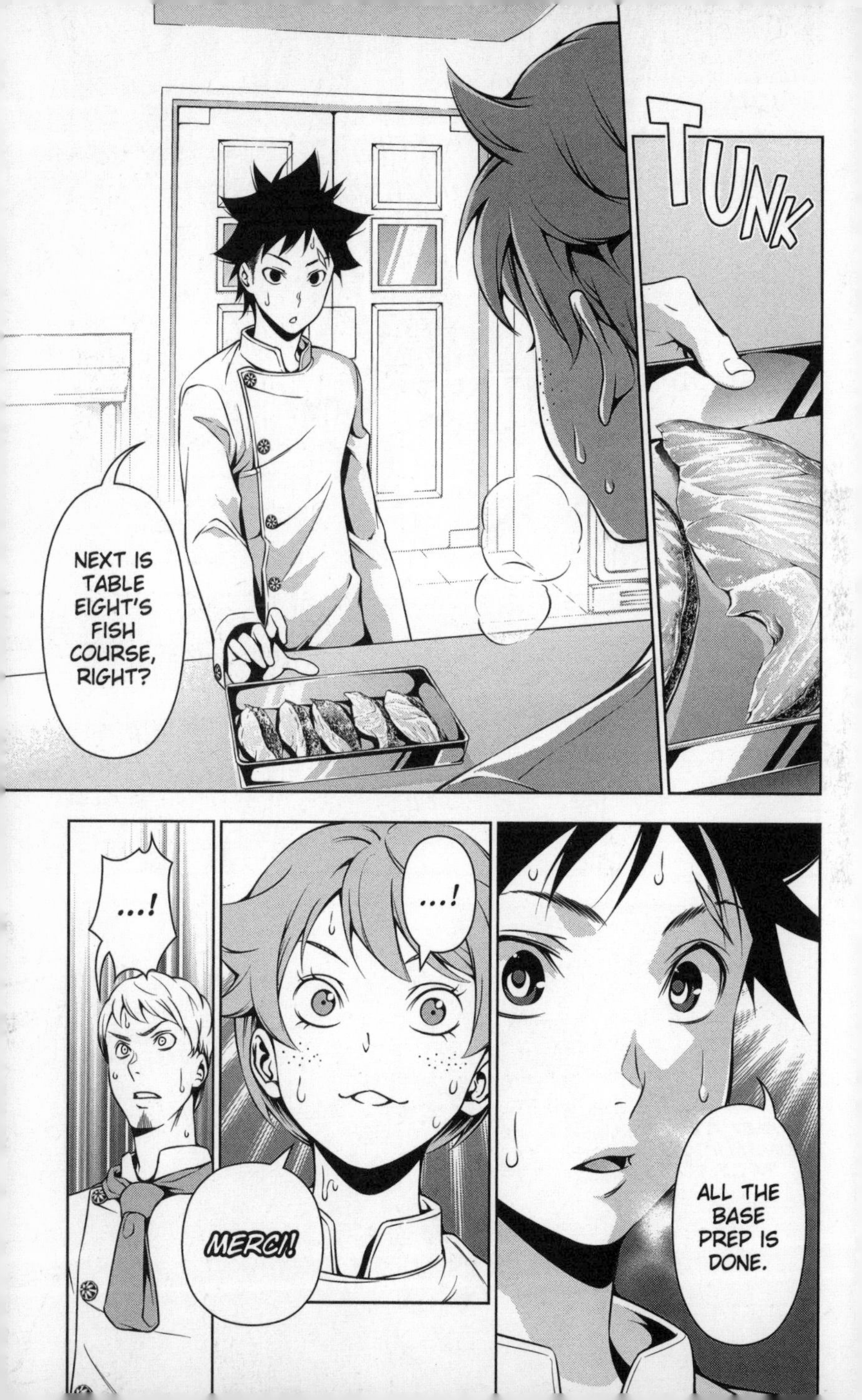
TUNK
NEXT IS TABLE EIGHT'S FISH COURSE, RIGHT?
ALL THE BASE PREP IS DONE.
...!
MERCI!
...!

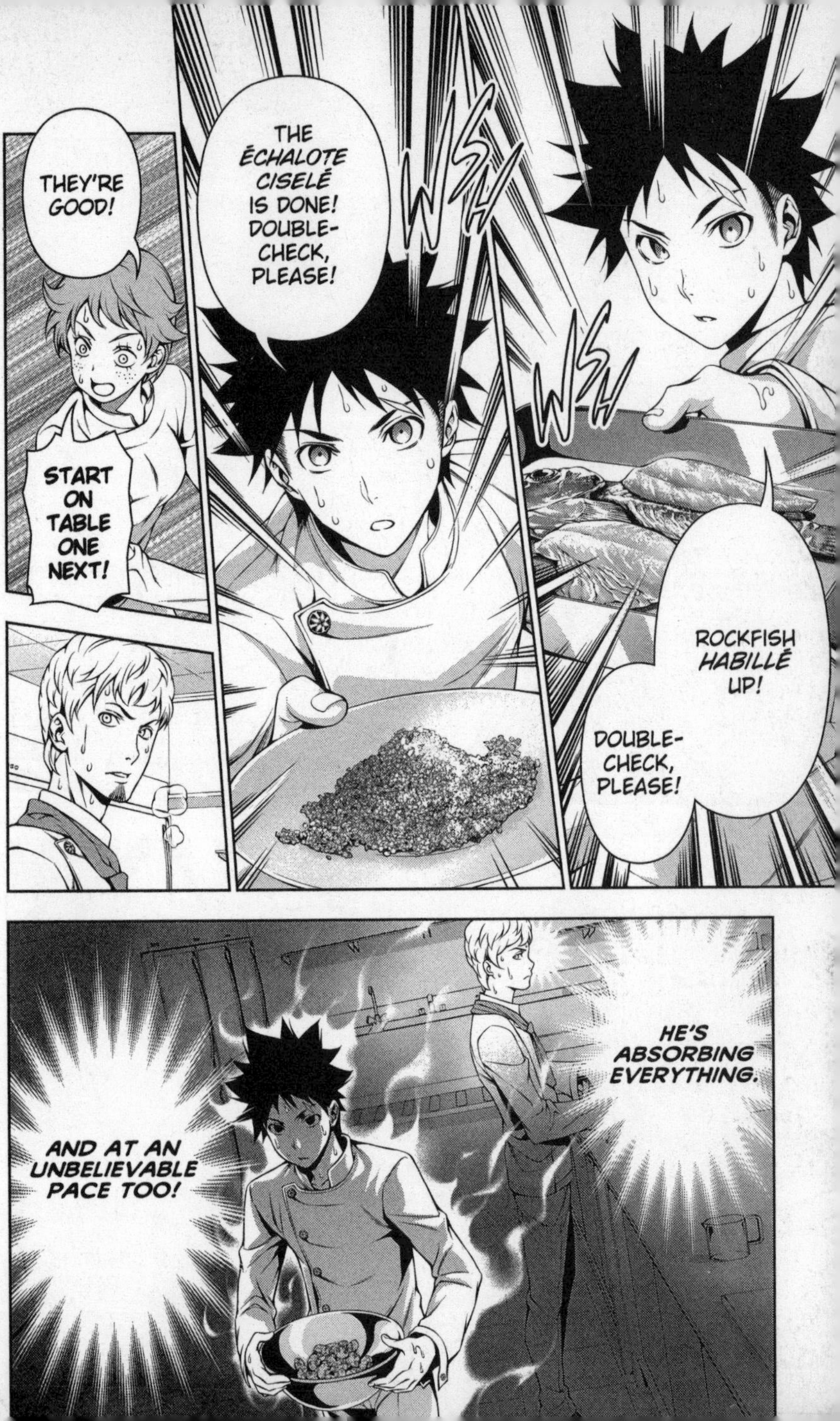
WSH
ROCKFISH HABILLÉ UP!
DOUBLE-CHECK, PLEASE!
WSH
THE ÉCHALOTE CISELÉ IS DONE! DOUBLE-CHECK, PLEASE!
THEY'RE GOOD!
START ON TABLE ONE NEXT!
HE'S ABSORBING EVERYTHING.
AND AT AN UNBELIEVABLE PACE TOO!

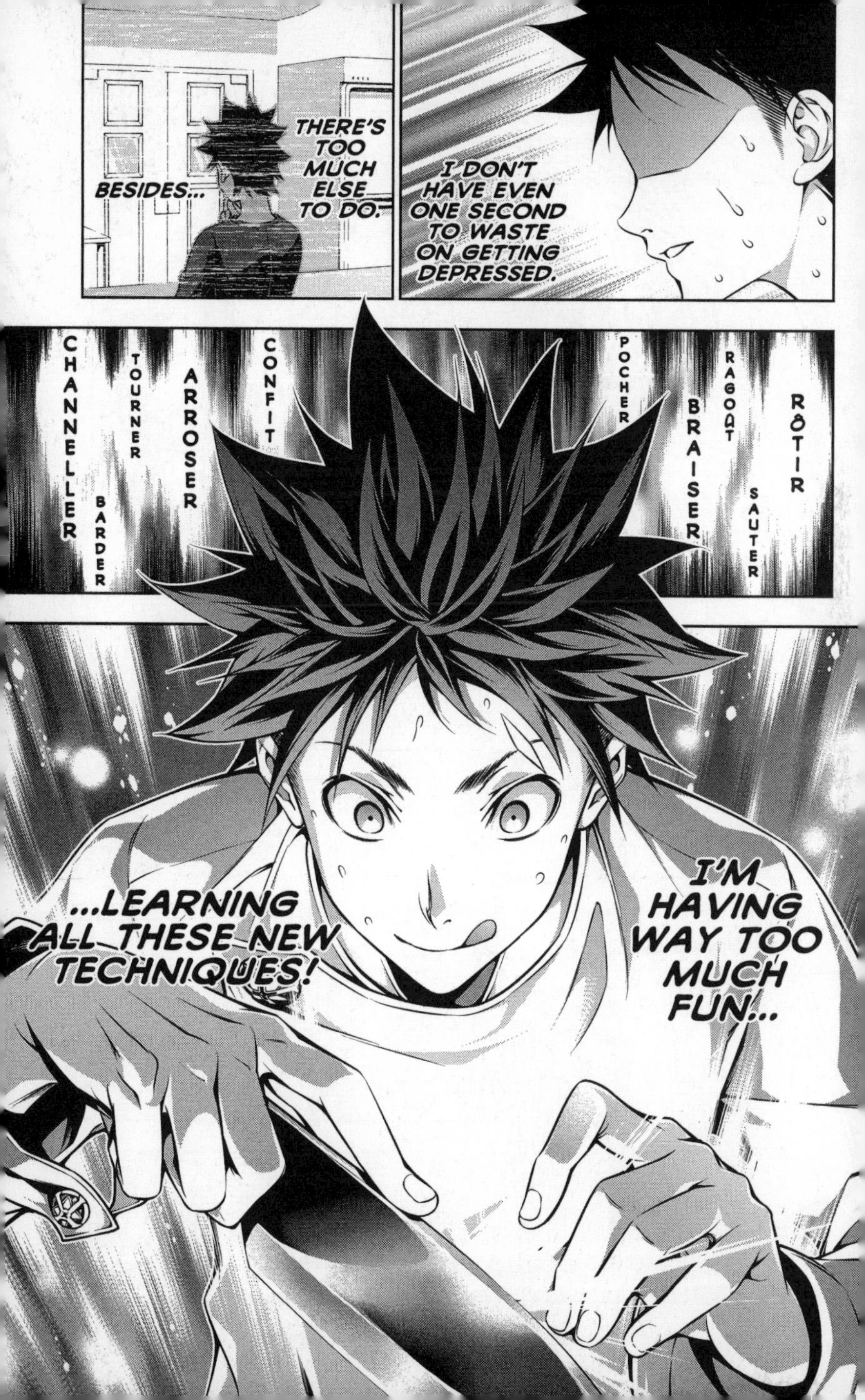
I DON'T HAVE EVEN ONE SECOND TO WASTE ON GETTING DEPRESSED.
THERE'S TOO MUCH ELSE TO DO.
BESIDES...
RÔTIR
SAUTER
RAGOÛT
BRAISER
POCHER
CONFIT
ARROSER
TOURNER
BARDER
CHANNELLER
I'M HAVING WAY TOO MUCH FUN...
...LEARNING ALL THESE NEW TECHNIQUES!

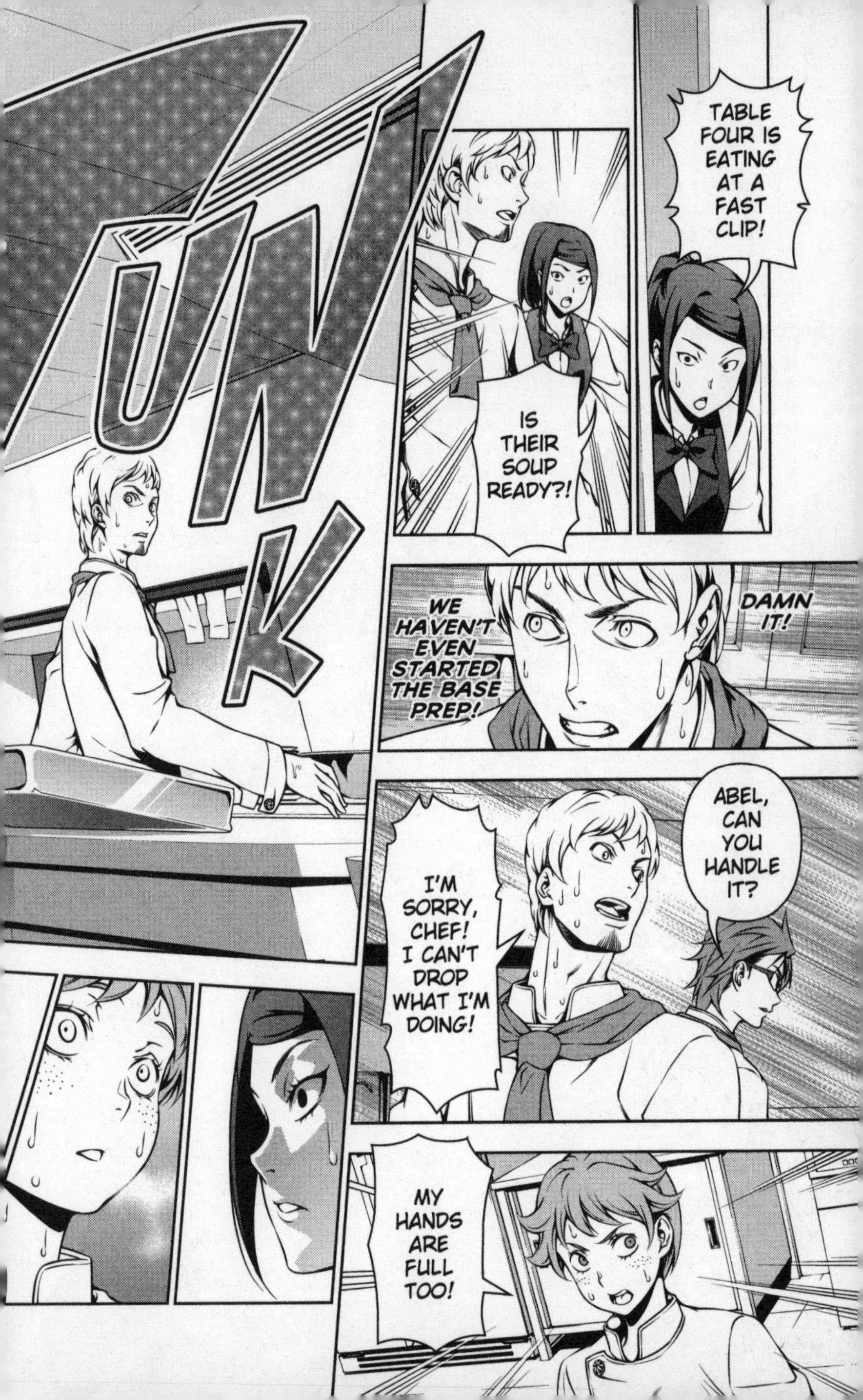
TABLE FOUR IS EATING AT A FAST CLIP!
IS THEIR SOUP READY?!
DAMN IT!
WE HAVEN'T EVEN STARTED THE BASE PREP!
ABEL, CAN YOU HANDLE IT?
I'M SORRY, CHEF! I CAN'T DROP WHAT I'M DOING!
MY HANDS ARE FULL TOO!

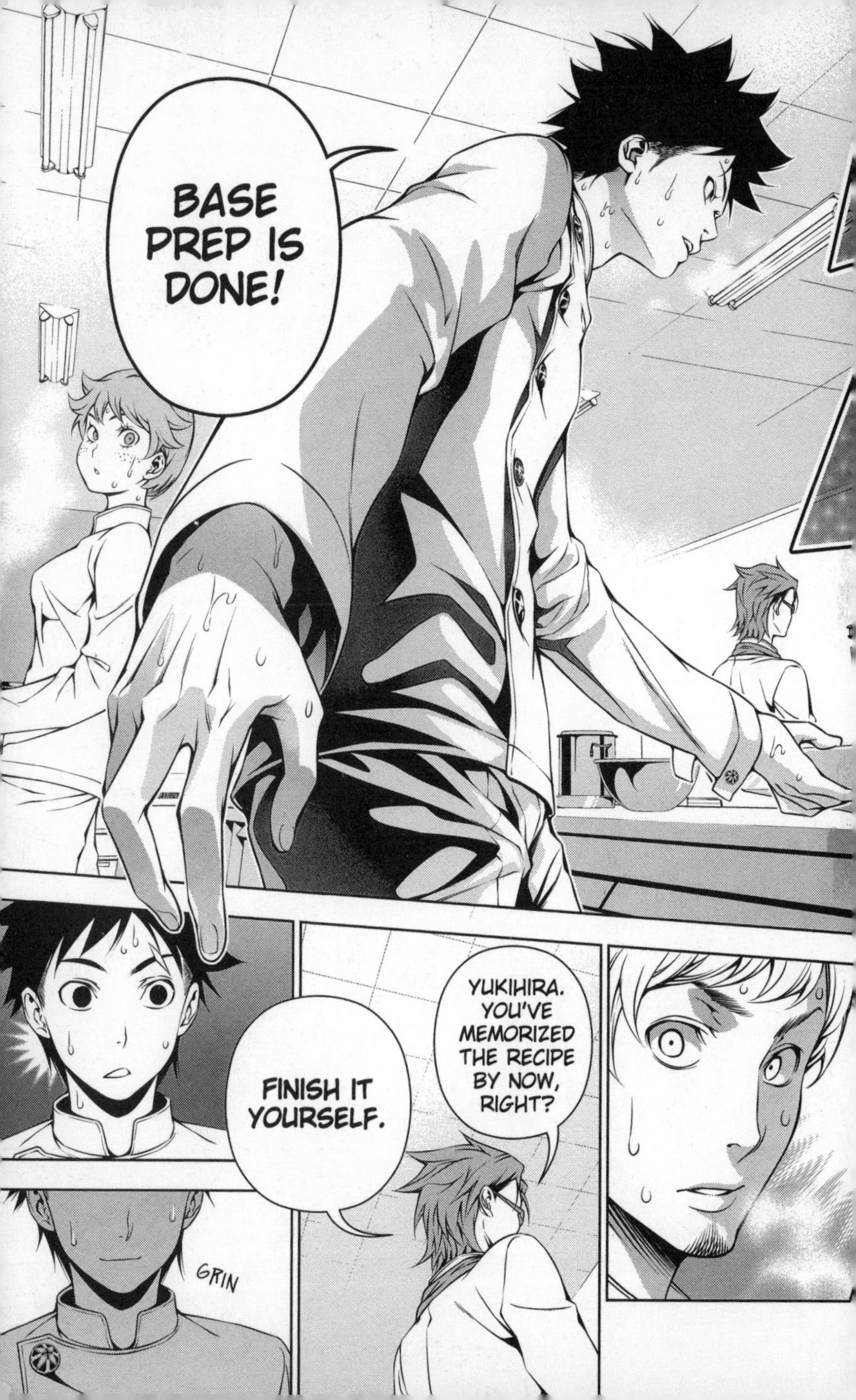
BASE PREP IS DONE!
YUKIHIRA. YOU'VE MEMORIZED THE RECIPE BY NOW, RIGHT?
FINISH IT YOURSELF.
GRIN

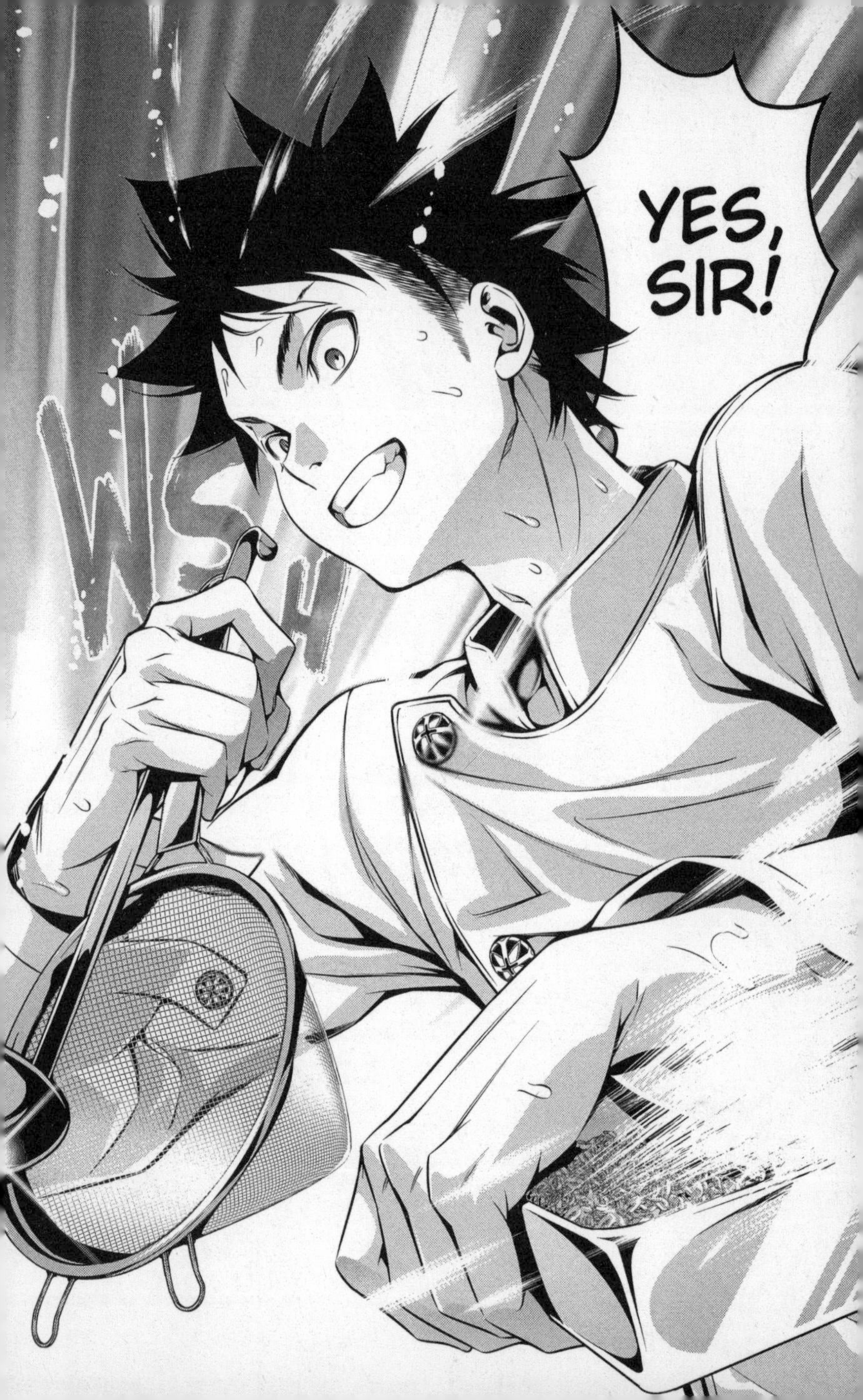
YES, SIR!

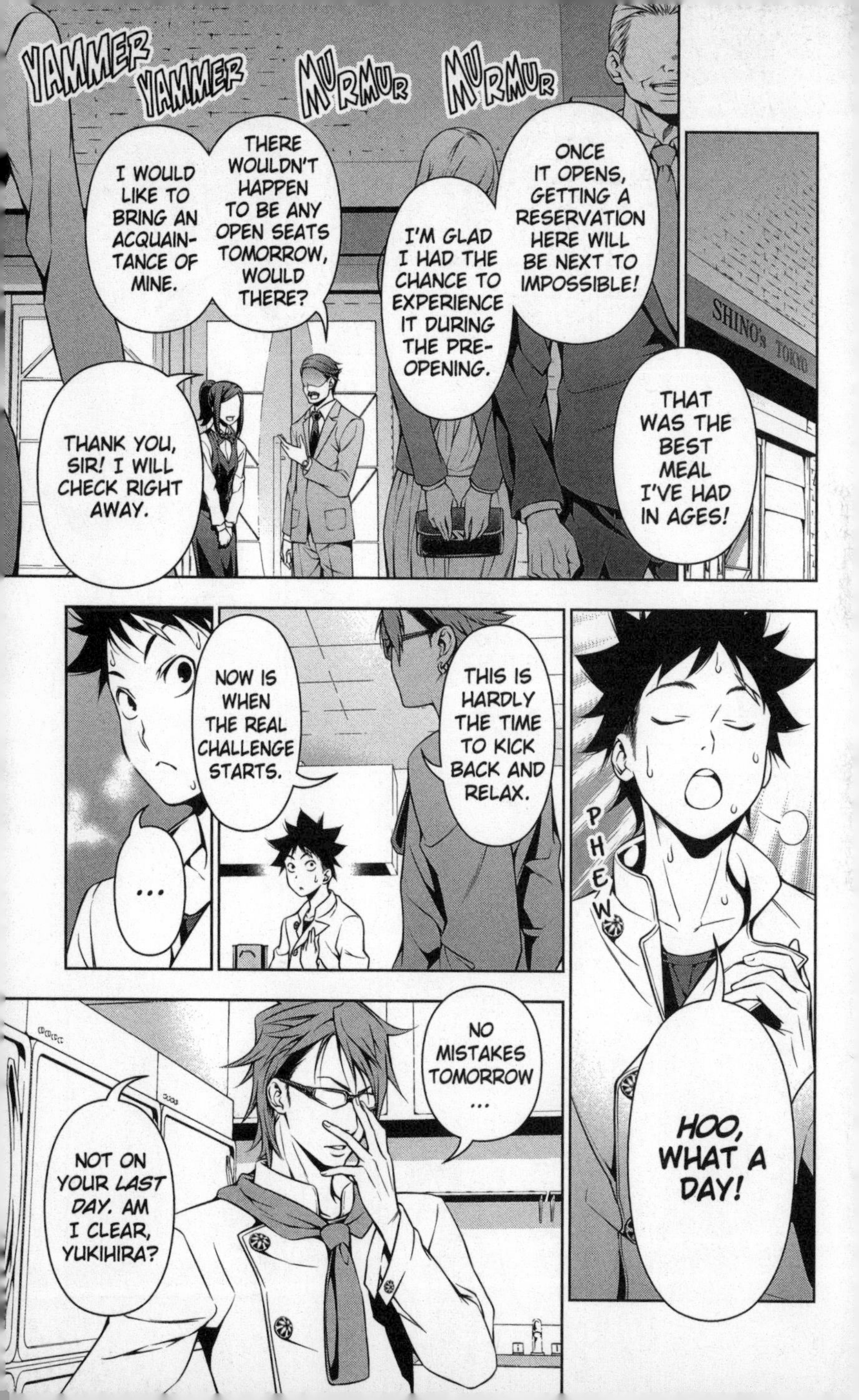
MURMUR MURMUR
YAMMER YAMMER
ONCE IT OPENS, GETTING A RESERVATION HERE WILL BE NEXT TO IMPOSSIBLE!
SHINO's TOKYO
THAT WAS THE BEST MEAL I'VE HAD IN AGES!
I'M GLAD I HAD THE CHANCE TO EXPERIENCE IT DURING THE PRE-OPENING.
THERE WOULDN'T HAPPEN TO BE ANY OPEN SEATS TOMORROW, WOULD THERE?
I WOULD LIKE TO BRING AN ACQUAINTANCE OF MINE.
THANK YOU, SIR! I WILL CHECK RIGHT AWAY.
PHEW
HOO, WHAT A DAY!
THIS IS HARDLY THE TIME TO KICK BACK AND RELAX.
NOW IS WHEN THE REAL CHALLENGE STARTS.
...
NO MISTAKES TOMORROW...
NOT ON YOUR *LAST* DAY. AM I CLEAR, YUKIHIRA?

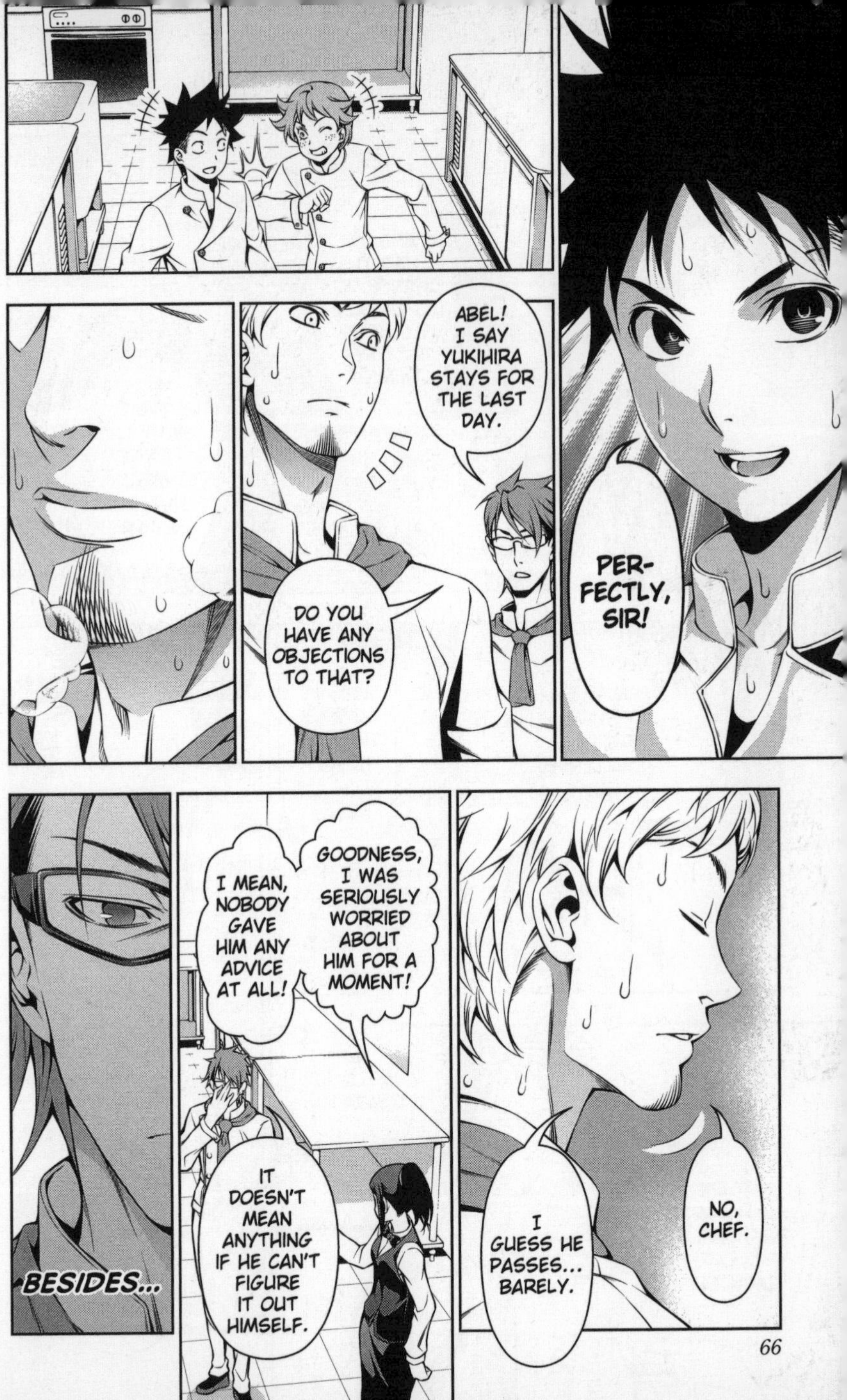
PER-FECTLY, SIR!
ABEL! I SAY YUKIHIRA STAYS FOR THE LAST DAY.
DO YOU HAVE ANY OBJECTIONS TO THAT?
NO, CHEF.
I GUESS HE PASSES... BARELY.
GOODNESS, I WAS SERIOUSLY WORRIED ABOUT HIM FOR A MOMENT!
I MEAN, NOBODY GAVE HIM ANY ADVICE AT ALL!
IT DOESN'T MEAN ANYTHING IF HE CAN'T FIGURE IT OUT HIMSELF.
BESIDES...

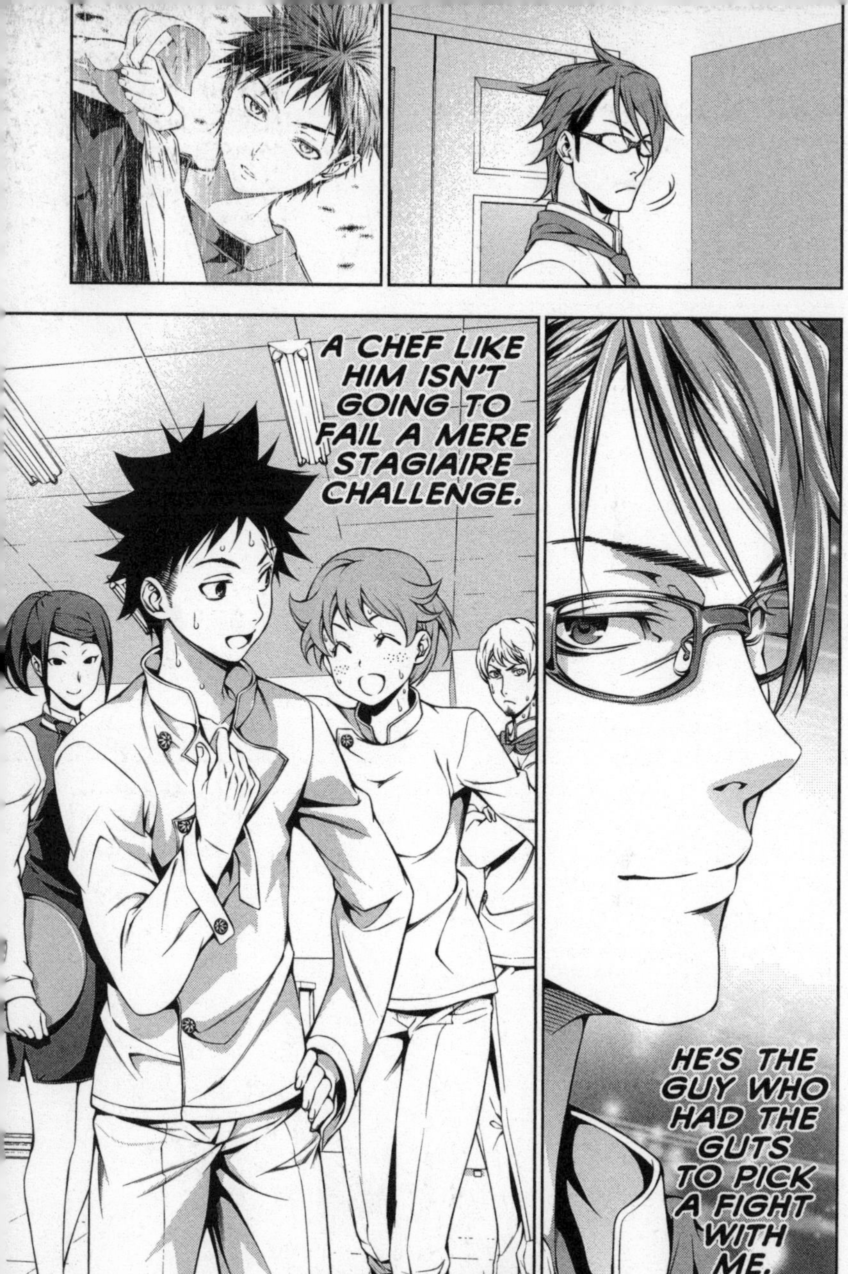
HE'S THE GUY WHO HAD THE GUTS TO PICK A FIGHT WITH ME.
A CHEF LIKE HIM ISN'T GOING TO FAIL A MERE STAGIAIRE CHALLENGE.

THAT NIGHT
HE WAS
ASLEEP
BEFORE HIS
HEAD HIT
THE PILLOW.

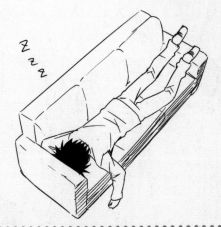

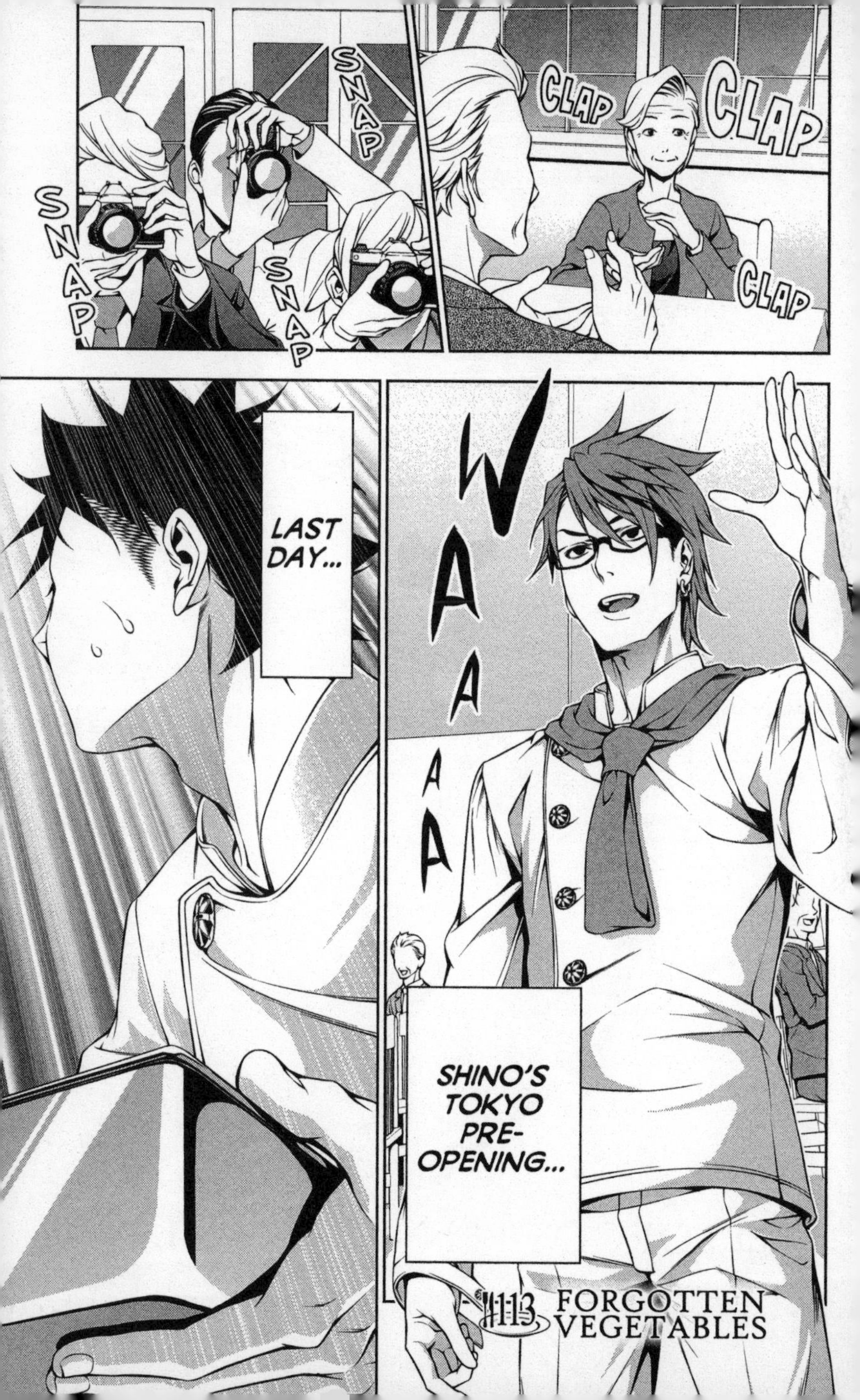
CLAP
CLAP
CLAP
SNAP
SNAP
SNAP
WAAAA
SHINO'S TOKYO PRE-OPENING...
LAST DAY...
#113 FORGOTTEN VEGETABLES

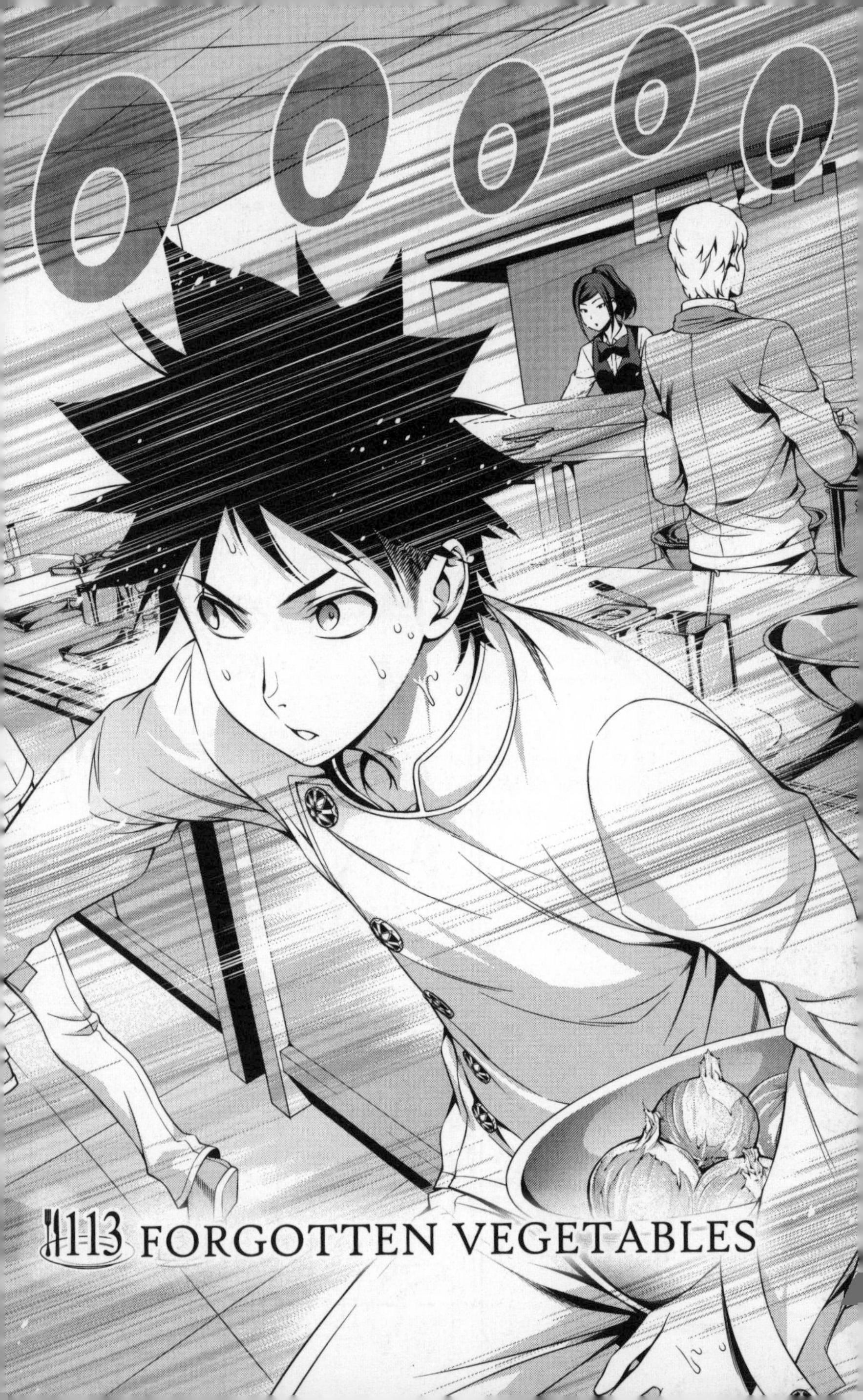
113 FORGOTTEN VEGETABLES

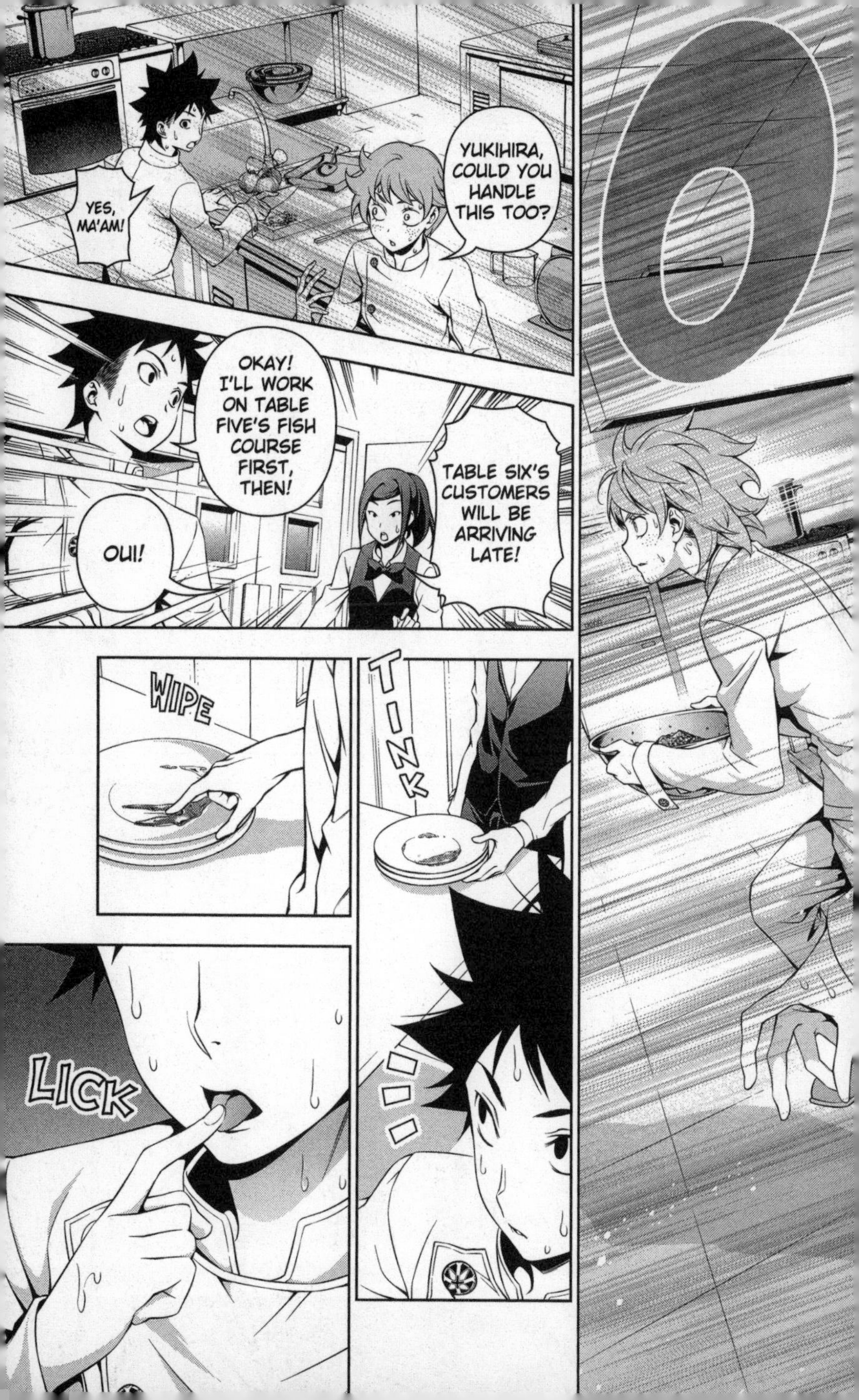
YUKIHIRA, COULD YOU HANDLE THIS TOO?
YES, MA'AM!
TABLE SIX'S CUSTOMERS WILL BE ARRIVING LATE!
OKAY! I'LL WORK ON TABLE FIVE'S FISH COURSE FIRST, THEN!
OUI!
TINK
WIPE
...
LICK

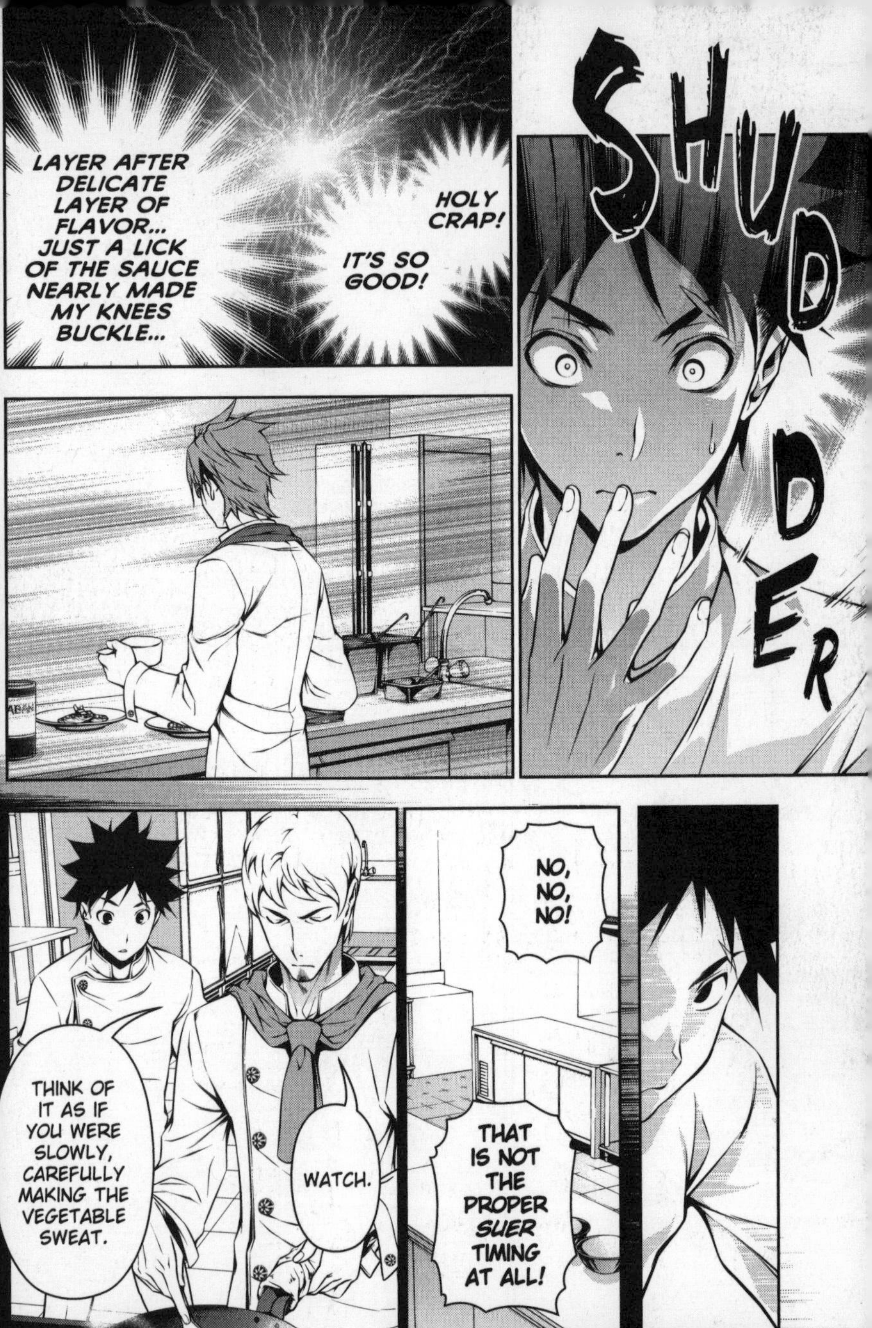
SHUDDER
HOLY CRAP!
IT'S SO GOOD!
LAYER AFTER DELICATE LAYER OF FLAVOR... JUST A LICK OF THE SAUCE NEARLY MADE MY KNEES BUCKLE...
NO, NO, NO!
THAT IS NOT THE PROPER *SUER* TIMING AT ALL!
WATCH.
THINK OF IT AS IF YOU WERE SLOWLY, CAREFULLY MAKING THE VEGETABLE SWEAT.

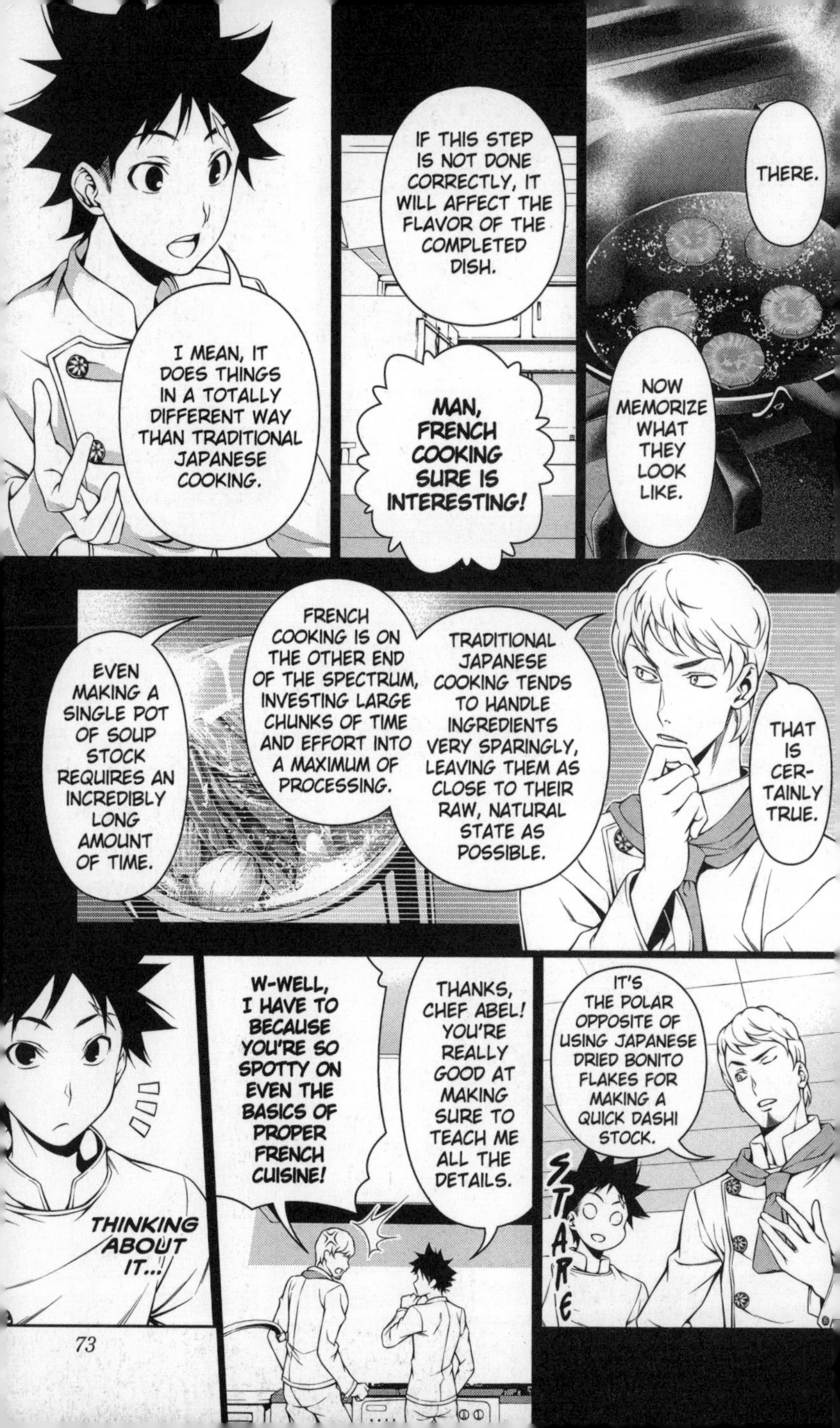
THERE.
NOW MEMORIZE WHAT THEY LOOK LIKE.
IF THIS STEP IS NOT DONE CORRECTLY, IT WILL AFFECT THE FLAVOR OF THE COMPLETED DISH.
MAN, FRENCH COOKING SURE IS INTERESTING!
I MEAN, IT DOES THINGS IN A TOTALLY DIFFERENT WAY THAN TRADITIONAL JAPANESE COOKING.
THAT IS CER- TAINLY TRUE.
TRADITIONAL JAPANESE COOKING TENDS TO HANDLE INGREDIENTS VERY SPARINGLY, LEAVING THEM AS CLOSE TO THEIR RAW, NATURAL STATE AS POSSIBLE.
FRENCH COOKING IS ON THE OTHER END OF THE SPECTRUM, INVESTING LARGE CHUNKS OF TIME AND EFFORT INTO A MAXIMUM OF PROCESSING.
EVEN MAKING A SINGLE POT OF SOUP STOCK REQUIRES AN INCREDIBLY LONG AMOUNT OF TIME.
IT'S THE POLAR OPPOSITE OF USING JAPANESE DRIED BONITO FLAKES FOR MAKING A QUICK DASHI STOCK.
STARE
THANKS, CHEF ABEL! YOU'RE REALLY GOOD AT MAKING SURE TO TEACH ME ALL THE DETAILS.
W-WELL, I HAVE TO BECAUSE YOU'RE SO SPOTTY ON EVEN THE BASICS OF PROPER FRENCH CUISINE!
THINKING ABOUT IT...!

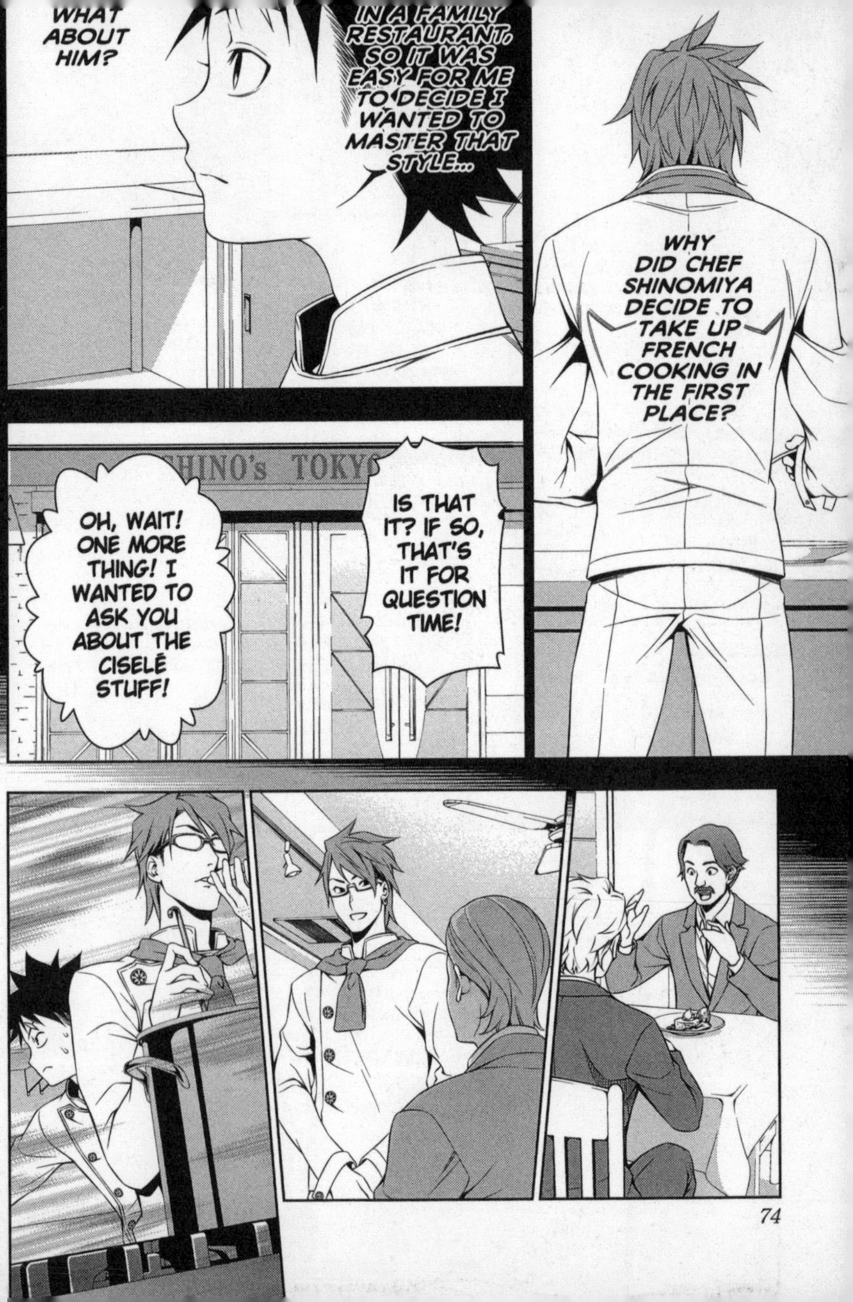
WHY DID CHEF SHINOMIYA DECIDE TO TAKE UP FRENCH COOKING IN THE FIRST PLACE?
IN A FAMILY RESTAURANT, SO IT WAS EASY FOR ME TO DECIDE I WANTED TO MASTER THAT STYLE...
WHAT ABOUT HIM?
HINO's TOKY
IS THAT IT? IF SO, THAT'S IT FOR QUESTION TIME!
OH, WAIT! ONE MORE THING! I WANTED TO ASK YOU ABOUT THE CISELÉ STUFF!

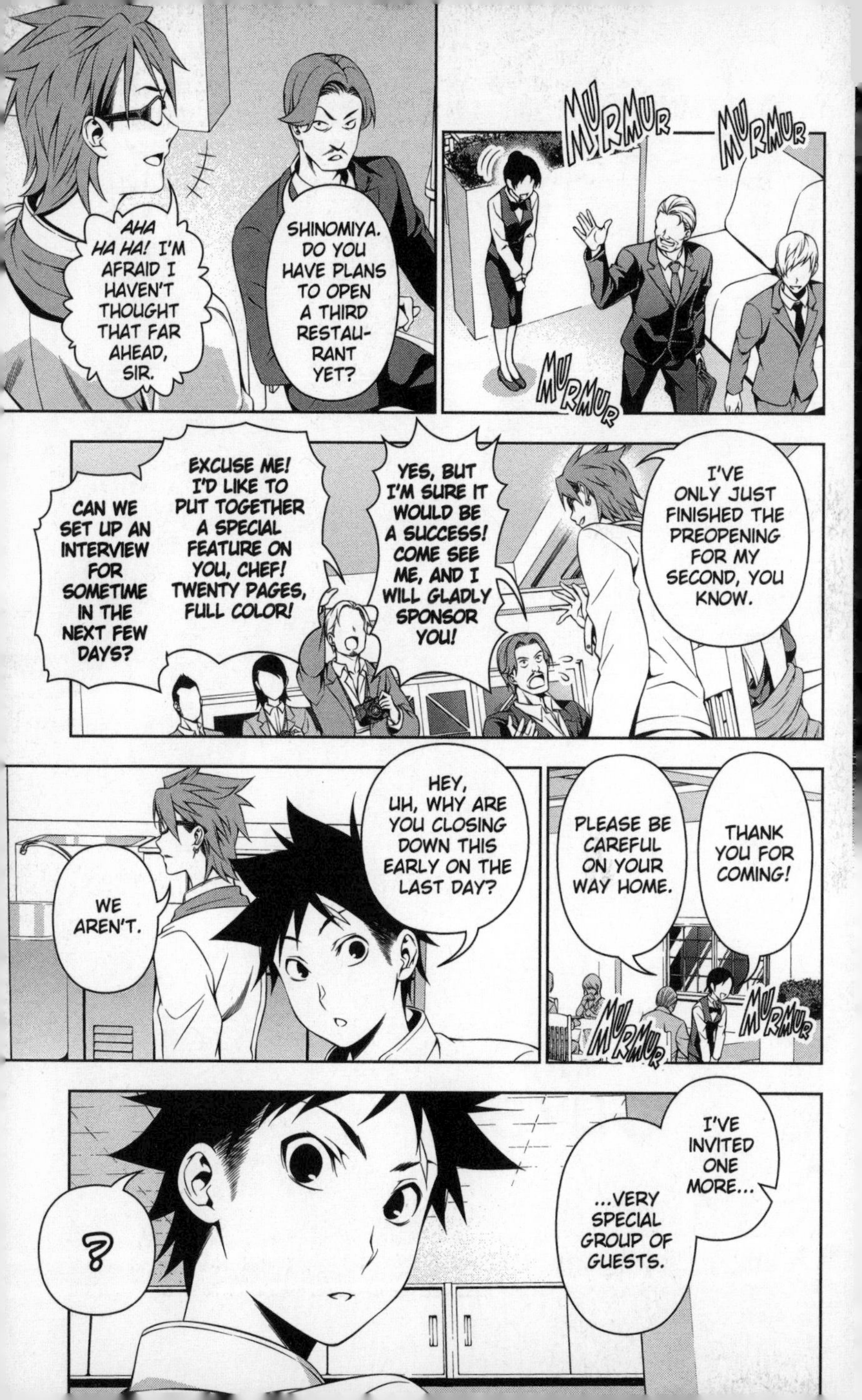
MURMUR
MURMUR
MURMUR
SHINOMIYA. DO YOU HAVE PLANS TO OPEN A THIRD RESTAU-RANT YET?
AHA HA HA! I'M AFRAID I HAVEN'T THOUGHT THAT FAR AHEAD, SIR.
I'VE ONLY JUST FINISHED THE PREOPENING FOR MY SECOND, YOU KNOW.
YES, BUT I'M SURE IT WOULD BE A SUCCESS! COME SEE ME, AND I WILL GLADLY SPONSOR YOU!
EXCUSE ME! I'D LIKE TO PUT TOGETHER A SPECIAL FEATURE ON YOU, CHEF! TWENTY PAGES, FULL COLOR!
CAN WE SET UP AN INTERVIEW FOR SOMETIME IN THE NEXT FEW DAYS?
THANK YOU FOR COMING!
PLEASE BE CAREFUL ON YOUR WAY HOME.
MURMUR
MURMUR
HEY, UH, WHY ARE YOU CLOSING DOWN THIS EARLY ON THE LAST DAY?
WE AREN'T.
I'VE INVITED ONE MORE...
...VERY SPECIAL GROUP OF GUESTS.
?

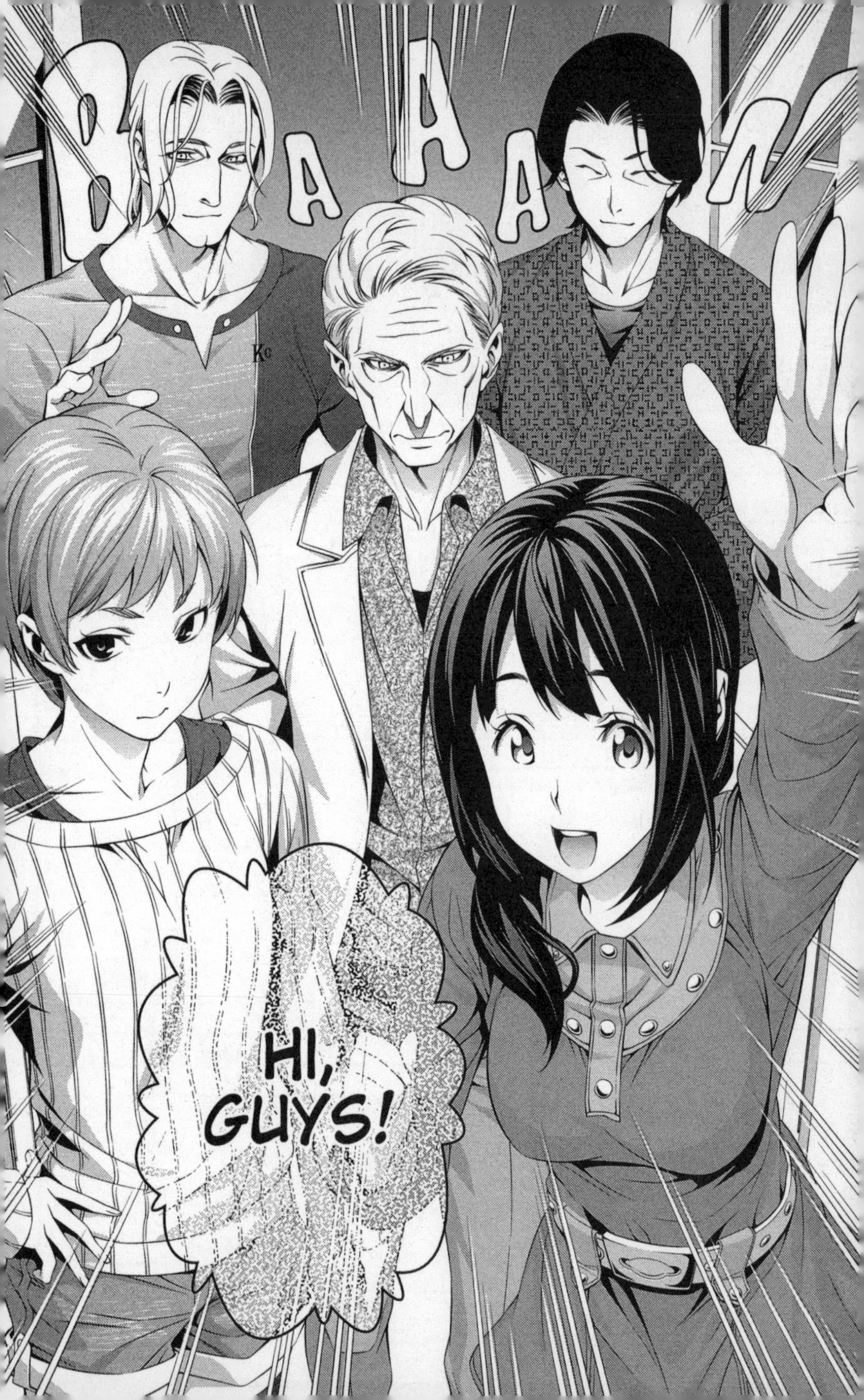
BAAAN
HI, GUYS!

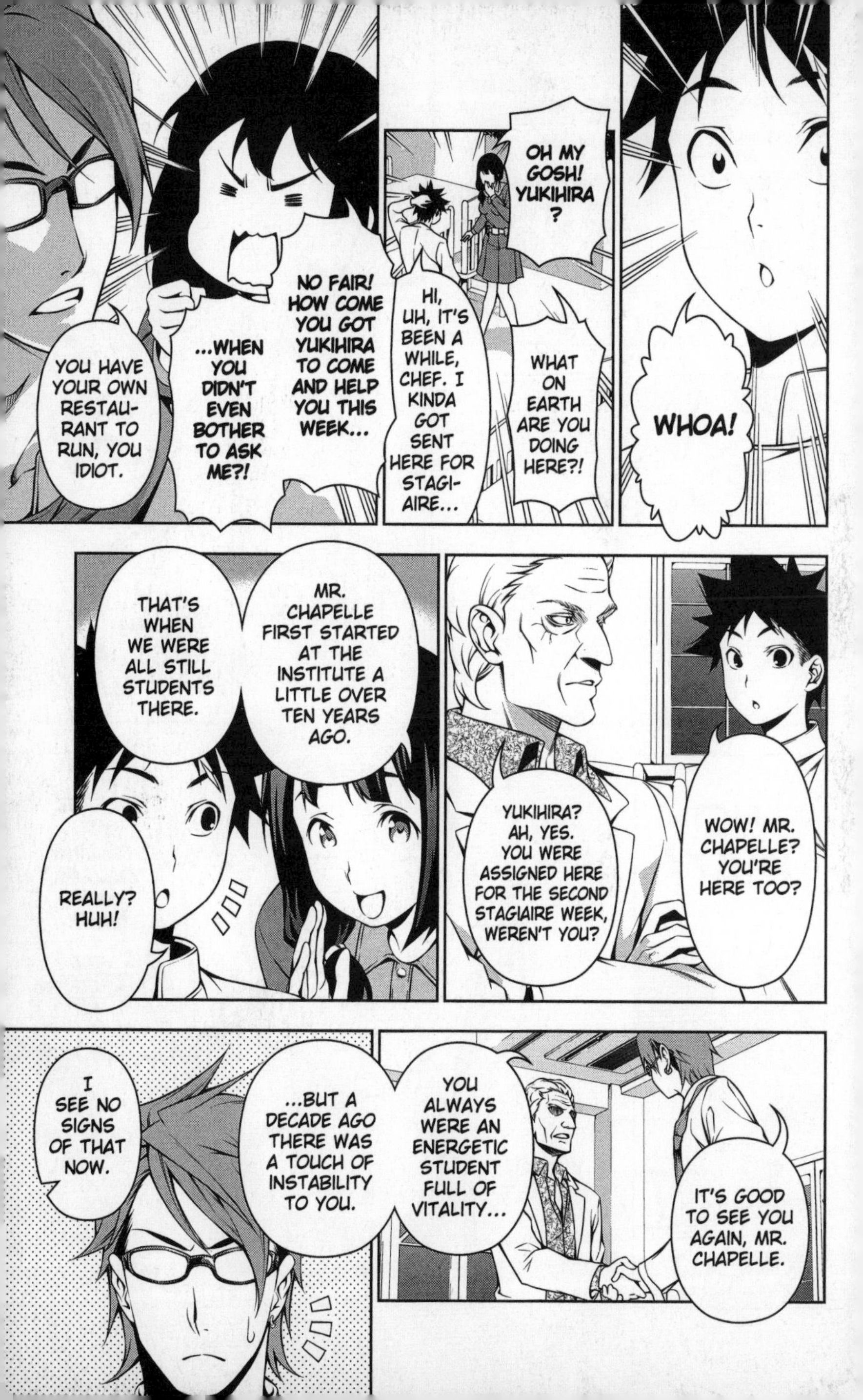
WHOA!
OH MY GOSH! YUKIHIRA?
WHAT ON EARTH ARE YOU DOING HERE?!
HI, UH, IT'S BEEN A WHILE, CHEF. I KINDA GOT SENT HERE FOR STAGIAIRE...
NO FAIR! HOW COME YOU GOT YUKIHIRA TO COME AND HELP YOU THIS WEEK...
...WHEN YOU DIDN'T EVEN BOTHER TO ASK ME?!
YOU HAVE YOUR OWN RESTAURANT TO RUN, YOU IDIOT.
WOW! MR. CHAPELLE? YOU'RE HERE TOO?
YUKIHIRA? AH, YES. YOU WERE ASSIGNED HERE FOR THE SECOND STAGIAIRE WEEK, WEREN'T YOU?
MR. CHAPELLE FIRST STARTED AT THE INSTITUTE A LITTLE OVER TEN YEARS AGO.
THAT'S WHEN WE WERE ALL STILL STUDENTS THERE.
REALLY? HUH!
IT'S GOOD TO SEE YOU AGAIN, MR. CHAPELLE.
YOU ALWAYS WERE AN ENERGETIC STUDENT FULL OF VITALITY...
...BUT A DECADE AGO THERE WAS A TOUCH OF INSTABILITY TO YOU.
I SEE NO SIGNS OF THAT NOW.

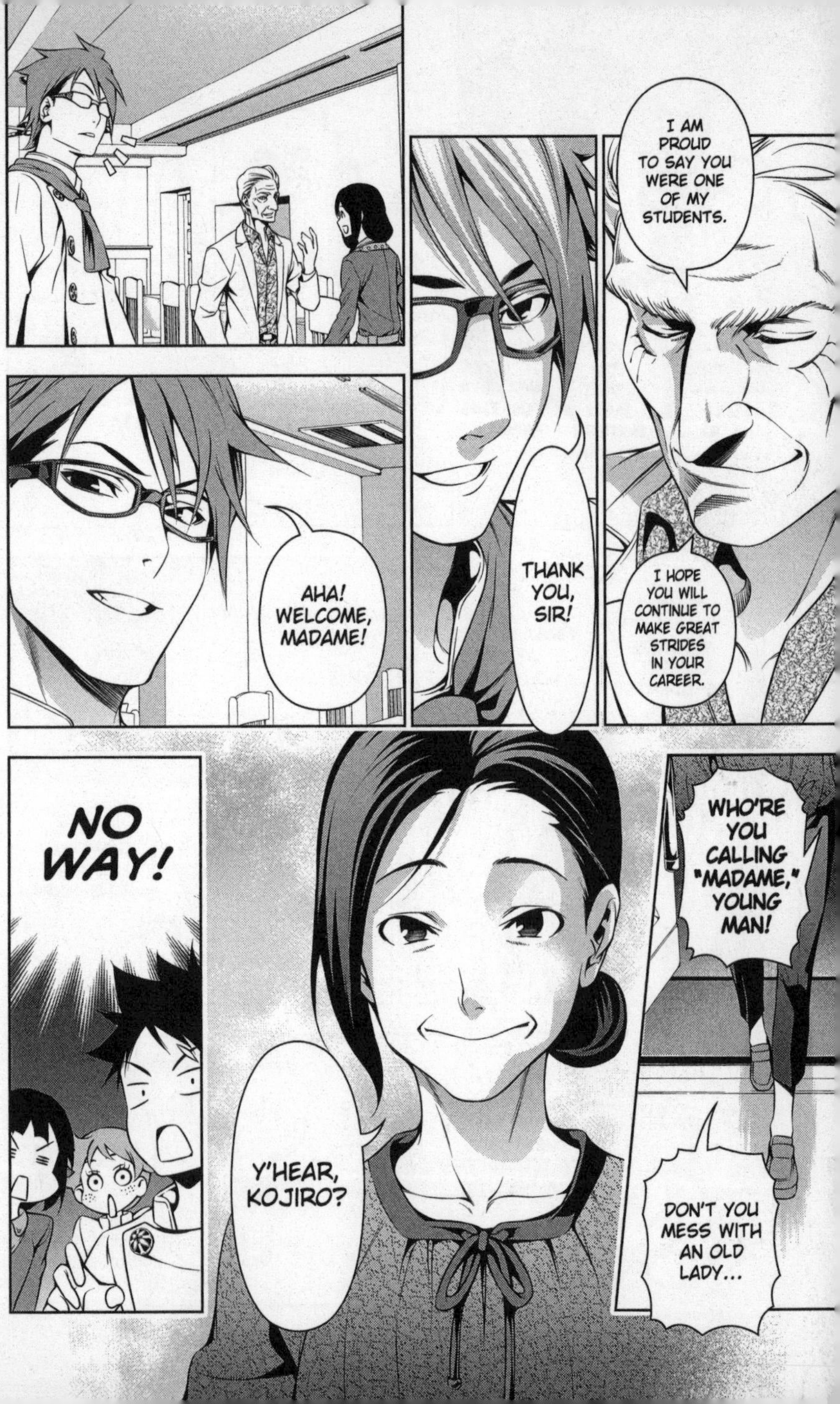
I AM PROUD TO SAY YOU WERE ONE OF MY STUDENTS.
I HOPE YOU WILL CONTINUE TO MAKE GREAT STRIDES IN YOUR CAREER.
THANK YOU, SIR!
AHA! WELCOME, MADAME!
WHO'RE YOU CALLING "MADAME," YOUNG MAN!
DON'T YOU MESS WITH AN OLD LADY...
Y'HEAR, KOJIRO?
NO WAY!

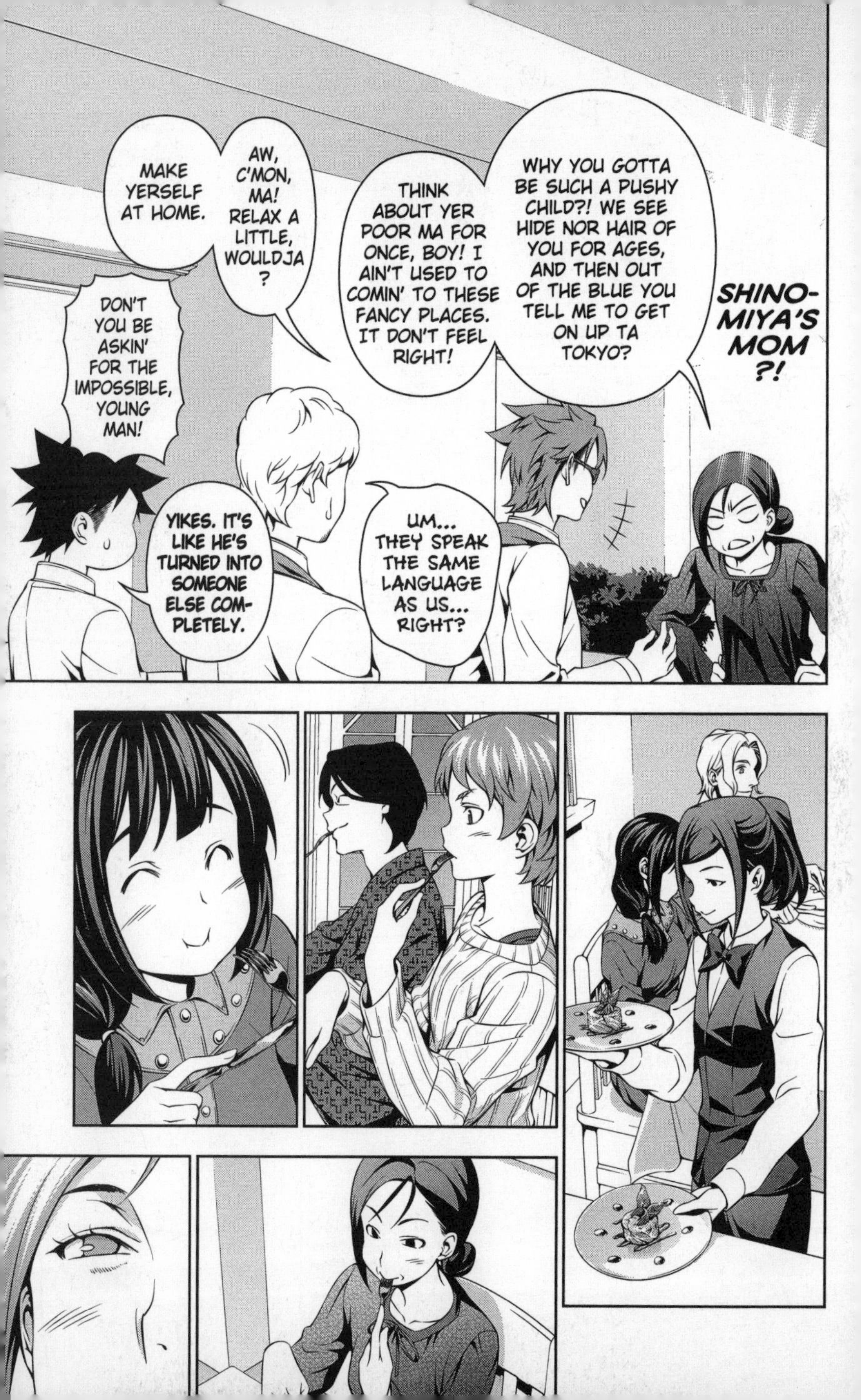
SHINO-MIYA'S MOM ?!
WHY YOU GOTTA BE SUCH A PUSHY CHILD?! WE SEE HIDE NOR HAIR OF YOU FOR AGES, AND THEN OUT OF THE BLUE YOU TELL ME TO GET ON UP TA TOKYO?
THINK ABOUT YER POOR MA FOR ONCE, BOY! I AIN'T USED TO COMIN' TO THESE FANCY PLACES. IT DON'T FEEL RIGHT!
AW, C'MON, MA! RELAX A LITTLE, WOULDJA?
MAKE YERSELF AT HOME.
DON'T YOU BE ASKIN' FOR THE IMPOSSIBLE, YOUNG MAN!
UM... THEY SPEAK THE SAME LANGUAGE AS US... RIGHT?
YIKES. IT'S LIKE HE'S TURNED INTO SOMEONE ELSE COMPLETELY.

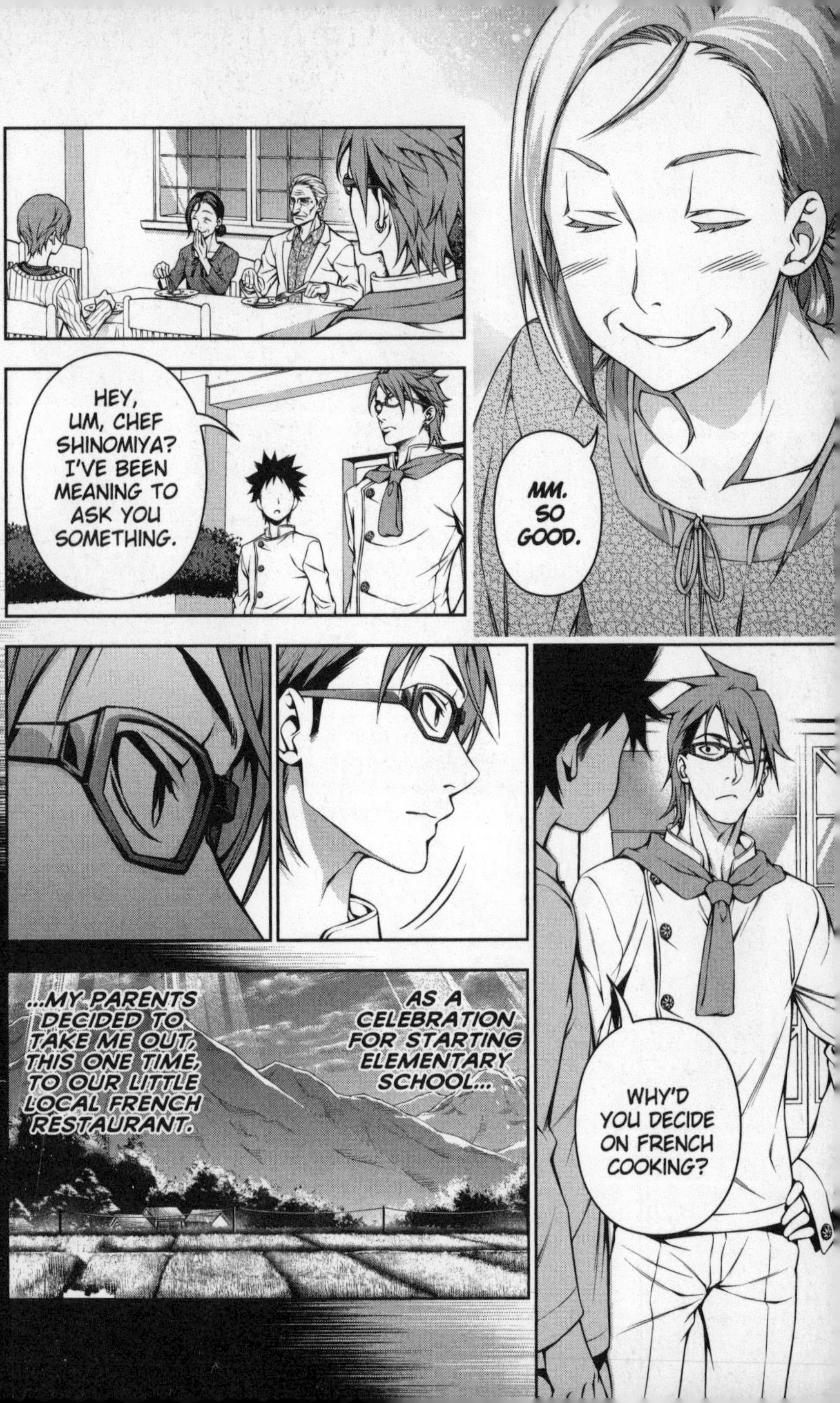
MM. SO GOOD.
HEY, UM, CHEF SHINOMIYA? I'VE BEEN MEANING TO ASK YOU SOMETHING.
WHY'D YOU DECIDE ON FRENCH COOKING?
AS A CELEBRATION FOR STARTING ELEMENTARY SCHOOL...
...MY PARENTS DECIDED TO TAKE ME OUT, THIS ONE TIME, TO OUR LITTLE LOCAL FRENCH RESTAURANT.

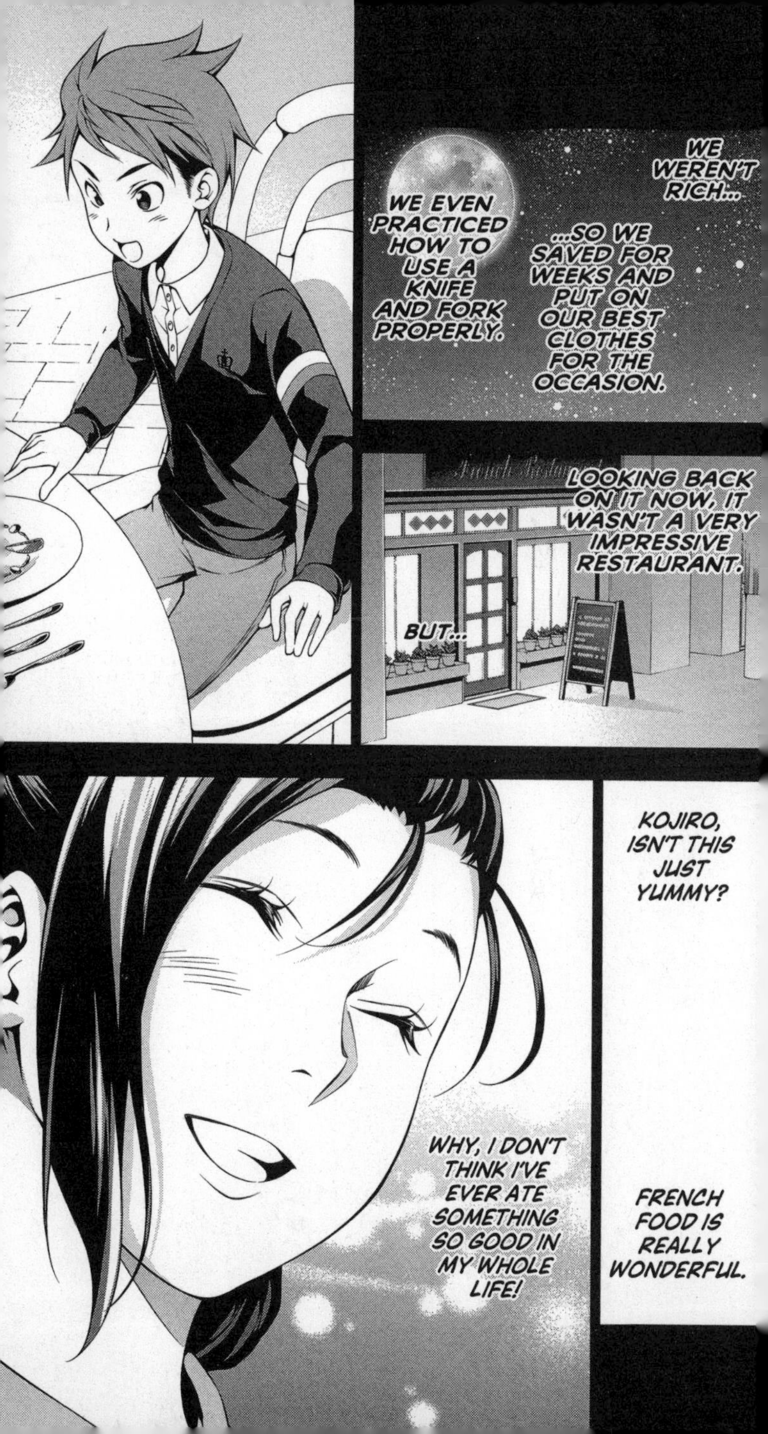
WE WEREN'T RICH...
...SO WE SAVED FOR WEEKS AND PUT ON OUR BEST CLOTHES FOR THE OCCASION.
WE EVEN PRACTICED HOW TO USE A KNIFE AND FORK PROPERLY.
LOOKING BACK ON IT NOW, IT WASN'T A VERY IMPRESSIVE RESTAURANT.
BUT...
KOJIRO, ISN'T THIS JUST YUMMY?
FRENCH FOOD IS REALLY WONDERFUL.
WHY, I DON'T THINK I'VE EVER ATE SOMETHING SO GOOD IN MY WHOLE LIFE!

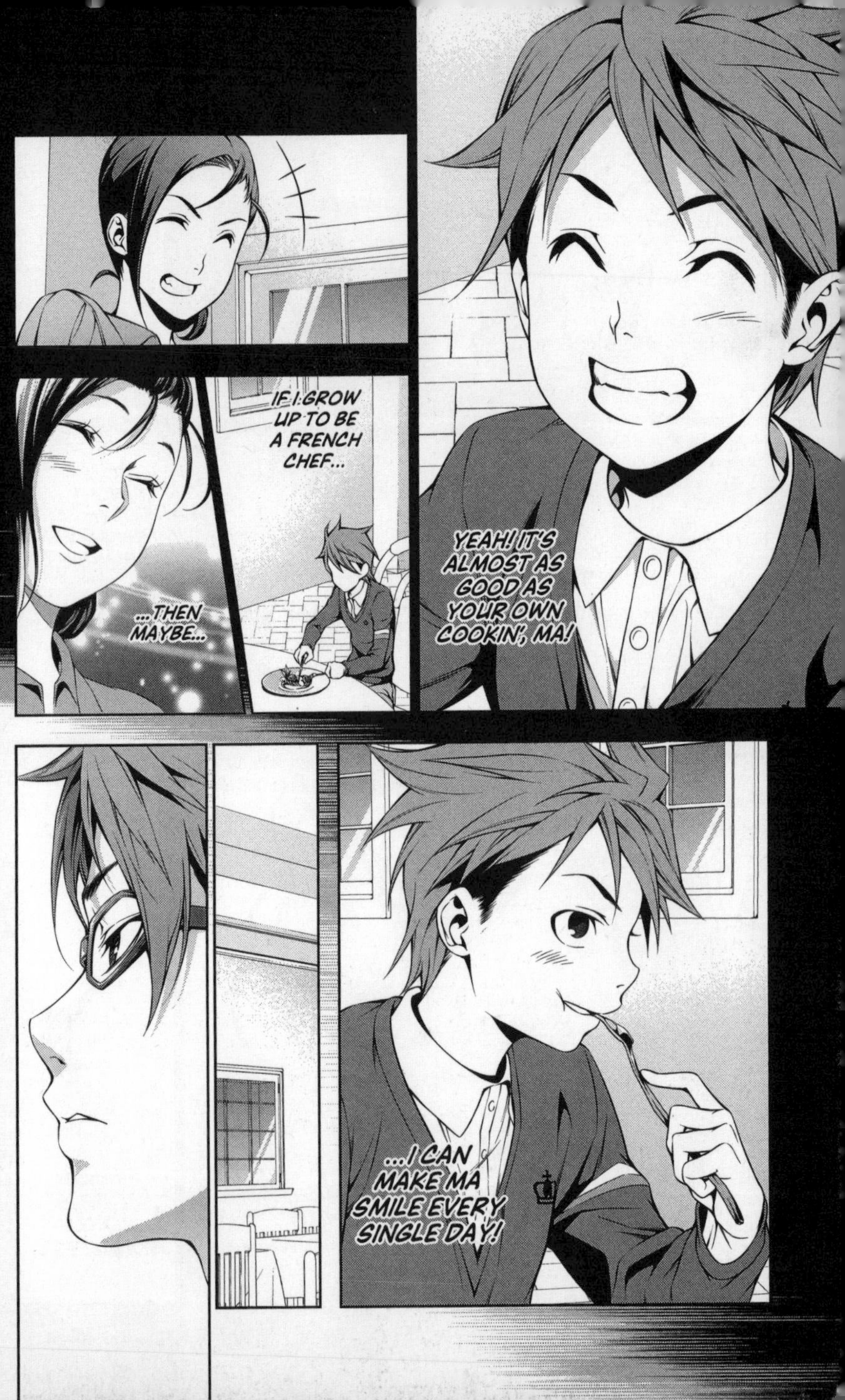
YEAH! IT'S ALMOST AS GOOD AS YOUR OWN COOKIN', MA!
IF I GROW UP TO BE A FRENCH CHEF...
...THEN MAYBE...
...I CAN MAKE MA SMILE EVERY SINGLE DAY!

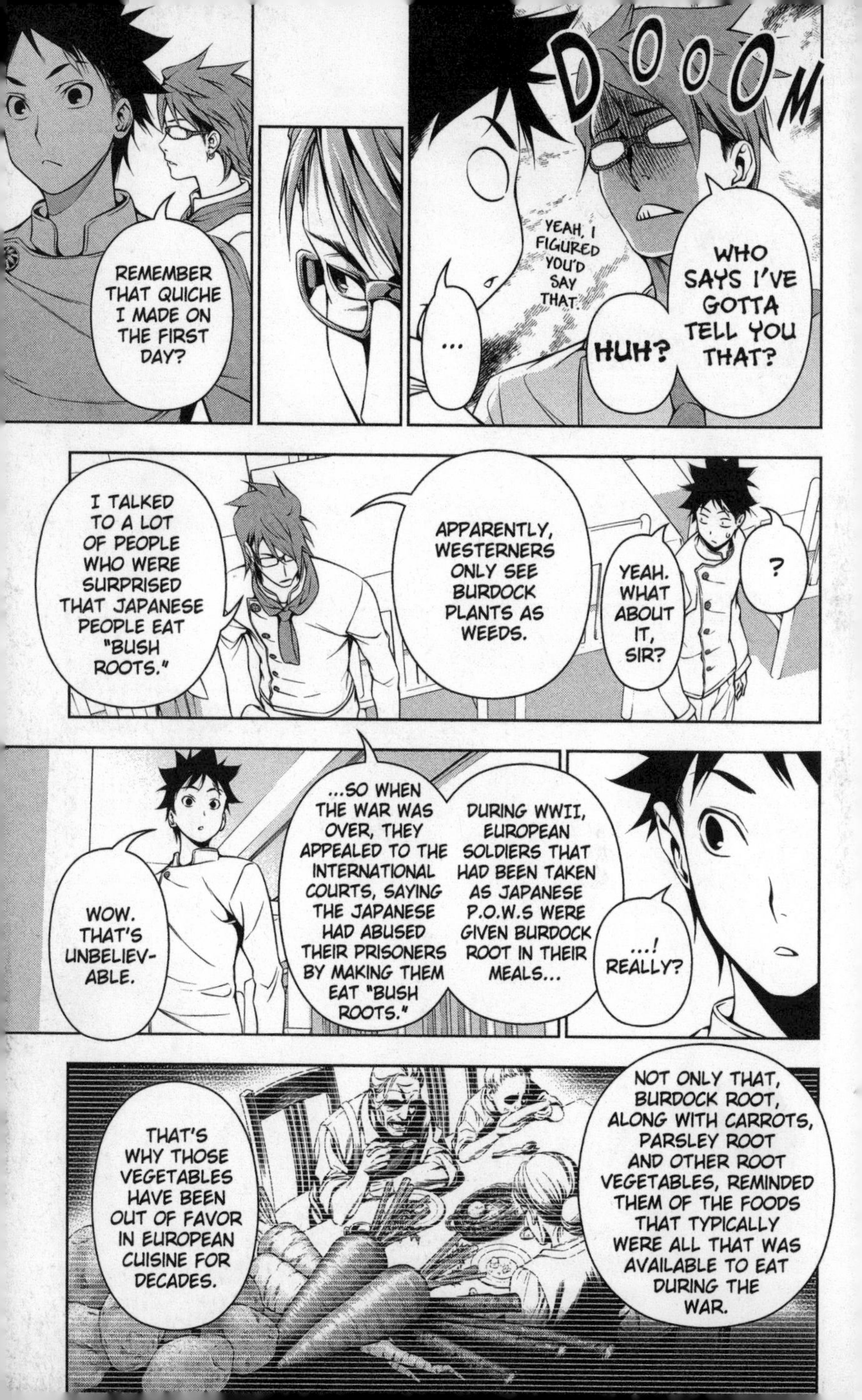
DOOOM
HUH?
WHO SAYS I'VE GOTTA TELL YOU THAT?
YEAH, I FIGURED YOU'D SAY THAT.
...
REMEMBER THAT QUICHE I MADE ON THE FIRST DAY?
?
YEAH. WHAT ABOUT IT, SIR?
APPARENTLY, WESTERNERS ONLY SEE BURDOCK PLANTS AS WEEDS.
I TALKED TO A LOT OF PEOPLE WHO WERE SURPRISED THAT JAPANESE PEOPLE EAT "BUSH ROOTS."
...! REALLY?
DURING WWII, EUROPEAN SOLDIERS THAT HAD BEEN TAKEN AS JAPANESE P.O.W.S WERE GIVEN BURDOCK ROOT IN THEIR MEALS...
...SO WHEN THE WAR WAS OVER, THEY APPEALED TO THE INTERNATIONAL COURTS, SAYING THE JAPANESE HAD ABUSED THEIR PRISONERS BY MAKING THEM EAT "BUSH ROOTS."
WOW. THAT'S UNBELIEV-ABLE.
NOT ONLY THAT, BURDOCK ROOT, ALONG WITH CARROTS, PARSLEY ROOT AND OTHER ROOT VEGETABLES, REMINDED THEM OF THE FOODS THAT TYPICALLY WERE ALL THAT WAS AVAILABLE TO EAT DURING THE WAR.
THAT'S WHY THOSE VEGETABLES HAVE BEEN OUT OF FAVOR IN EUROPEAN CUISINE FOR DECADES.

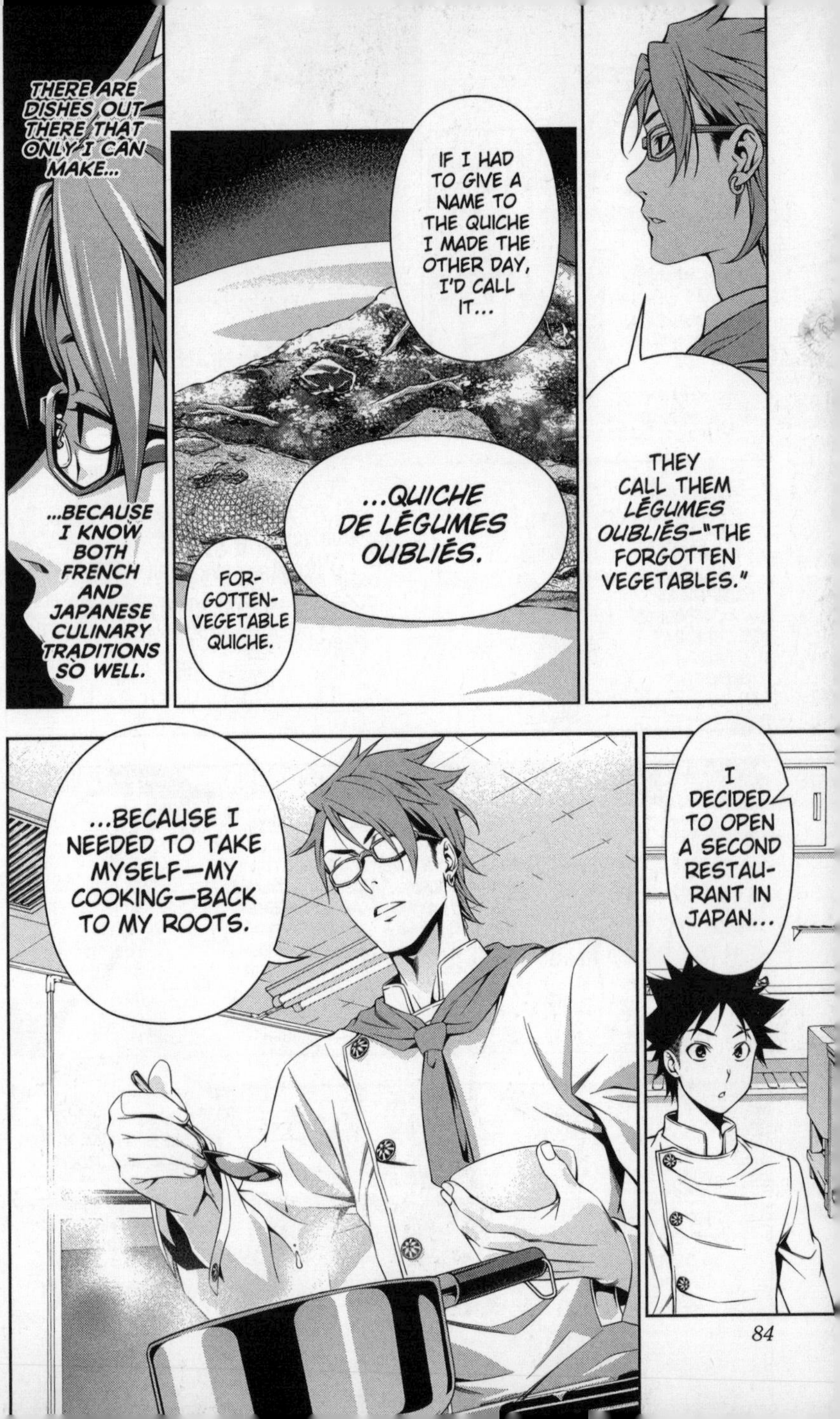
THEY CALL THEM LÉGUMES OUBLIÉS—"THE FORGOTTEN VEGETABLES."
IF I HAD TO GIVE A NAME TO THE QUICHE I MADE THE OTHER DAY, I'D CALL IT...
...QUICHE DE LÉGUMES OUBLIÉS.
FOR-GOTTEN-VEGETABLE QUICHE.
THERE ARE DISHES OUT THERE THAT ONLY I CAN MAKE...
...BECAUSE I KNOW BOTH FRENCH AND JAPANESE CULINARY TRADITIONS SO WELL.
I DECIDED TO OPEN A SECOND RESTAU-RANT IN JAPAN...
...BECAUSE I NEEDED TO TAKE MYSELF—MY COOKING—BACK TO MY ROOTS.

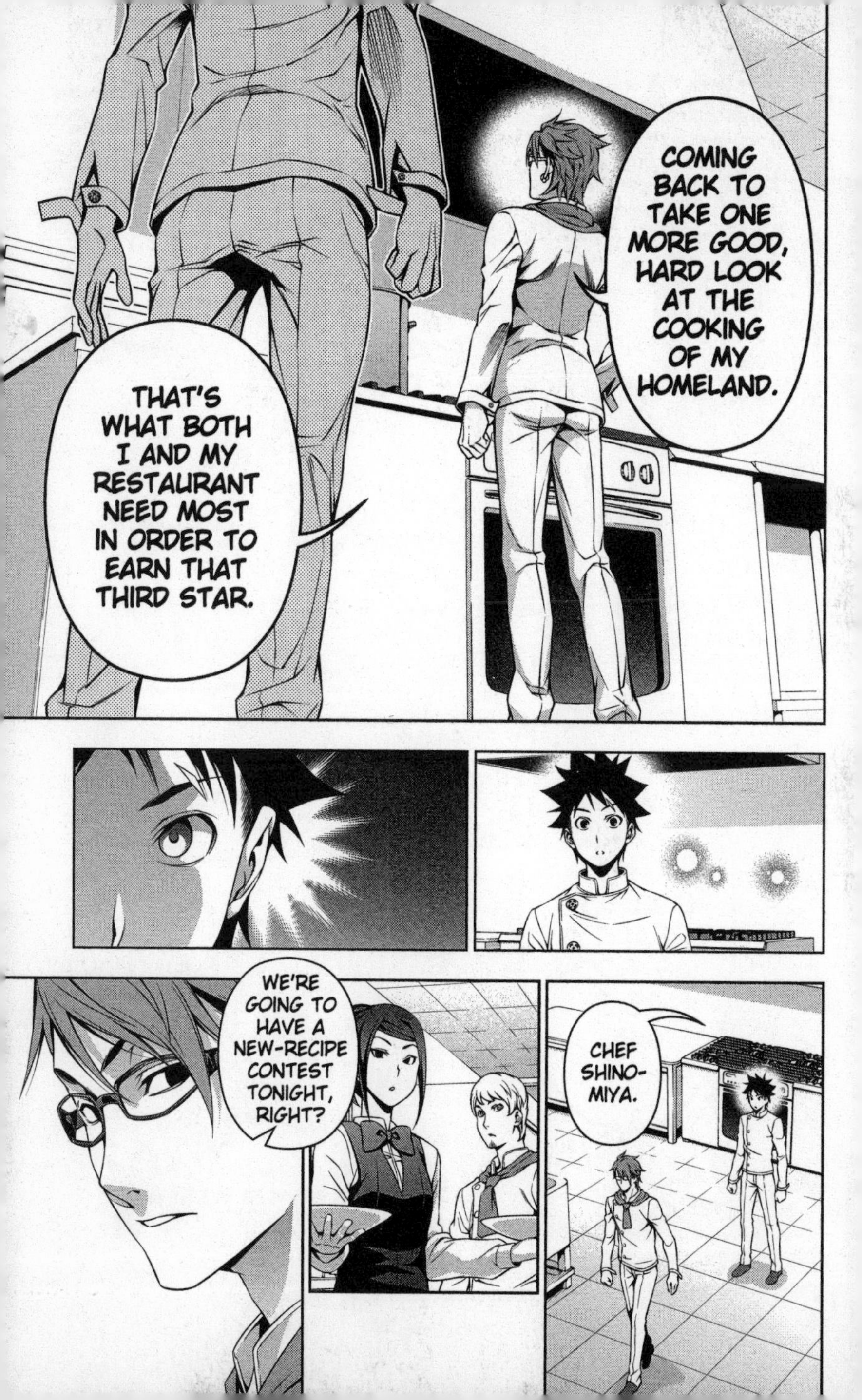
COMING BACK TO TAKE ONE MORE GOOD, HARD LOOK AT THE COOKING OF MY HOMELAND.
THAT'S WHAT BOTH I AND MY RESTAURANT NEED MOST IN ORDER TO EARN THAT THIRD STAR.
CHEF SHINO-MIYA.
WE'RE GOING TO HAVE A NEW-RECIPE CONTEST TONIGHT, RIGHT?

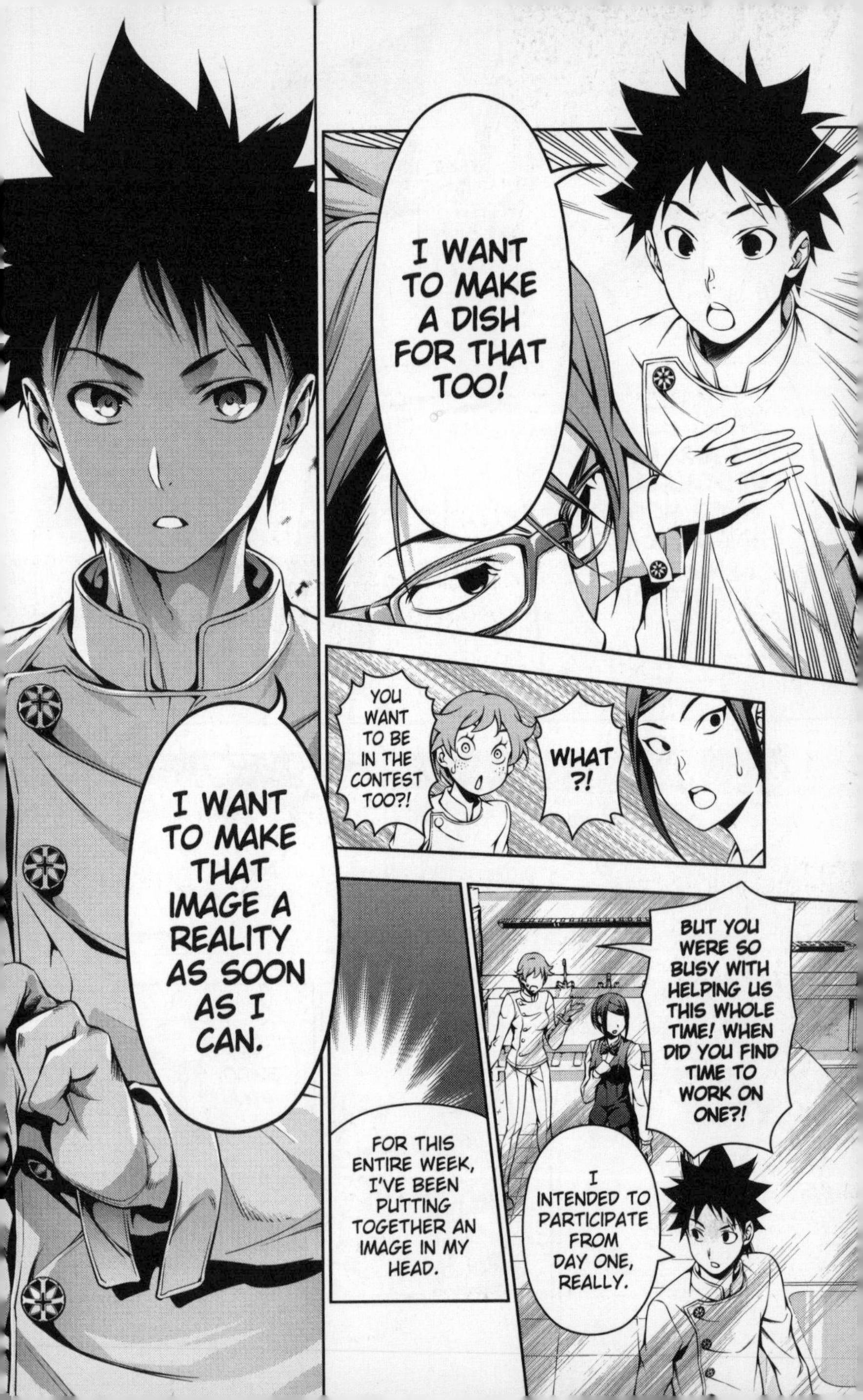
I WANT TO MAKE A DISH FOR THAT TOO!
WHAT?!
YOU WANT TO BE IN THE CONTEST TOO?!
BUT YOU WERE SO BUSY WITH HELPING US THIS WHOLE TIME! WHEN DID YOU FIND TIME TO WORK ON ONE?!
I INTENDED TO PARTICIPATE FROM DAY ONE, REALLY.
FOR THIS ENTIRE WEEK, I'VE BEEN PUTTING TOGETHER AN IMAGE IN MY HEAD.
I WANT TO MAKE THAT IMAGE A REALITY AS SOON AS I CAN.

YES.

YOU THINK YOU CAN PUT TOGETHER A QUALITY DISH?

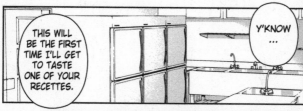

THIS WILL BE THE FIRST TIME I'LL GET TO TASTE ONE OF YOUR RECETTES.

Y'KNOW...

ALL RIGHT. YOU CAN DO IT. BUT...

SHINO's

...DON'T COME WHINING TO ME IF THIS NEW SENSE OF CONFIDENCE OF YOURS GETS CRUSHED.

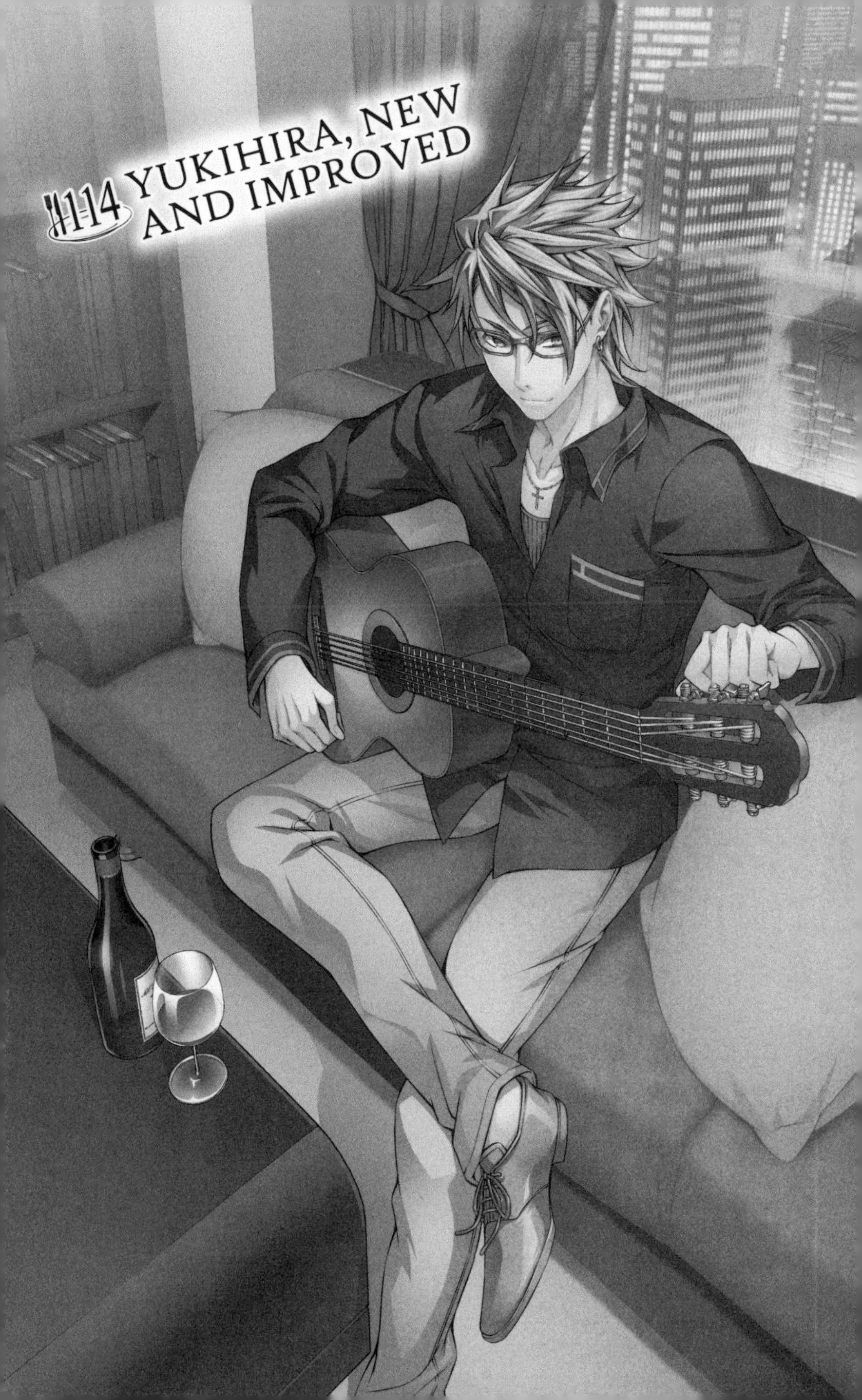
114
YUKIHIRA, NEW
AND IMPROVED

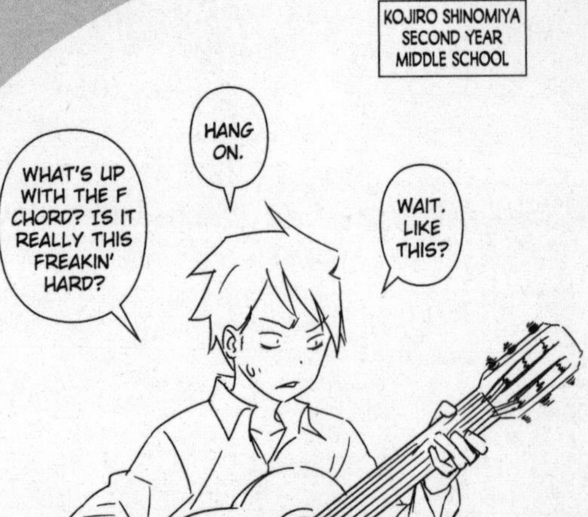
KOJIRO SHINOMIYA SECOND YEAR MIDDLE SCHOOL
WAIT. LIKE THIS?
HANG ON.
WHAT'S UP WITH THE F CHORD? IS IT REALLY THIS FREAKIN' HARD?

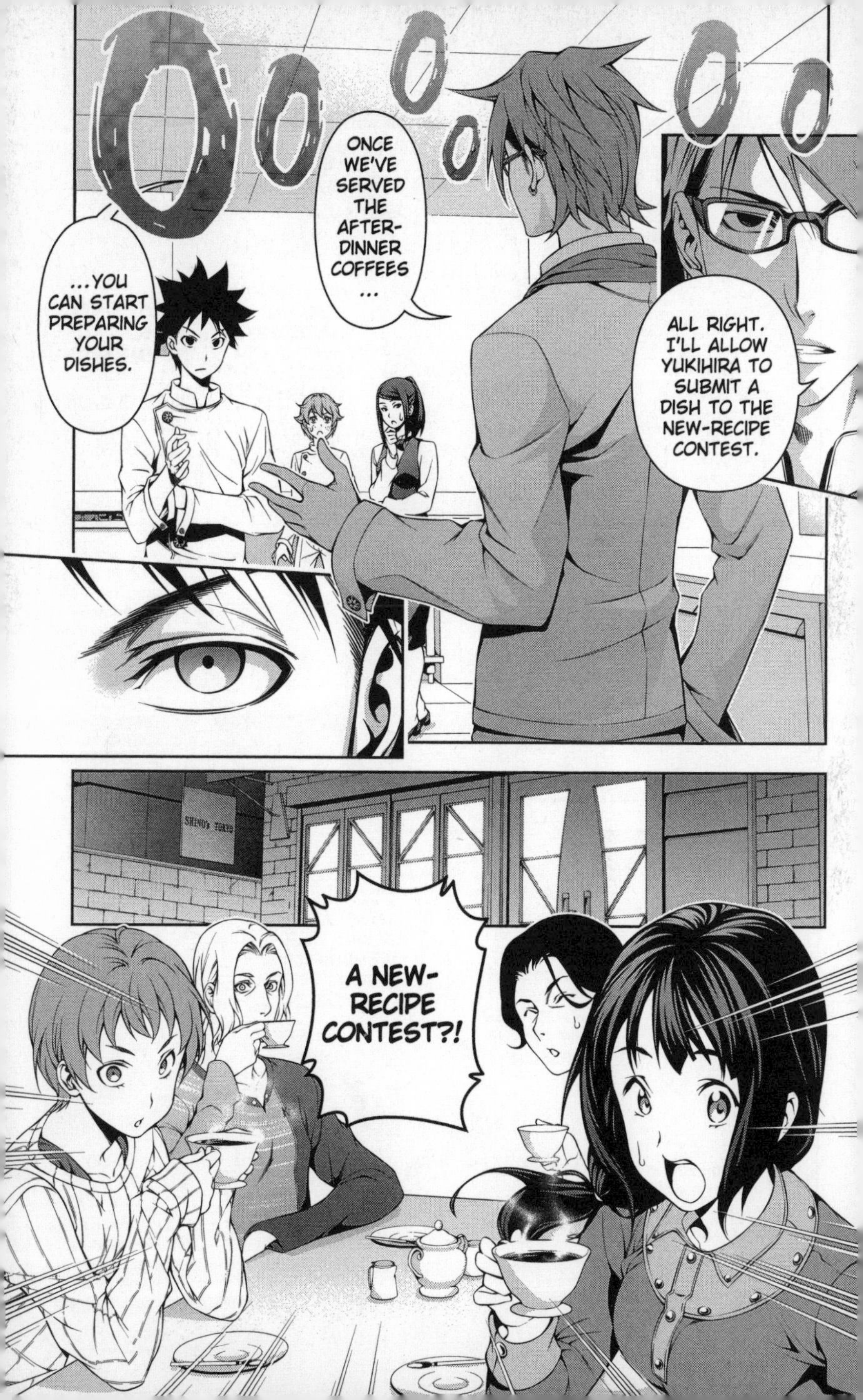
ALL RIGHT. I'LL ALLOW YUKIHIRA TO SUBMIT A DISH TO THE NEW-RECIPE CONTEST.
ONCE WE'VE SERVED THE AFTER-DINNER COFFEES ...
...YOU CAN START PREPARING YOUR DISHES.
SHINO's TOKYO
A NEW-RECIPE CONTEST?!

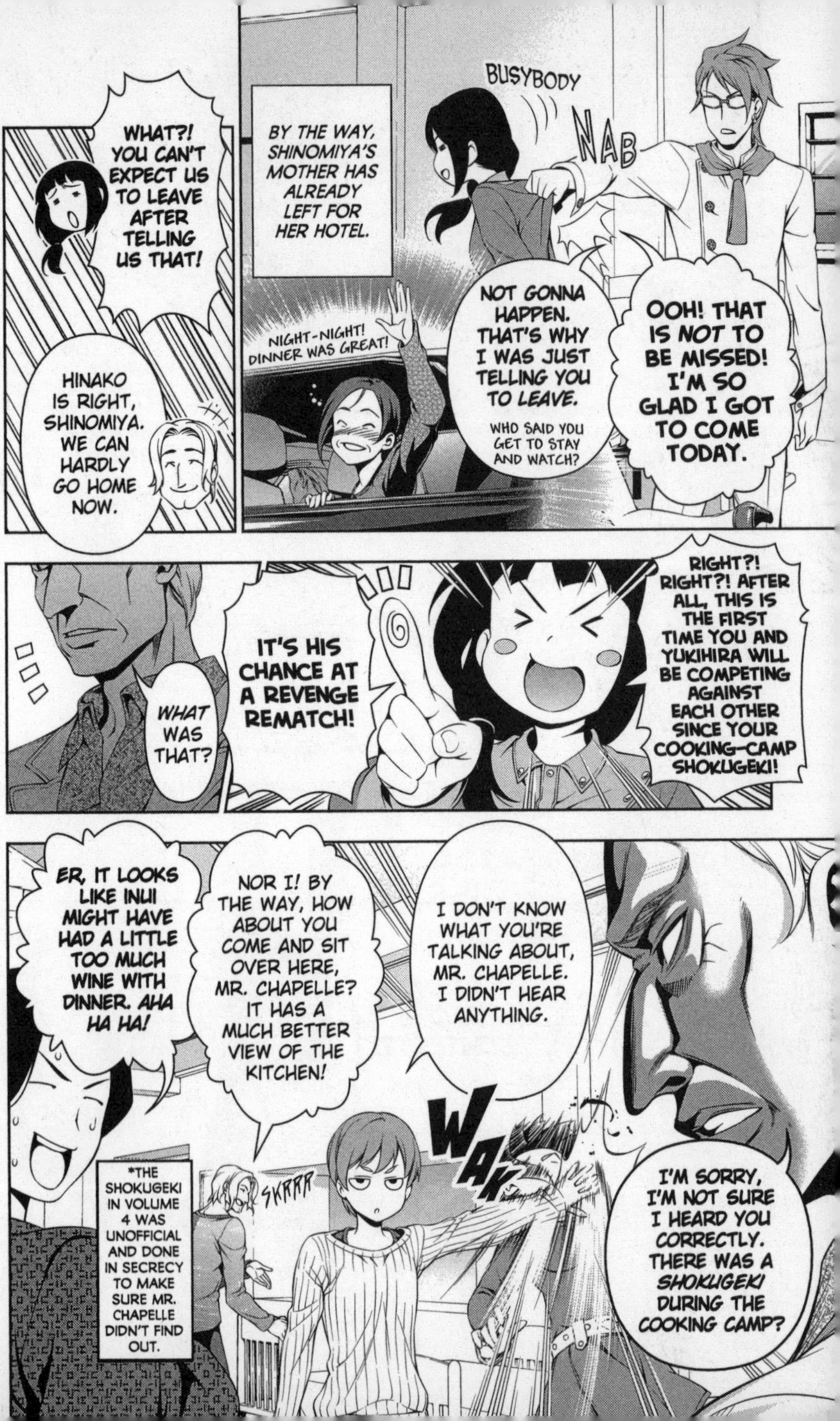

BUSYBODY
NAB
OOH! THAT IS *NOT* TO BE MISSED! I'M SO GLAD I GOT TO COME TODAY.
NOT GONNA HAPPEN. THAT'S WHY I WAS JUST TELLING YOU TO *LEAVE*.
WHO SAID YOU GET TO STAY AND WATCH?
BY THE WAY, SHINOMIYA'S MOTHER HAS ALREADY LEFT FOR HER HOTEL.
NIGHT-NIGHT! DINNER WAS GREAT!
WHAT?! YOU CAN'T EXPECT US TO LEAVE AFTER TELLING US THAT!
HINAKO IS RIGHT, SHINOMIYA. WE CAN HARDLY GO HOME NOW.
RIGHT?! RIGHT?! AFTER ALL, THIS IS THE FIRST TIME YOU AND YUKIHIRA WILL BE COMPETING AGAINST EACH OTHER SINCE YOUR COOKING-CAMP SHOKUGEKI!
IT'S HIS CHANCE AT A REVENGE REMATCH!
*WHAT* WAS THAT?
I'M SORRY, I'M NOT SURE I HEARD YOU CORRECTLY. THERE WAS A *SHOKUGEKI* DURING THE COOKING CAMP?
WAK
I DON'T KNOW WHAT YOU'RE TALKING ABOUT, MR. CHAPELLE. I DIDN'T HEAR ANYTHING.
NOR I! BY THE WAY, HOW ABOUT YOU COME AND SIT OVER HERE, MR. CHAPELLE? IT HAS A MUCH BETTER VIEW OF THE KITCHEN!
ER, IT LOOKS LIKE INUI MIGHT HAVE HAD A LITTLE TOO MUCH WINE WITH DINNER. AHA HA HA!
SKRRR
*THE SHOKUGEKI IN VOLUME 4 WAS UNOFFICIAL AND DONE IN SECRECY TO MAKE SURE MR. CHAPELLE DIDN'T FIND OUT.

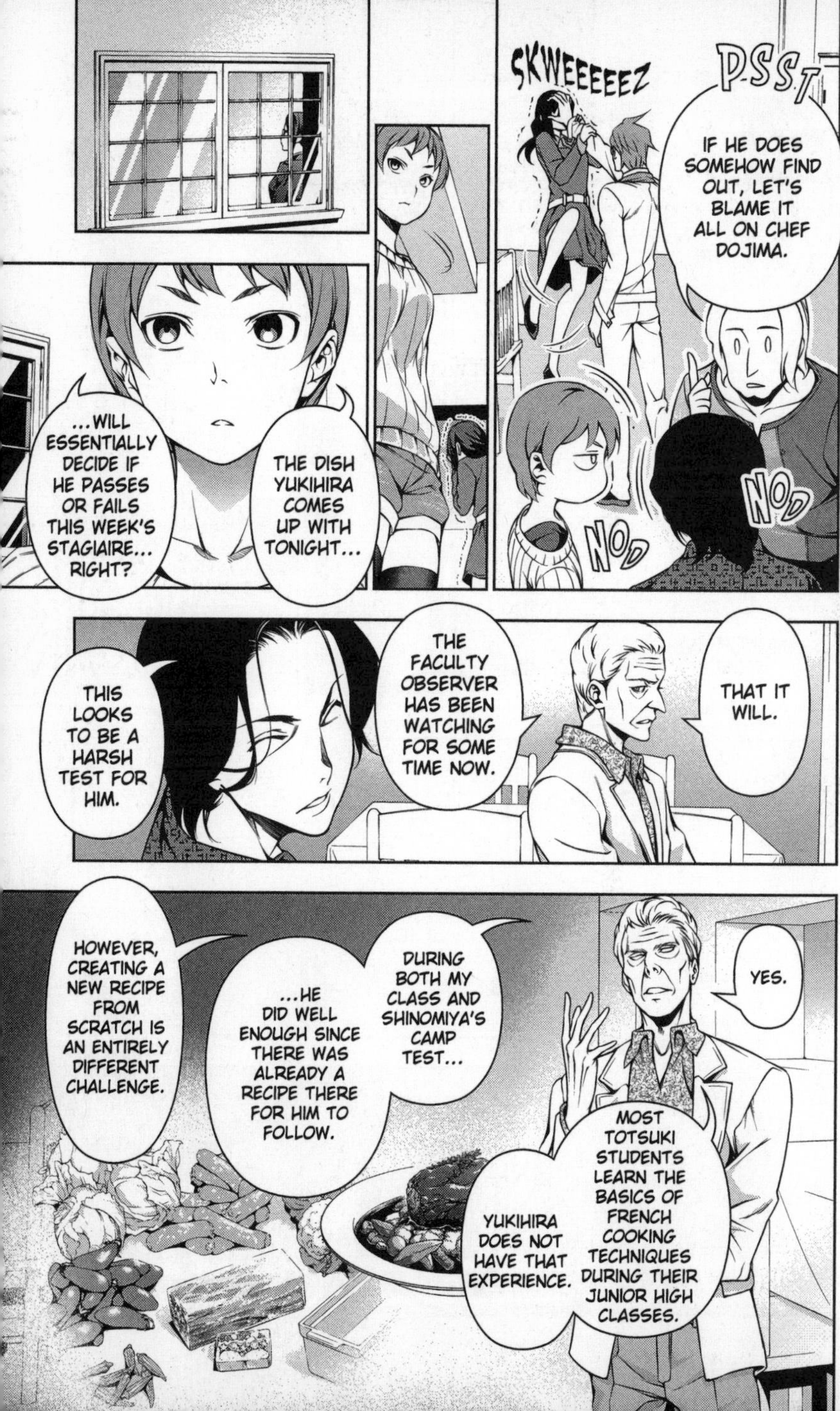
PSST
IF HE DOES SOMEHOW FIND OUT, LET'S BLAME IT ALL ON CHEF DOJIMA.
SKWEEEEEZ
NOD
NOD
THE DISH YUKIHIRA COMES UP WITH TONIGHT...
...WILL ESSENTIALLY DECIDE IF HE PASSES OR FAILS THIS WEEK'S STAGIAIRE... RIGHT?
THAT IT WILL.
THE FACULTY OBSERVER HAS BEEN WATCHING FOR SOME TIME NOW.
THIS LOOKS TO BE A HARSH TEST FOR HIM.
YES.
MOST TOTSUKI STUDENTS LEARN THE BASICS OF FRENCH COOKING TECHNIQUES DURING THEIR JUNIOR HIGH CLASSES.
YUKIHIRA DOES NOT HAVE THAT EXPERIENCE.
DURING BOTH MY CLASS AND SHINOMIYA'S CAMP TEST...
...HE DID WELL ENOUGH SINCE THERE WAS ALREADY A RECIPE THERE FOR HIM TO FOLLOW.
HOWEVER, CREATING A NEW RECIPE FROM SCRATCH IS AN ENTIRELY DIFFERENT CHALLENGE.

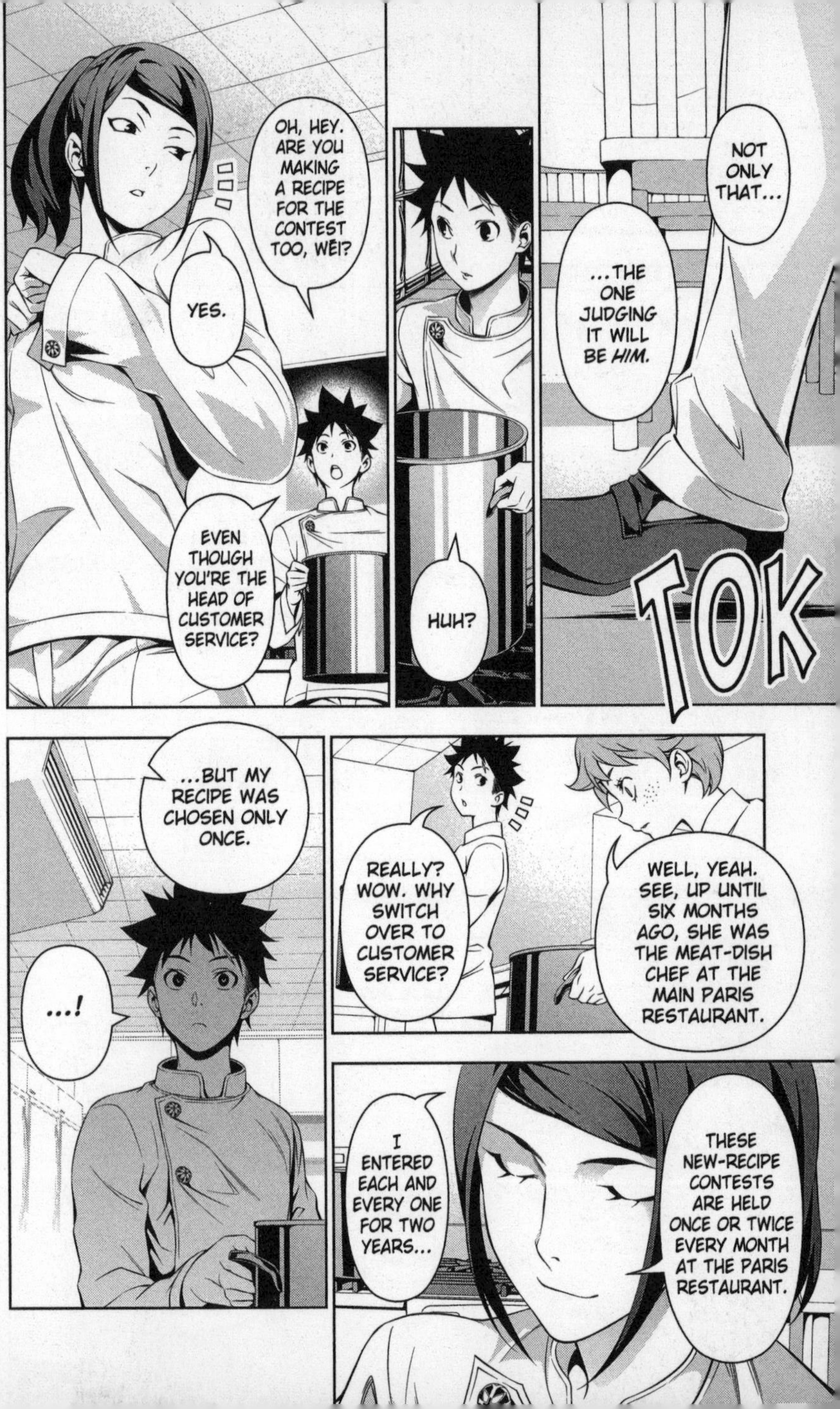
NOT ONLY THAT...
...THE ONE JUDGING IT WILL BE *HIM*.
TOK
HUH?
OH, HEY. ARE YOU MAKING A RECIPE FOR THE CONTEST TOO, WÉI?
YES.
EVEN THOUGH YOU'RE THE HEAD OF CUSTOMER SERVICE?
WELL, YEAH. SEE, UP UNTIL SIX MONTHS AGO, SHE WAS THE MEAT-DISH CHEF AT THE MAIN PARIS RESTAURANT.
REALLY? WOW. WHY SWITCH OVER TO CUSTOMER SERVICE?
THESE NEW-RECIPE CONTESTS ARE HELD ONCE OR TWICE EVERY MONTH AT THE PARIS RESTAURANT.
I ENTERED EACH AND EVERY ONE FOR TWO YEARS...
...BUT MY RECIPE WAS CHOSEN ONLY ONCE.
...!

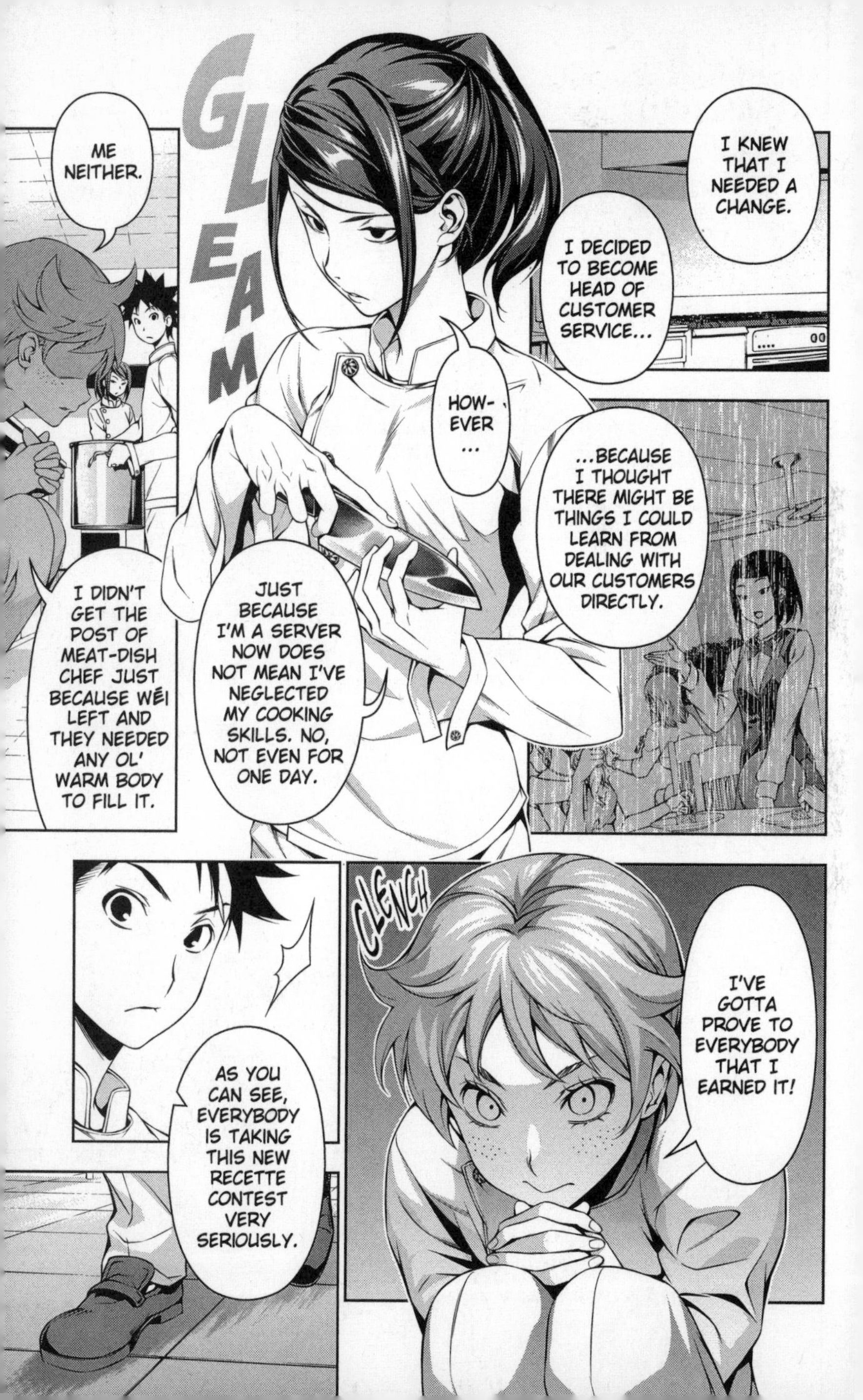
I KNEW THAT I NEEDED A CHANGE.
I DECIDED TO BECOME HEAD OF CUSTOMER SERVICE...
...BECAUSE I THOUGHT THERE MIGHT BE THINGS I COULD LEARN FROM DEALING WITH OUR CUSTOMERS DIRECTLY.
GLEAM
HOW-EVER...
JUST BECAUSE I'M A SERVER NOW DOES NOT MEAN I'VE NEGLECTED MY COOKING SKILLS. NO, NOT EVEN FOR ONE DAY.
ME NEITHER.
I DIDN'T GET THE POST OF MEAT-DISH CHEF JUST BECAUSE WÉI LEFT AND THEY NEEDED ANY OL' WARM BODY TO FILL IT.
CLENCH
I'VE GOTTA PROVE TO EVERYBODY THAT I EARNED IT!
AS YOU CAN SEE, EVERYBODY IS TAKING THIS NEW RECETTE CONTEST VERY SERIOUSLY.

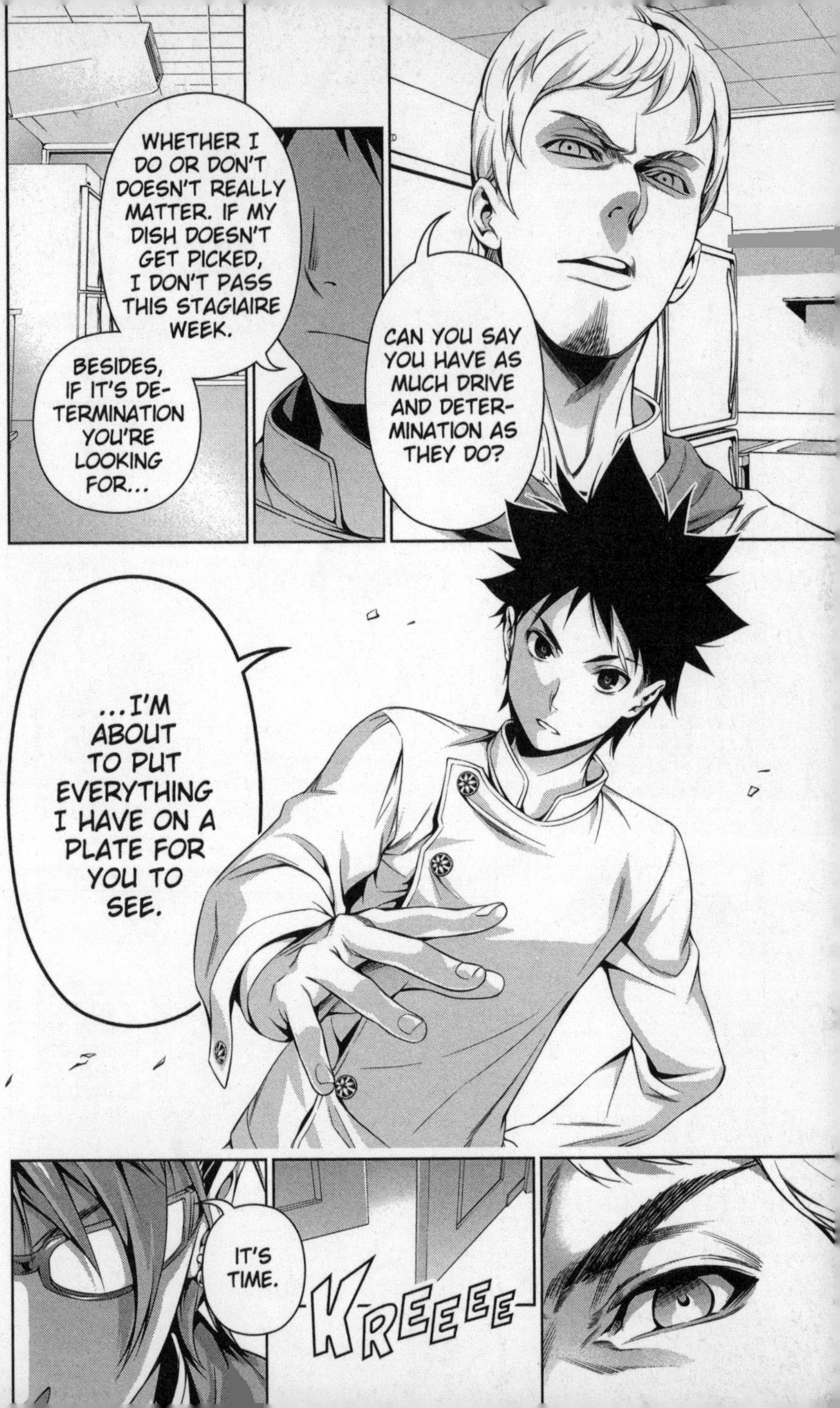
CAN YOU SAY YOU HAVE AS MUCH DRIVE AND DETERMINATION AS THEY DO?
WHETHER I DO OR DON'T DOESN'T REALLY MATTER. IF MY DISH DOESN'T GET PICKED, I DON'T PASS THIS STAGIAIRE WEEK.
BESIDES, IF IT'S DETERMINATION YOU'RE LOOKING FOR...
...I'M ABOUT TO PUT EVERYTHING I HAVE ON A PLATE FOR YOU TO SEE.
KREEEEE
IT'S TIME.

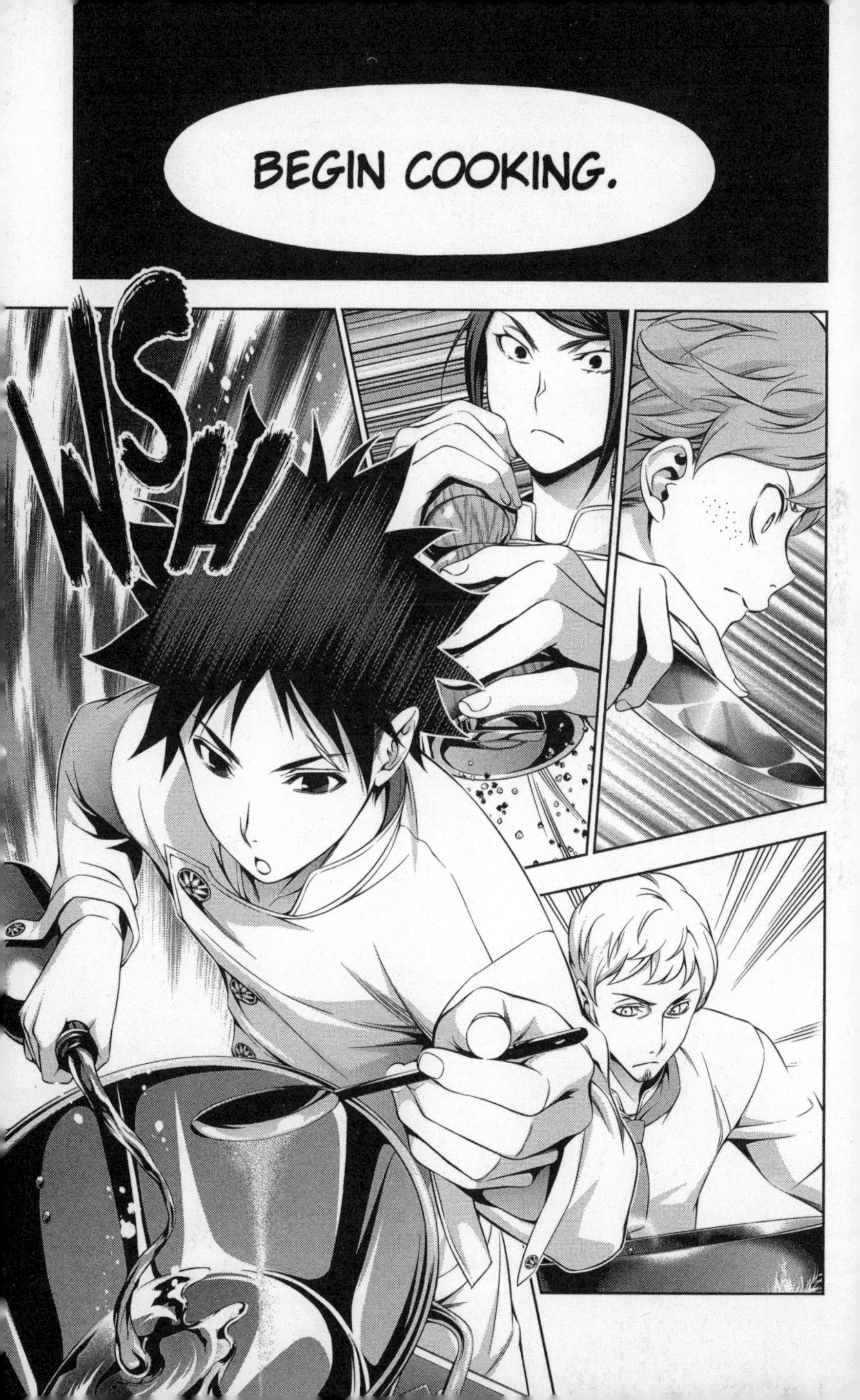
BEGIN COOKING.
WSH

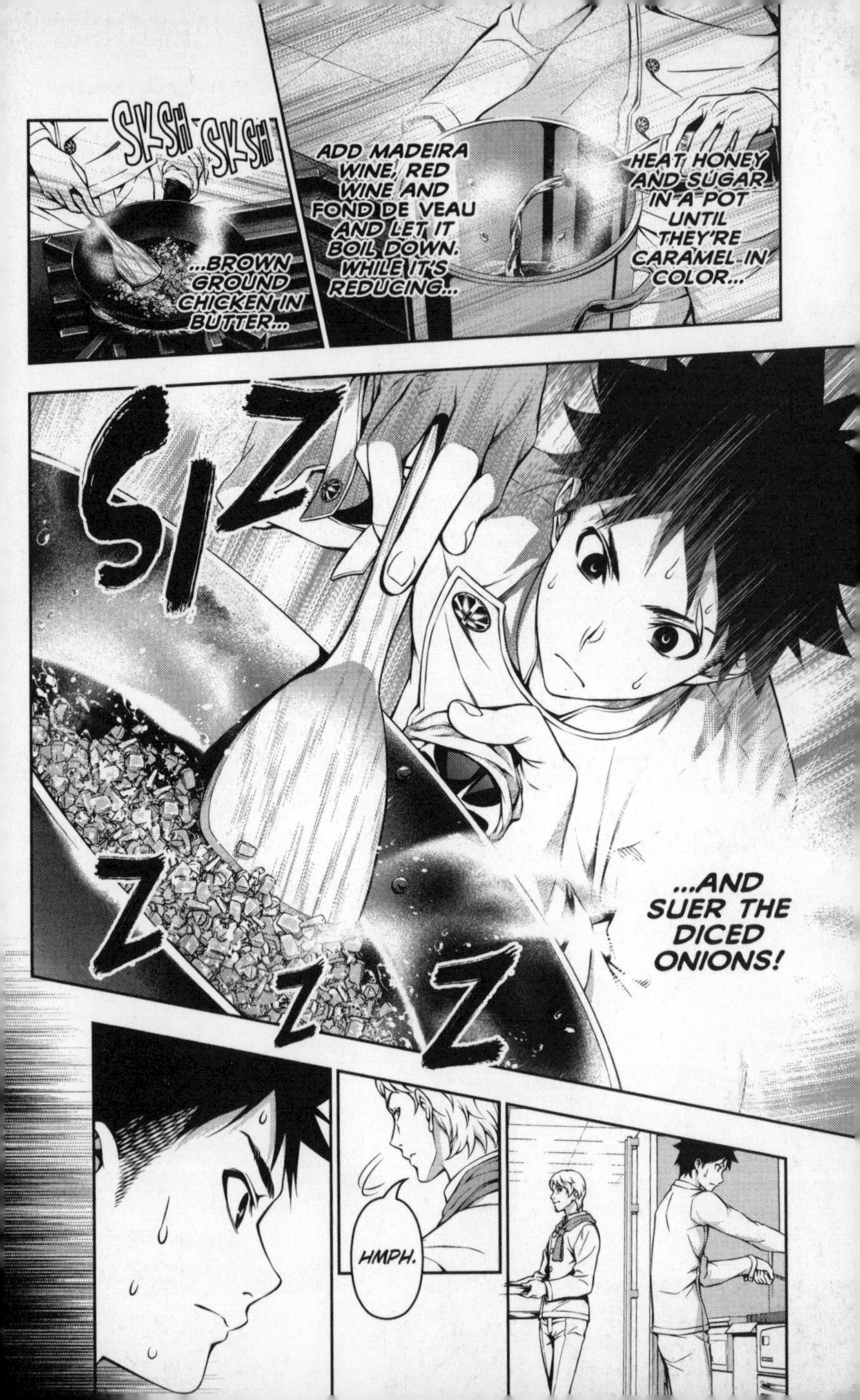
HEAT HONEY AND SUGAR IN A POT UNTIL THEY'RE CARAMEL IN COLOR...
ADD MADEIRA WINE, RED WINE AND FOND DE VEAU AND LET IT BOIL DOWN. WHILE IT'S REDUCING...
SKSH SKSH
...BROWN GROUND CHICKEN IN BUTTER...
SIZ
ZZZZ
...AND SUER THE DICED ONIONS!
HMPH.

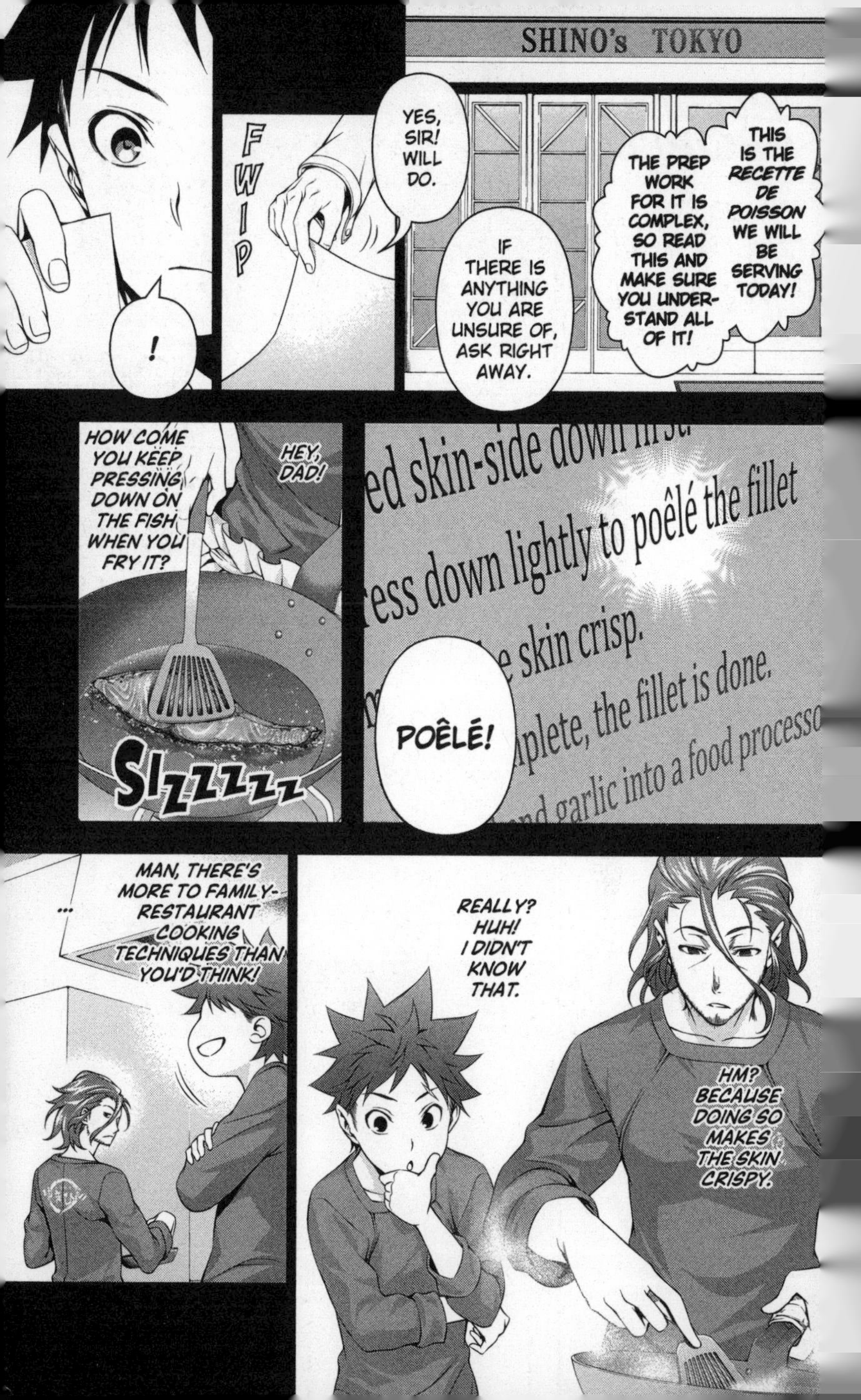
SHINO's TOKYO
THIS IS THE RECETTE DE POISSON WE WILL BE SERVING TODAY!
THE PREP WORK FOR IT IS COMPLEX, SO READ THIS AND MAKE SURE YOU UNDERSTAND ALL OF IT!
IF THERE IS ANYTHING YOU ARE UNSURE OF, ASK RIGHT AWAY.
YES, SIR! WILL DO.
FWIP
!
ed skin-side down first.
ess down lightly to poêlé the fillet
e skin crisp.
plete, the fillet is done.
nd garlic into a food processo
POÊLÉ!
HEY, DAD!
HOW COME YOU KEEP PRESSING DOWN ON THE FISH WHEN YOU FRY IT?
SIZZZZZZ
HM? BECAUSE DOING SO MAKES THE SKIN CRISPY.
REALLY? HUH! I DIDN'T KNOW THAT.
MAN, THERE'S MORE TO FAMILY-RESTAURANT COOKING TECHNIQUES THAN YOU'D THINK!
...

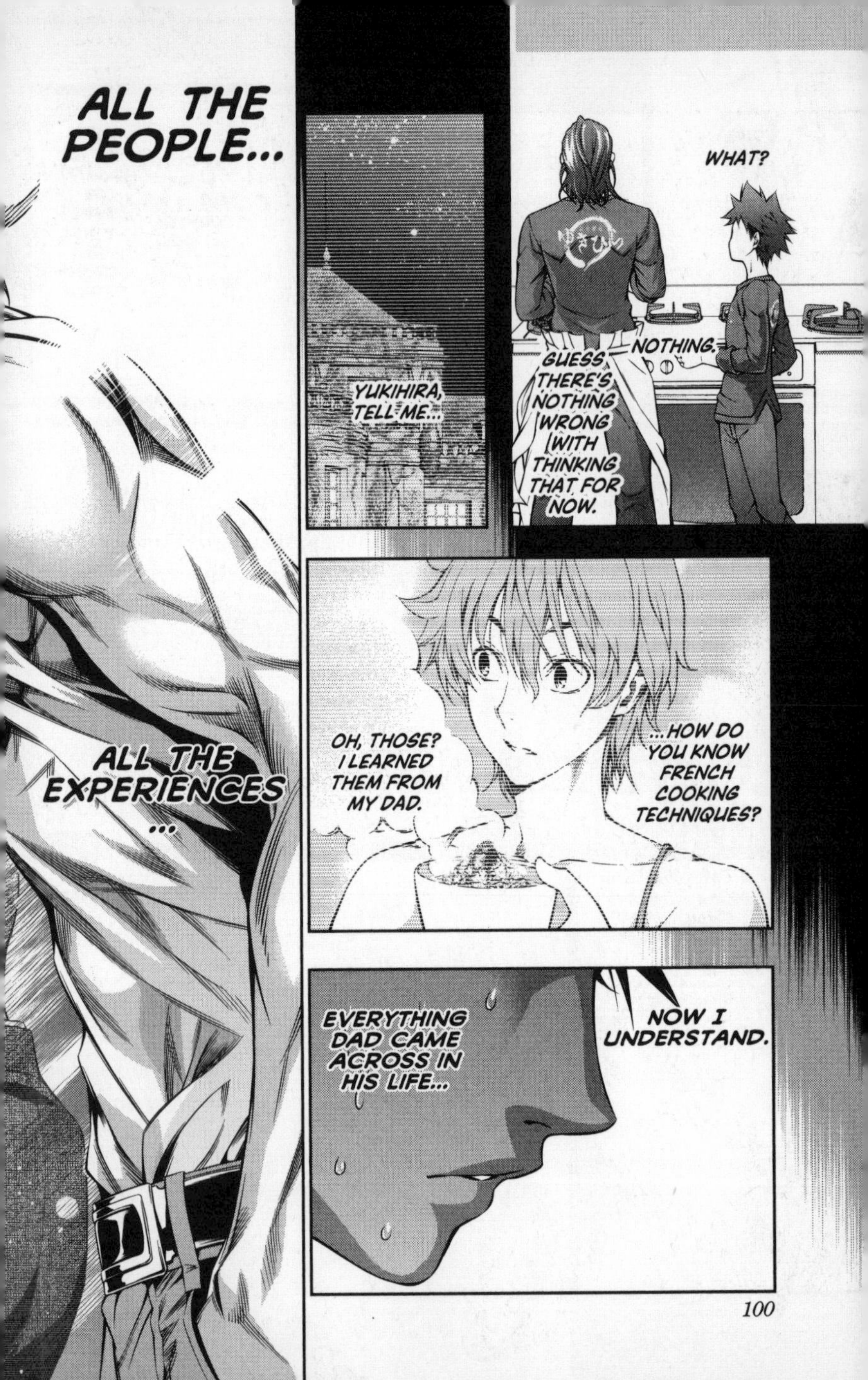
WHAT?
NOTHING.
GUESS THERE'S NOTHING WRONG WITH THINKING THAT FOR NOW.
YUKIHIRA, TELL ME...
...HOW DO YOU KNOW FRENCH COOKING TECHNIQUES?
OH, THOSE? I LEARNED THEM FROM MY DAD.
NOW I UNDERSTAND.
EVERYTHING DAD CAME ACROSS IN HIS LIFE...
ALL THE PEOPLE...
ALL THE EXPERIENCES...

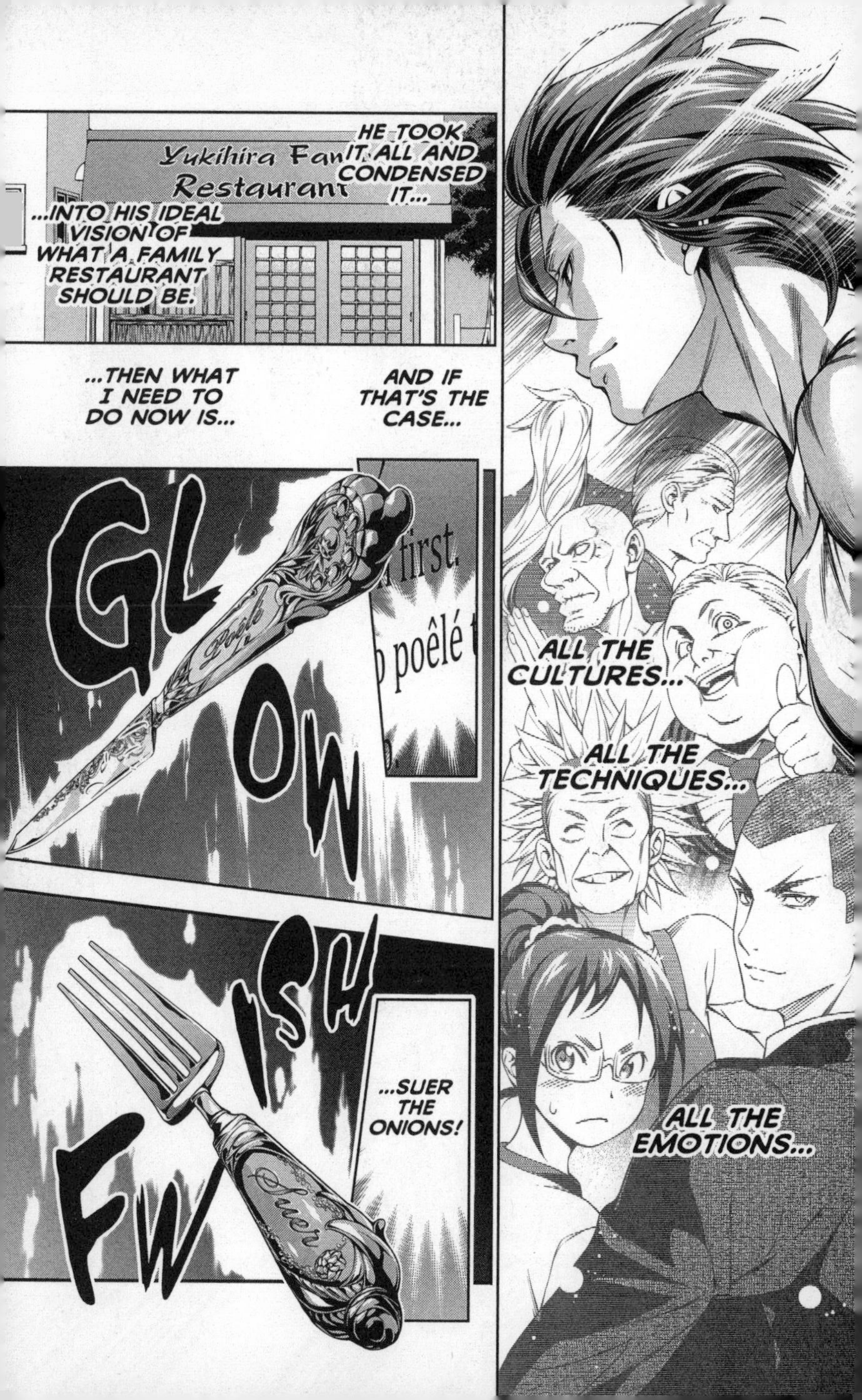
ALL THE CULTURES...
ALL THE TECHNIQUES...
ALL THE EMOTIONS...
Yukihira Fan
Restaurant
HE TOOK IT ALL AND CONDENSED IT...
...INTO HIS IDEAL VISION OF WHAT A FAMILY RESTAURANT SHOULD BE.
AND IF THAT'S THE CASE...
...THEN WHAT I NEED TO DO NOW IS...
GLOW
Poêle
first.
poêlé
FWISH
Suer
...SUER THE ONIONS!

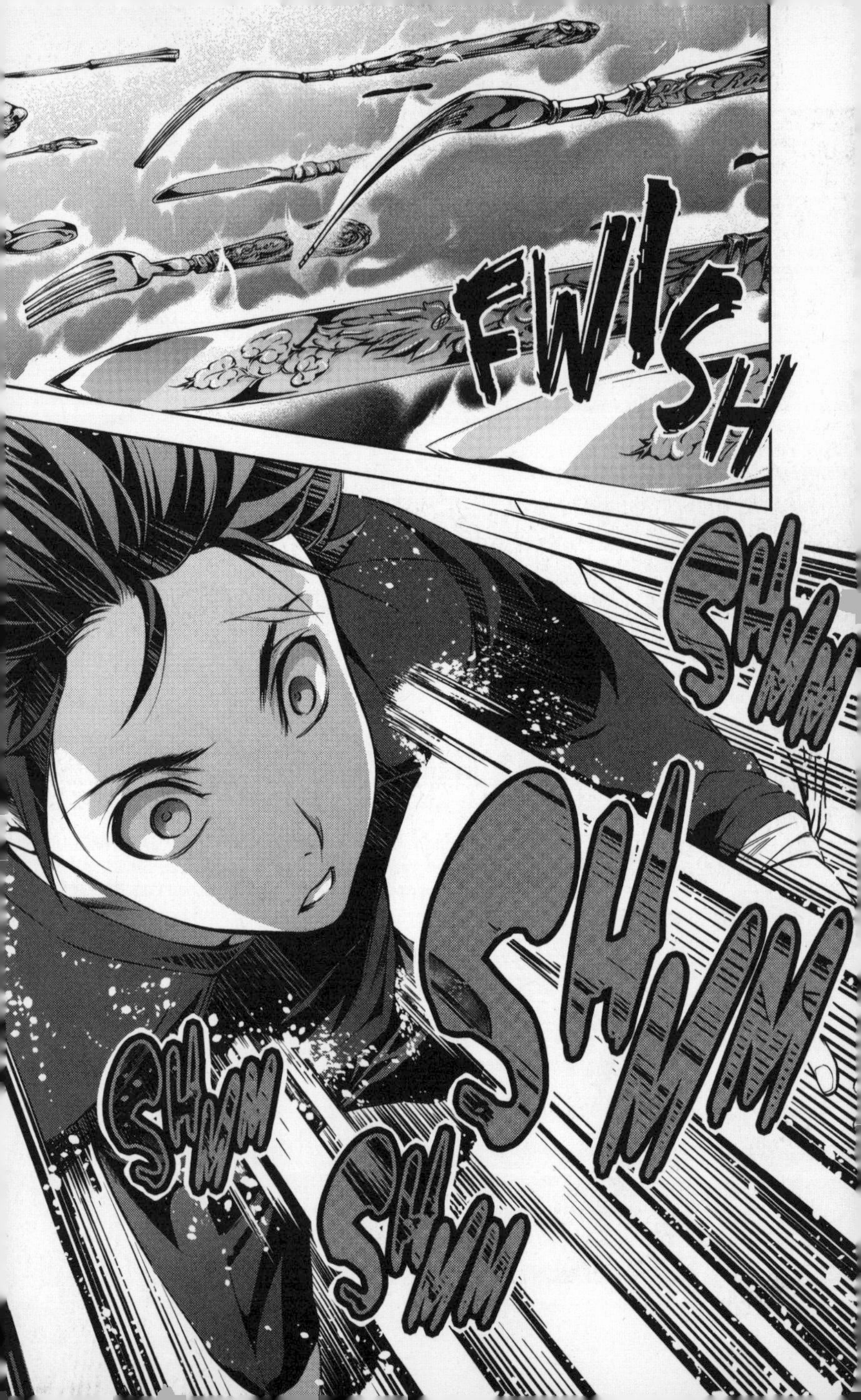
FWISH

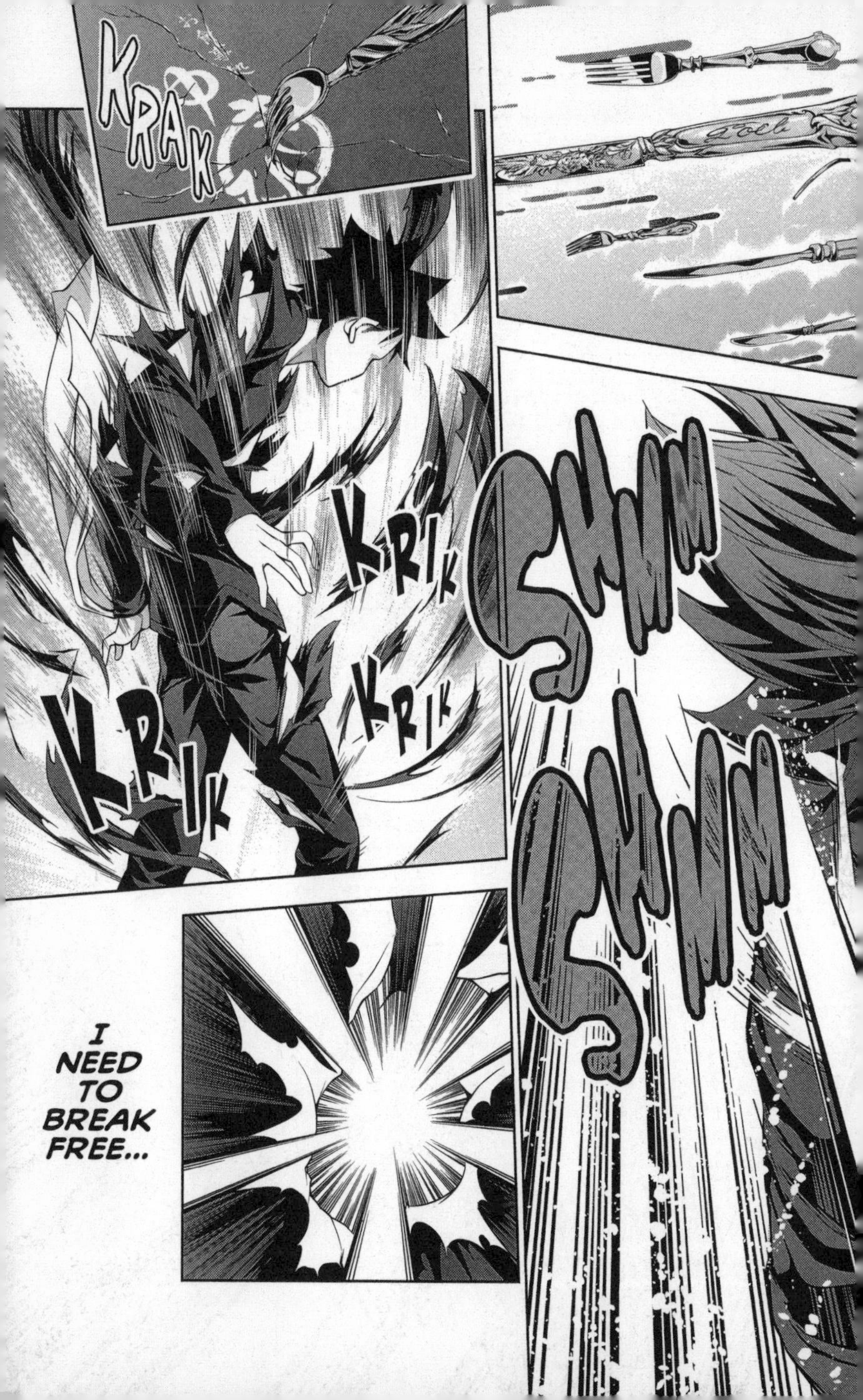
KRAK
SHWM
SHWM
KRIK
KRIK
KRIK
I NEED TO BREAK FREE...

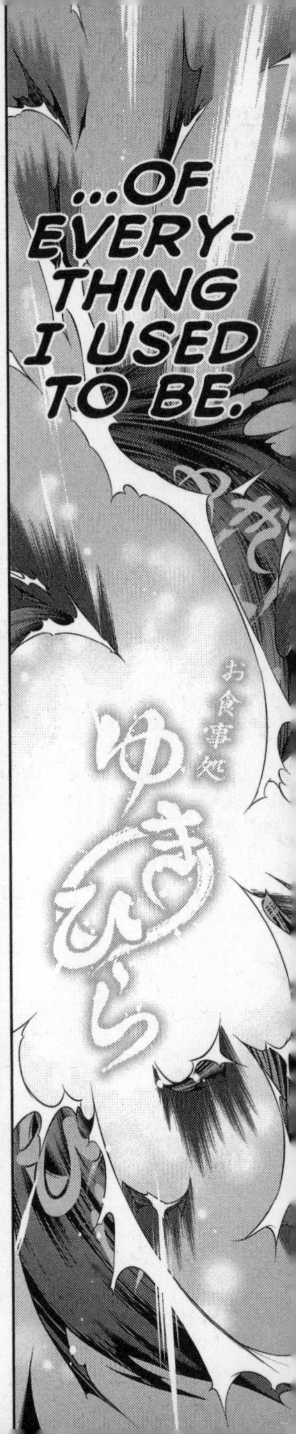
...OF EVERY-THING I USED TO BE.
お食事処
ゆきひら

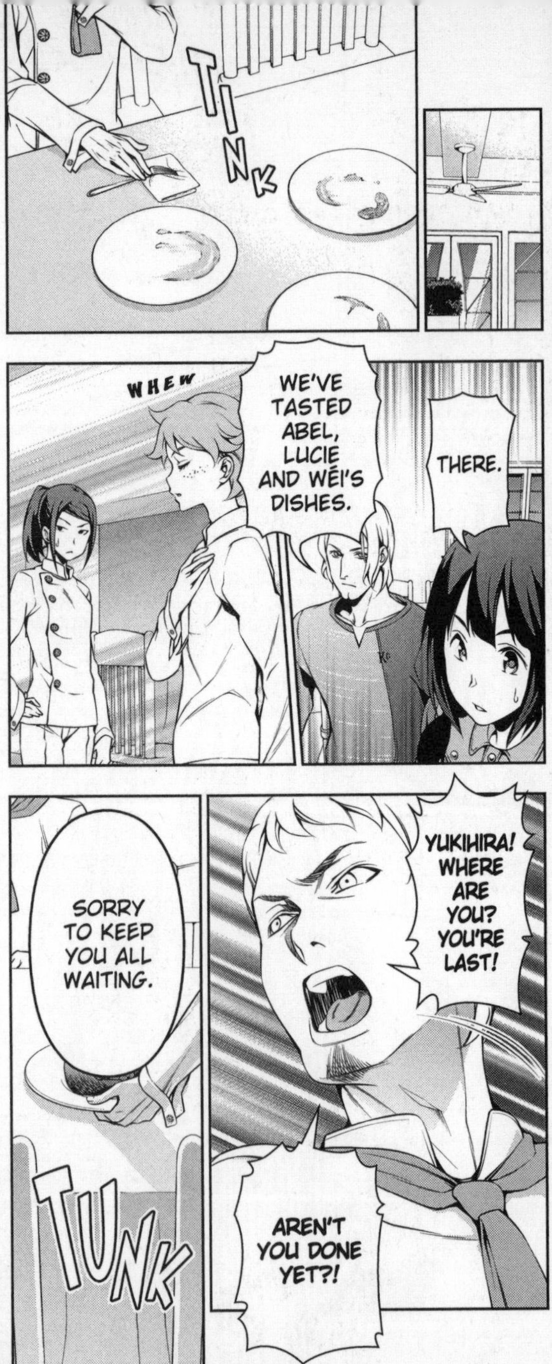
TINK
THERE.
WHEW
WE'VE TASTED ABEL, LUCIE AND WÈI'S DISHES.
YUKIHIRA! WHERE ARE YOU? YOU'RE LAST!
AREN'T YOU DONE YET?!
SORRY TO KEEP YOU ALL WAITING.
TUNK

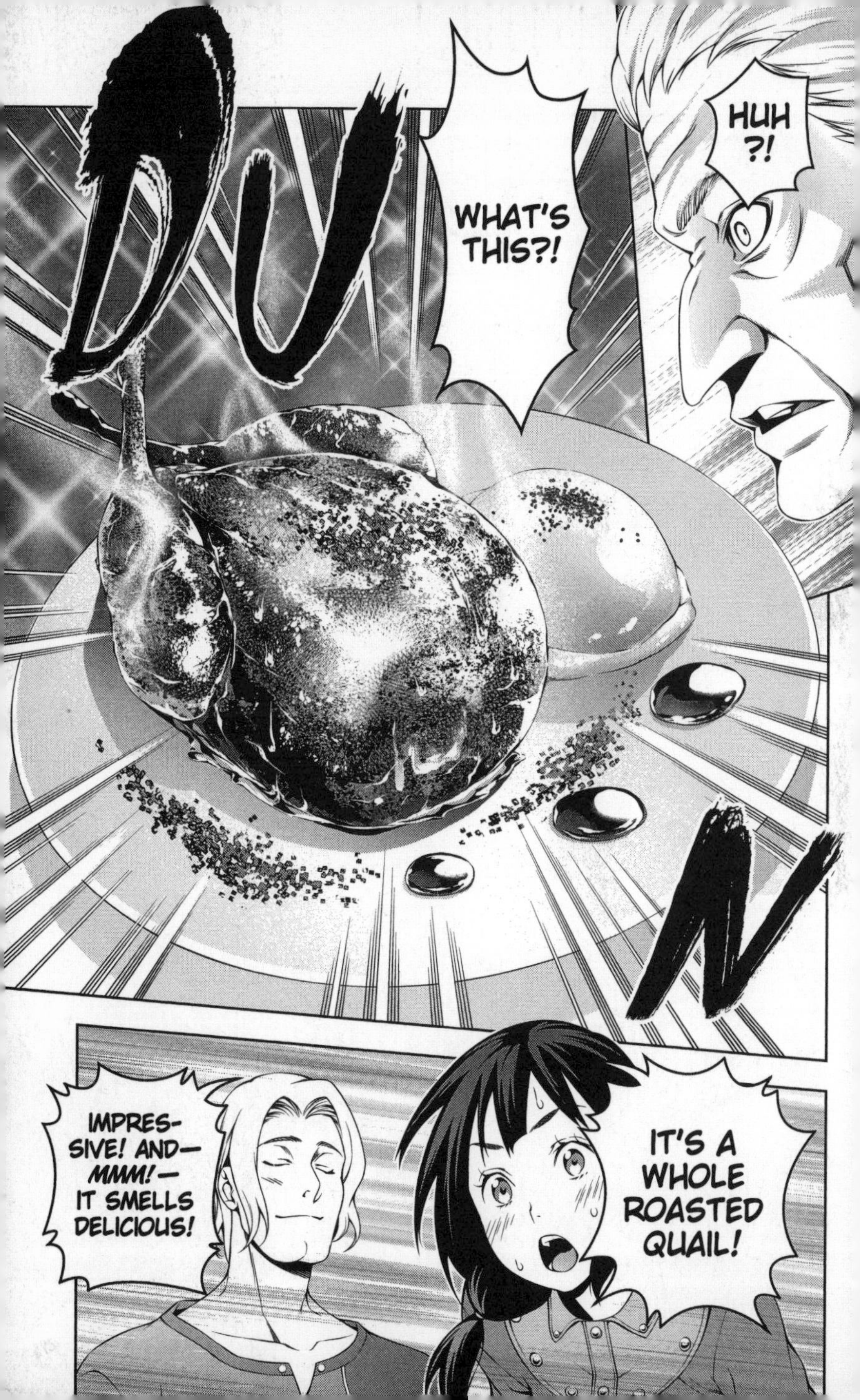
HUH ?!
WHAT'S THIS?!
DU
N
IT'S A WHOLE ROASTED QUAIL!
IMPRES-SIVE! AND— MMM!— IT SMELLS DELICIOUS!

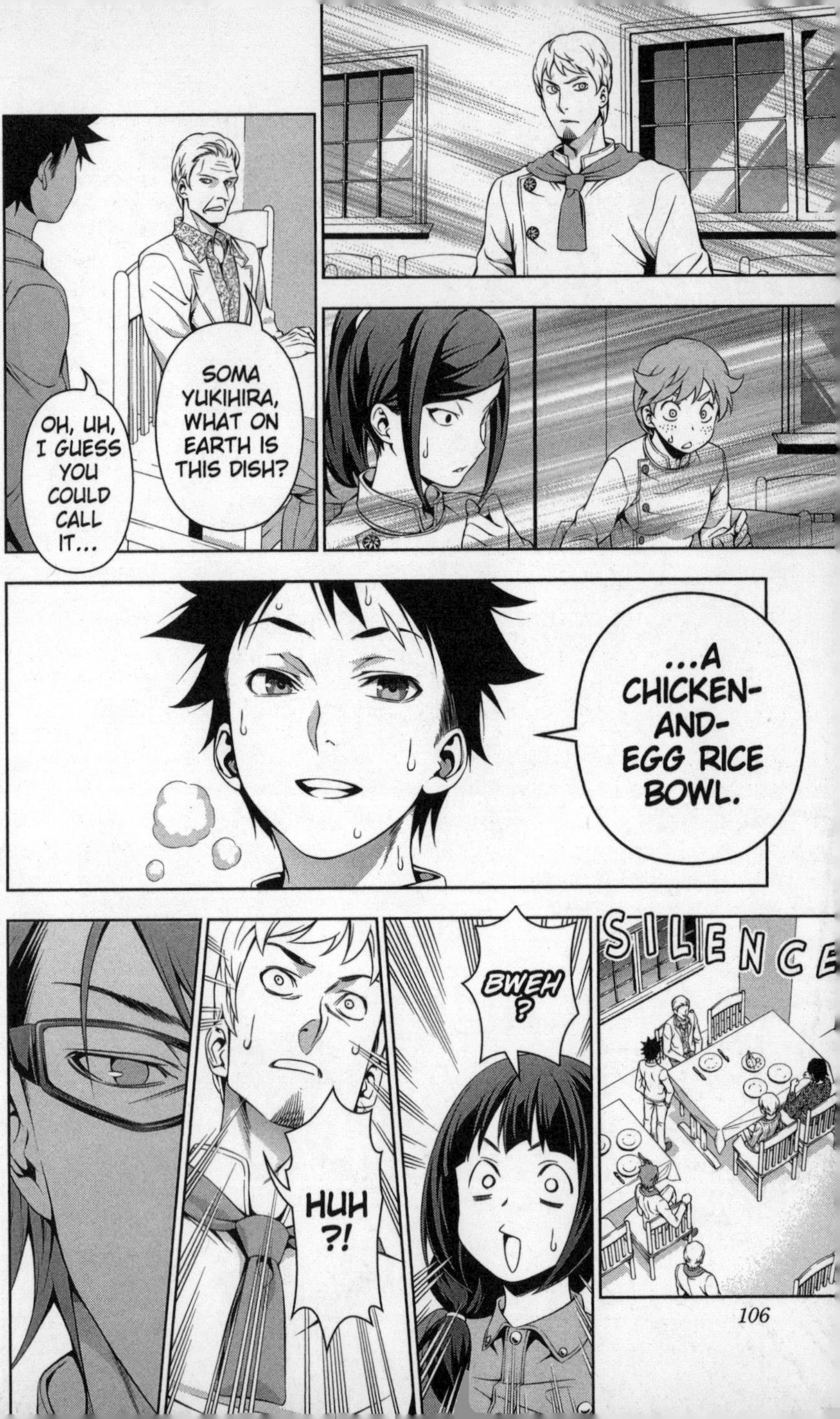
SOMA YUKIHIRA, WHAT ON EARTH IS THIS DISH?
OH, UH, I GUESS YOU COULD CALL IT...
...A CHICKEN-AND-EGG RICE BOWL.
SILENCE
BWEH?
HUH?!

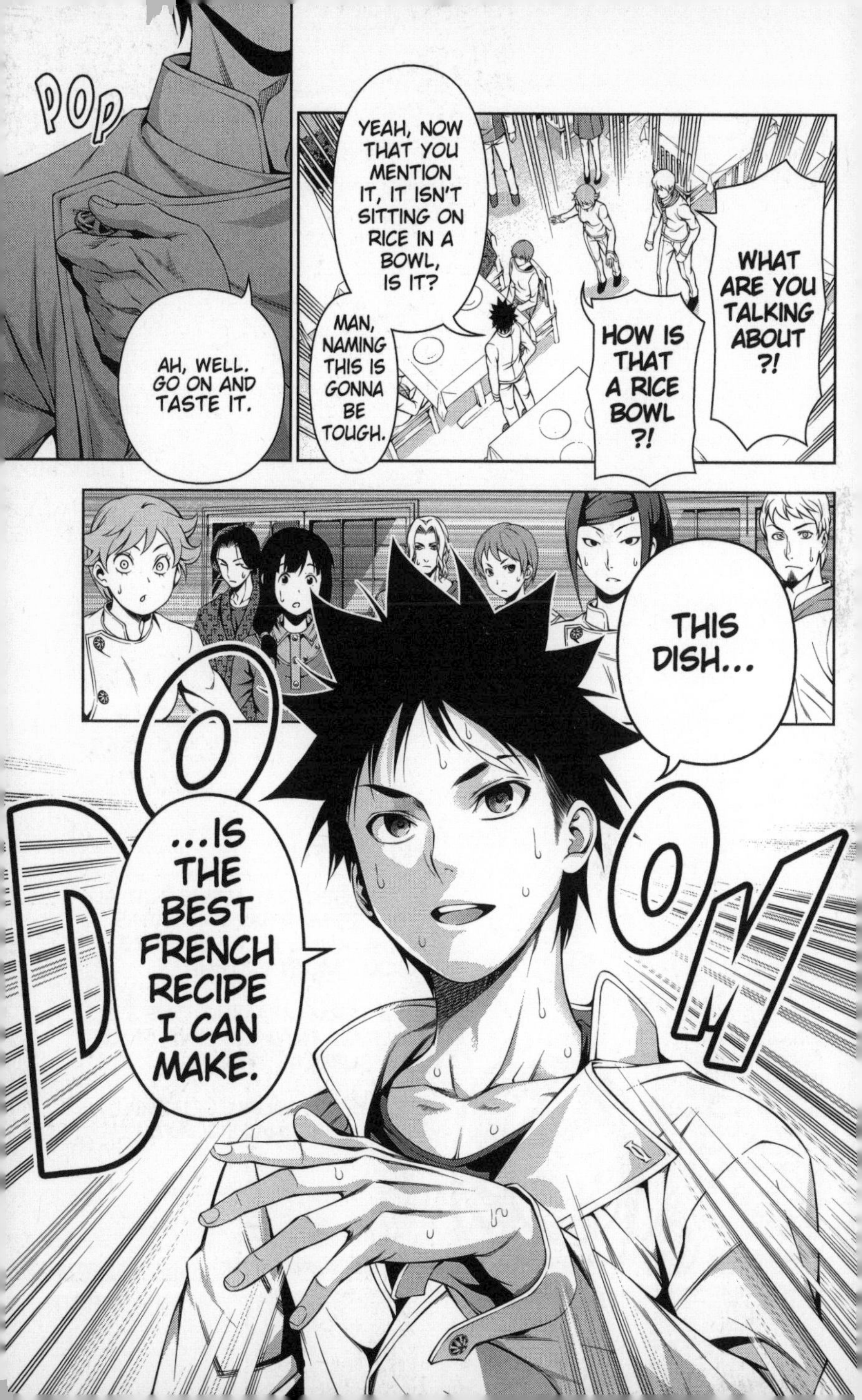
WHAT ARE YOU TALKING ABOUT?!
HOW IS THAT A RICE BOWL?!
YEAH, NOW THAT YOU MENTION IT, IT ISN'T SITTING ON RICE IN A BOWL, IS IT?
MAN, NAMING THIS IS GONNA BE TOUGH.
POP
AH, WELL. GO ON AND TASTE IT.
THIS DISH...
DOOM
...IS THE BEST FRENCH RECIPE I CAN MAKE.

## *KUNG FU IS...

1. THE GENERAL NAME FOR ALL CHINESE MARTIAL ARTS. THIS IS THE KUNG FU ONE HEARS ABOUT MOST OFTEN.

2. A TERM MEANING ONE'S OVERALL TRAINING AND SKILL IN A SUBJECT.

**EXAMPLE:** "YOUR COOKING KUNG FU IS INADEQUATE!"

IF SOMEONE YOU KNOW IS POOR OR STRUGGLING IN A SUBJECT, CHEER THEM ON BY SAYING THEY SHOULD INCREASE THEIR KUNG FU.

WÉI

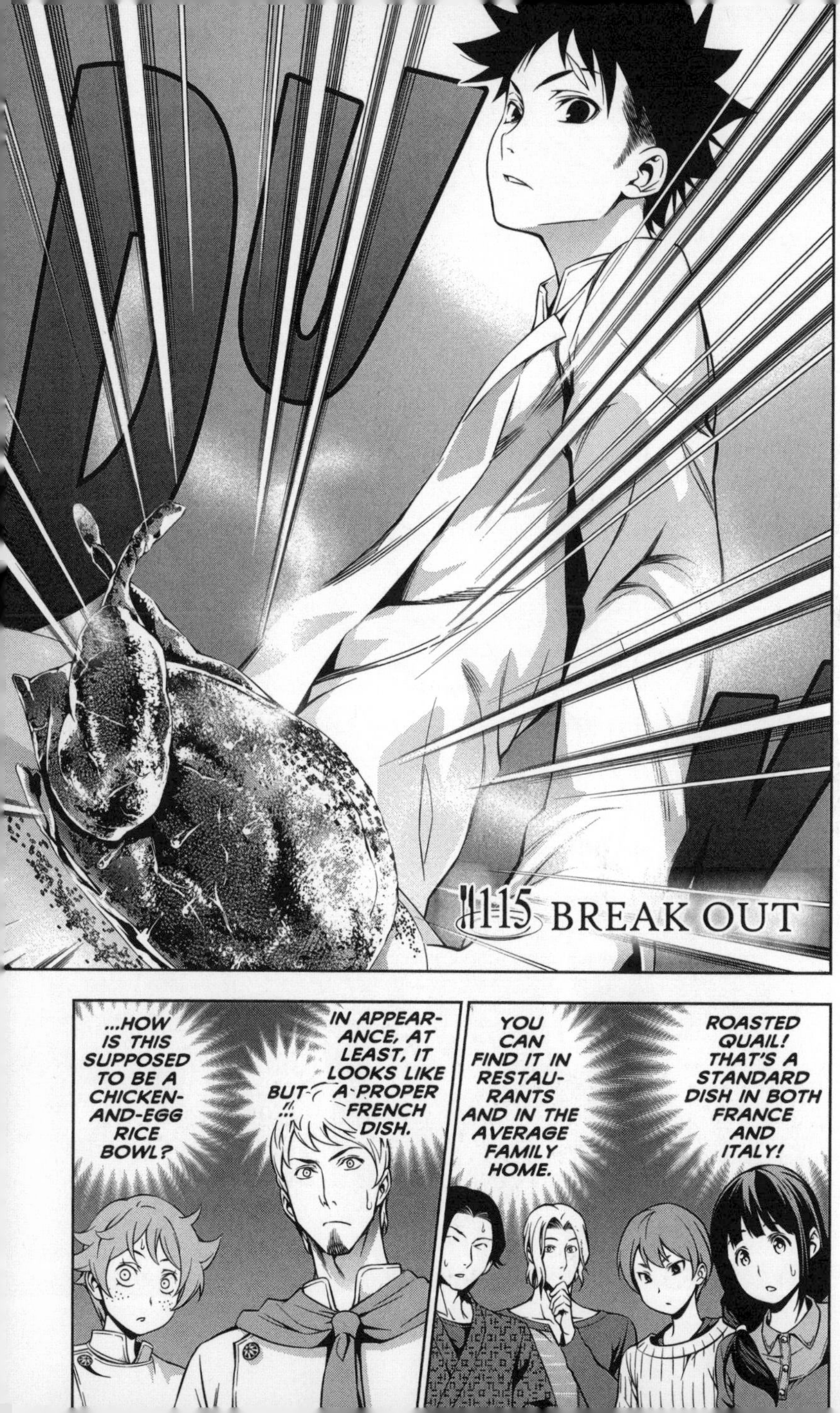
115 BREAK OUT
ROASTED QUAIL! THAT'S A STANDARD DISH IN BOTH FRANCE AND ITALY!
YOU CAN FIND IT IN RESTAURANTS AND IN THE AVERAGE FAMILY HOME.
IN APPEARANCE, AT LEAST, IT LOOKS LIKE A PROPER FRENCH DISH.
BUT...!!
...HOW IS THIS SUPPOSED TO BE A CHICKEN-AND-EGG RICE BOWL?

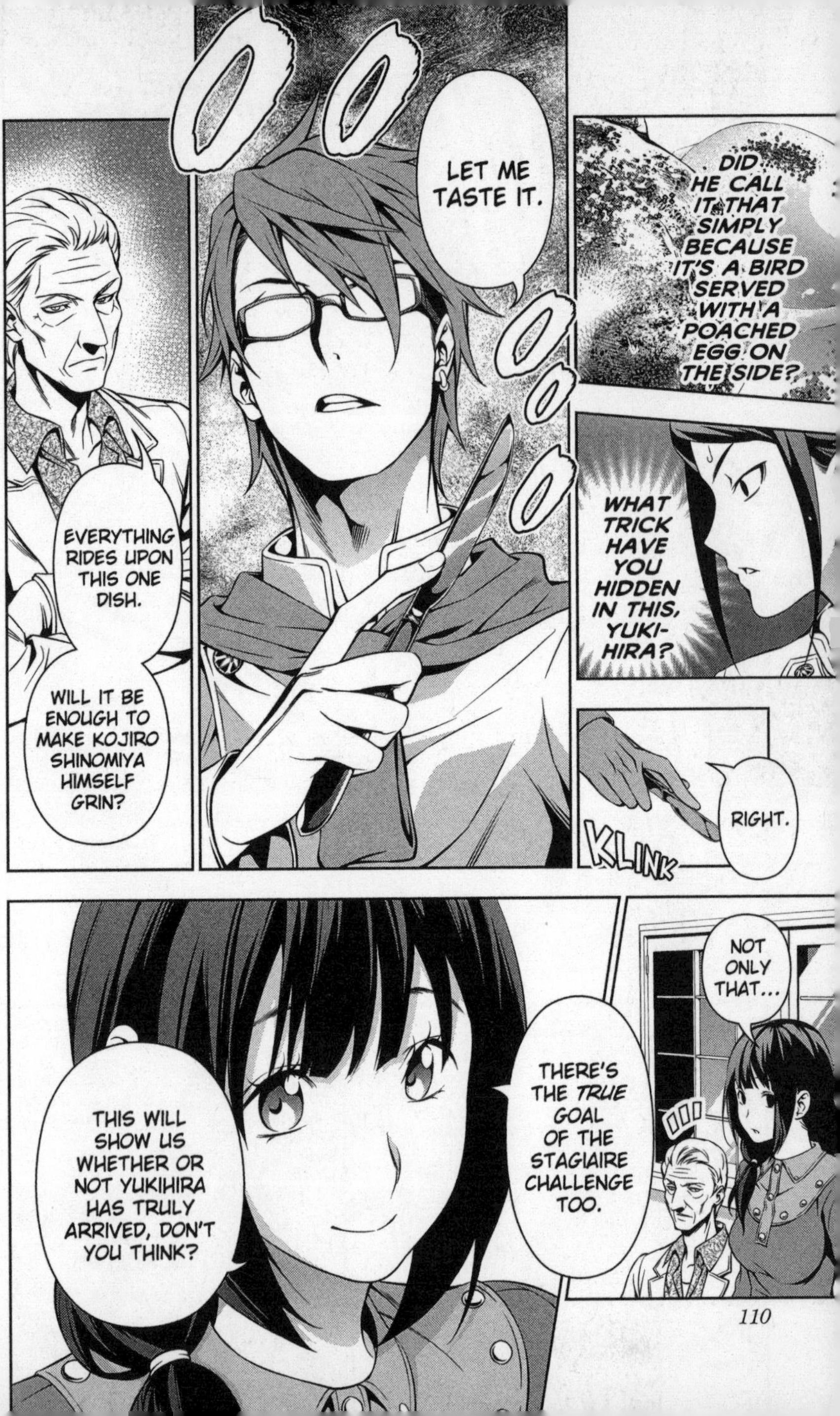
DID HE CALL IT THAT SIMPLY BECAUSE IT'S A BIRD SERVED WITH A POACHED EGG ON THE SIDE?
WHAT TRICK HAVE YOU HIDDEN IN THIS, YUKI-HIRA?
RIGHT.
KLINK
LET ME TASTE IT.
EVERYTHING RIDES UPON THIS ONE DISH.
WILL IT BE ENOUGH TO MAKE KOJIRO SHINOMIYA HIMSELF GRIN?
NOT ONLY THAT...
THERE'S THE *TRUE* GOAL OF THE STAGIAIRE CHALLENGE TOO.
THIS WILL SHOW US WHETHER OR NOT YUKIHIRA HAS TRULY ARRIVED, DON'T YOU THINK?

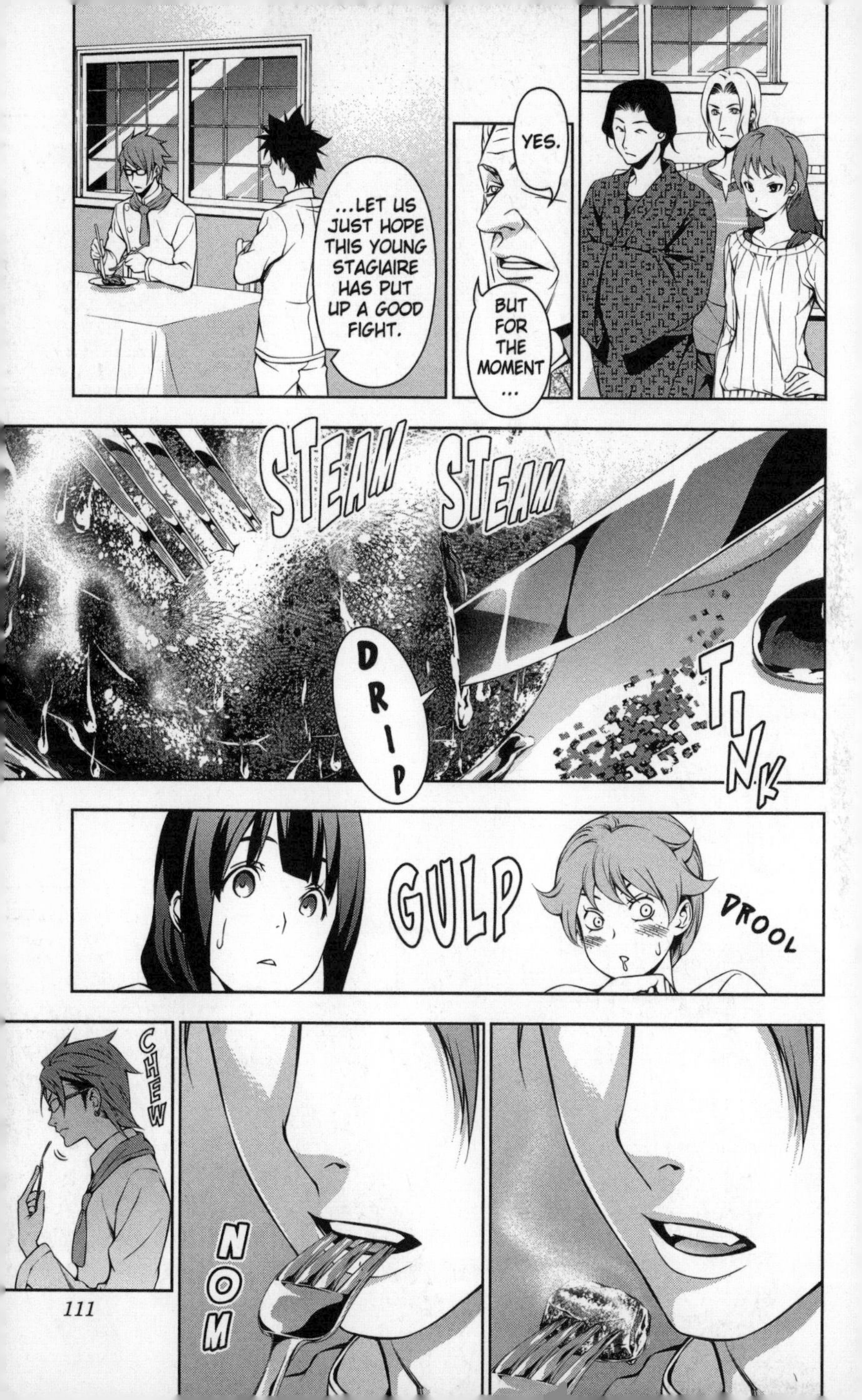
YES.
BUT FOR THE MOMENT ...
...LET US JUST HOPE THIS YOUNG STAGIAIRE HAS PUT UP A GOOD FIGHT.
STEAM STEAM
TINK
DRIP
DROOL
GULP
NOM
CHEW

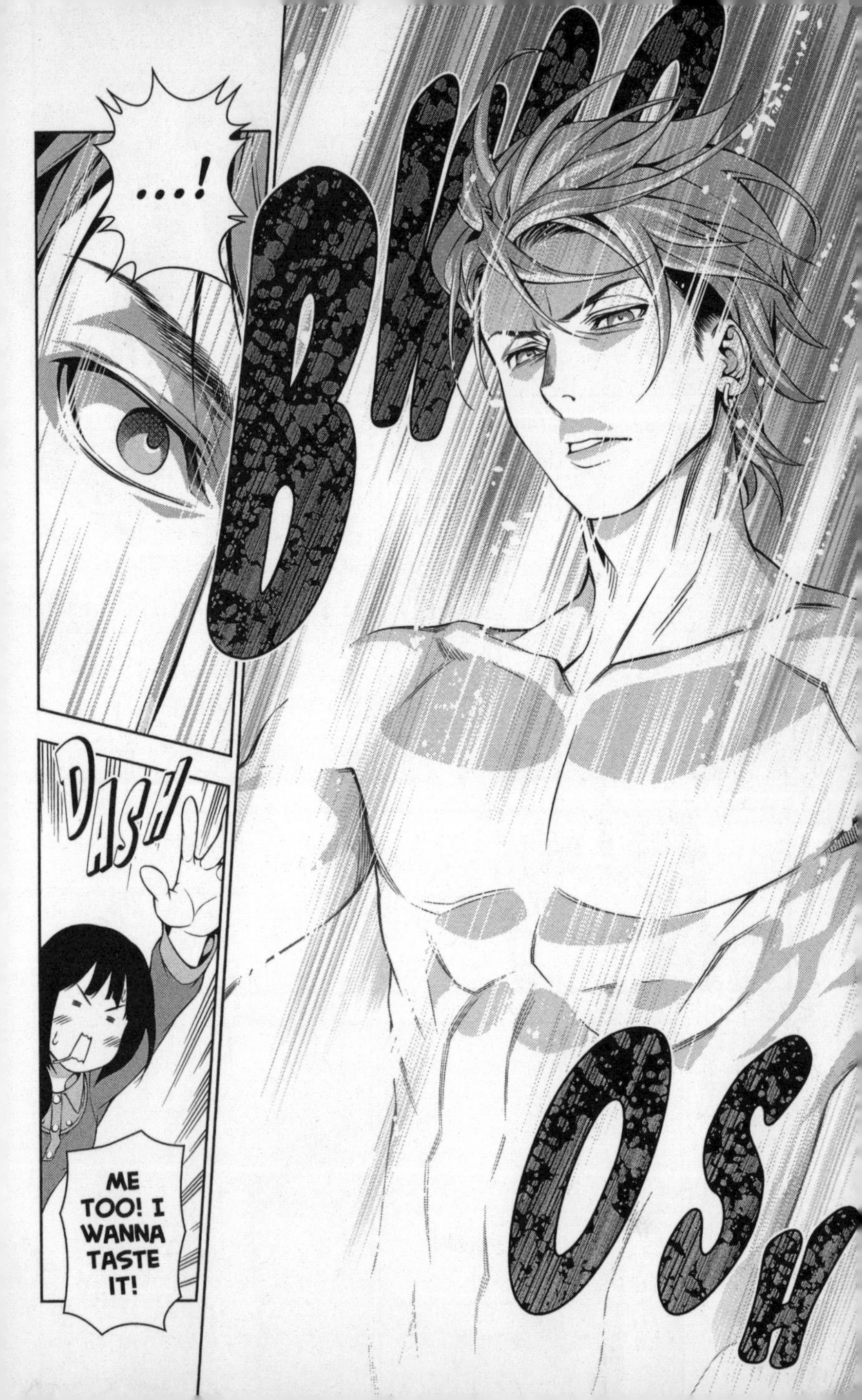

BWOOOSH
...!
DASH
ME TOO! I WANNA TASTE IT!

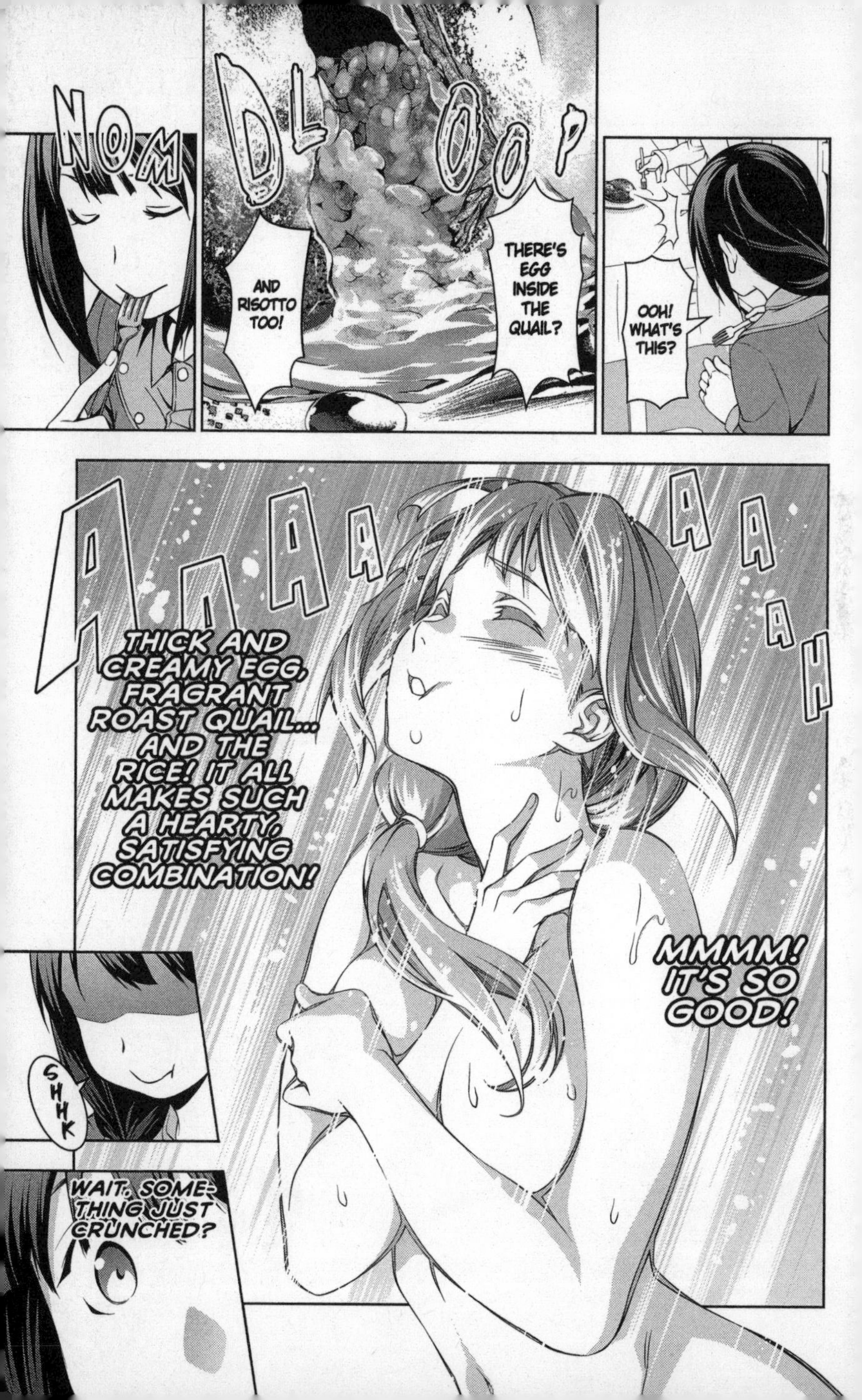
OOH! WHAT'S THIS?
THERE'S EGG INSIDE THE QUAIL?
AND RISOTTO TOO!
DLOOP
NOM
AAAAAAAH
THICK AND CREAMY EGG, FRAGRANT ROAST QUAIL... AND THE RICE! IT ALL MAKES SUCH A HEARTY, SATISFYING COMBINATION!
MMMM! IT'S SO GOOD!
SHHK
WAIT, SOME-THING JUST CRUNCHED?

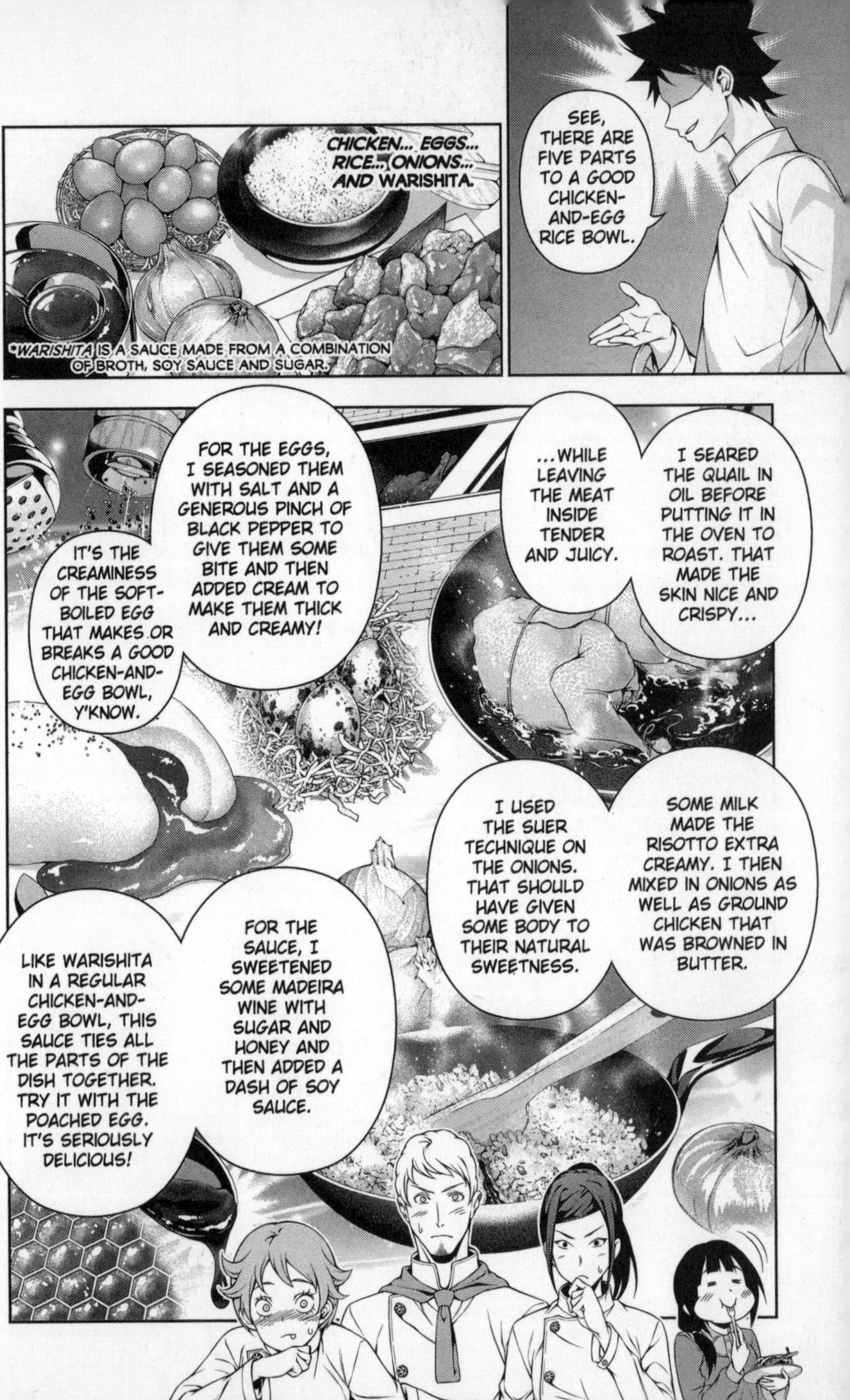
SEE, THERE ARE FIVE PARTS TO A GOOD CHICKEN-AND-EGG RICE BOWL.
CHICKEN... EGGS... RICE... ONIONS... AND WARISHITA.
*WARISHITA IS A SAUCE MADE FROM A COMBINATION OF BROTH, SOY SAUCE AND SUGAR.
I SEARED THE QUAIL IN OIL BEFORE PUTTING IT IN THE OVEN TO ROAST. THAT MADE THE SKIN NICE AND CRISPY...
...WHILE LEAVING THE MEAT INSIDE TENDER AND JUICY.
FOR THE EGGS, I SEASONED THEM WITH SALT AND A GENEROUS PINCH OF BLACK PEPPER TO GIVE THEM SOME BITE AND THEN ADDED CREAM TO MAKE THEM THICK AND CREAMY!
IT'S THE CREAMINESS OF THE SOFT-BOILED EGG THAT MAKES OR BREAKS A GOOD CHICKEN-AND-EGG BOWL, Y'KNOW.
SOME MILK MADE THE RISOTTO EXTRA CREAMY. I THEN MIXED IN ONIONS AS WELL AS GROUND CHICKEN THAT WAS BROWNED IN BUTTER.
I USED THE SUER TECHNIQUE ON THE ONIONS. THAT SHOULD HAVE GIVEN SOME BODY TO THEIR NATURAL SWEETNESS.
FOR THE SAUCE, I SWEETENED SOME MADEIRA WINE WITH SUGAR AND HONEY AND THEN ADDED A DASH OF SOY SAUCE.
LIKE WARISHITA IN A REGULAR CHICKEN-AND-EGG BOWL, THIS SAUCE TIES ALL THE PARTS OF THE DISH TOGETHER. TRY IT WITH THE POACHED EGG. IT'S SERIOUSLY DELICIOUS!

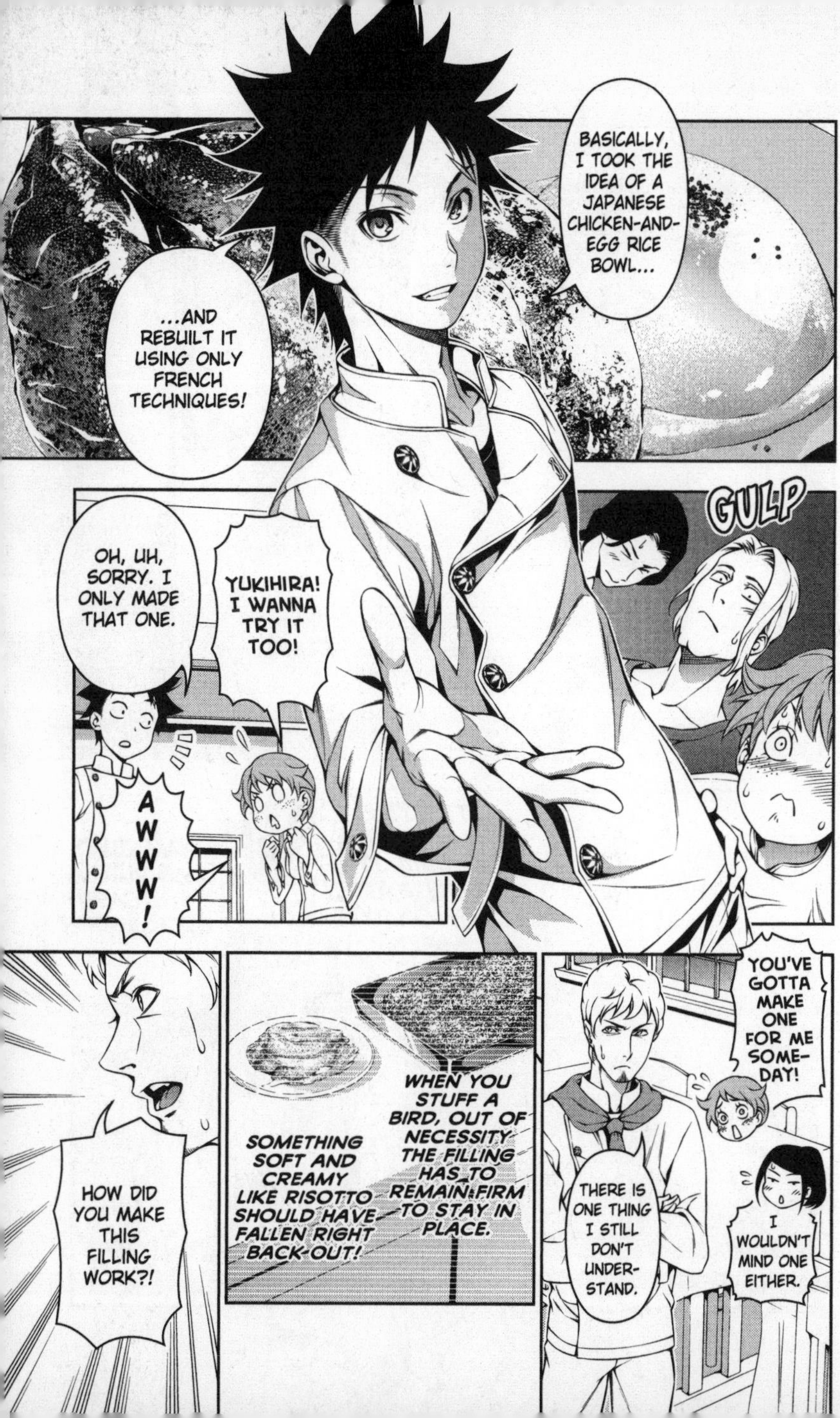
BASICALLY, I TOOK THE IDEA OF A JAPANESE CHICKEN-AND-EGG RICE BOWL...
...AND REBUILT IT USING ONLY FRENCH TECHNIQUES!
GULP
YUKIHIRA! I WANNA TRY IT TOO!
OH, UH, SORRY. I ONLY MADE THAT ONE.
AWWW!
YOU'VE GOTTA MAKE ONE FOR ME SOME-DAY!
I WOULDN'T MIND ONE EITHER.
THERE IS ONE THING I STILL DON'T UNDER-STAND.
WHEN YOU STUFF A BIRD, OUT OF NECESSITY THE FILLING HAS TO REMAIN FIRM TO STAY IN PLACE.
SOMETHING SOFT AND CREAMY LIKE RISOTTO SHOULD HAVE FALLEN RIGHT BACK OUT!
HOW DID YOU MAKE THIS FILLING WORK?!

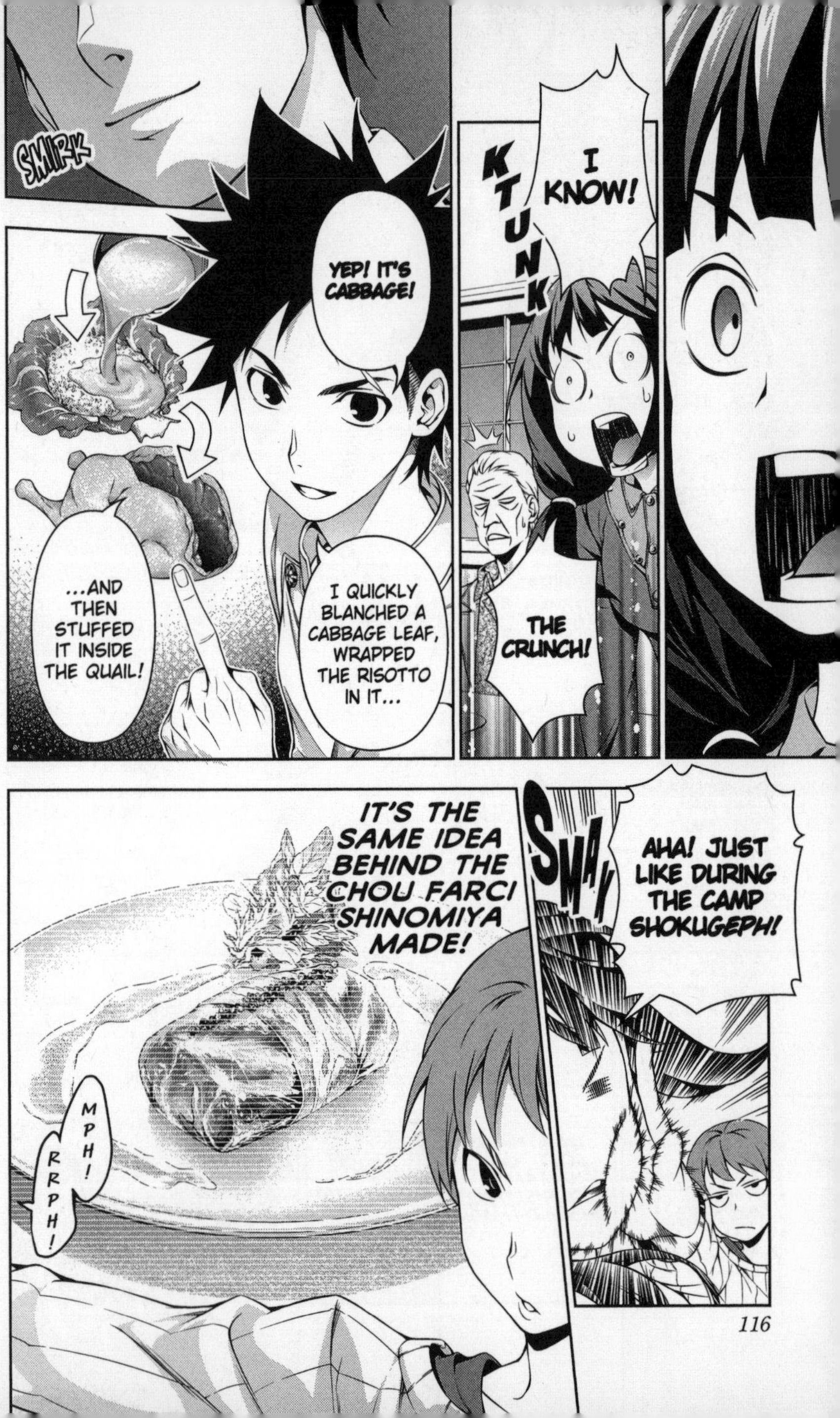
KTUNK
I KNOW!
THE CRUNCH!
SMIRK
YEP! IT'S CABBAGE!
I QUICKLY BLANCHED A CABBAGE LEAF, WRAPPED THE RISOTTO IN IT...
...AND THEN STUFFED IT INSIDE THE QUAIL!
AHA! JUST LIKE DURING THE CAMP SHOKUGEPH!
IT'S THE SAME IDEA BEHIND THE CHOU FARCI SHINOMIYA MADE!
MPH!
RRPH!

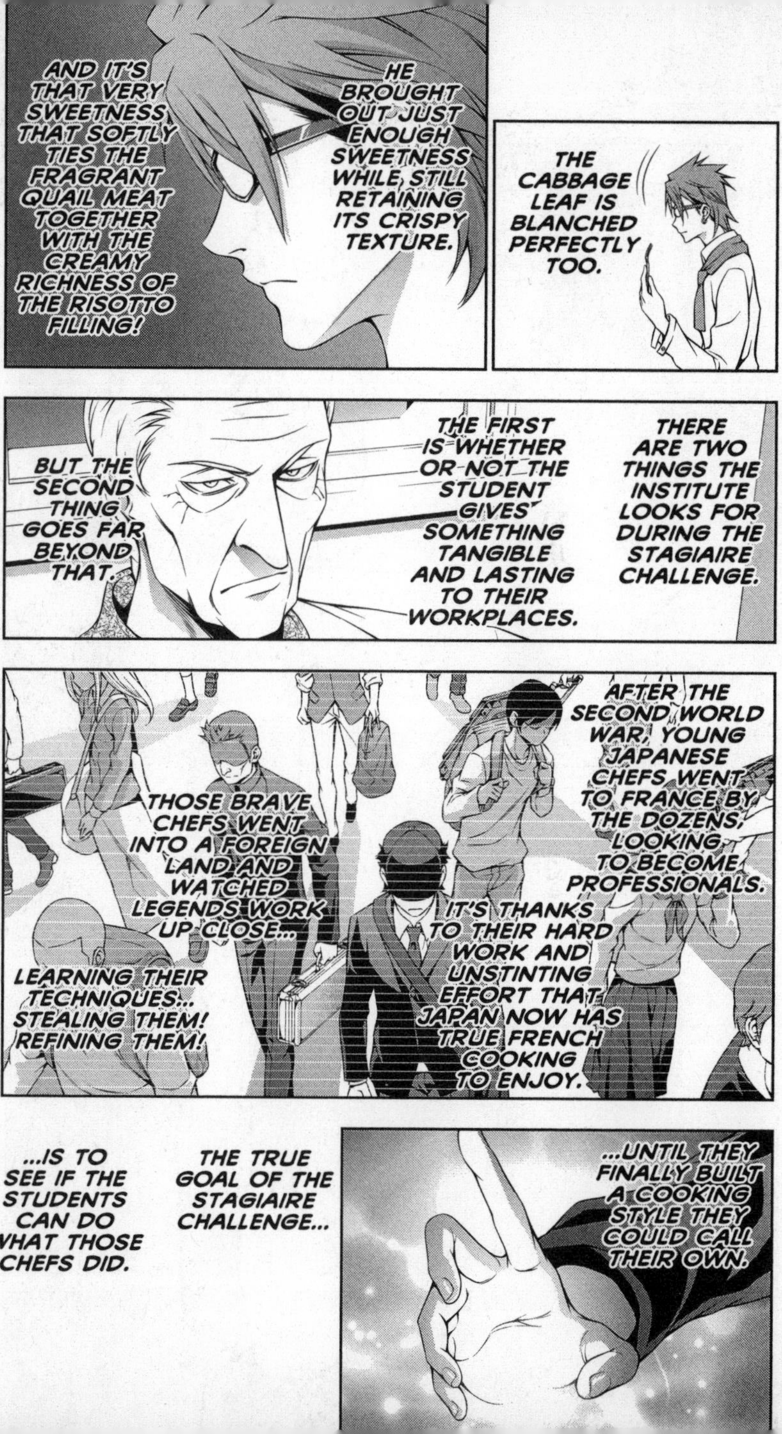
THE CABBAGE LEAF IS BLANCHED PERFECTLY TOO.
HE BROUGHT OUT JUST ENOUGH SWEETNESS WHILE STILL RETAINING ITS CRISPY TEXTURE.
AND IT'S THAT VERY SWEETNESS THAT SOFTLY TIES THE FRAGRANT QUAIL MEAT TOGETHER WITH THE CREAMY RICHNESS OF THE RISOTTO FILLING!
THERE ARE TWO THINGS THE INSTITUTE LOOKS FOR DURING THE STAGIAIRE CHALLENGE.
THE FIRST IS WHETHER OR NOT THE STUDENT GIVES SOMETHING TANGIBLE AND LASTING TO THEIR WORKPLACES.
BUT THE SECOND THING GOES FAR BEYOND THAT.
AFTER THE SECOND WORLD WAR, YOUNG JAPANESE CHEFS WENT TO FRANCE BY THE DOZENS, LOOKING TO BECOME PROFESSIONALS.
THOSE BRAVE CHEFS WENT INTO A FOREIGN LAND AND WATCHED LEGENDS WORK UP CLOSE...
IT'S THANKS TO THEIR HARD WORK AND UNSTINTING EFFORT THAT JAPAN NOW HAS TRUE FRENCH COOKING TO ENJOY.
LEARNING THEIR TECHNIQUES... STEALING THEM! REFINING THEM!
...UNTIL THEY FINALLY BUILT A COOKING STYLE THEY COULD CALL THEIR OWN.
THE TRUE GOAL OF THE STAGIAIRE CHALLENGE...
...IS TO SEE IF THE STUDENTS CAN DO WHAT THOSE CHEFS DID.

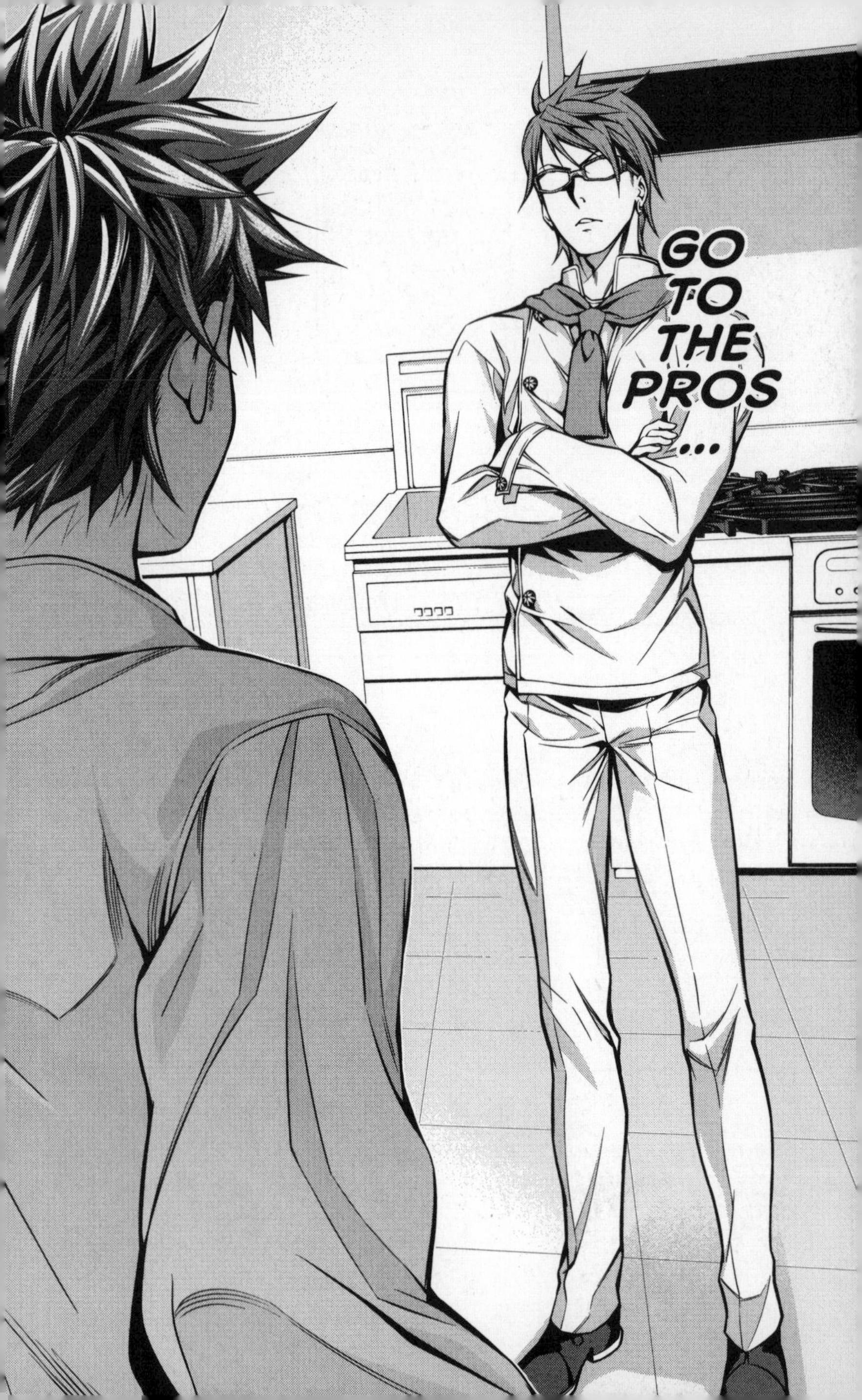
GO TO THE PROS...

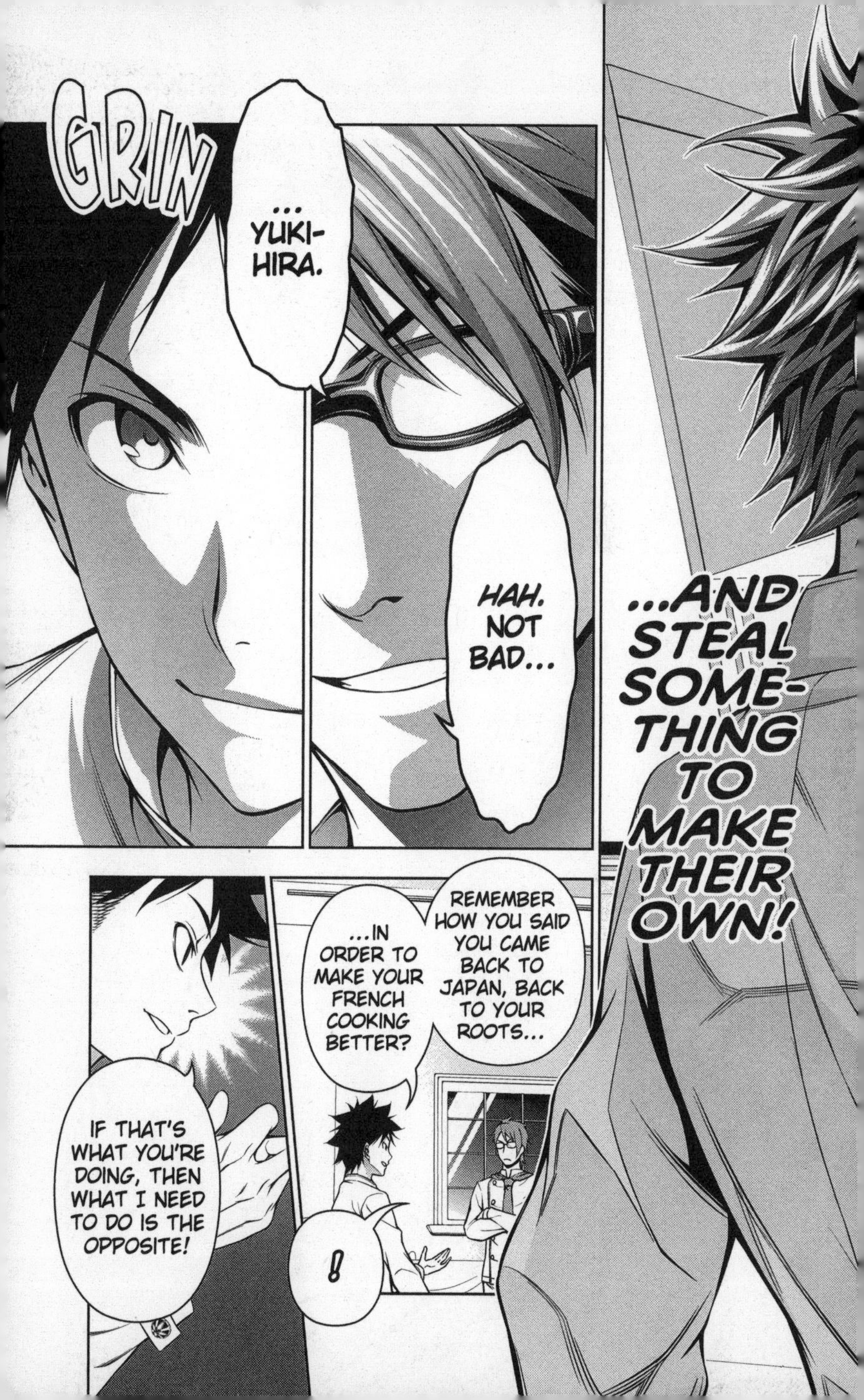
...AND STEAL SOME-THING TO MAKE THEIR OWN!
... YUKI-HIRA.
HAH. NOT BAD...
GRIN
REMEMBER HOW YOU SAID YOU CAME BACK TO JAPAN, BACK TO YOUR ROOTS...
...IN ORDER TO MAKE YOUR FRENCH COOKING BETTER?
!
IF THAT'S WHAT YOU'RE DOING, THEN WHAT I NEED TO DO IS THE OPPOSITE!

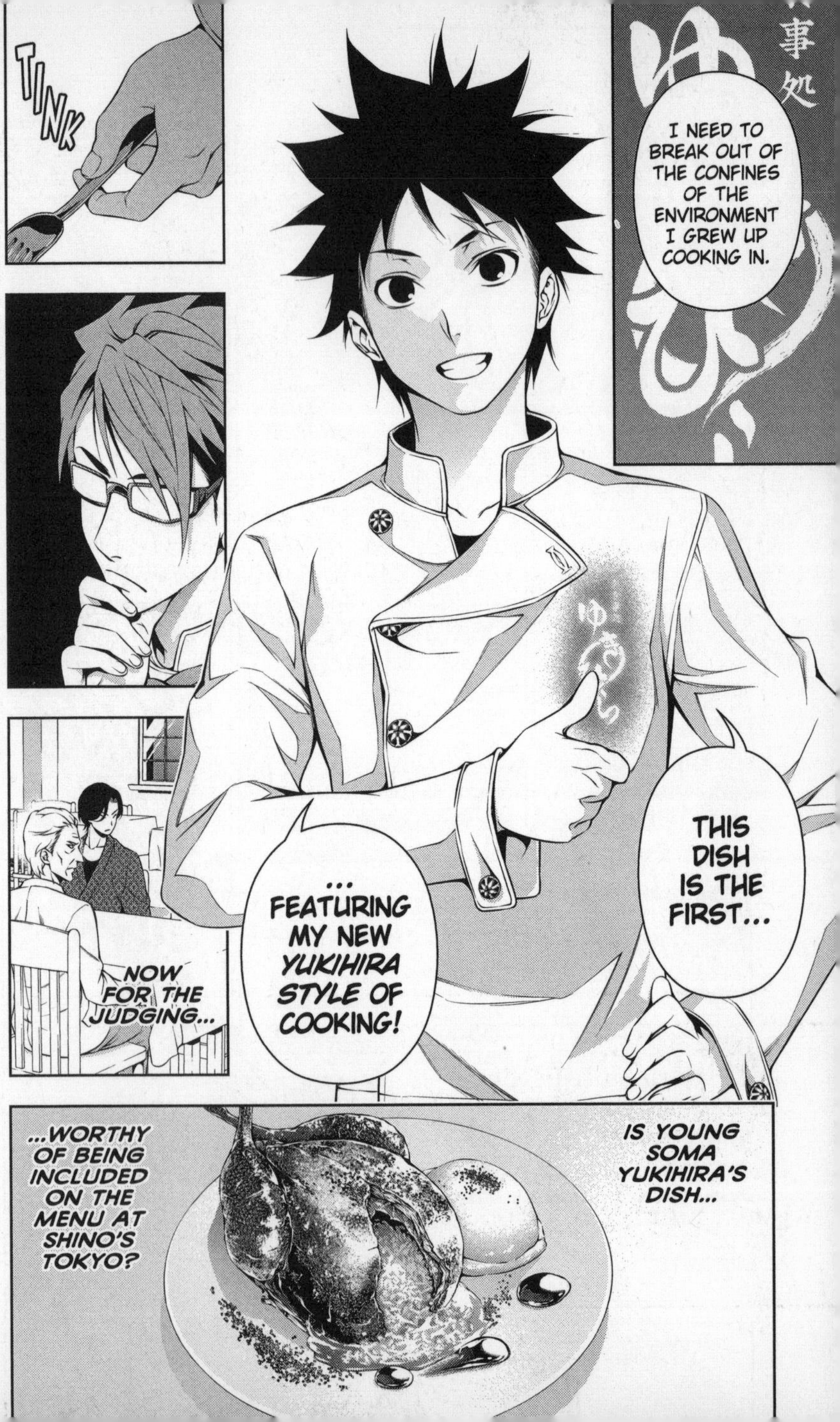
I NEED TO BREAK OUT OF THE CONFINES OF THE ENVIRONMENT I GREW UP COOKING IN.
THIS DISH IS THE FIRST...
... FEATURING MY NEW YUKIHIRA STYLE OF COOKING!
TINK
NOW FOR THE JUDGING...
IS YOUNG SOMA YUKIHIRA'S DISH...
...WORTHY OF BEING INCLUDED ON THE MENU AT SHINO'S TOKYO?

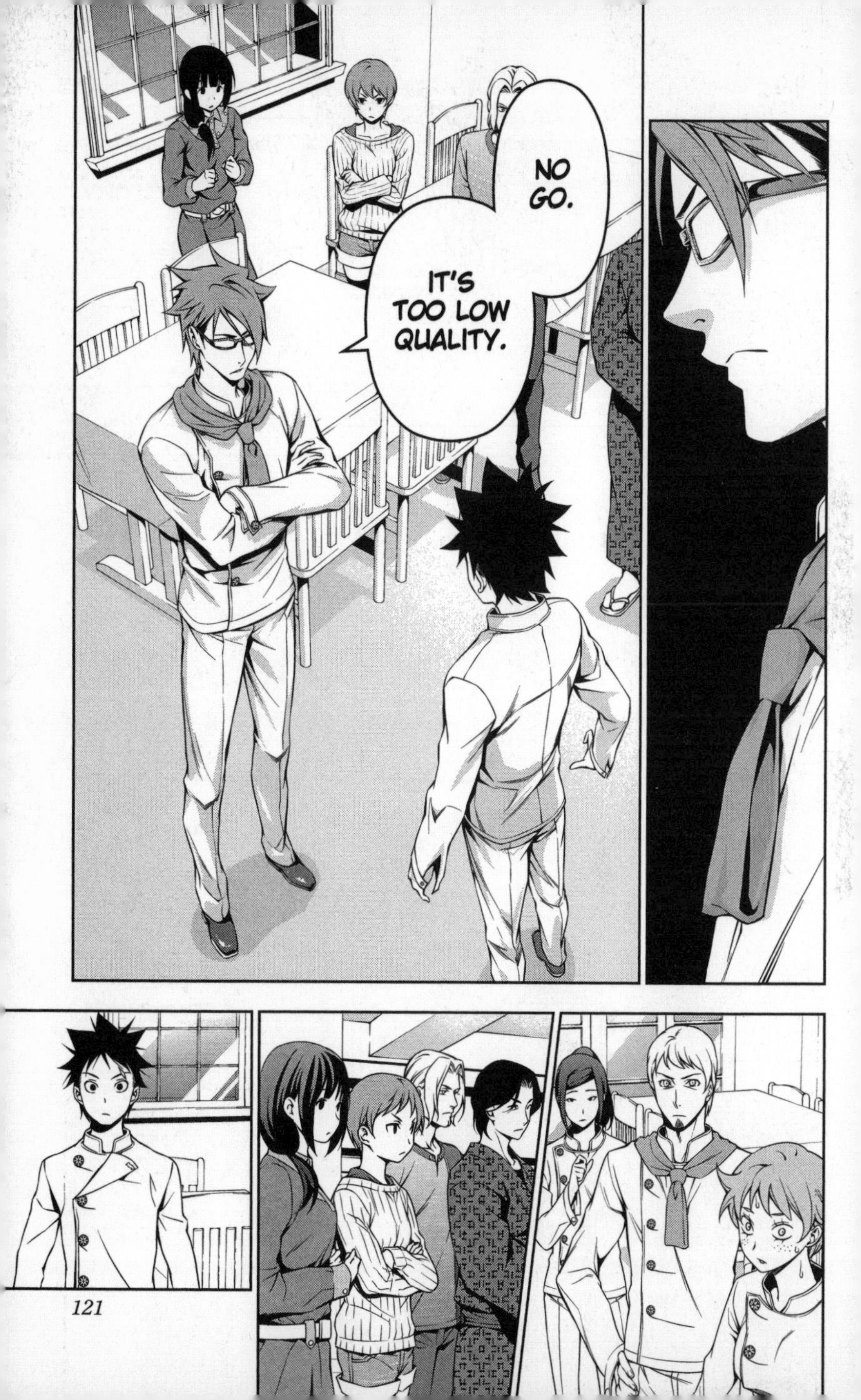
NO GO.
IT'S TOO LOW QUALITY.

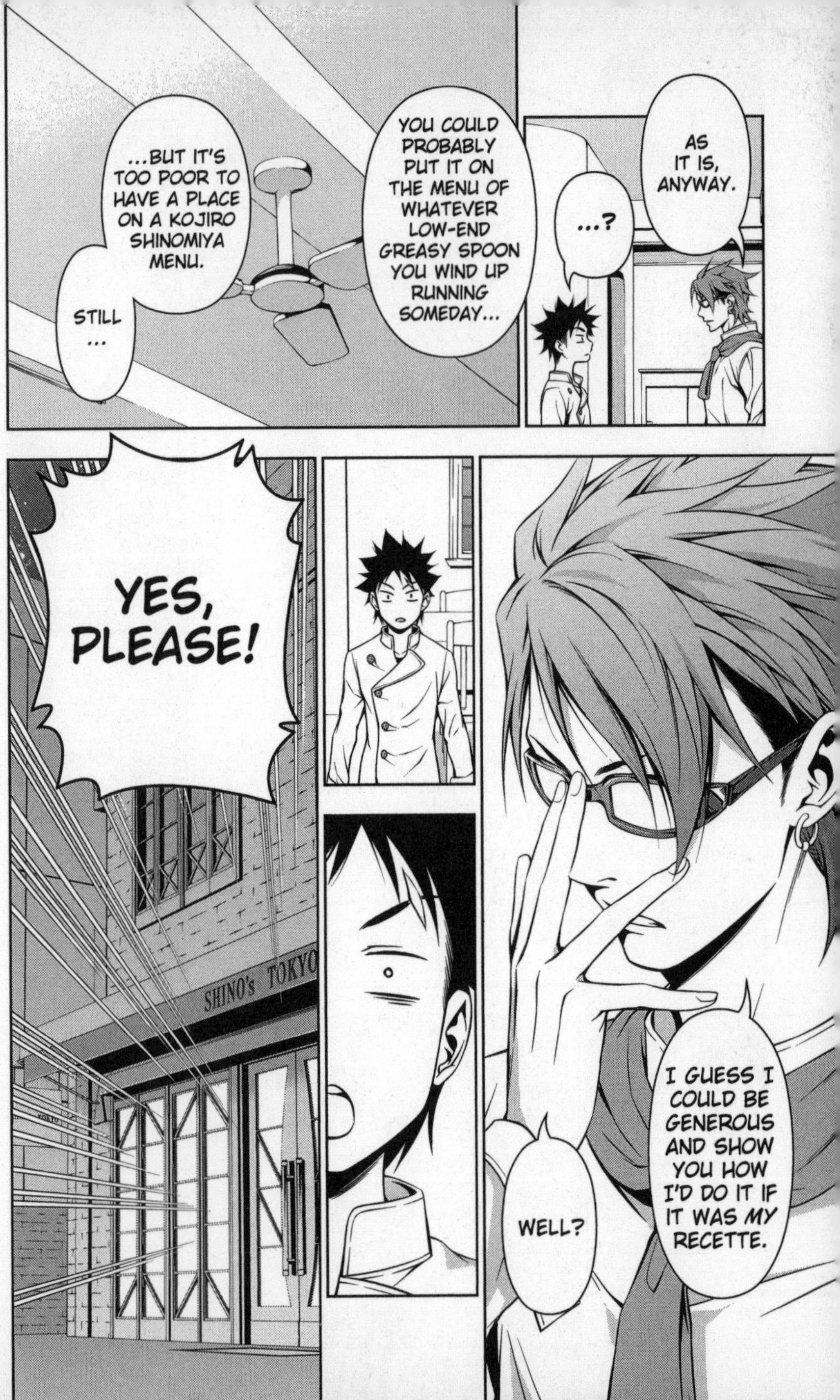
AS IT IS, ANYWAY.
...?
YOU COULD PROBABLY PUT IT ON THE MENU OF WHATEVER LOW-END GREASY SPOON YOU WIND UP RUNNING SOMEDAY...
...BUT IT'S TOO POOR TO HAVE A PLACE ON A KOJIRO SHINOMIYA MENU.
STILL ...
I GUESS I COULD BE GENEROUS AND SHOW YOU HOW I'D DO IT IF IT WAS *MY* RECETTE.
WELL?
YES, PLEASE!
SHINO's TOKYO

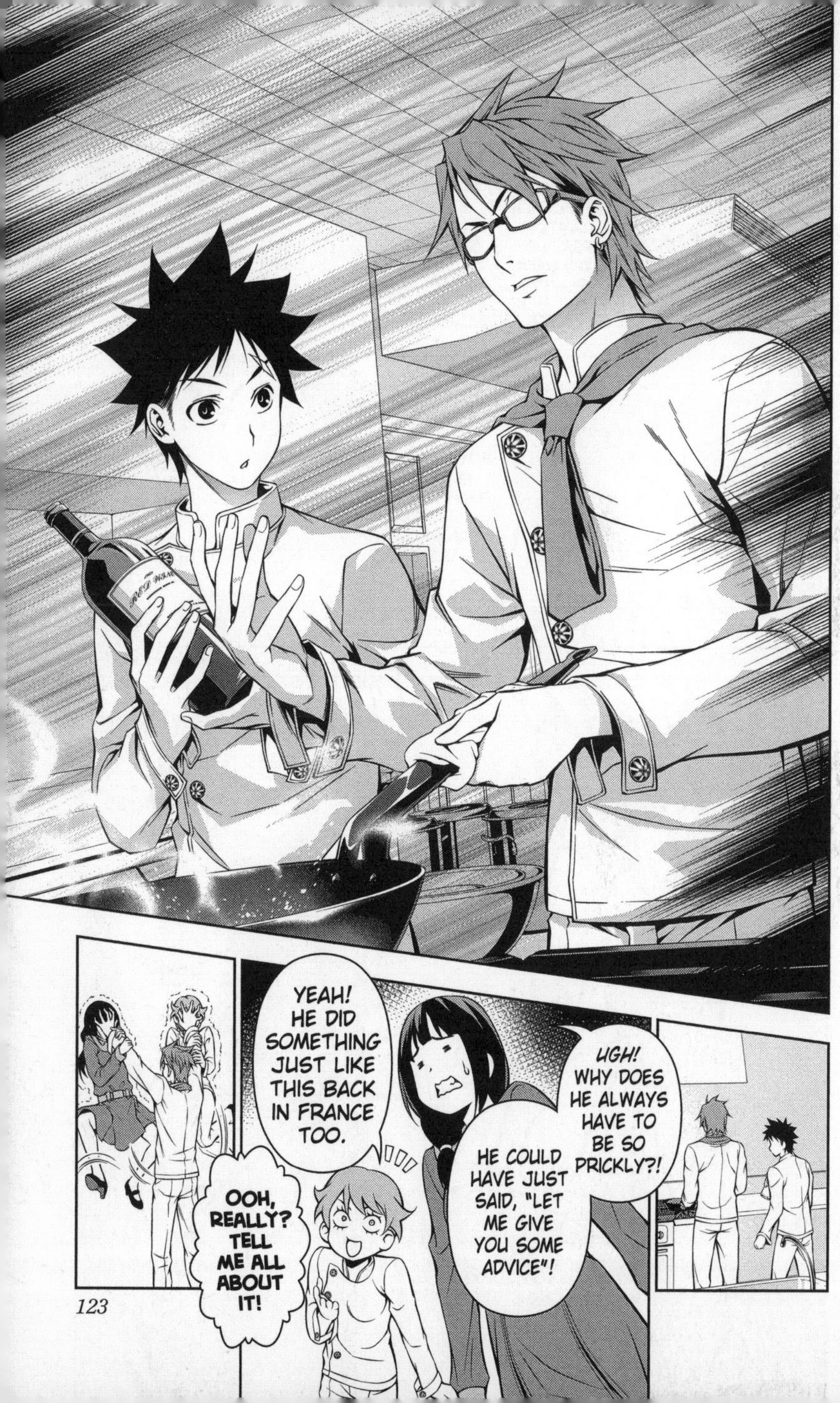
UGH! WHY DOES HE ALWAYS HAVE TO BE SO PRICKLY?!
HE COULD HAVE JUST SAID, "LET ME GIVE YOU SOME ADVICE"!
YEAH! HE DID SOMETHING JUST LIKE THIS BACK IN FRANCE TOO.
OOH, REALLY? TELL ME ALL ABOUT IT!

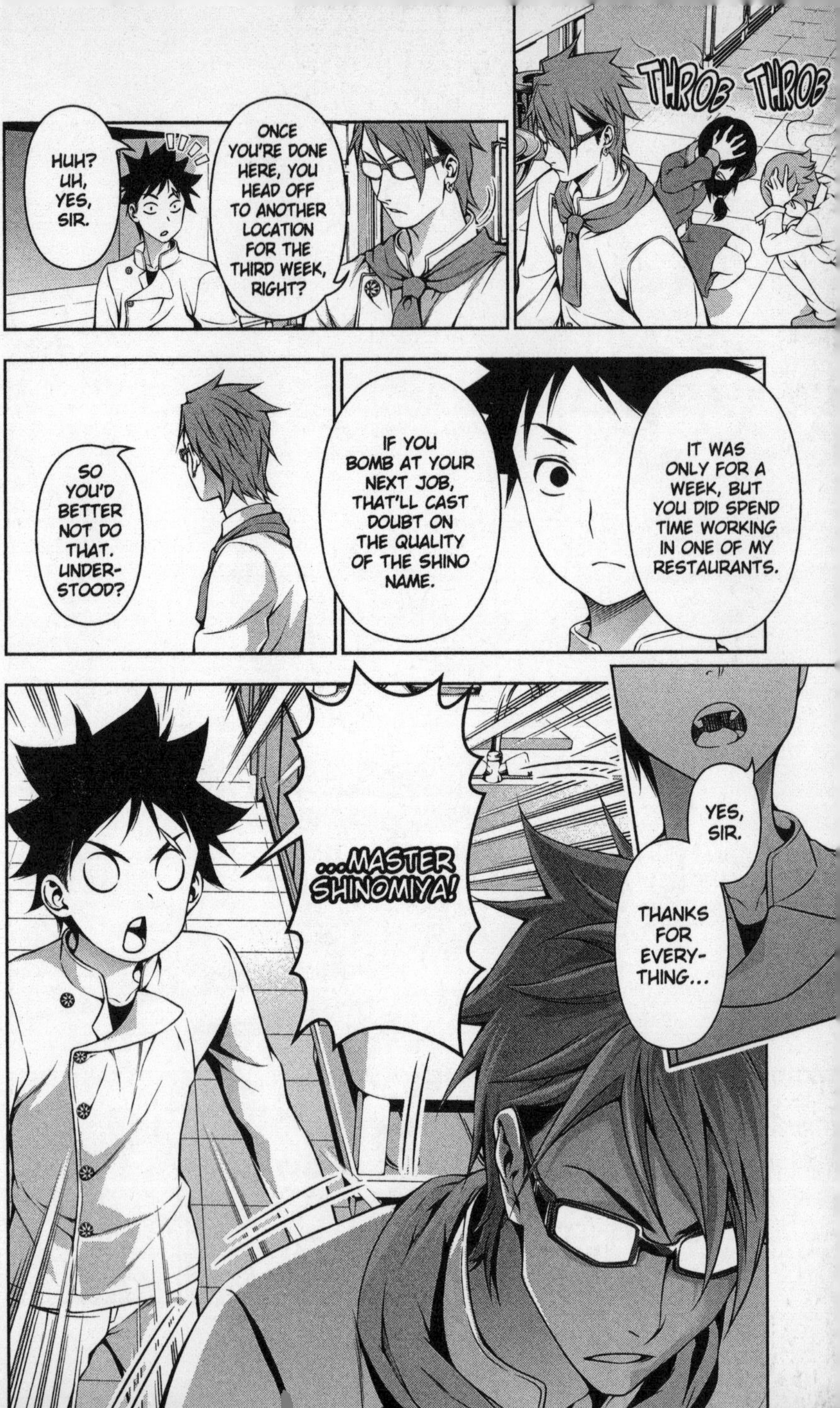
THROB THROB
ONCE YOU'RE DONE HERE, YOU HEAD OFF TO ANOTHER LOCATION FOR THE THIRD WEEK, RIGHT?
HUH? UH, YES, SIR.
IT WAS ONLY FOR A WEEK, BUT YOU DID SPEND TIME WORKING IN ONE OF MY RESTAURANTS.
IF YOU BOMB AT YOUR NEXT JOB, THAT'LL CAST DOUBT ON THE QUALITY OF THE SHINO NAME.
SO YOU'D BETTER NOT DO THAT. UNDER-STOOD?
YES, SIR.
THANKS FOR EVERY-THING...
...MASTER SHINOMIYA!

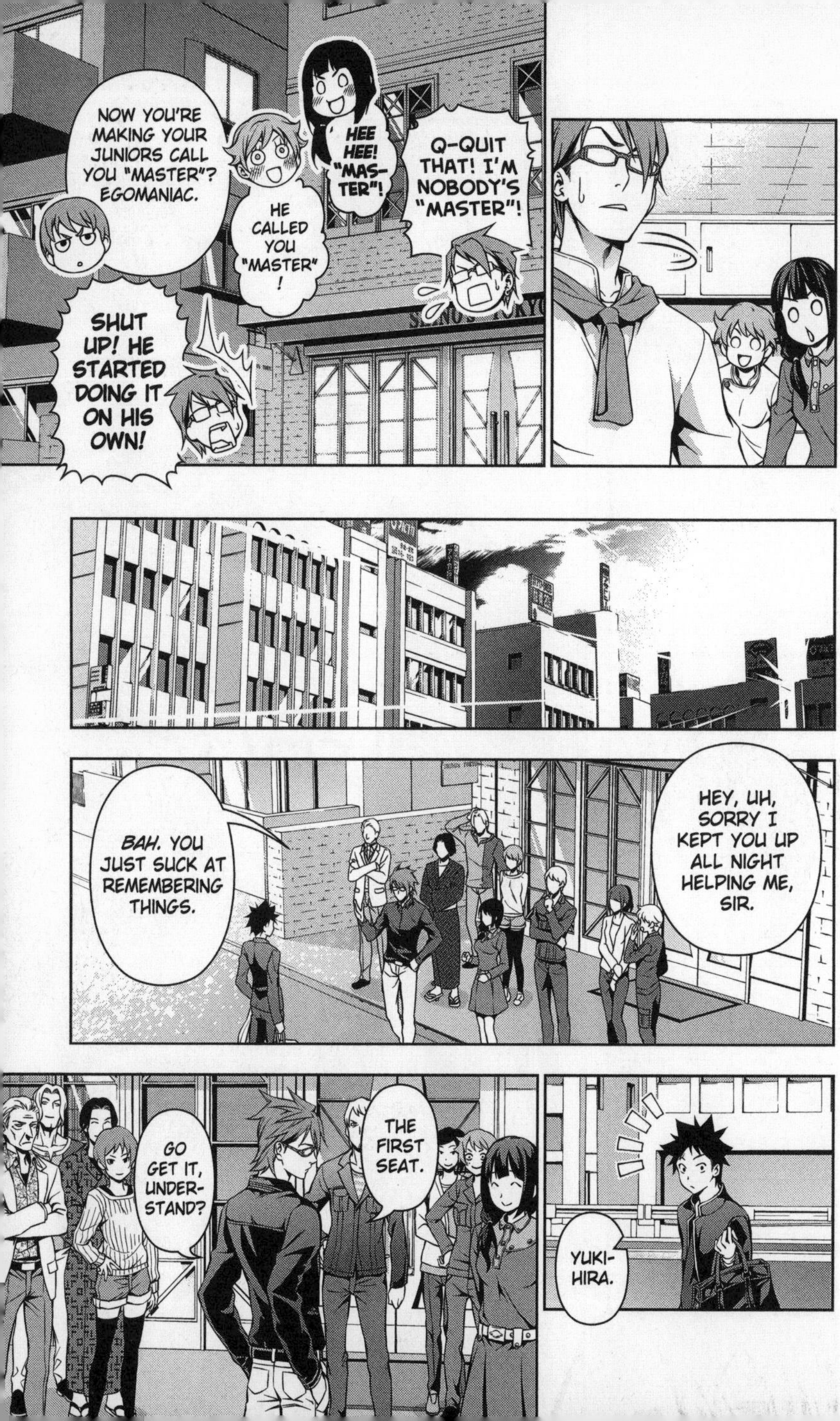
Q-QUIT THAT! I'M NOBODY'S "MASTER"!
HEE HEE! "MAS-TER"!
HE CALLED YOU "MASTER"!
NOW YOU'RE MAKING YOUR JUNIORS CALL YOU "MASTER"? EGOMANIAC.
SHUT UP! HE STARTED DOING IT ON HIS OWN!
HEY, UH, SORRY I KEPT YOU UP ALL NIGHT HELPING ME, SIR.
BAH. YOU JUST SUCK AT REMEMBERING THINGS.
YUKI-HIRA.
THE FIRST SEAT.
GO GET IT, UNDER-STAND?

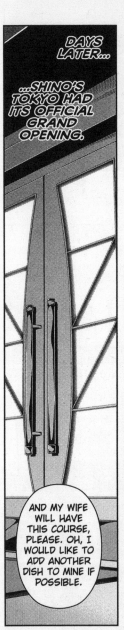

DAYS LATER...

...SHINO'S TOKYO HAD ITS OFFICIAL GRAND OPENING.

AND MY WIFE WILL HAVE THIS COURSE, PLEASE. OH, I WOULD LIKE TO ADD ANOTHER DISH TO MINE IF POSSIBLE.

YES, SIR!

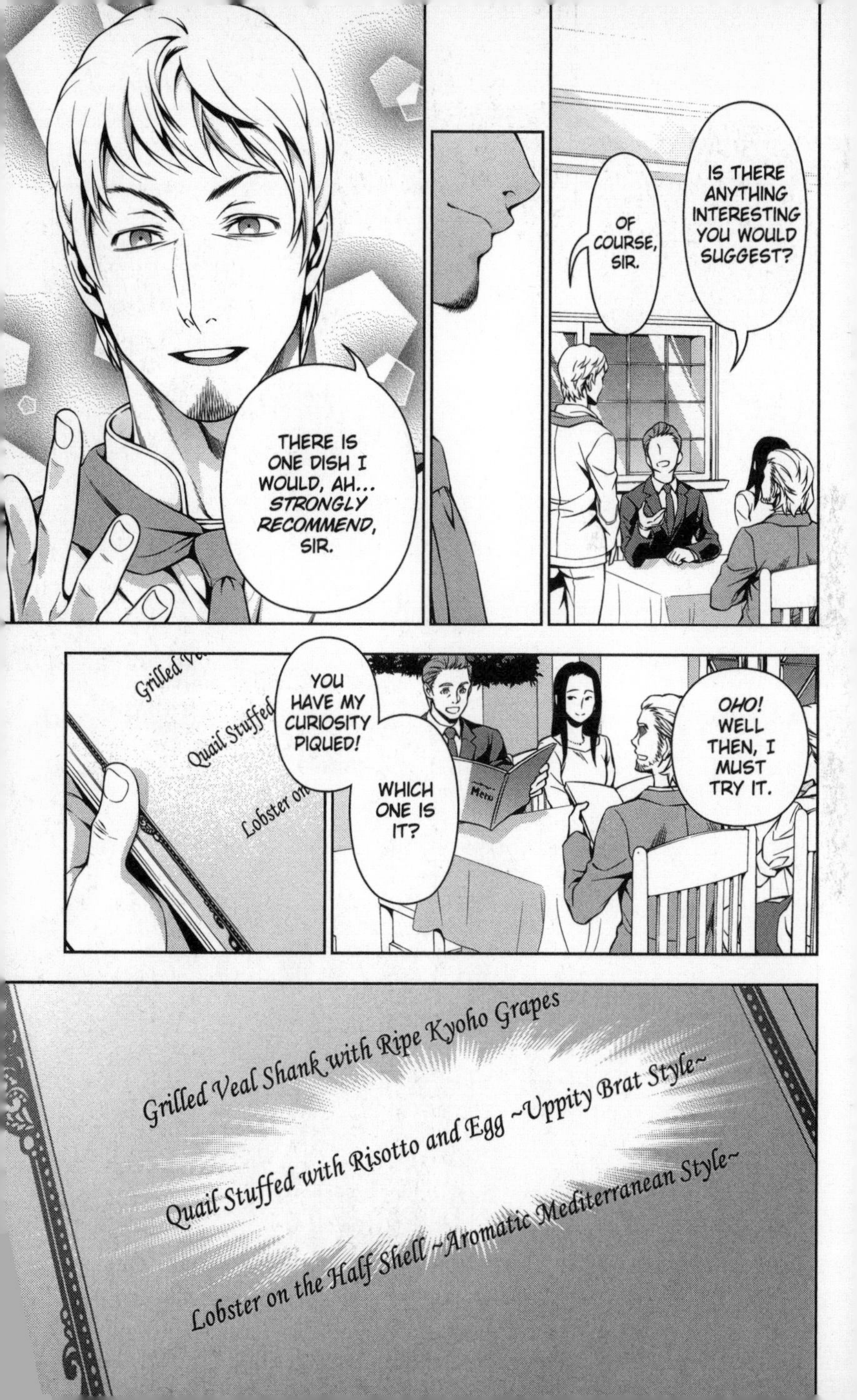
IS THERE ANYTHING INTERESTING YOU WOULD SUGGEST?
OF COURSE, SIR.
THERE IS ONE DISH I WOULD, AH... *STRONGLY RECOMMEND*, SIR.
*OHO!* WELL THEN, I MUST TRY IT.
YOU HAVE MY CURIOSITY PIQUED!
WHICH ONE IS IT?
Grilled Ve
Quail Stuffed
Lobster on
Grilled Veal Shank with Ripe Kyoho Grapes
Quail Stuffed with Risotto and Egg ~Uppity Brat Style~
Lobster on the Half Shell ~Aromatic Mediterranean Style~

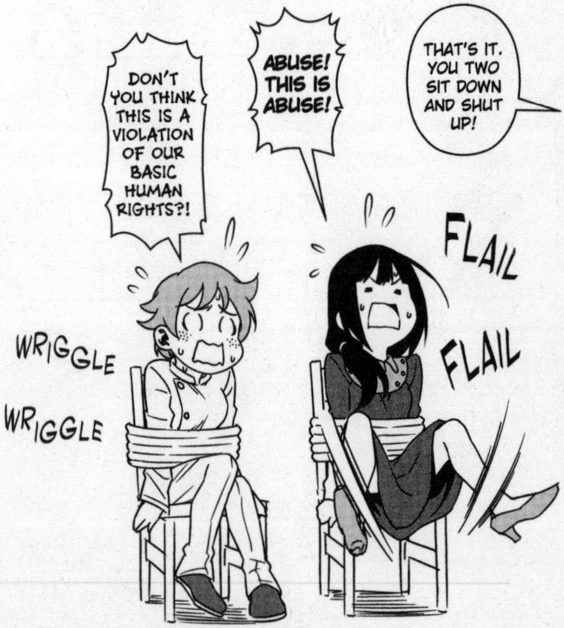
THAT'S IT. YOU TWO SIT DOWN AND SHUT UP!
ABUSE! THIS IS ABUSE!
DON'T YOU THINK THIS IS A VIOLATION OF OUR BASIC HUMAN RIGHTS?!
FLAIL
FLAIL
WRIGGLE
WRIGGLE

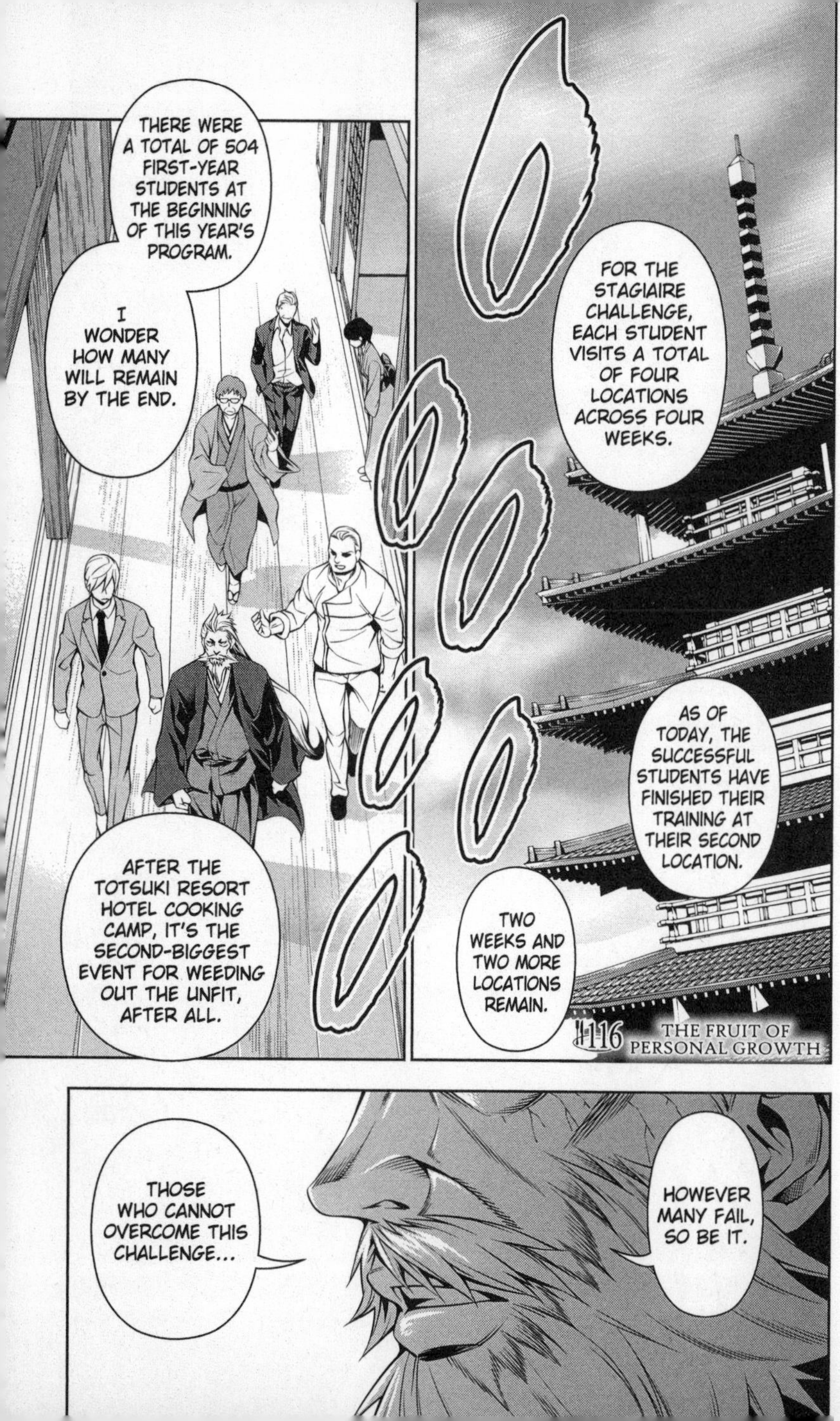
FOR THE STAGIAIRE CHALLENGE, EACH STUDENT VISITS A TOTAL OF FOUR LOCATIONS ACROSS FOUR WEEKS.
AS OF TODAY, THE SUCCESSFUL STUDENTS HAVE FINISHED THEIR TRAINING AT THEIR SECOND LOCATION.
TWO WEEKS AND TWO MORE LOCATIONS REMAIN.
116 THE FRUIT OF PERSONAL GROWTH
THERE WERE A TOTAL OF 504 FIRST-YEAR STUDENTS AT THE BEGINNING OF THIS YEAR'S PROGRAM.
I WONDER HOW MANY WILL REMAIN BY THE END.
AFTER THE TOTSUKI RESORT HOTEL COOKING CAMP, IT'S THE SECOND-BIGGEST EVENT FOR WEEDING OUT THE UNFIT, AFTER ALL.
HOWEVER MANY FAIL, SO BE IT.
THOSE WHO CANNOT OVERCOME THIS CHALLENGE...

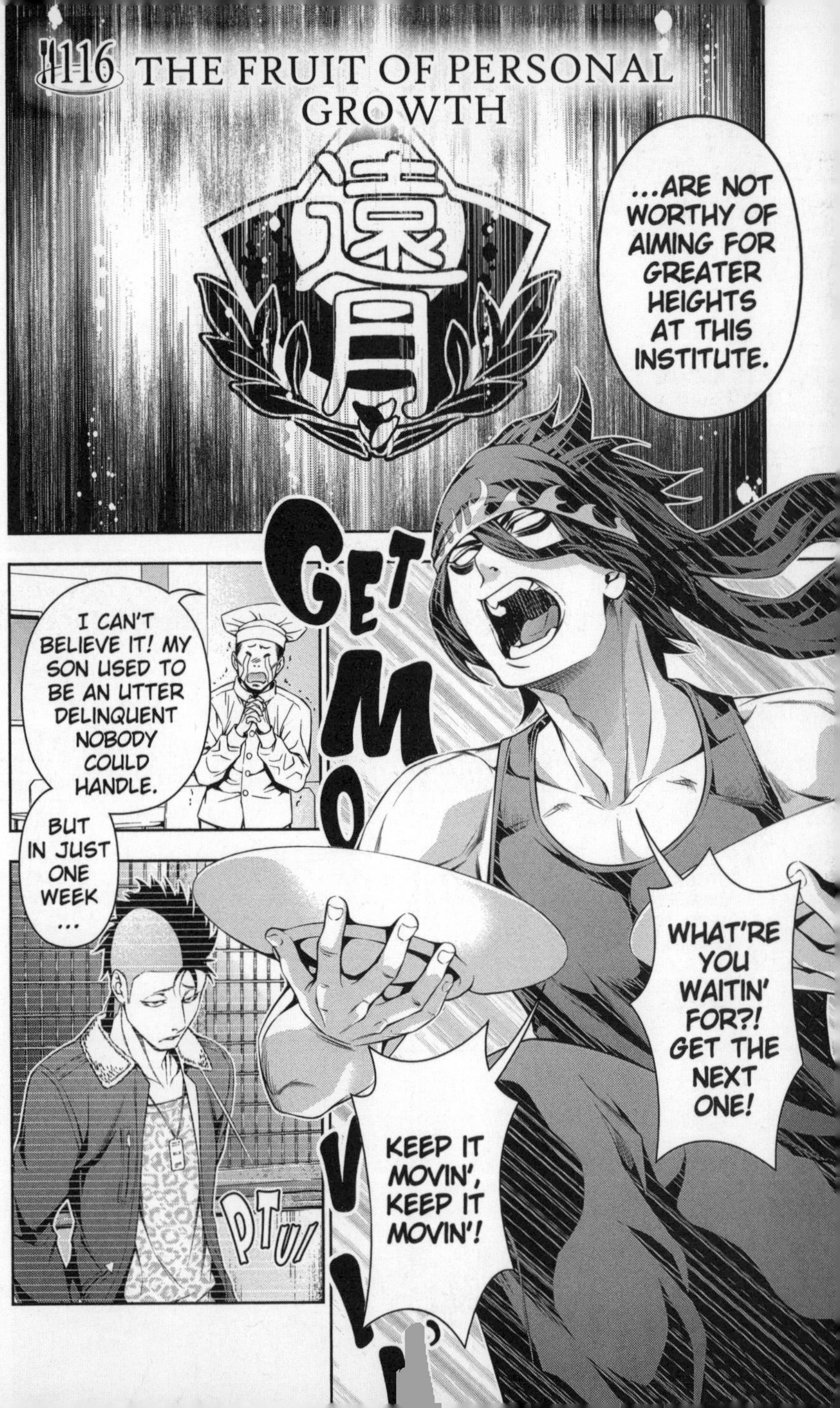
#116 THE FRUIT OF PERSONAL GROWTH
...ARE NOT WORTHY OF AIMING FOR GREATER HEIGHTS AT THIS INSTITUTE.
GET MOVIN'!
WHAT'RE YOU WAITIN' FOR?! GET THE NEXT ONE!
KEEP IT MOVIN', KEEP IT MOVIN'!
I CAN'T BELIEVE IT! MY SON USED TO BE AN UTTER DELINQUENT NOBODY COULD HANDLE.
BUT IN JUST ONE WEEK...
PTUI

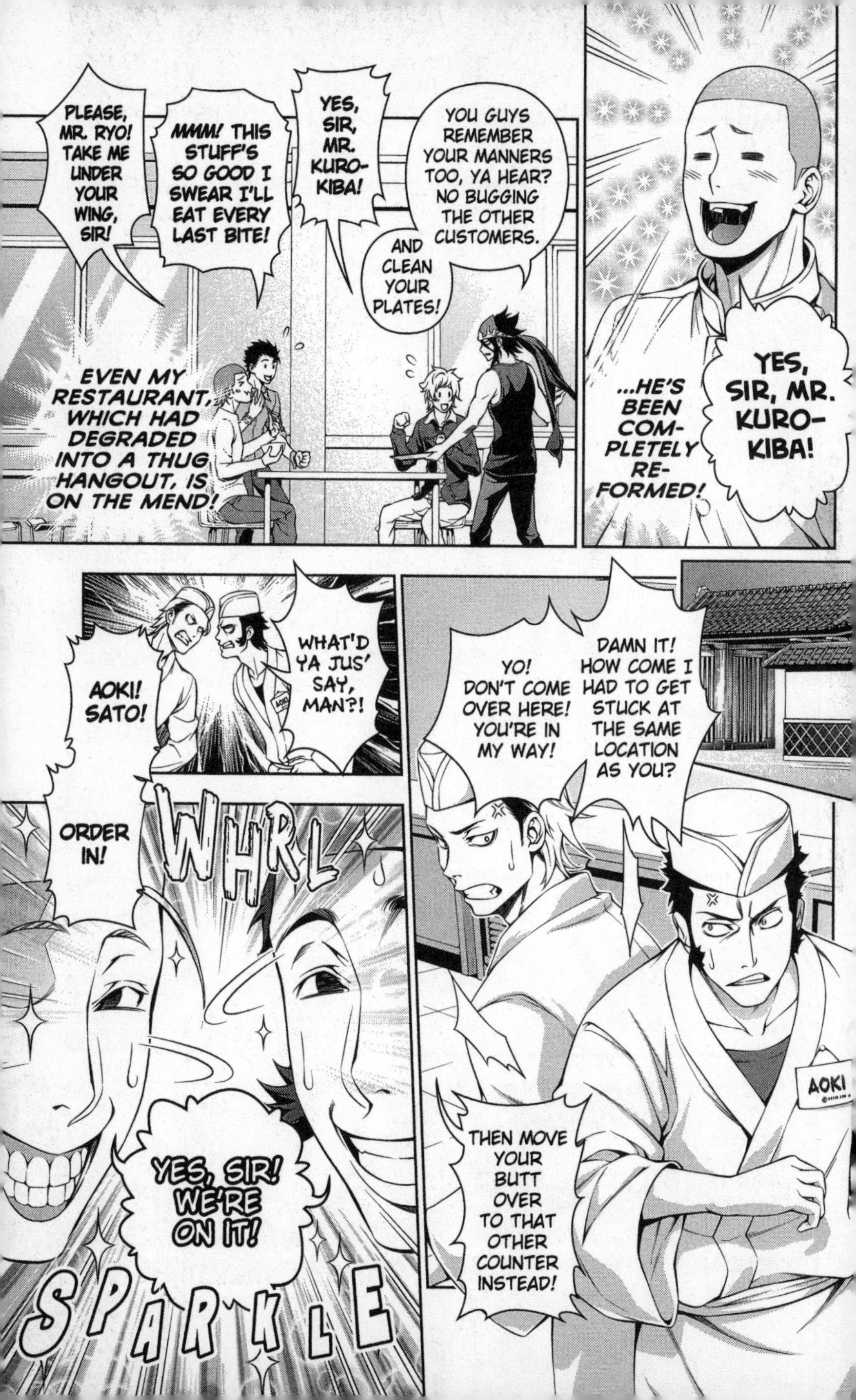
YES, SIR, MR. KURO-KIBA!
...HE'S BEEN COM-PLETELY RE-FORMED!
YOU GUYS REMEMBER YOUR MANNERS TOO, YA HEAR? NO BUGGING THE OTHER CUSTOMERS.
AND CLEAN YOUR PLATES!
YES, SIR, MR. KURO-KIBA!
MMM! THIS STUFF'S SO GOOD I SWEAR I'LL EAT EVERY LAST BITE!
PLEASE, MR. RYO! TAKE ME UNDER YOUR WING, SIR!
EVEN MY RESTAURANT, WHICH HAD DEGRADED INTO A THUG HANGOUT, IS ON THE MEND!
DAMN IT! HOW COME I HAD TO GET STUCK AT THE SAME LOCATION AS YOU?
YO! DON'T COME OVER HERE! YOU'RE IN MY WAY!
AOKI
THEN MOVE YOUR BUTT OVER TO THAT OTHER COUNTER INSTEAD!
WHAT'D YA JUS' SAY, MAN?!
AOKI! SATO!
ORDER IN!
WHRL
YES, SIR! WE'RE ON IT!
SPARKLE

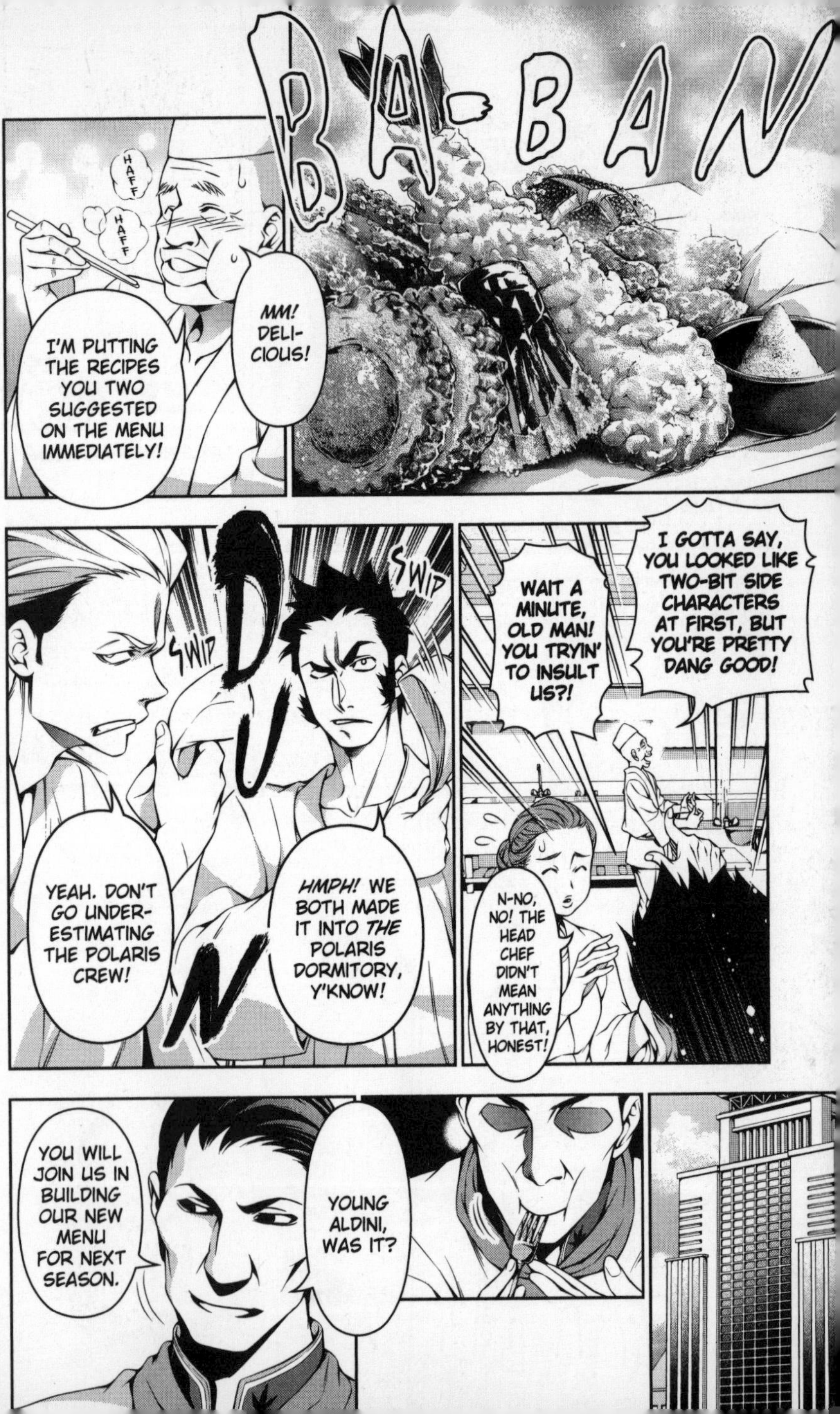
BA-BAN
HAFF HAFF
MM! DELICIOUS!
I'M PUTTING THE RECIPES YOU TWO SUGGESTED ON THE MENU IMMEDIATELY!
I GOTTA SAY, YOU LOOKED LIKE TWO-BIT SIDE CHARACTERS AT FIRST, BUT YOU'RE PRETTY DANG GOOD!
WAIT A MINUTE, OLD MAN! YOU TRYIN' TO INSULT US?!
N-NO, NO! THE HEAD CHEF DIDN'T MEAN ANYTHING BY THAT, HONEST!
SWIP
DUN
SWIP
HMPH! WE BOTH MADE IT INTO *THE* POLARIS DORMITORY, Y'KNOW!
YEAH. DON'T GO UNDER-ESTIMATING THE POLARIS CREW!
YOUNG ALDINI, WAS IT?
YOU WILL JOIN US IN BUILDING OUR NEW MENU FOR NEXT SEASON.

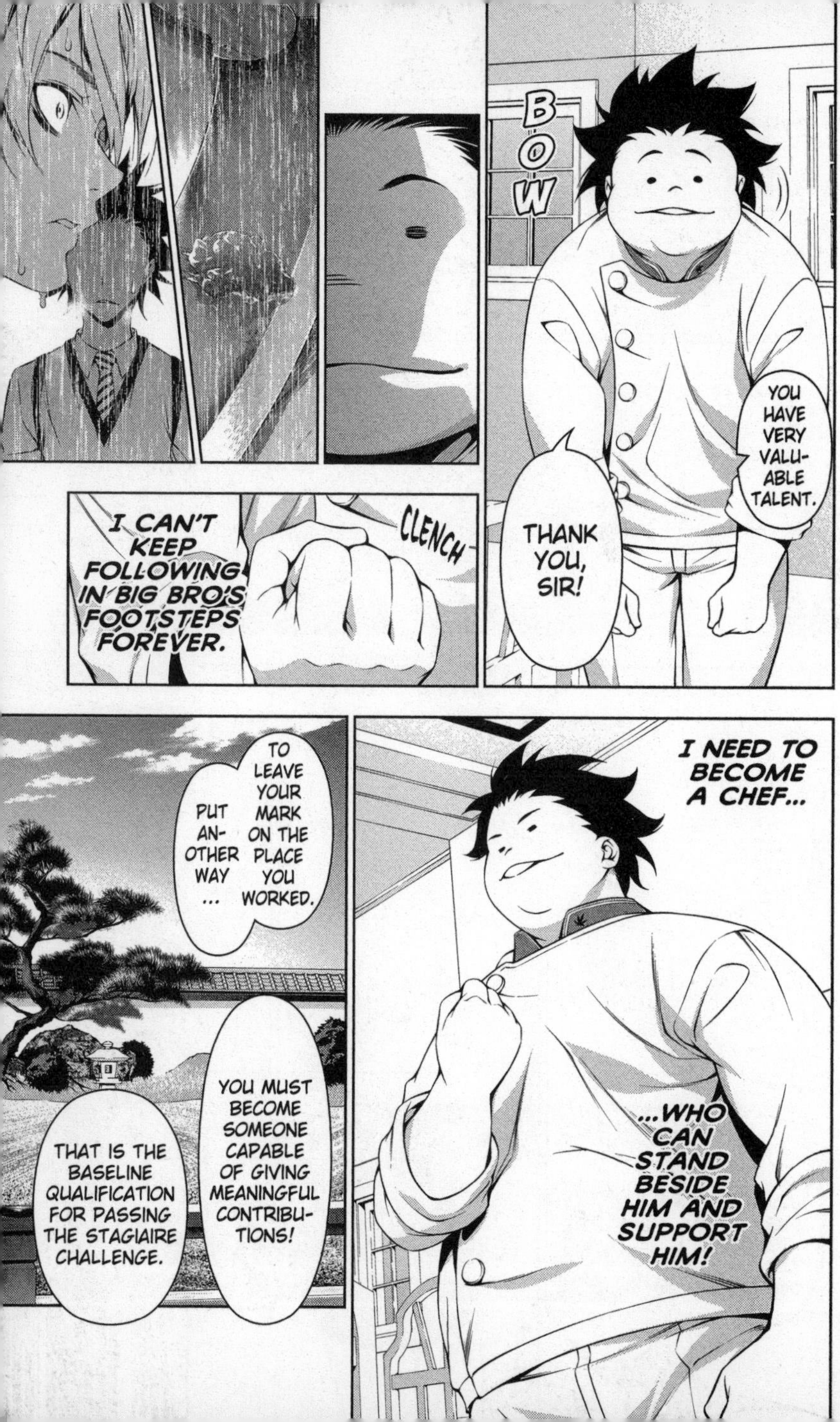
BOW
YOU HAVE VERY VALUABLE TALENT.
THANK YOU, SIR!
CLENCH
I CAN'T KEEP FOLLOWING IN BIG BRO'S FOOTSTEPS FOREVER.
I NEED TO BECOME A CHEF...
...WHO CAN STAND BESIDE HIM AND SUPPORT HIM!
TO LEAVE YOUR MARK ON THE PLACE YOU WORKED.
PUT ANOTHER WAY...
YOU MUST BECOME SOMEONE CAPABLE OF GIVING MEANINGFUL CONTRIBUTIONS!
THAT IS THE BASELINE QUALIFICATION FOR PASSING THE STAGIAIRE CHALLENGE.

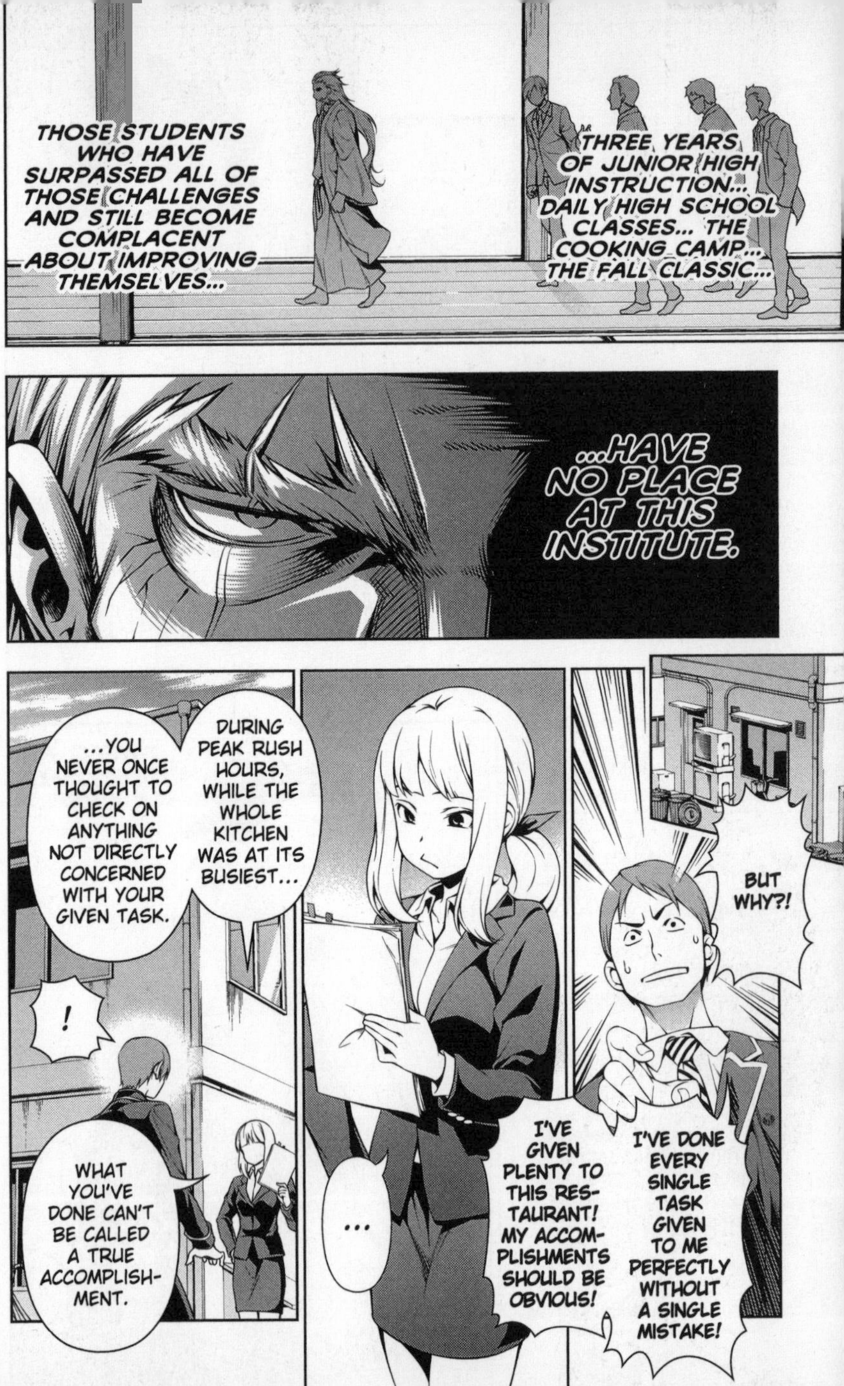
THREE YEARS OF JUNIOR HIGH INSTRUCTION... DAILY HIGH SCHOOL CLASSES... THE COOKING CAMP... THE FALL CLASSIC...
THOSE STUDENTS WHO HAVE SURPASSED ALL OF THOSE CHALLENGES AND STILL BECOME COMPLACENT ABOUT IMPROVING THEMSELVES...
...HAVE NO PLACE AT THIS INSTITUTE.
BUT WHY?!
I'VE DONE EVERY SINGLE TASK GIVEN TO ME PERFECTLY WITHOUT A SINGLE MISTAKE!
I'VE GIVEN PLENTY TO THIS RES-TAURANT! MY ACCOM-PLISHMENTS SHOULD BE OBVIOUS!
...
DURING PEAK RUSH HOURS, WHILE THE WHOLE KITCHEN WAS AT ITS BUSIEST...
...YOU NEVER ONCE THOUGHT TO CHECK ON ANYTHING NOT DIRECTLY CONCERNED WITH YOUR GIVEN TASK.
!
WHAT YOU'VE DONE CAN'T BE CALLED A TRUE ACCOMPLISH-MENT.

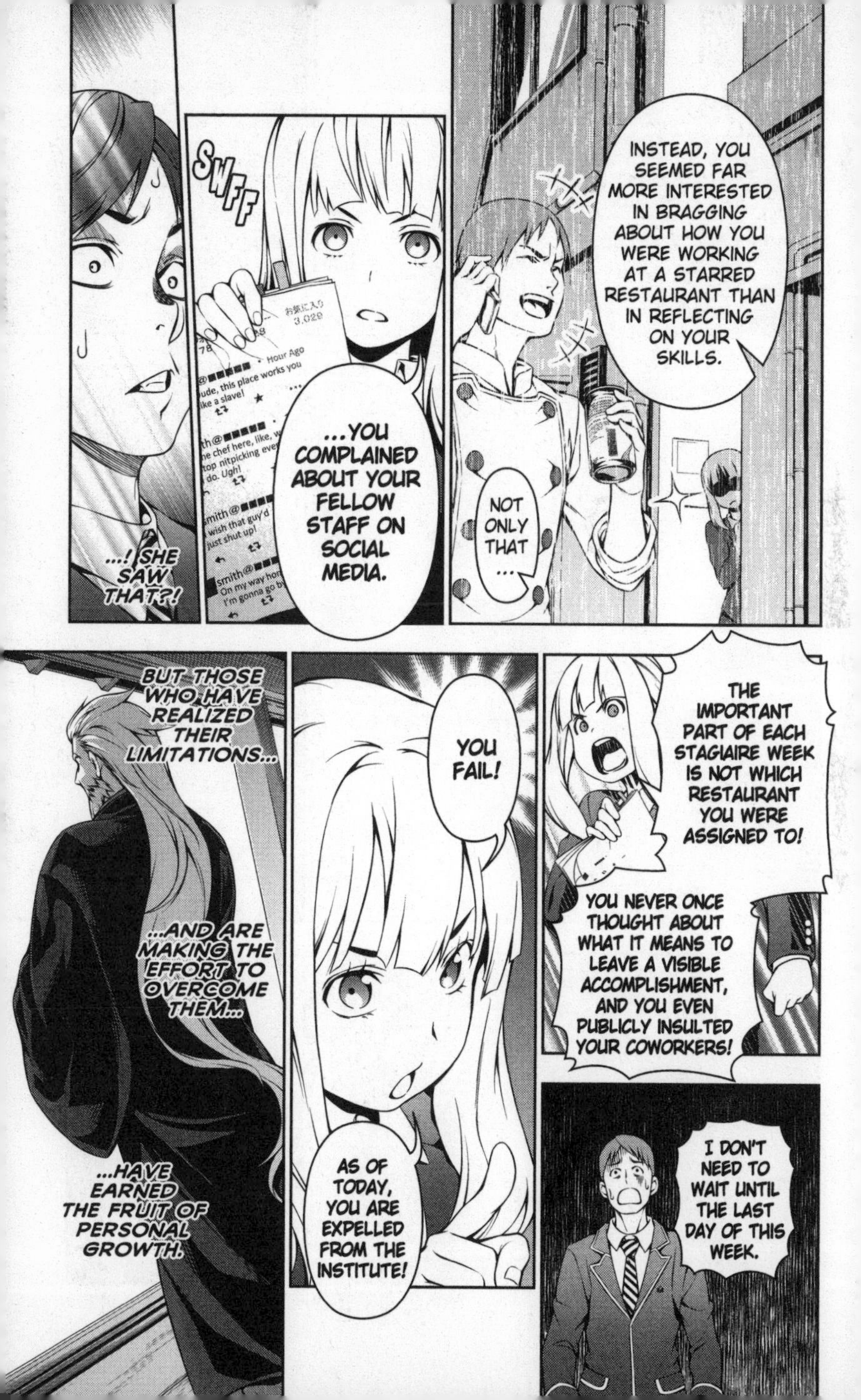
INSTEAD, YOU SEEMED FAR MORE INTERESTED IN BRAGGING ABOUT HOW YOU WERE WORKING AT A STARRED RESTAURANT THAN IN REFLECTING ON YOUR SKILLS.
NOT ONLY THAT...
SWFF
お気に入り 3,029
Hour Ago
...YOU COMPLAINED ABOUT YOUR FELLOW STAFF ON SOCIAL MEDIA.
...! SHE SAW THAT?!
THE IMPORTANT PART OF EACH STAGIAIRE WEEK IS NOT WHICH RESTAURANT YOU WERE ASSIGNED TO!
YOU NEVER ONCE THOUGHT ABOUT WHAT IT MEANS TO LEAVE A VISIBLE ACCOMPLISHMENT, AND YOU EVEN PUBLICLY INSULTED YOUR COWORKERS!
I DON'T NEED TO WAIT UNTIL THE LAST DAY OF THIS WEEK.
YOU FAIL!
AS OF TODAY, YOU ARE EXPELLED FROM THE INSTITUTE!
BUT THOSE WHO HAVE REALIZED THEIR LIMITATIONS...
...AND ARE MAKING THE EFFORT TO OVERCOME THEM...
...HAVE EARNED THE FRUIT OF PERSONAL GROWTH.

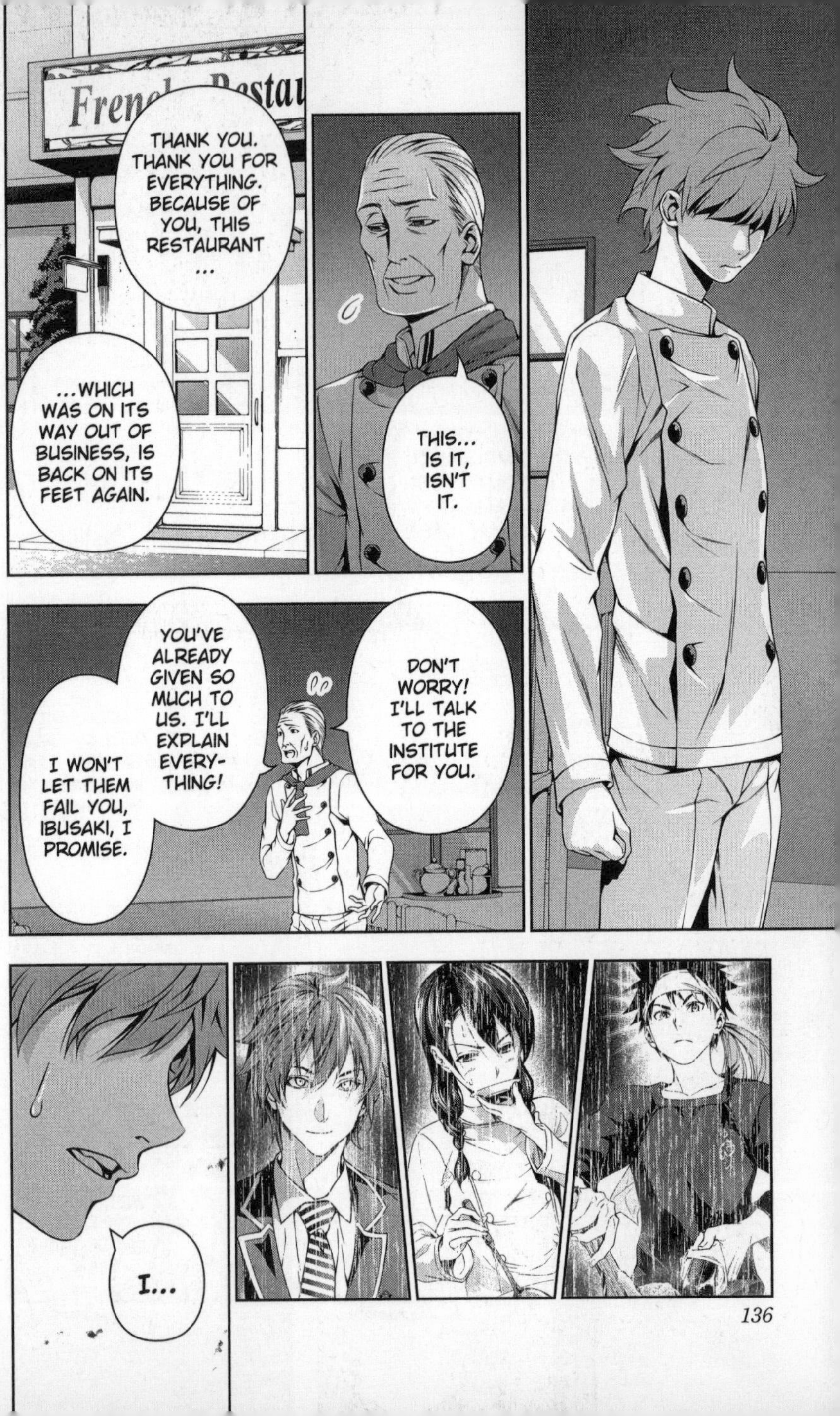
THIS... IS IT, ISN'T IT.
THANK YOU. THANK YOU FOR EVERYTHING. BECAUSE OF YOU, THIS RESTAURANT ...
...WHICH WAS ON ITS WAY OUT OF BUSINESS, IS BACK ON ITS FEET AGAIN.
DON'T WORRY! I'LL TALK TO THE INSTITUTE FOR YOU.
YOU'VE ALREADY GIVEN SO MUCH TO US. I'LL EXPLAIN EVERY-THING!
I WON'T LET THEM FAIL YOU, IBUSAKI, I PROMISE.
I...

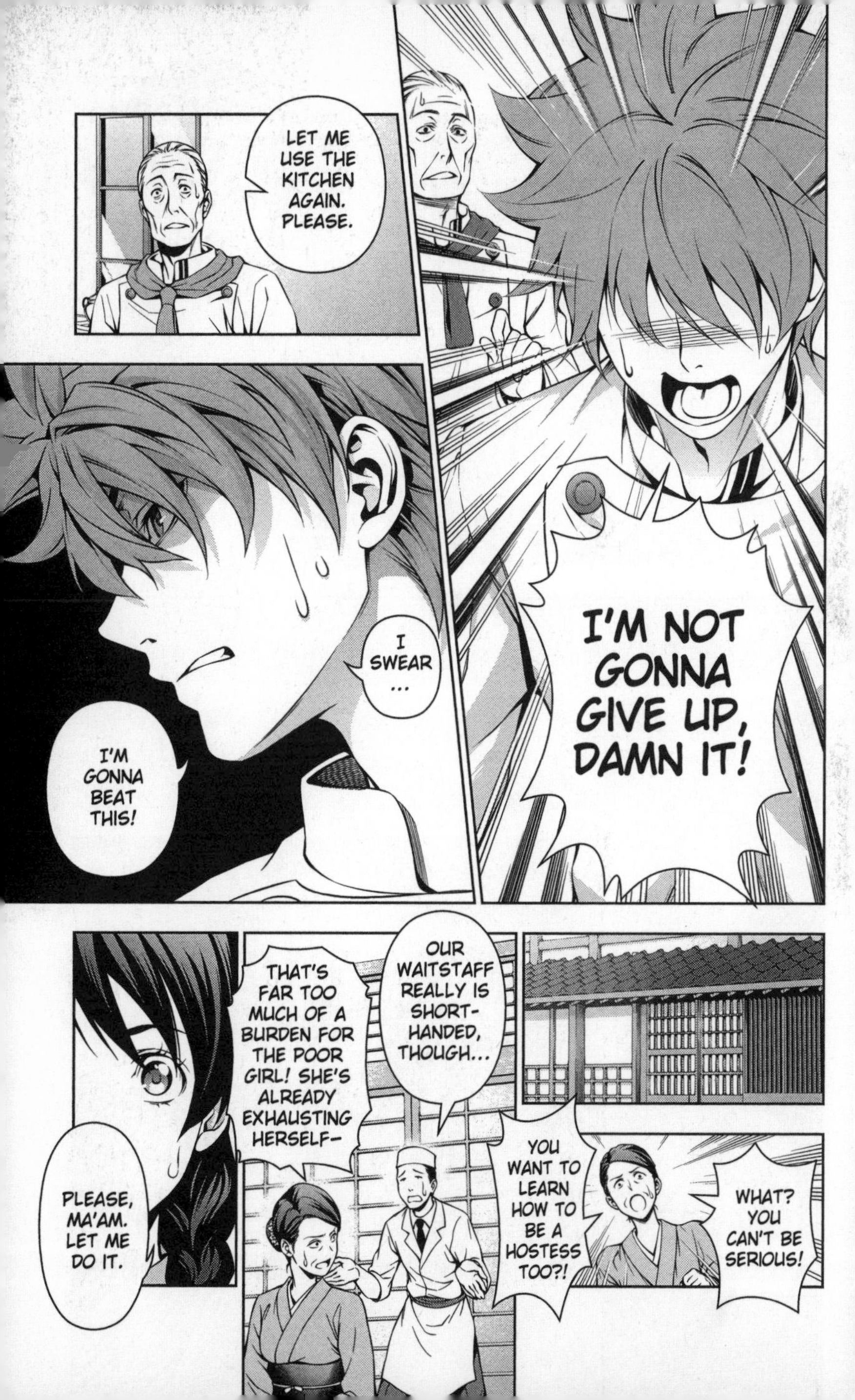
I'M NOT GONNA GIVE UP, DAMN IT!
LET ME USE THE KITCHEN AGAIN. PLEASE.
I SWEAR...
I'M GONNA BEAT THIS!
WHAT? YOU CAN'T BE SERIOUS!
YOU WANT TO LEARN HOW TO BE A HOSTESS TOO?!
OUR WAITSTAFF REALLY IS SHORT-HANDED, THOUGH...
THAT'S FAR TOO MUCH OF A BURDEN FOR THE POOR GIRL! SHE'S ALREADY EXHAUSTING HERSELF-
PLEASE, MA'AM. LET ME DO IT.

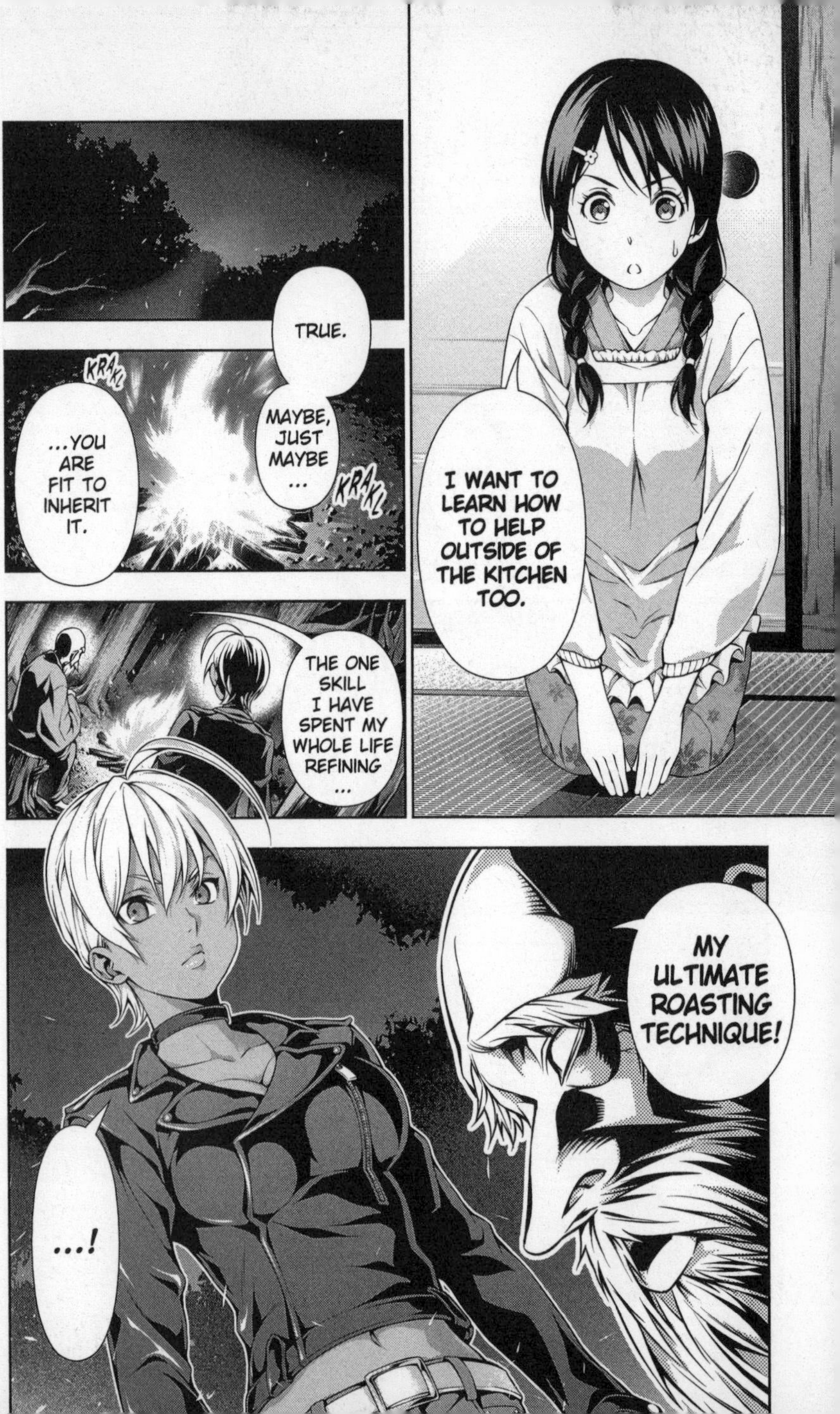

I WANT TO LEARN HOW TO HELP OUTSIDE OF THE KITCHEN TOO.
TRUE.
KRAKL
MAYBE, JUST MAYBE...
...YOU ARE FIT TO INHERIT IT.
KRAKL
THE ONE SKILL I HAVE SPENT MY WHOLE LIFE REFINING...
MY ULTIMATE ROASTING TECHNIQUE!
...!

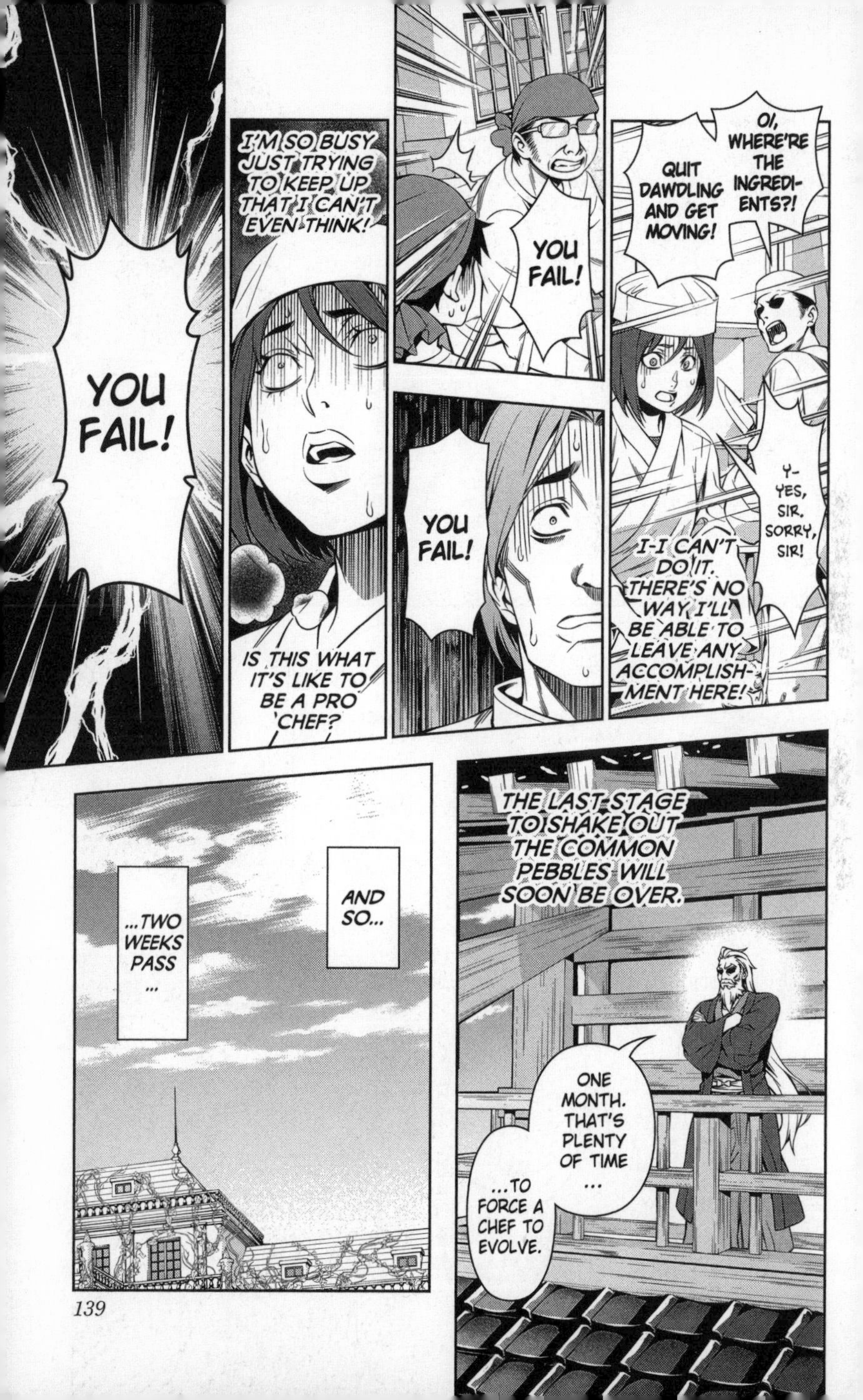
OI, WHERE'RE THE INGREDI-ENTS?!
QUIT DAWDLING AND GET MOVING!
Y-YES, SIR. SORRY, SIR!
I-I CAN'T DO IT. THERE'S NO WAY I'LL BE ABLE TO LEAVE ANY ACCOMPLISH-MENT HERE!
YOU FAIL!
YOU FAIL!
I'M SO BUSY JUST TRYING TO KEEP UP THAT I CAN'T EVEN THINK!
IS THIS WHAT IT'S LIKE TO BE A PRO CHEF?
YOU FAIL!
THE LAST STAGE TO SHAKE OUT THE COMMON PEBBLES WILL SOON BE OVER.
ONE MONTH. THAT'S PLENTY OF TIME ...
...TO FORCE A CHEF TO EVOLVE.
AND SO...
...TWO WEEKS PASS ...

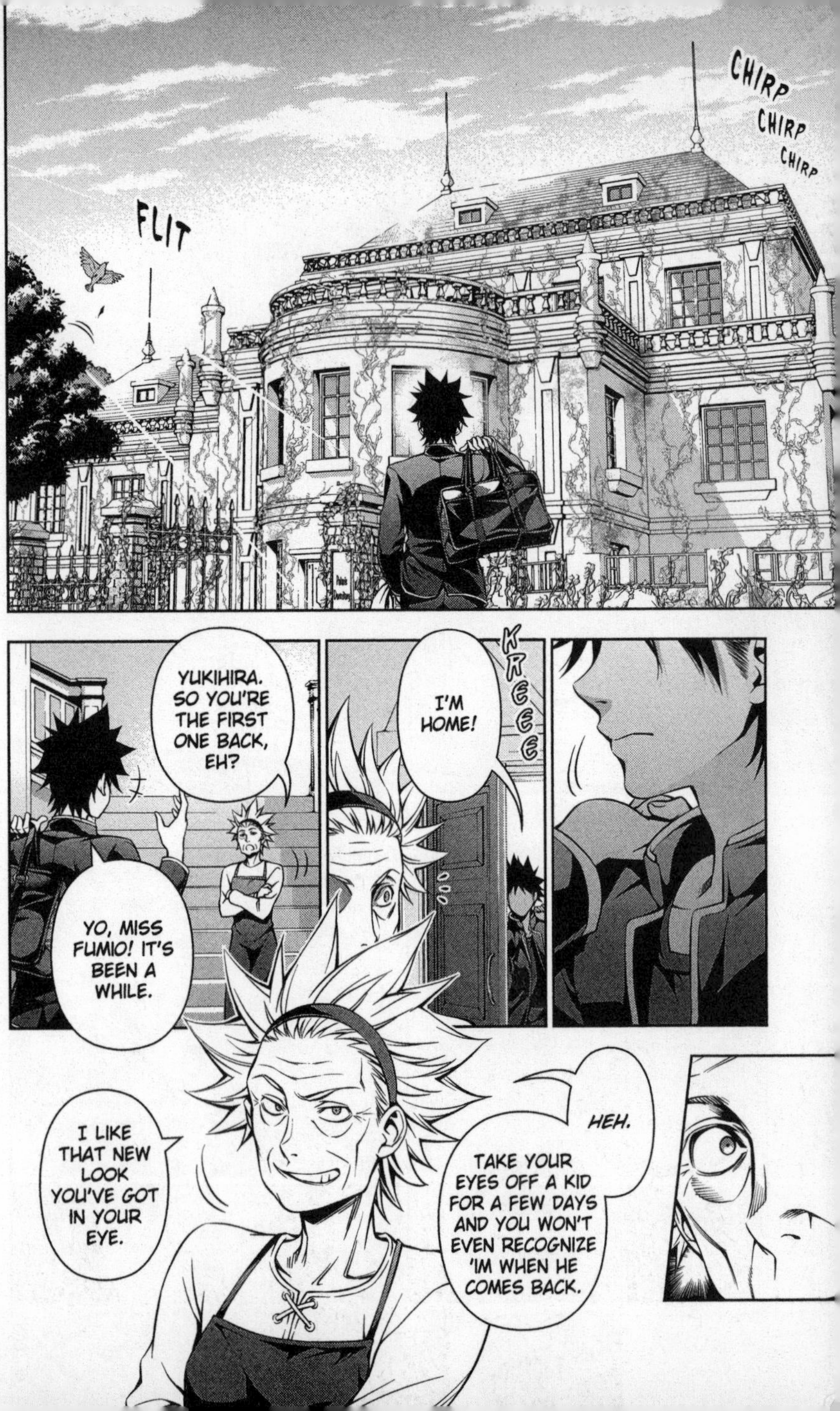
CHIRP
CHIRP
CHIRP
FLIT
KREEE
I'M HOME!
YUKIHIRA. SO YOU'RE THE FIRST ONE BACK, EH?
YO, MISS FUMIO! IT'S BEEN A WHILE.
HEH.
TAKE YOUR EYES OFF A KID FOR A FEW DAYS AND YOU WON'T EVEN RECOGNIZE 'IM WHEN HE COMES BACK.
I LIKE THAT NEW LOOK YOU'VE GOT IN YOUR EYE.

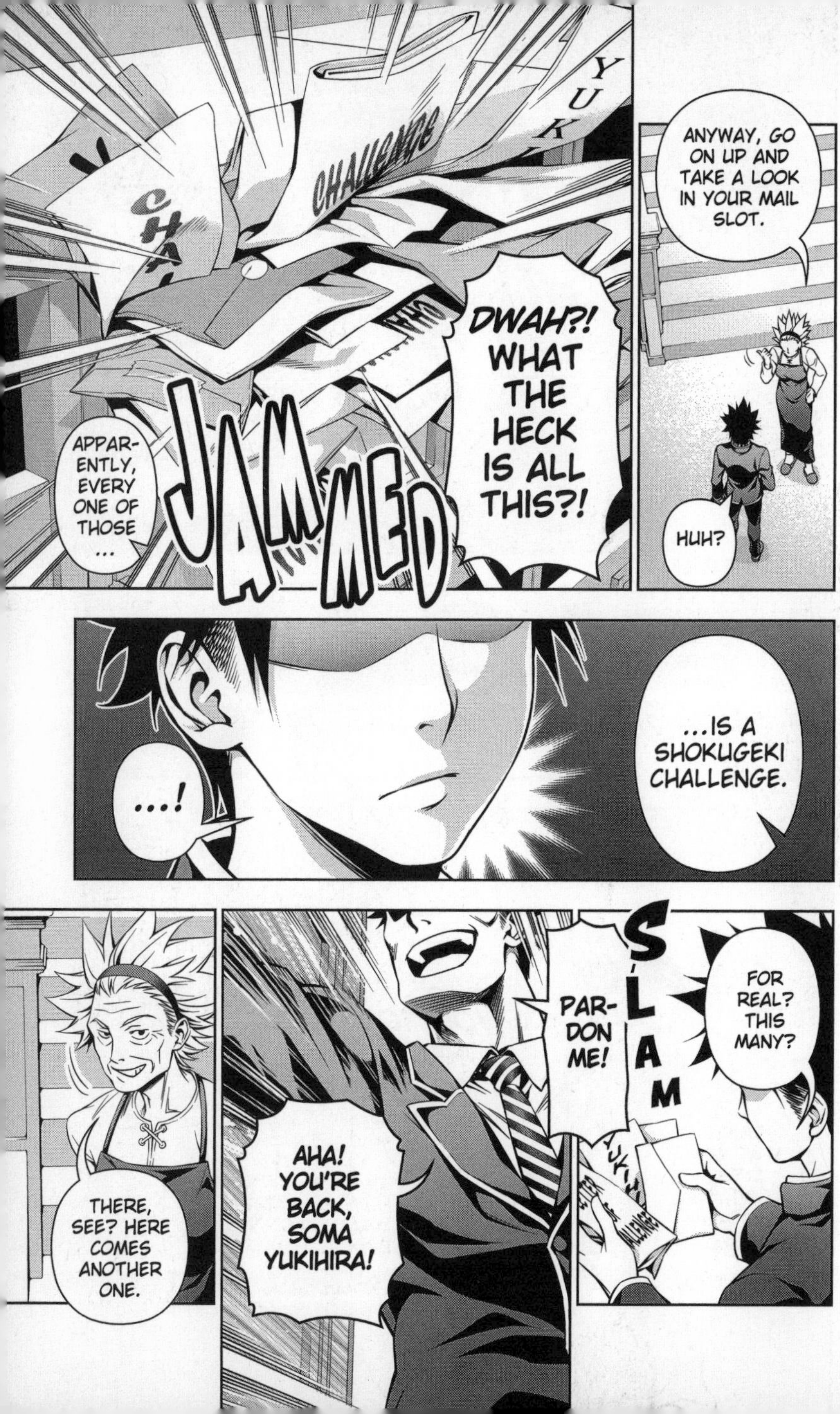
ANYWAY, GO ON UP AND TAKE A LOOK IN YOUR MAIL SLOT.
HUH?
DWAH?! WHAT THE HECK IS ALL THIS?!
JAMMED
APPAR-ENTLY, EVERY ONE OF THOSE ...
...IS A SHOKUGEKI CHALLENGE.
...!
FOR REAL? THIS MANY?
SLAM
PAR-DON ME!
AHA! YOU'RE BACK, SOMA YUKIHIRA!
THERE, SEE? HERE COMES ANOTHER ONE.

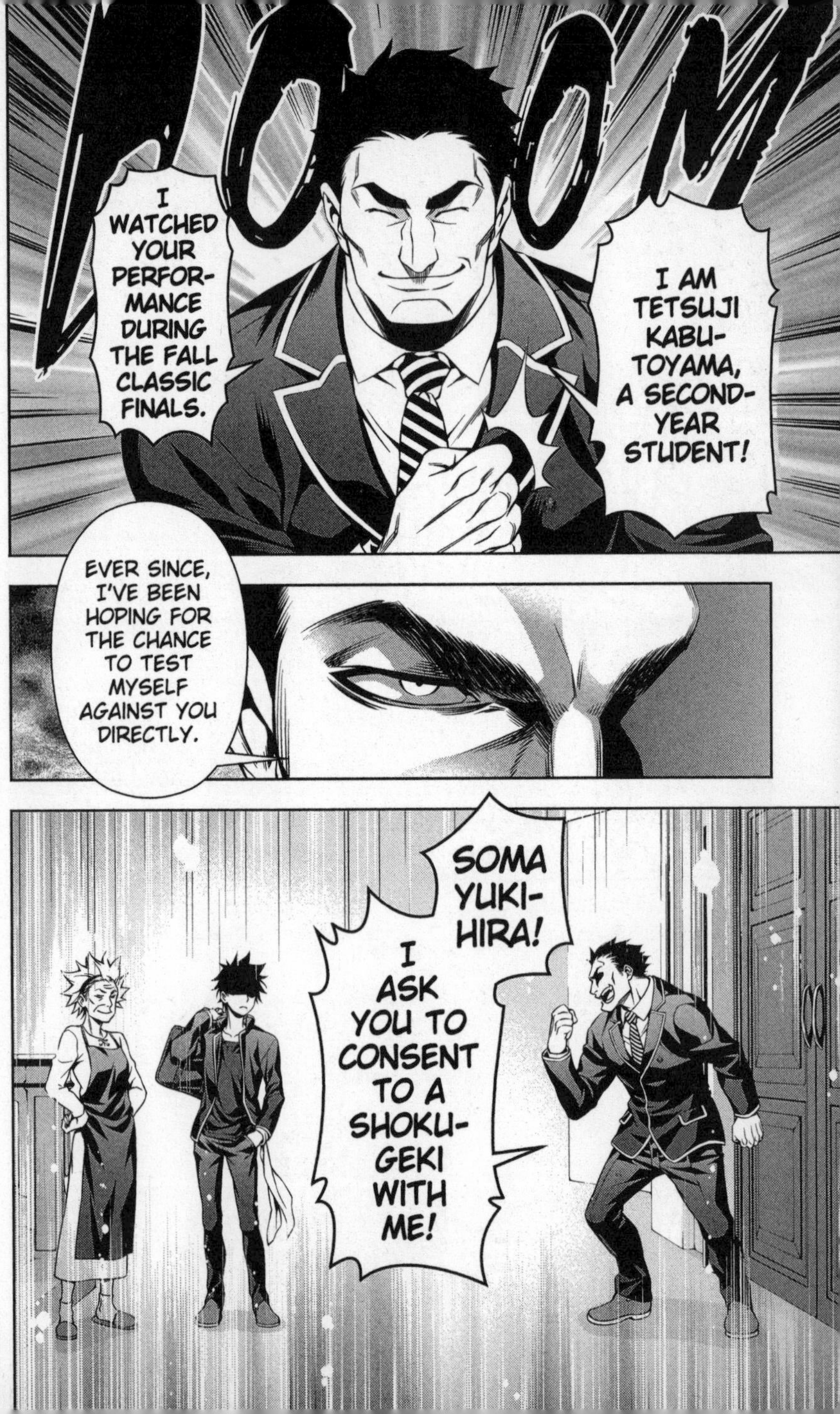
I AM TETSUJI KABU-TOYAMA, A SECOND-YEAR STUDENT!
I WATCHED YOUR PERFOR-MANCE DURING THE FALL CLASSIC FINALS.
EVER SINCE, I'VE BEEN HOPING FOR THE CHANCE TO TEST MYSELF AGAINST YOU DIRECTLY.
SOMA YUKI-HIRA!
I ASK YOU TO CONSENT TO A SHOKU-GEKI WITH ME!

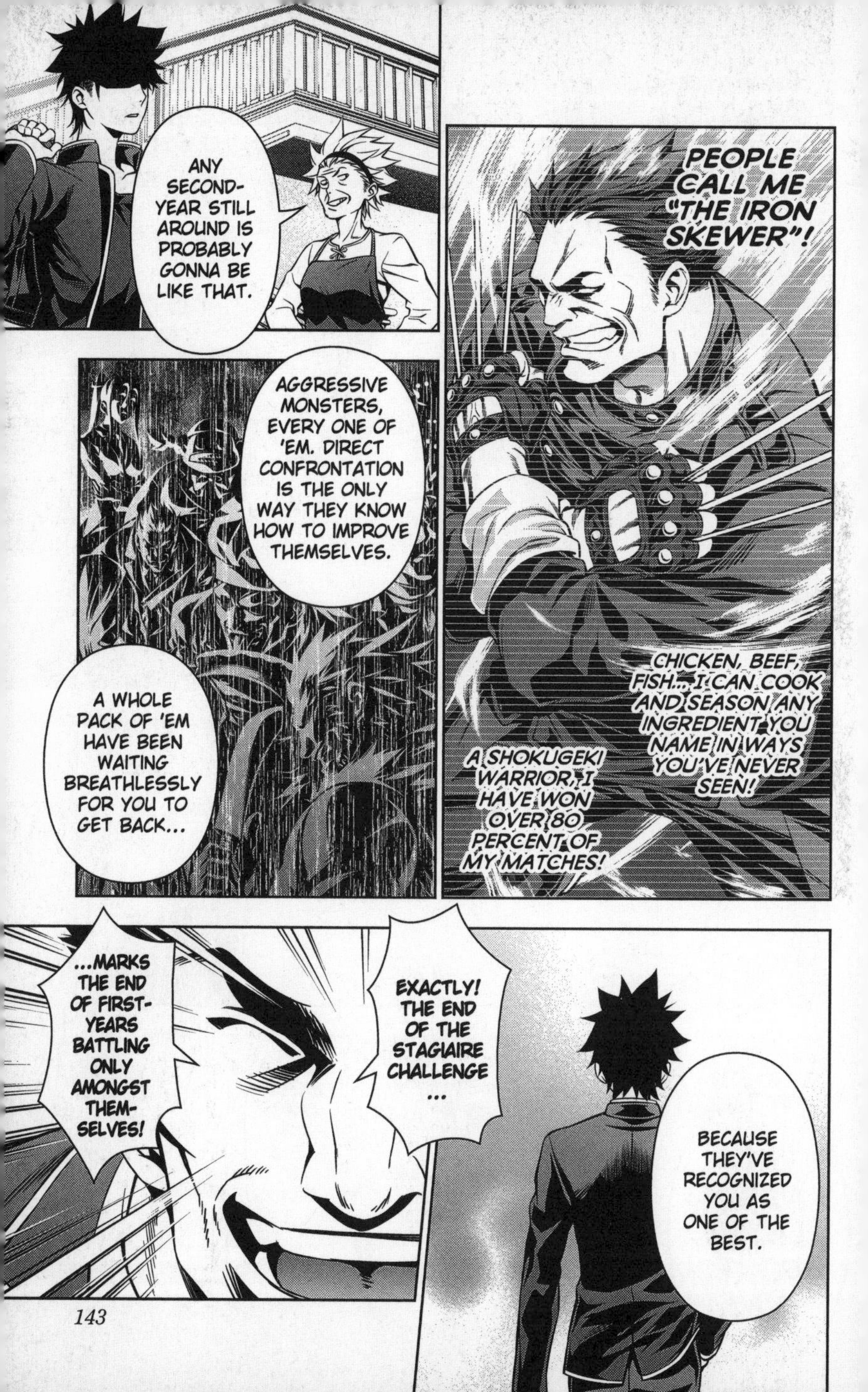
PEOPLE CALL ME "THE IRON SKEWER"!
CHICKEN, BEEF, FISH... I CAN COOK AND SEASON ANY INGREDIENT YOU NAME IN WAYS YOU'VE NEVER SEEN!
A SHOKUGEKI WARRIOR, I HAVE WON OVER 80 PERCENT OF MY MATCHES!
ANY SECOND-YEAR STILL AROUND IS PROBABLY GONNA BE LIKE THAT.
AGGRESSIVE MONSTERS, EVERY ONE OF 'EM. DIRECT CONFRONTATION IS THE ONLY WAY THEY KNOW HOW TO IMPROVE THEMSELVES.
A WHOLE PACK OF 'EM HAVE BEEN WAITING BREATHLESSLY FOR YOU TO GET BACK...
BECAUSE THEY'VE RECOGNIZED YOU AS ONE OF THE BEST.
EXACTLY! THE END OF THE STAGIAIRE CHALLENGE...
...MARKS THE END OF FIRST-YEARS BATTLING ONLY AMONGST THEM-SELVES!

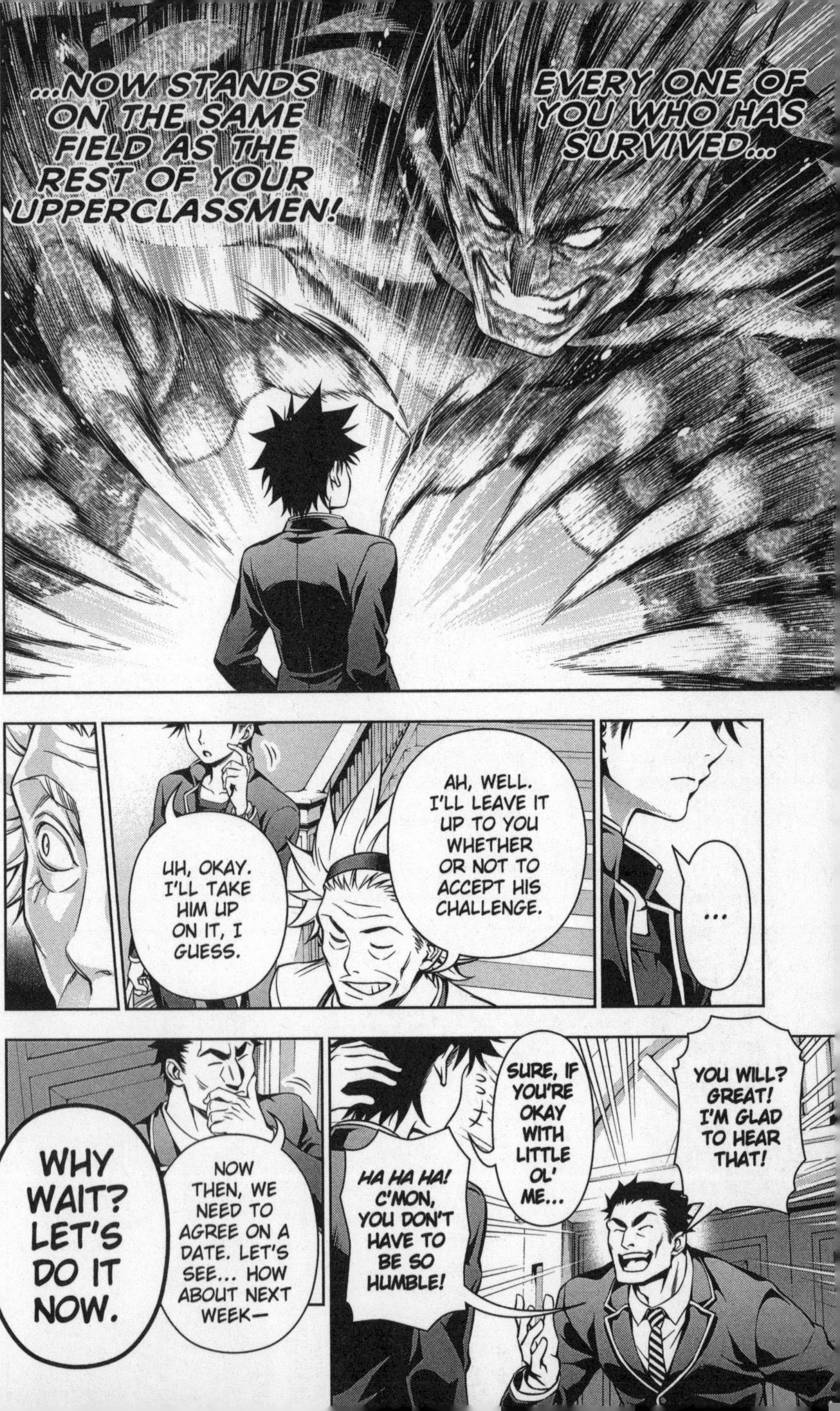

EVERY ONE OF YOU WHO HAS SURVIVED...
...NOW STANDS ON THE SAME FIELD AS THE REST OF YOUR UPPERCLASSMEN!
...
AH, WELL. I'LL LEAVE IT UP TO YOU WHETHER OR NOT TO ACCEPT HIS CHALLENGE.
UH, OKAY. I'LL TAKE HIM UP ON IT, I GUESS.
YOU WILL? GREAT! I'M GLAD TO HEAR THAT!
SURE, IF YOU'RE OKAY WITH LITTLE OL' ME...
HA HA HA! C'MON, YOU DON'T HAVE TO BE SO HUMBLE!
NOW THEN, WE NEED TO AGREE ON A DATE. LET'S SEE... HOW ABOUT NEXT WEEK—
WHY WAIT? LET'S DO IT NOW.

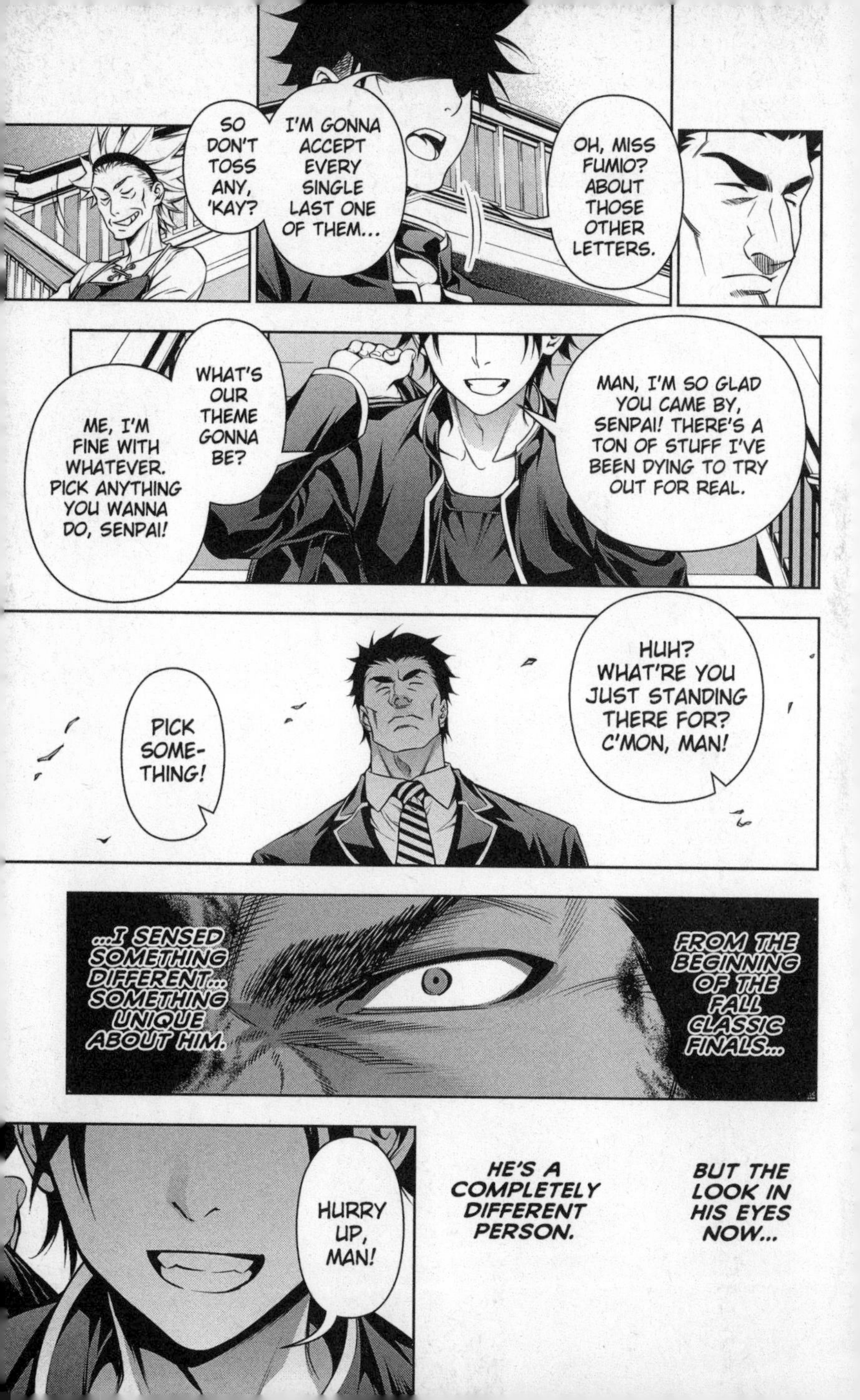
OH, MISS FUMIO? ABOUT THOSE OTHER LETTERS.
I'M GONNA ACCEPT EVERY SINGLE LAST ONE OF THEM...
SO DON'T TOSS ANY, 'KAY?
MAN, I'M SO GLAD YOU CAME BY, SENPAI! THERE'S A TON OF STUFF I'VE BEEN DYING TO TRY OUT FOR REAL.
WHAT'S OUR THEME GONNA BE?
ME, I'M FINE WITH WHATEVER. PICK ANYTHING YOU WANNA DO, SENPAI!
HUH? WHAT'RE YOU JUST STANDING THERE FOR? C'MON, MAN!
PICK SOME-THING!
FROM THE BEGINNING OF THE FALL CLASSIC FINALS...
...I SENSED SOMETHING DIFFERENT... SOMETHING UNIQUE ABOUT HIM.
BUT THE LOOK IN HIS EYES NOW...
HE'S A COMPLETELY DIFFERENT PERSON.
HURRY UP, MAN!

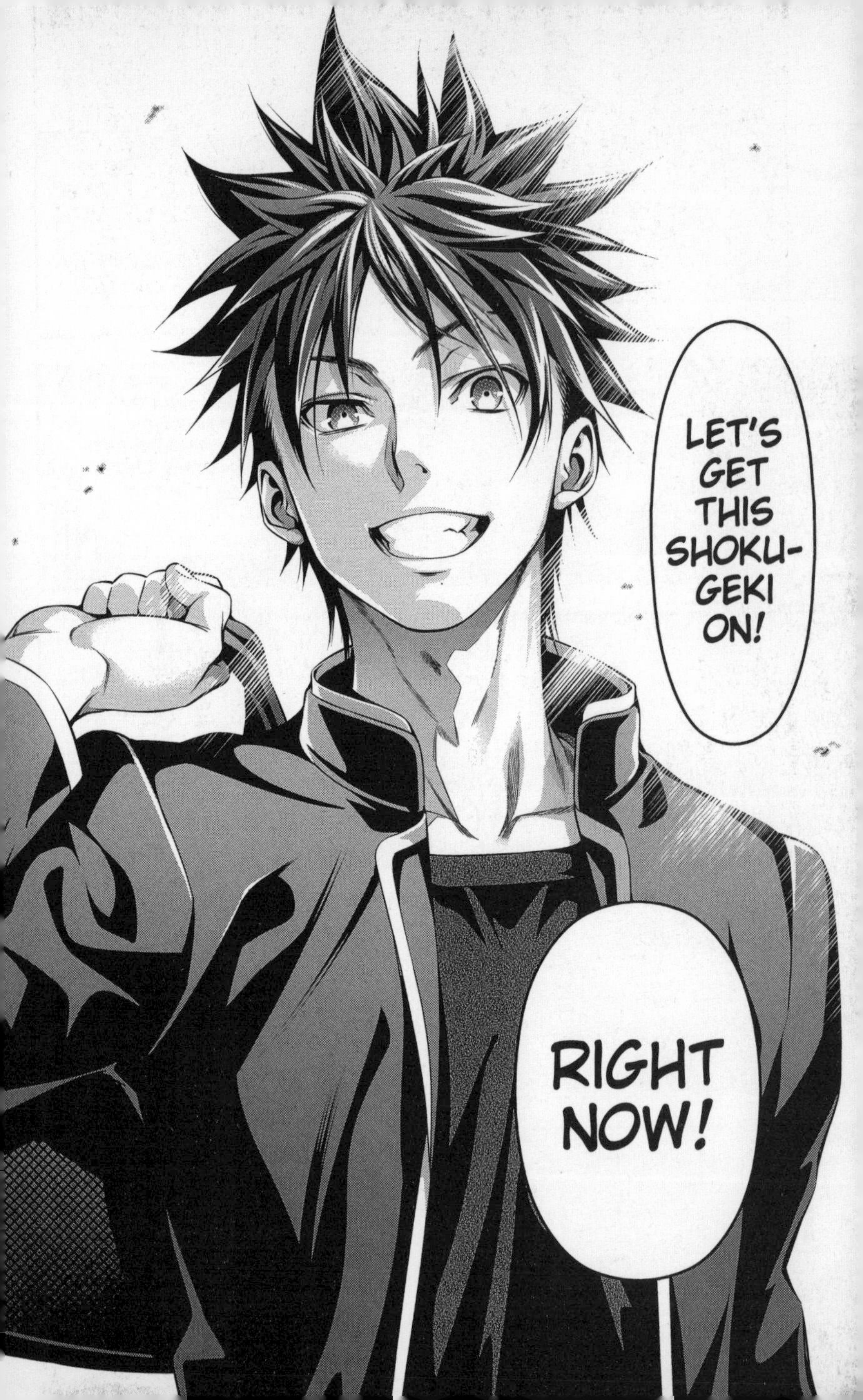
LET'S GET THIS SHOKU-GEKI ON!
RIGHT NOW!

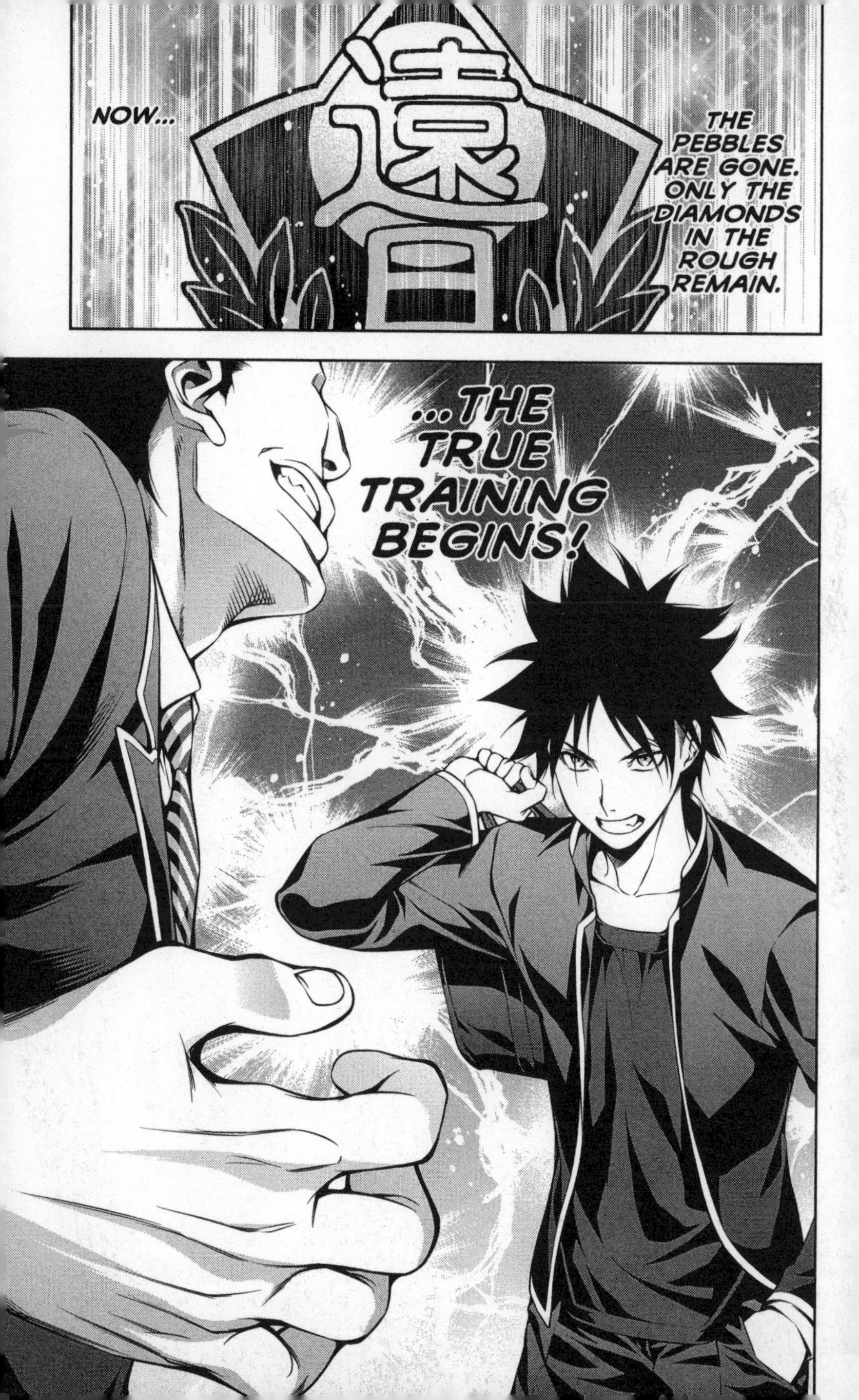
THE PEBBLES ARE GONE. ONLY THE DIAMONDS IN THE ROUGH REMAIN.
NOW...
...THE TRUE TRAINING BEGINS!

BING BONG
DING DONG

~OFFICIAL NOTICE~

ISAMI'S WEIGHT IS
BACK TO NORMAL.

BOW

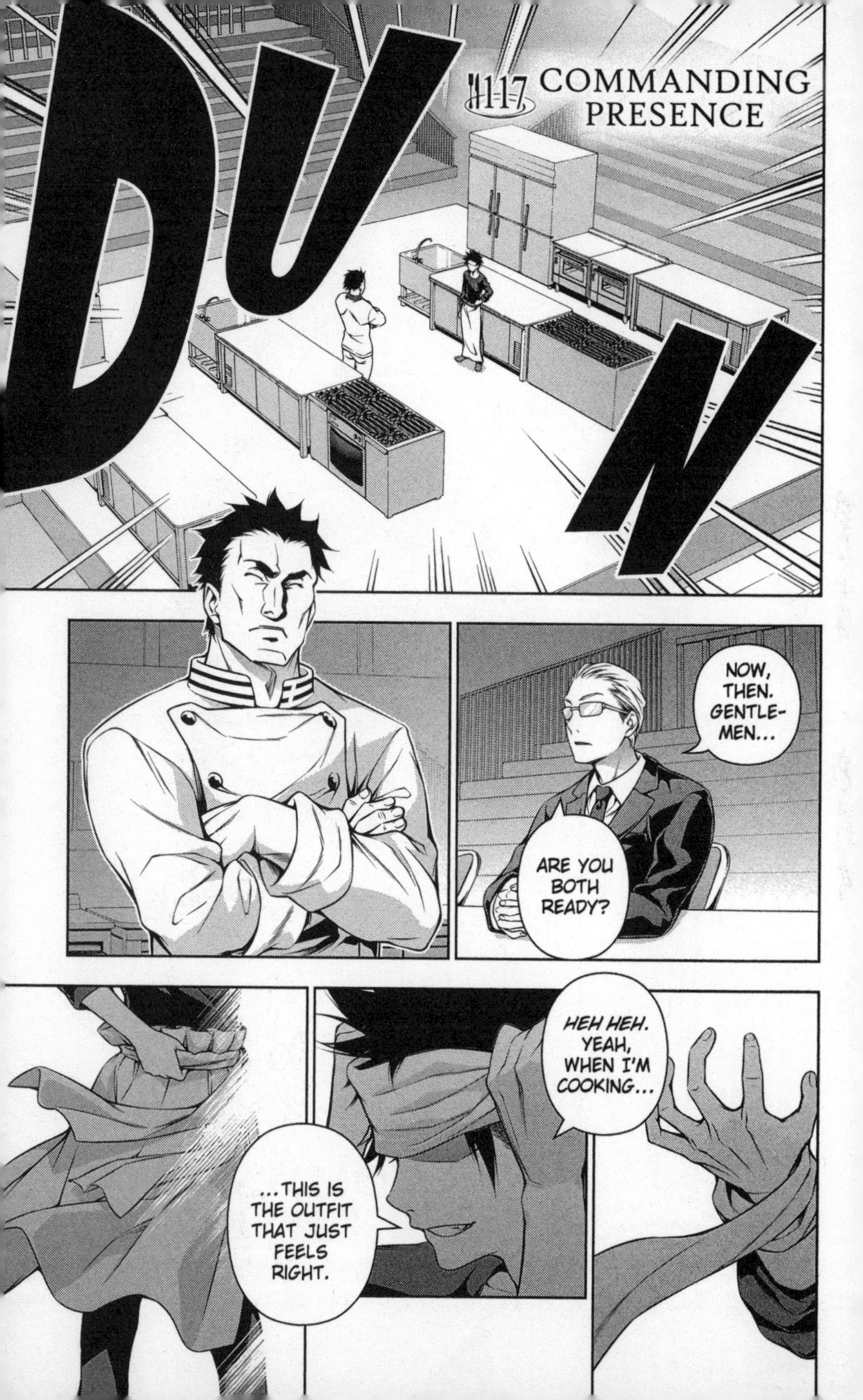
117 COMMANDING PRESENCE
DUN
NOW, THEN. GENTLEMEN...
ARE YOU BOTH READY?
HEH HEH. YEAH, WHEN I'M COOKING...
...THIS IS THE OUTFIT THAT JUST FEELS RIGHT.

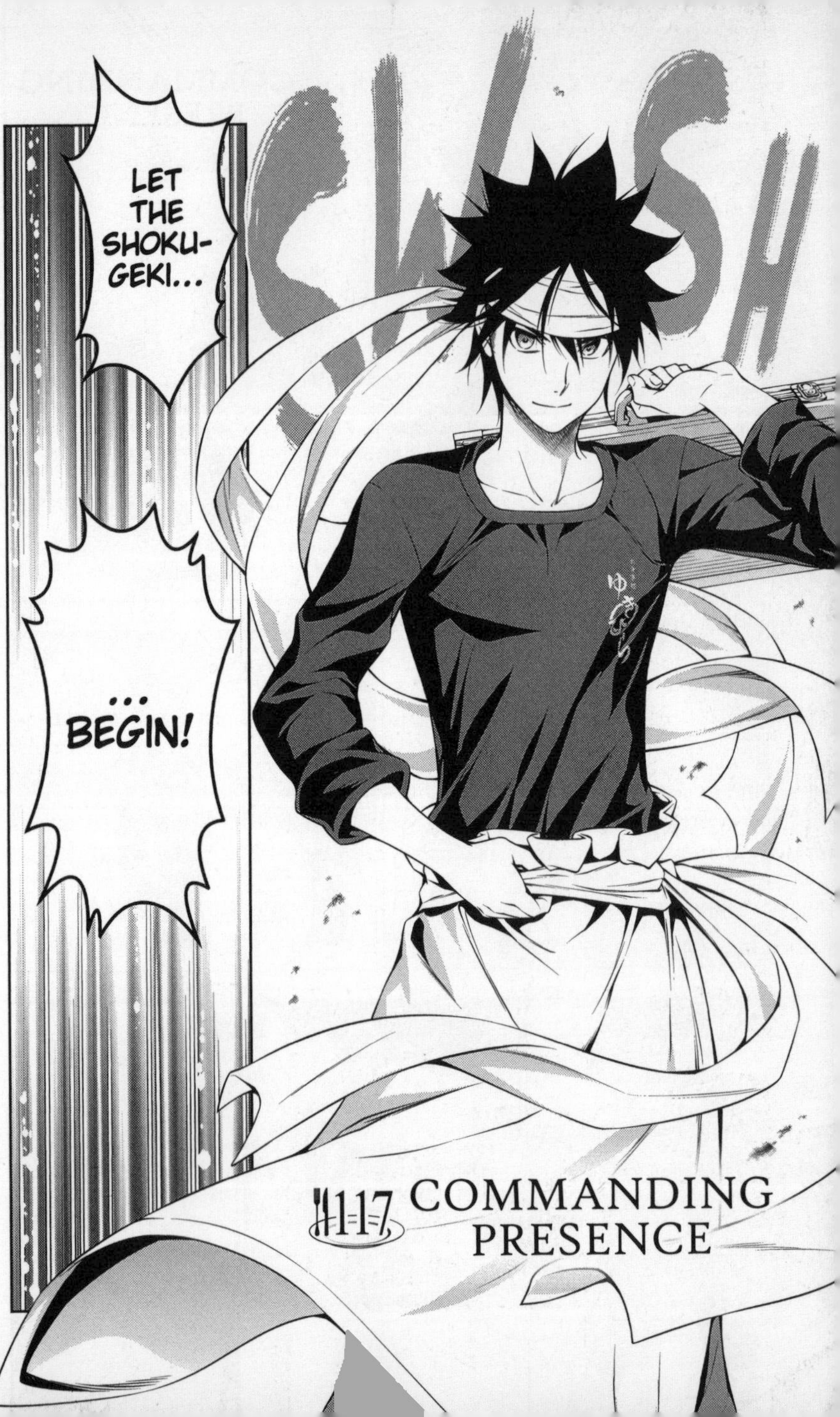
SWISH
LET THE SHOKUGEKI...
...BEGIN!
117 COMMANDING PRESENCE

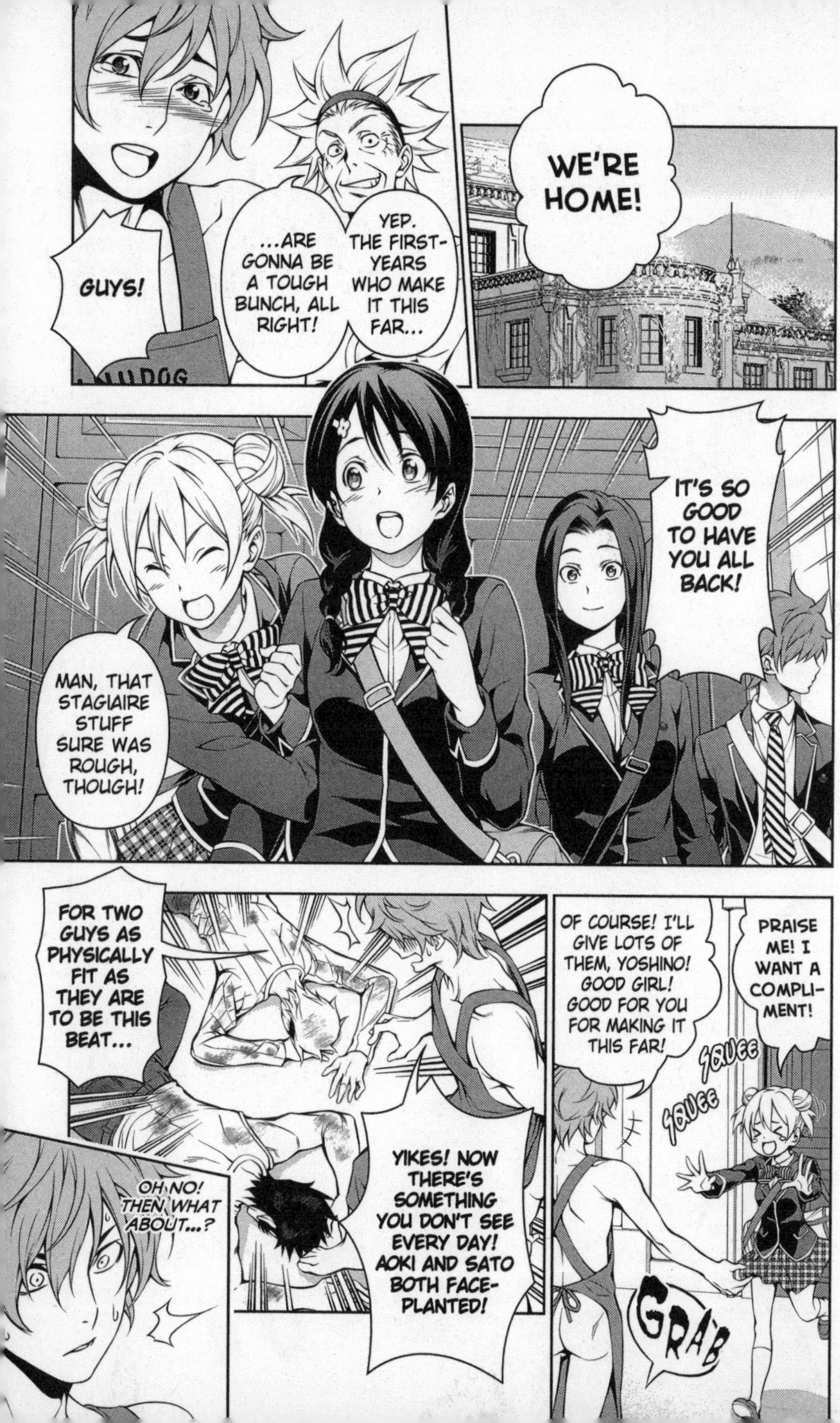
WE'RE HOME!
YEP. THE FIRST-YEARS WHO MAKE IT THIS FAR...
...ARE GONNA BE A TOUGH BUNCH, ALL RIGHT!
GUYS!
IT'S SO GOOD TO HAVE YOU ALL BACK!
MAN, THAT STAGIAIRE STUFF SURE WAS ROUGH, THOUGH!
PRAISE ME! I WANT A COMPLIMENT!
OF COURSE! I'LL GIVE LOTS OF THEM, YOSHINO! GOOD GIRL! GOOD FOR YOU FOR MAKING IT THIS FAR!
SQUEE
SQUEE
GRAB
FOR TWO GUYS AS PHYSICALLY FIT AS THEY ARE TO BE THIS BEAT...
YIKES! NOW THERE'S SOMETHING YOU DON'T SEE EVERY DAY! AOKI AND SATO BOTH FACE-PLANTED!
OH NO! THEN WHAT ABOUT...?

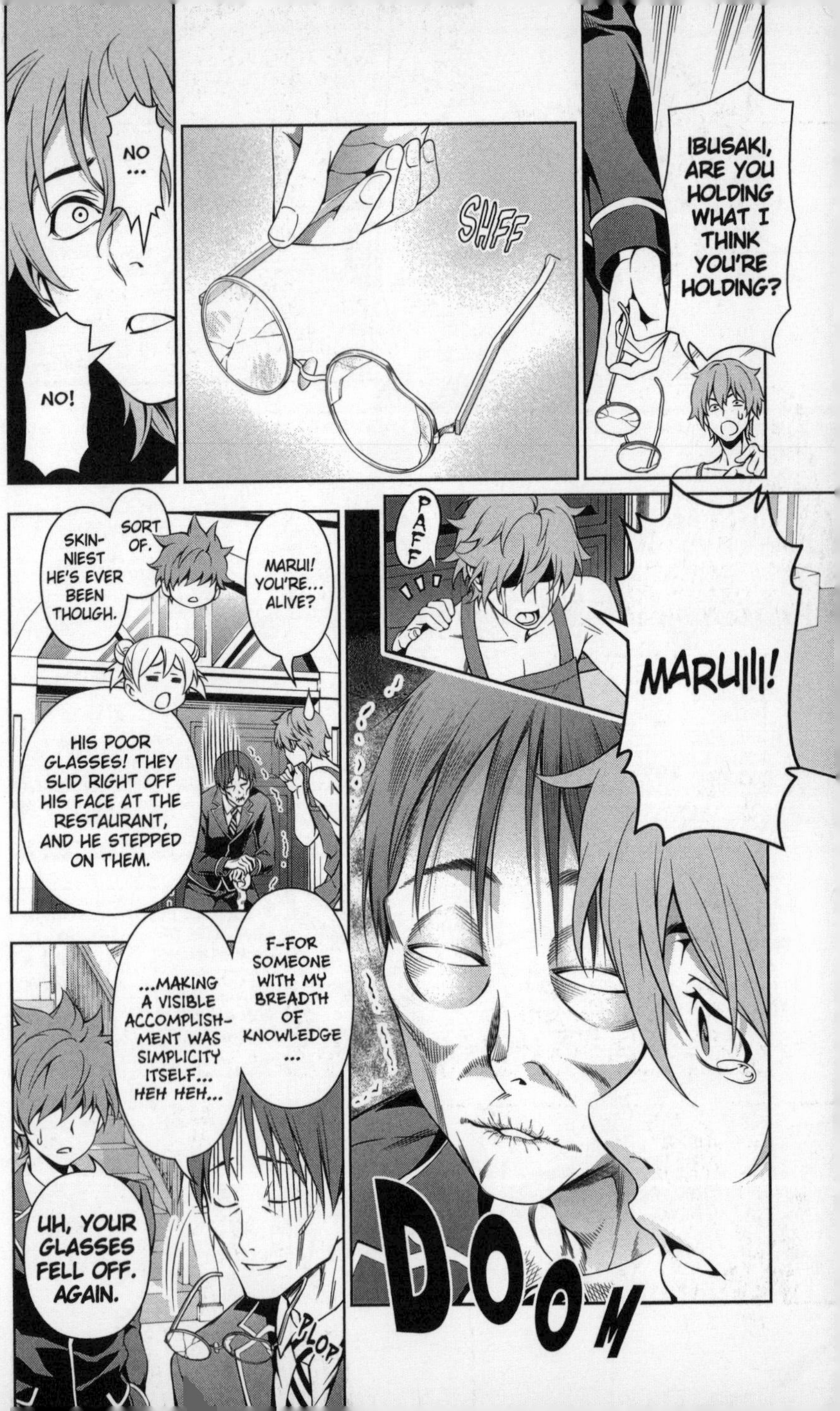
IBUSAKI, ARE YOU HOLDING WHAT I THINK YOU'RE HOLDING?
SHFF
NO ...
NO!
PAFF
MARUIIII!
DOOM
MARUI! YOU'RE... ALIVE?
SORT OF.
SKIN-NIEST HE'S EVER BEEN THOUGH.
HIS POOR GLASSES! THEY SLID RIGHT OFF HIS FACE AT THE RESTAURANT, AND HE STEPPED ON THEM.
F-FOR SOMEONE WITH MY BREADTH OF KNOWLEDGE ...
...MAKING A VISIBLE ACCOMPLISH-MENT WAS SIMPLICITY ITSELF... HEH HEH...
PLOP
UH, YOUR GLASSES FELL OFF. AGAIN.

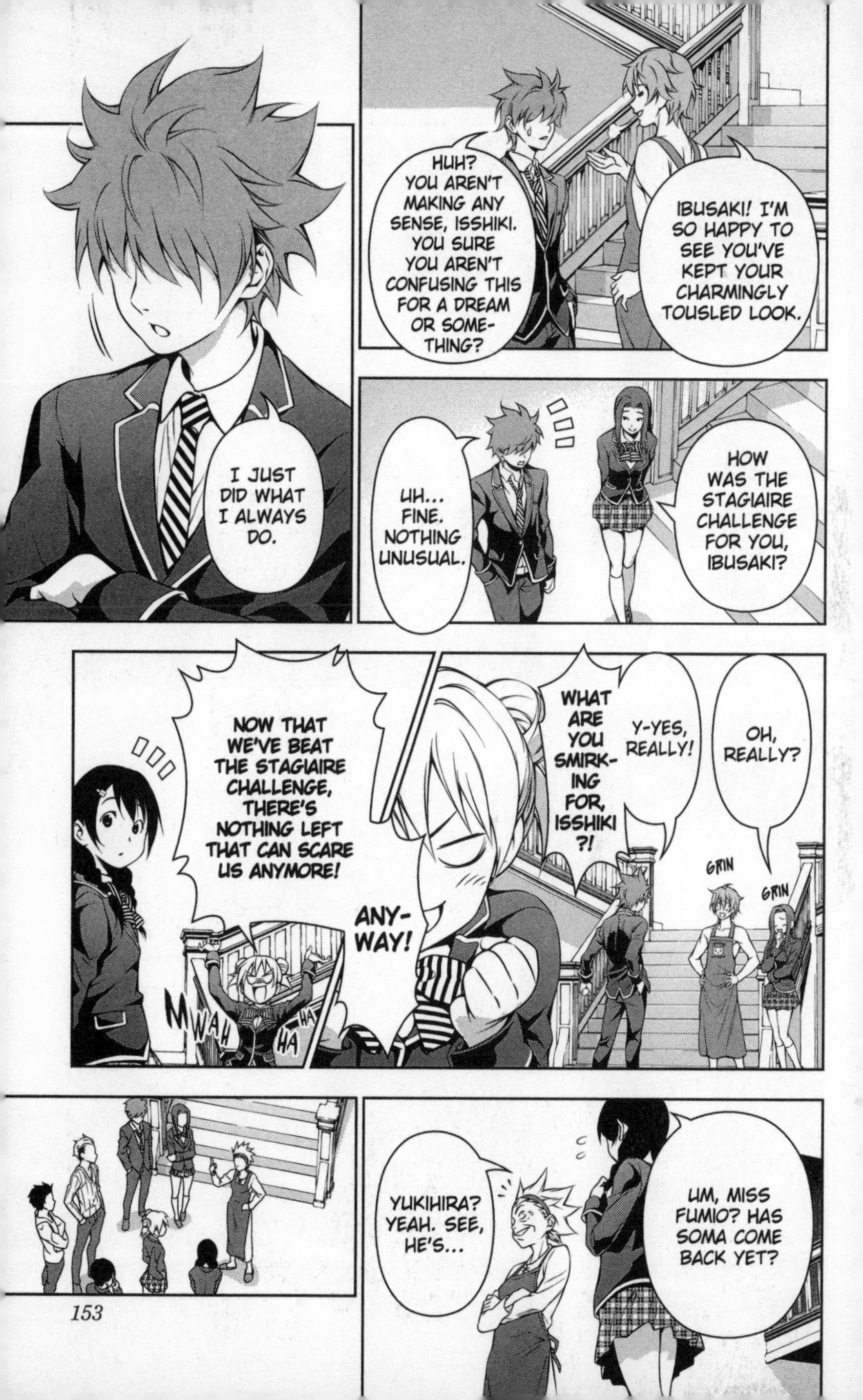
IBUSAKI! I'M SO HAPPY TO SEE YOU'VE KEPT YOUR CHARMINGLY TOUSLED LOOK.
HUH? YOU AREN'T MAKING ANY SENSE, ISSHIKI. YOU SURE YOU AREN'T CONFUSING THIS FOR A DREAM OR SOMETHING?
HOW WAS THE STAGIAIRE CHALLENGE FOR YOU, IBUSAKI?
UH... FINE. NOTHING UNUSUAL.
I JUST DID WHAT I ALWAYS DO.
OH, REALLY?
Y-YES, REALLY!
GRIN
GRIN
WHAT ARE YOU SMIRKING FOR, ISSHIKI?!
ANYWAY!
NOW THAT WE'VE BEAT THE STAGIAIRE CHALLENGE, THERE'S NOTHING LEFT THAT CAN SCARE US ANYMORE!
MWAH HA HA HA
UM, MISS FUMIO? HAS SOMA COME BACK YET?
YUKIHIRA? YEAH. SEE, HE'S...

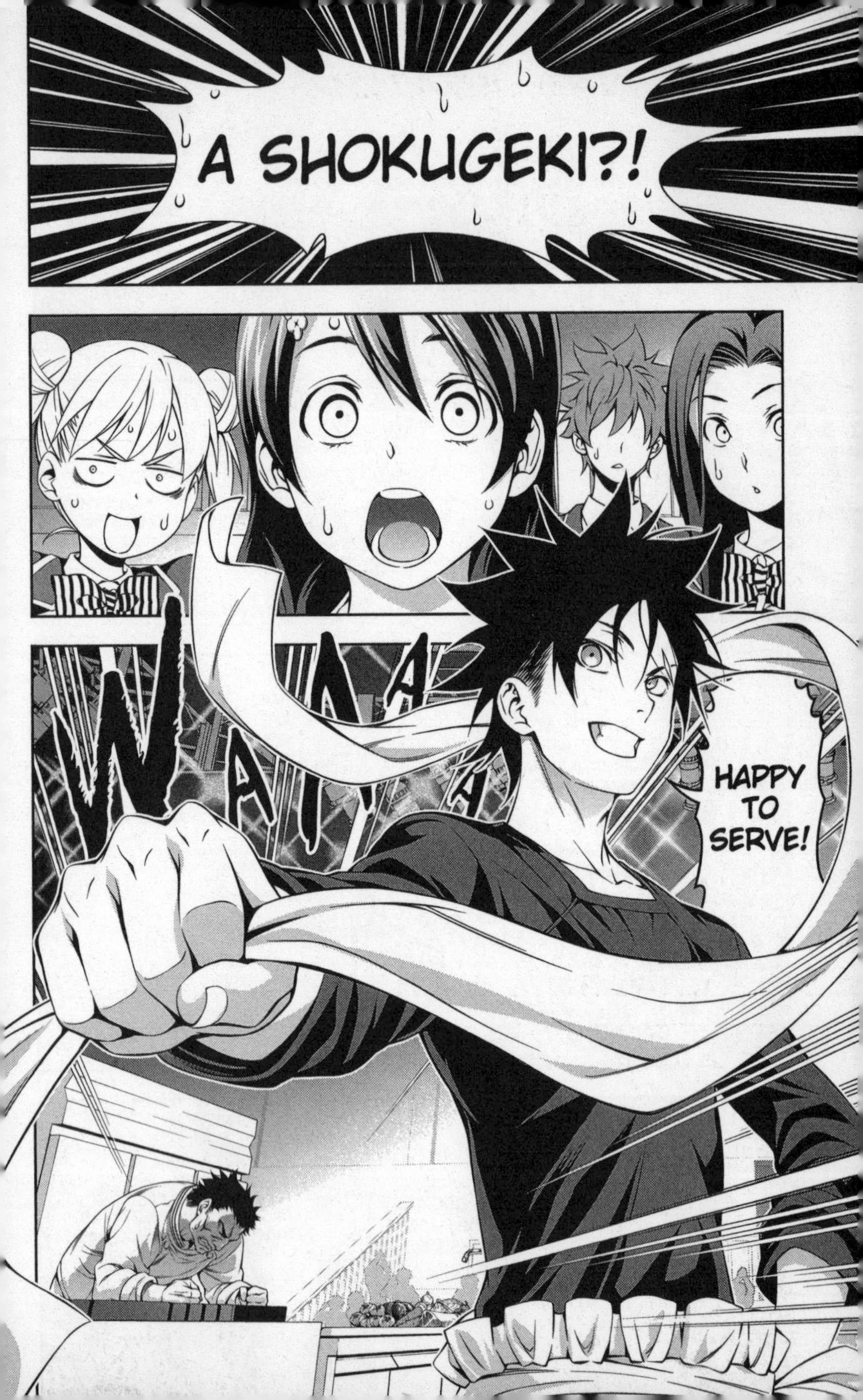
A SHOKUGEKI?!
HAPPY TO SERVE!
WAAAA

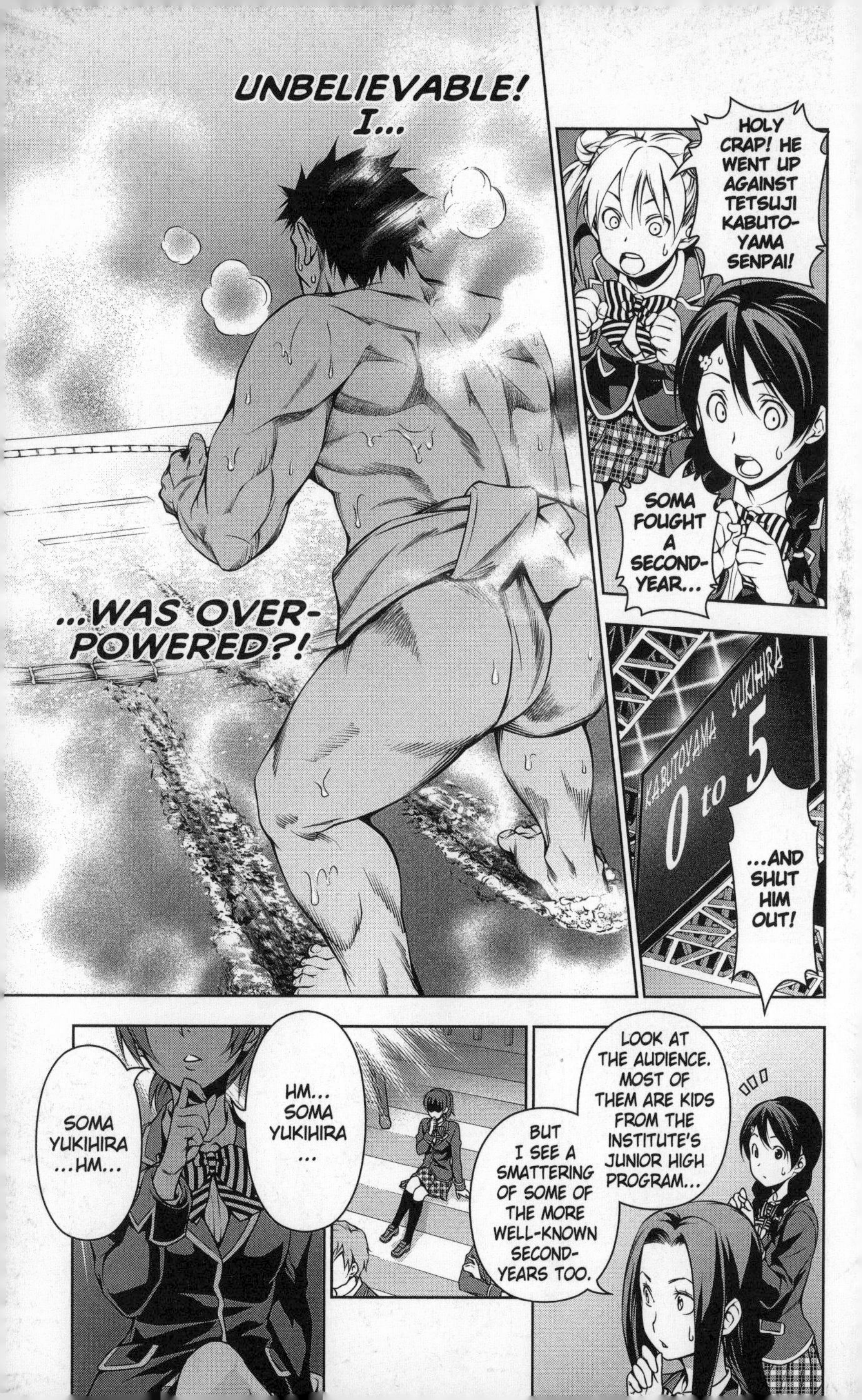
HOLY CRAP! HE WENT UP AGAINST TETSUJI KABUTOYAMA SENPAI!
SOMA FOUGHT A SECOND-YEAR...
KABUTOYAMA YUKIHIRA
0 to 5
...AND SHUT HIM OUT!
UNBELIEVABLE! I...
...WAS OVER-POWERED?!
LOOK AT THE AUDIENCE. MOST OF THEM ARE KIDS FROM THE INSTITUTE'S JUNIOR HIGH PROGRAM...
BUT I SEE A SMATTERING OF SOME OF THE MORE WELL-KNOWN SECOND-YEARS TOO.
HM... SOMA YUKIHIRA ...
SOMA YUKIHIRA ...HM...

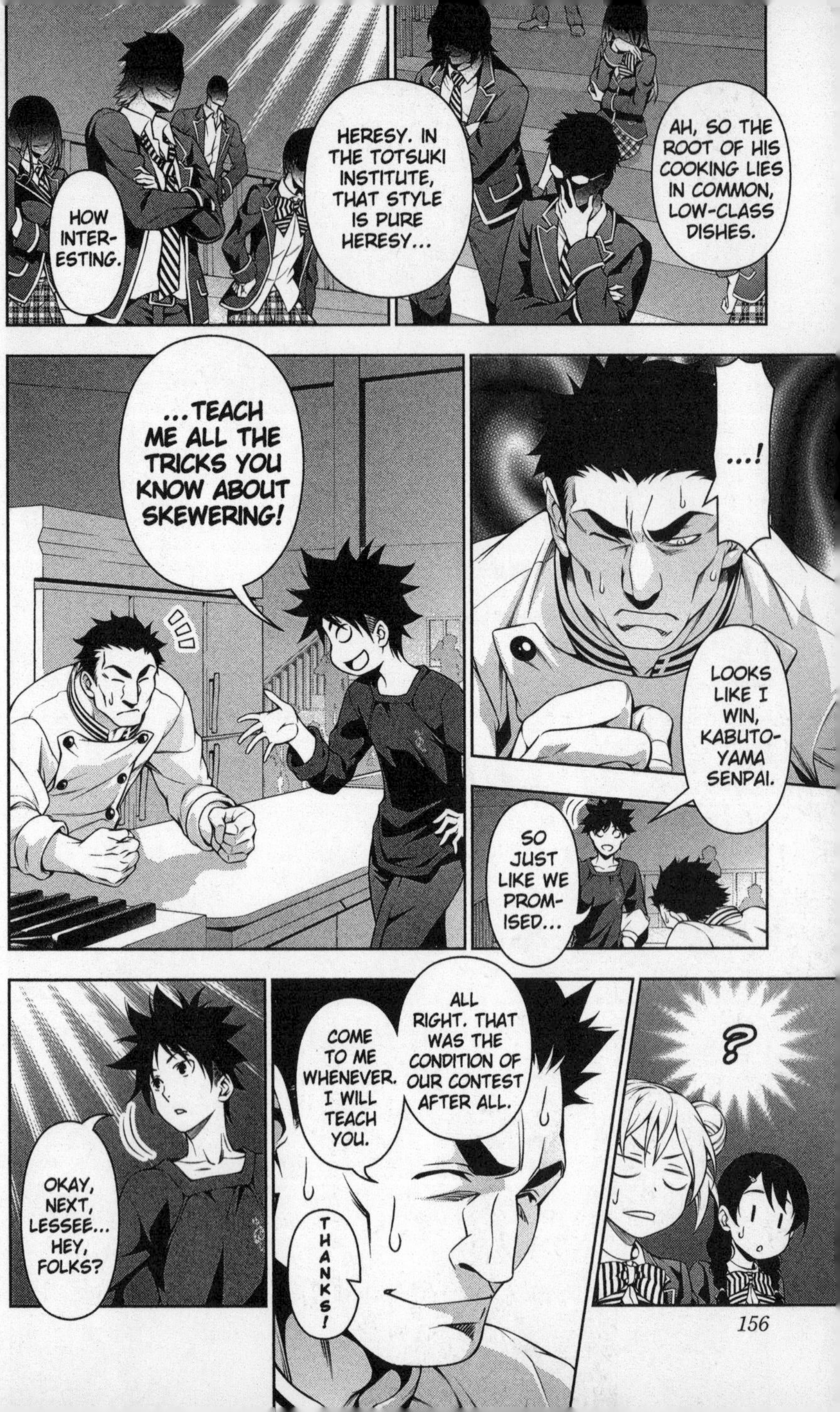

AH, SO THE ROOT OF HIS COOKING LIES IN COMMON, LOW-CLASS DISHES.
HERESY. IN THE TOTSUKI INSTITUTE, THAT STYLE IS PURE HERESY...
HOW INTER-ESTING.
...!
LOOKS LIKE I WIN, KABUTO-YAMA SENPAI.
SO JUST LIKE WE PROM-ISED...
...TEACH ME ALL THE TRICKS YOU KNOW ABOUT SKEWERING!
?
ALL RIGHT. THAT WAS THE CONDITION OF OUR CONTEST AFTER ALL.
COME TO ME WHENEVER. I WILL TEACH YOU.
THANKS!
OKAY, NEXT, LESSEE... HEY, FOLKS?

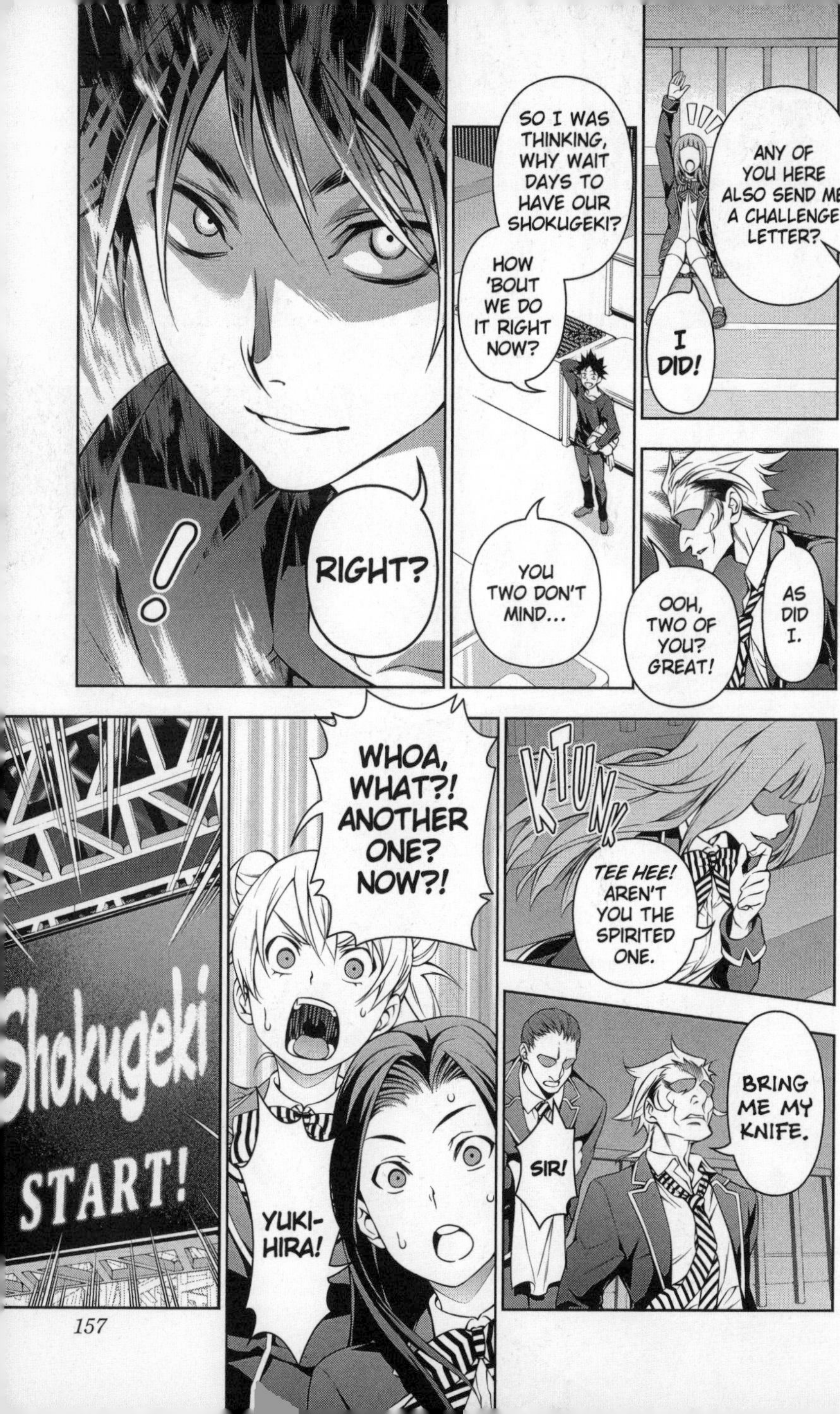
ANY OF YOU HERE ALSO SEND ME A CHALLENGE LETTER?
I DID!
AS DID I.
OOH, TWO OF YOU? GREAT!
SO I WAS THINKING, WHY WAIT DAYS TO HAVE OUR SHOKUGEKI?
HOW 'BOUT WE DO IT RIGHT NOW?
YOU TWO DON'T MIND...
RIGHT?
!
KTUNK
TEE HEE! AREN'T YOU THE SPIRITED ONE.
BRING ME MY KNIFE.
SIR!
WHOA, WHAT?! ANOTHER ONE? NOW?!
YUKI-HIRA!
Shokugeki START!

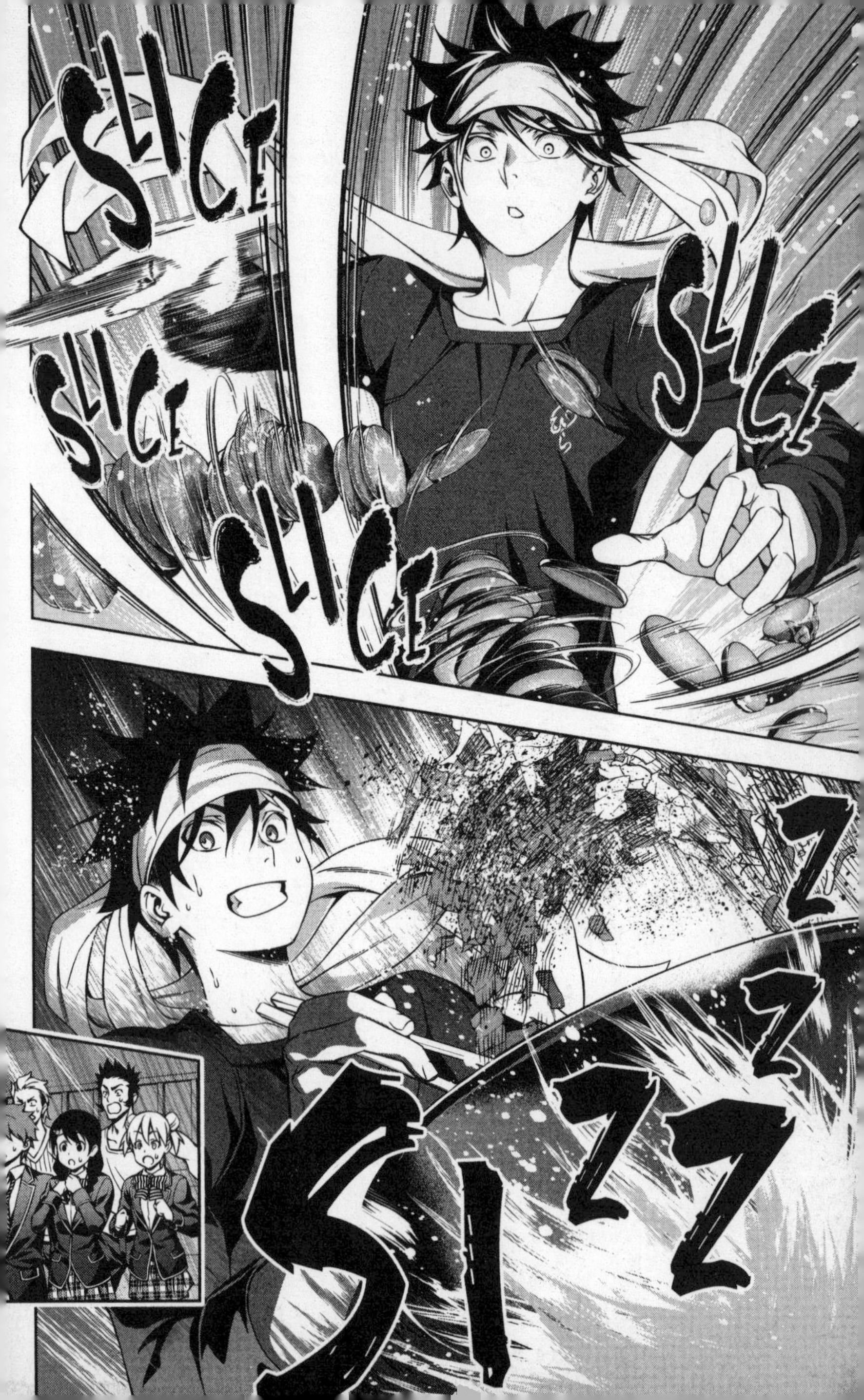
SLICE
SLICE
SLICE
SLICE
SIZZZZ

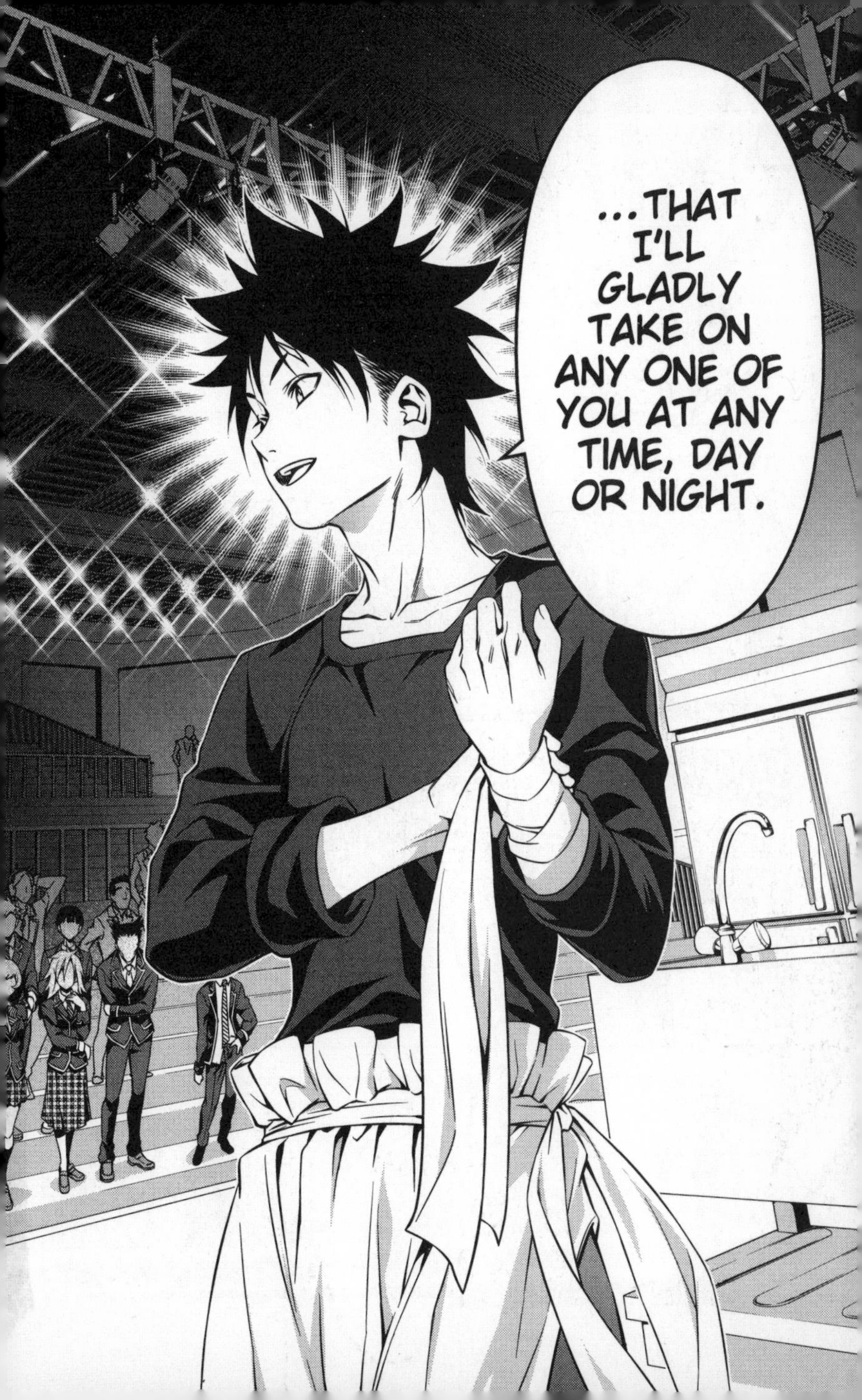
...THAT I'LL GLADLY TAKE ON ANY ONE OF YOU AT ANY TIME, DAY OR NIGHT.

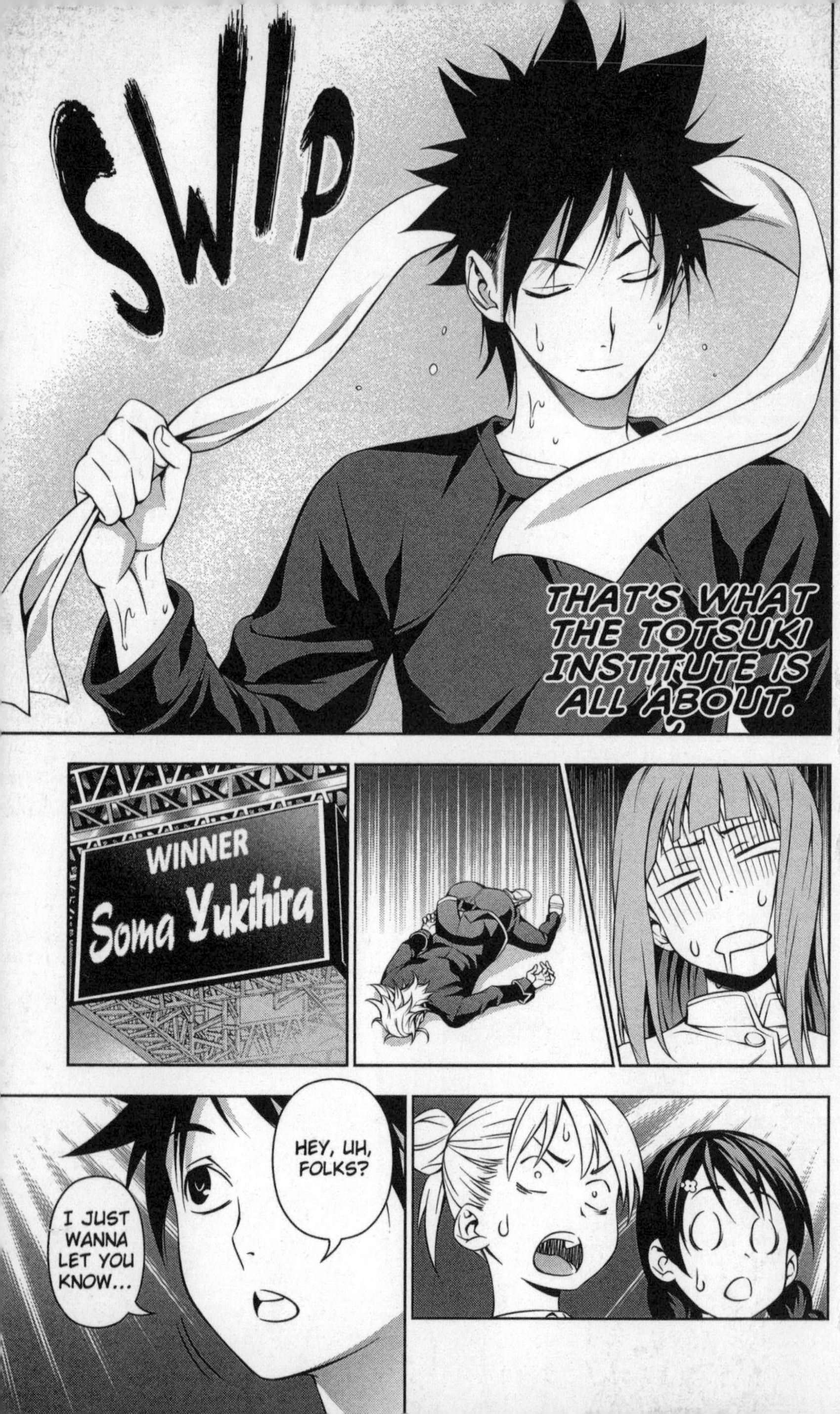
SWIP
THAT'S WHAT THE TOTSUKI INSTITUTE IS ALL ABOUT.
WINNER
Soma Yukihira
HEY, UH, FOLKS?
I JUST WANNA LET YOU KNOW...

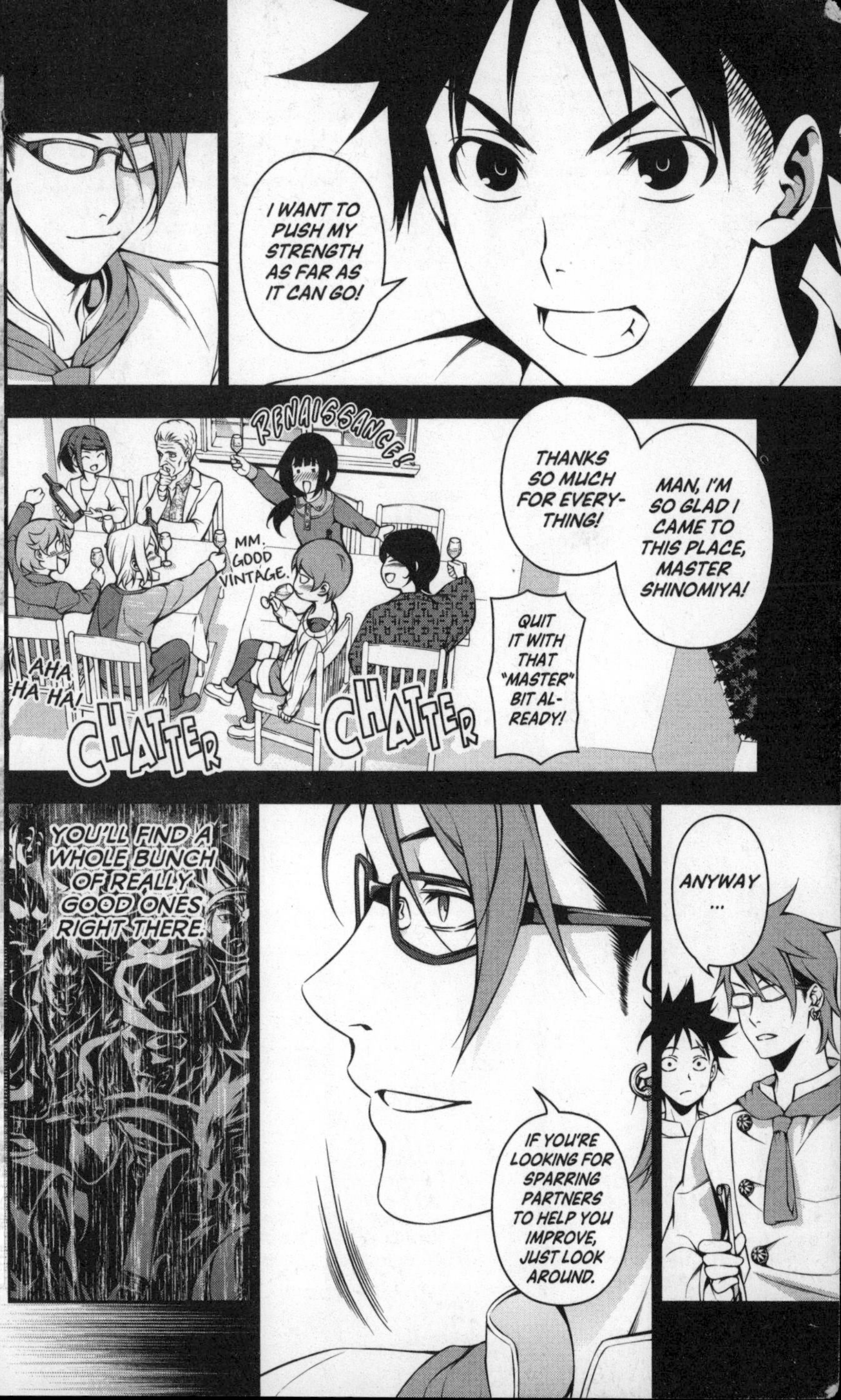
I WANT TO PUSH MY STRENGTH AS FAR AS IT CAN GO!
MAN, I'M SO GLAD I CAME TO THIS PLACE, MASTER SHINOMIYA!
THANKS SO MUCH FOR EVERY-THING!
QUIT IT WITH THAT "MASTER" BIT AL-READY!
RENAISSANCE!
MM. GOOD VINTAGE.
CHATTER
AHA HA HA!
CHATTER
ANYWAY ...
IF YOU'RE LOOKING FOR SPARRING PARTNERS TO HELP YOU IMPROVE, JUST LOOK AROUND.
YOU'LL FIND A WHOLE BUNCH OF REALLY GOOD ONES RIGHT THERE.

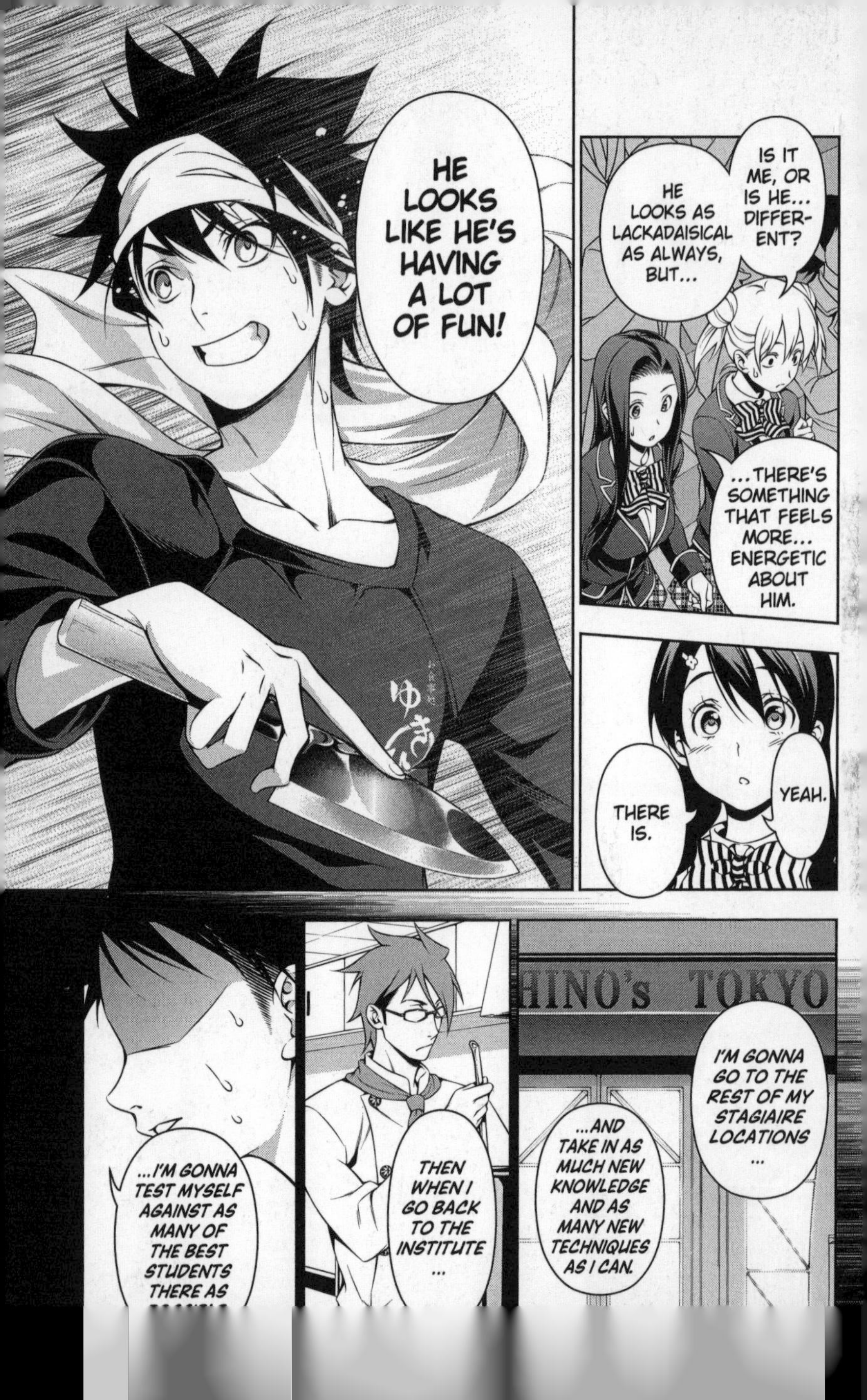
IS IT ME, OR IS HE... DIFFERENT?
HE LOOKS AS LACKADAISICAL AS ALWAYS, BUT...
...THERE'S SOMETHING THAT FEELS MORE... ENERGETIC ABOUT HIM.
YEAH.
THERE IS.
HE LOOKS LIKE HE'S HAVING A LOT OF FUN!
HINO's TOKYO
I'M GONNA GO TO THE REST OF MY STAGIAIRE LOCATIONS...
...AND TAKE IN AS MUCH NEW KNOWLEDGE AND AS MANY NEW TECHNIQUES AS I CAN.
THEN WHEN I GO BACK TO THE INSTITUTE...
...I'M GONNA TEST MYSELF AGAINST AS MANY OF THE BEST STUDENTS THERE AS

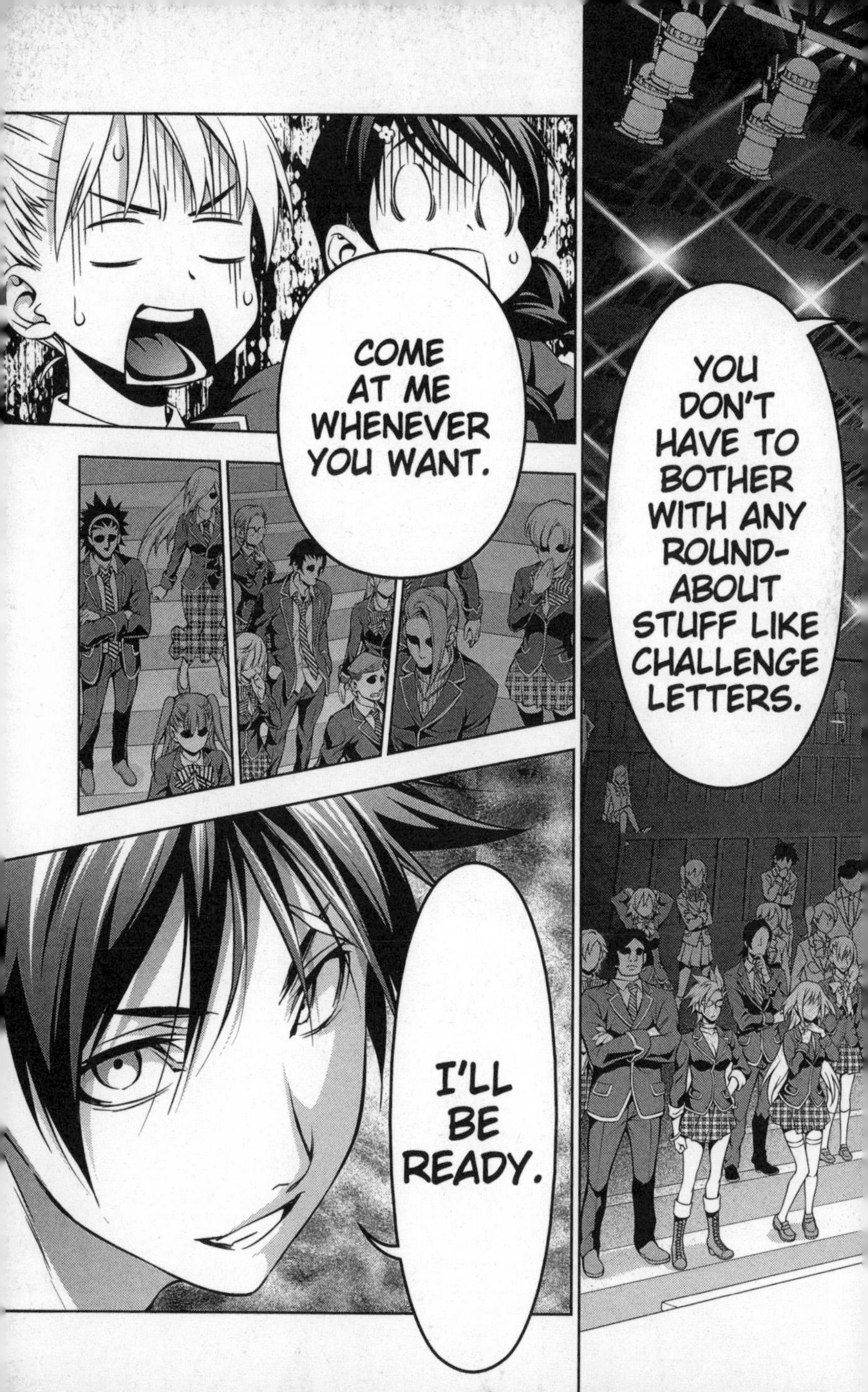
YOU DON'T HAVE TO BOTHER WITH ANY ROUND-ABOUT STUFF LIKE CHALLENGE LETTERS.
COME AT ME WHENEVER YOU WANT.
I'LL BE READY.

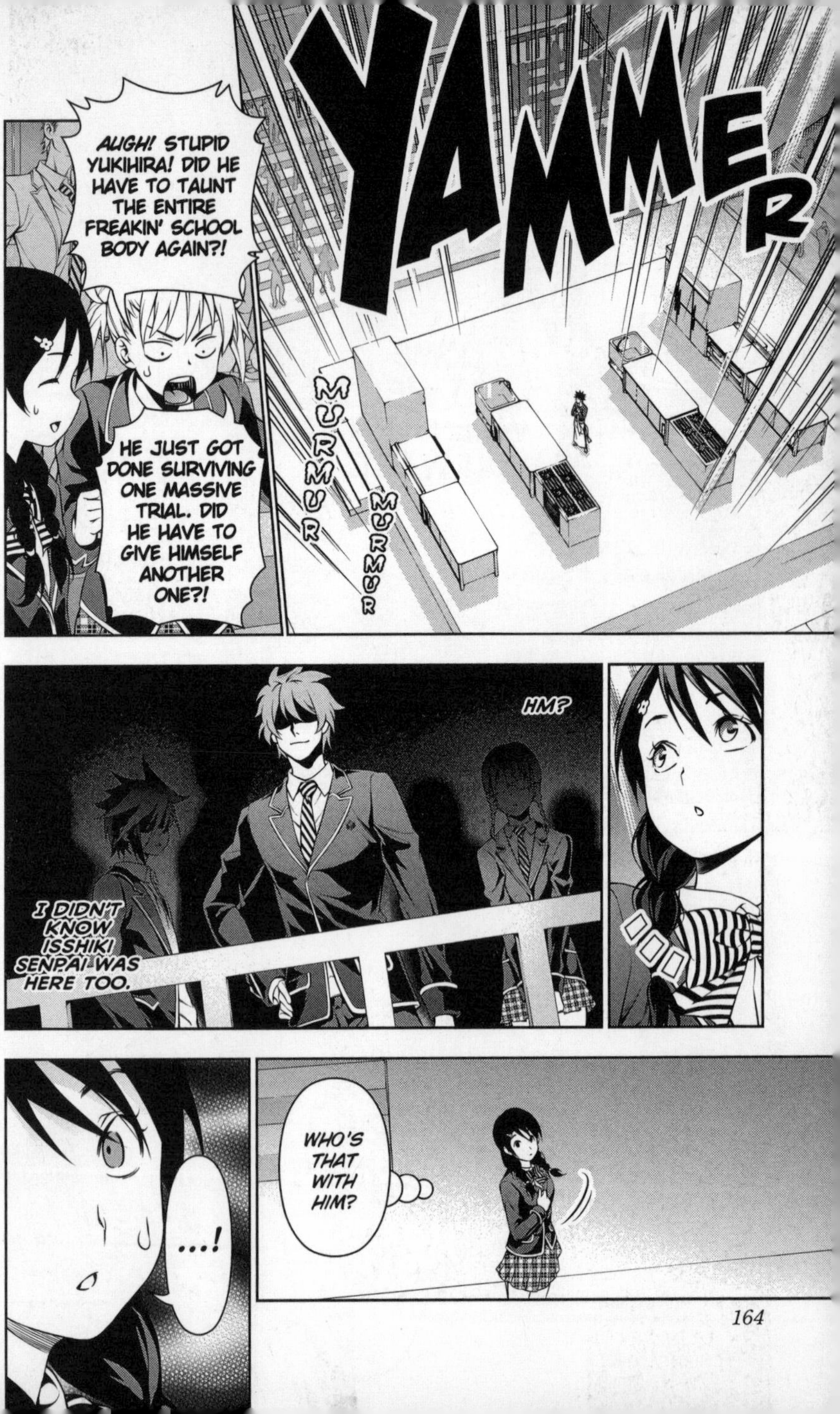

YAMMER
MURMUR
MURMUR
AUGH! STUPID YUKIHIRA! DID HE HAVE TO TAUNT THE ENTIRE FREAKIN' SCHOOL BODY AGAIN?!
HE JUST GOT DONE SURVIVING ONE MASSIVE TRIAL. DID HE HAVE TO GIVE HIMSELF ANOTHER ONE?!
HM?
I DIDN'T KNOW ISSHIKI SENPAI WAS HERE TOO.
WHO'S THAT WITH HIM?
...!

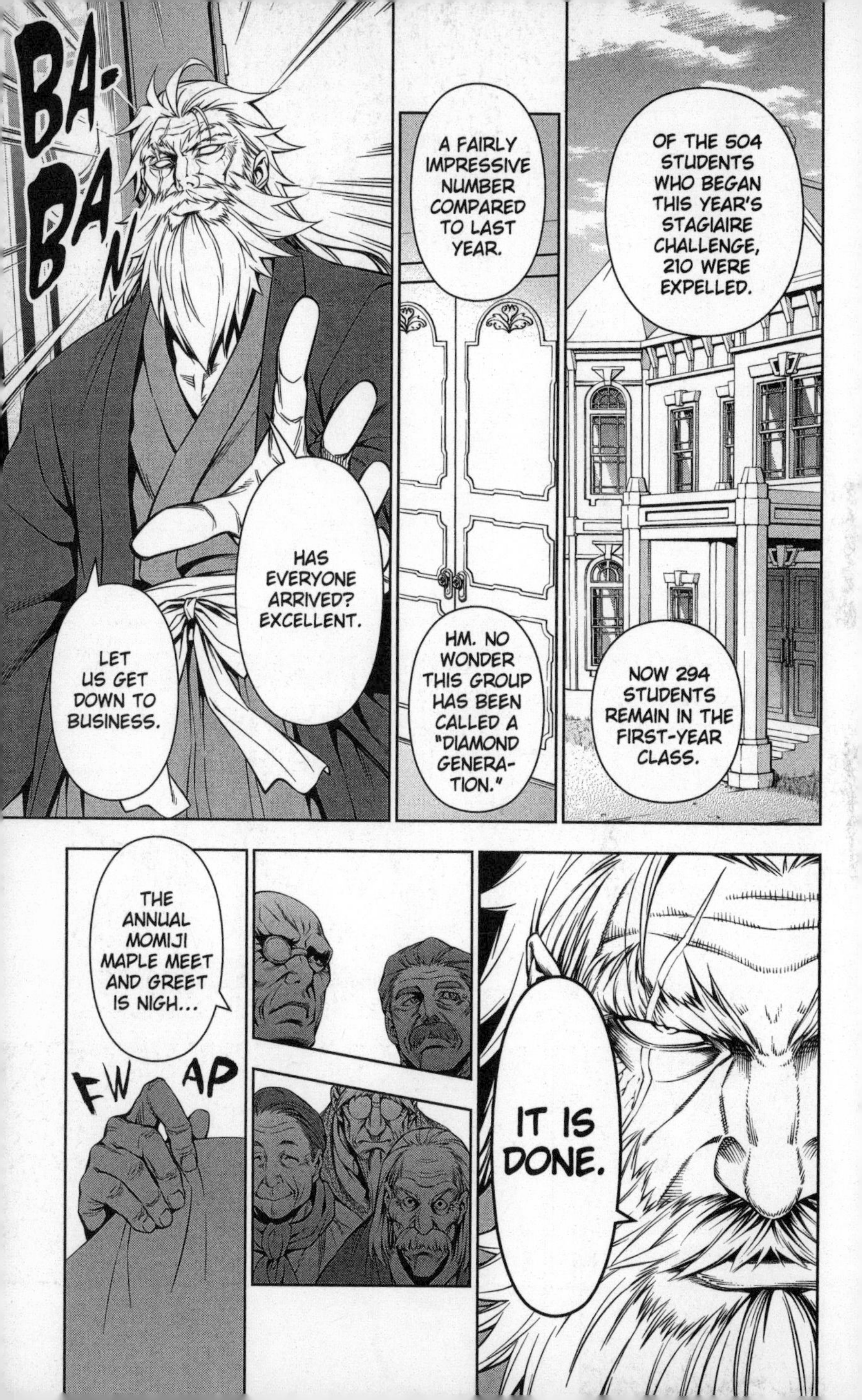
OF THE 504 STUDENTS WHO BEGAN THIS YEAR'S STAGIAIRE CHALLENGE, 210 WERE EXPELLED.
NOW 294 STUDENTS REMAIN IN THE FIRST-YEAR CLASS.
A FAIRLY IMPRESSIVE NUMBER COMPARED TO LAST YEAR.
HM. NO WONDER THIS GROUP HAS BEEN CALLED A "DIAMOND GENERATION."
BA-BA-N
HAS EVERYONE ARRIVED? EXCELLENT.
LET US GET DOWN TO BUSINESS.
IT IS DONE.
THE ANNUAL MOMIJI MAPLE MEET AND GREET IS NIGH...
FWAP

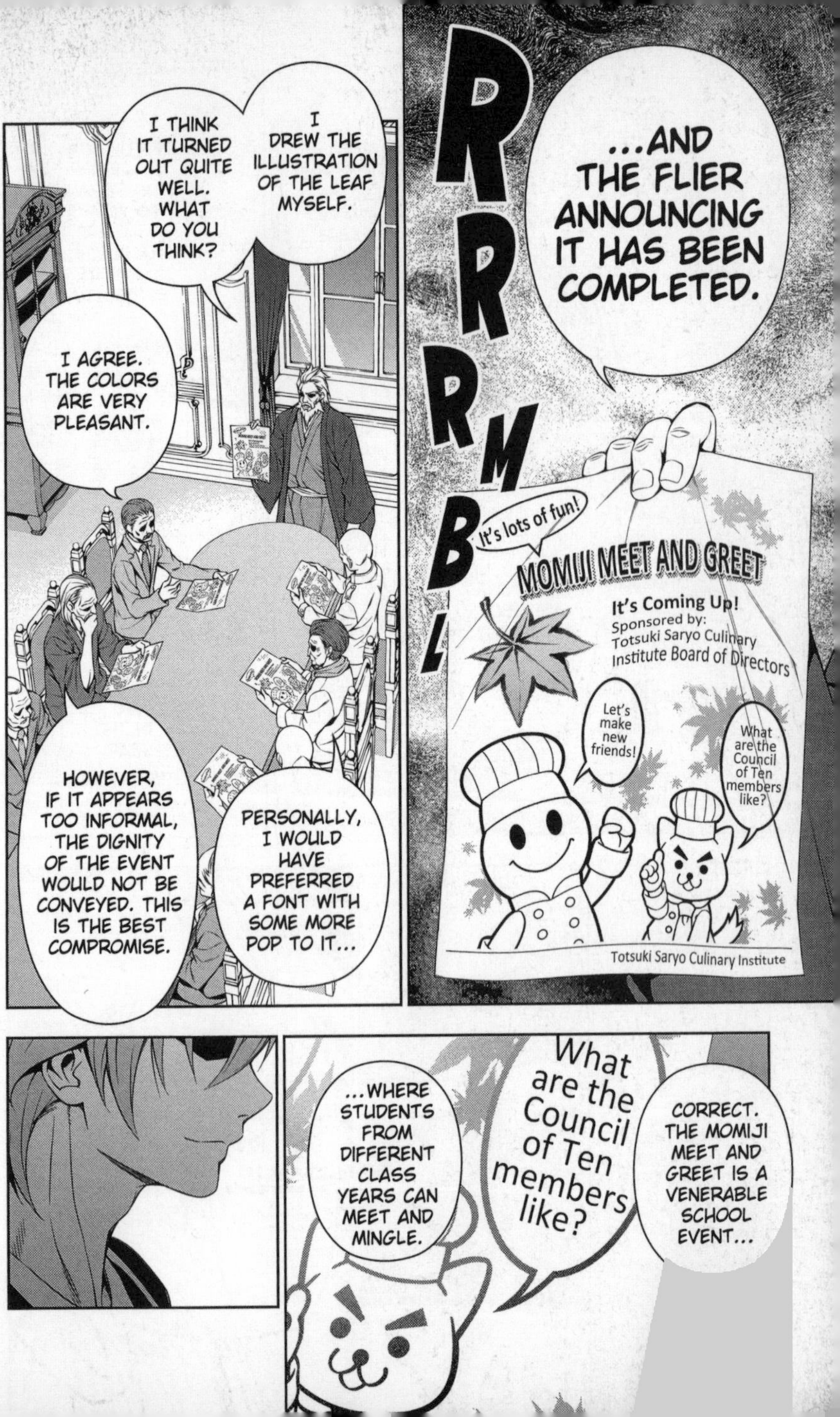
...AND THE FLIER ANNOUNCING IT HAS BEEN COMPLETED.
RRRRMBL
It's lots of fun!
MOMIJI MEET AND GREET
It's Coming Up!
Sponsored by: Totsuki Saryo Culinary Institute Board of Directors
Let's make new friends!
What are the Council of Ten members like?
Totsuki Saryo Culinary Institute
I DREW THE ILLUSTRATION OF THE LEAF MYSELF.
I THINK IT TURNED OUT QUITE WELL. WHAT DO YOU THINK?
I AGREE. THE COLORS ARE VERY PLEASANT.
PERSONALLY, I WOULD HAVE PREFERRED A FONT WITH SOME MORE POP TO IT...
HOWEVER, IF IT APPEARS TOO INFORMAL, THE DIGNITY OF THE EVENT WOULD NOT BE CONVEYED. THIS IS THE BEST COMPROMISE.
CORRECT. THE MOMIJI MEET AND GREET IS A VENERABLE SCHOOL EVENT...
What are the Council of Ten members like?
...WHERE STUDENTS FROM DIFFERENT CLASS YEARS CAN MEET AND MINGLE.

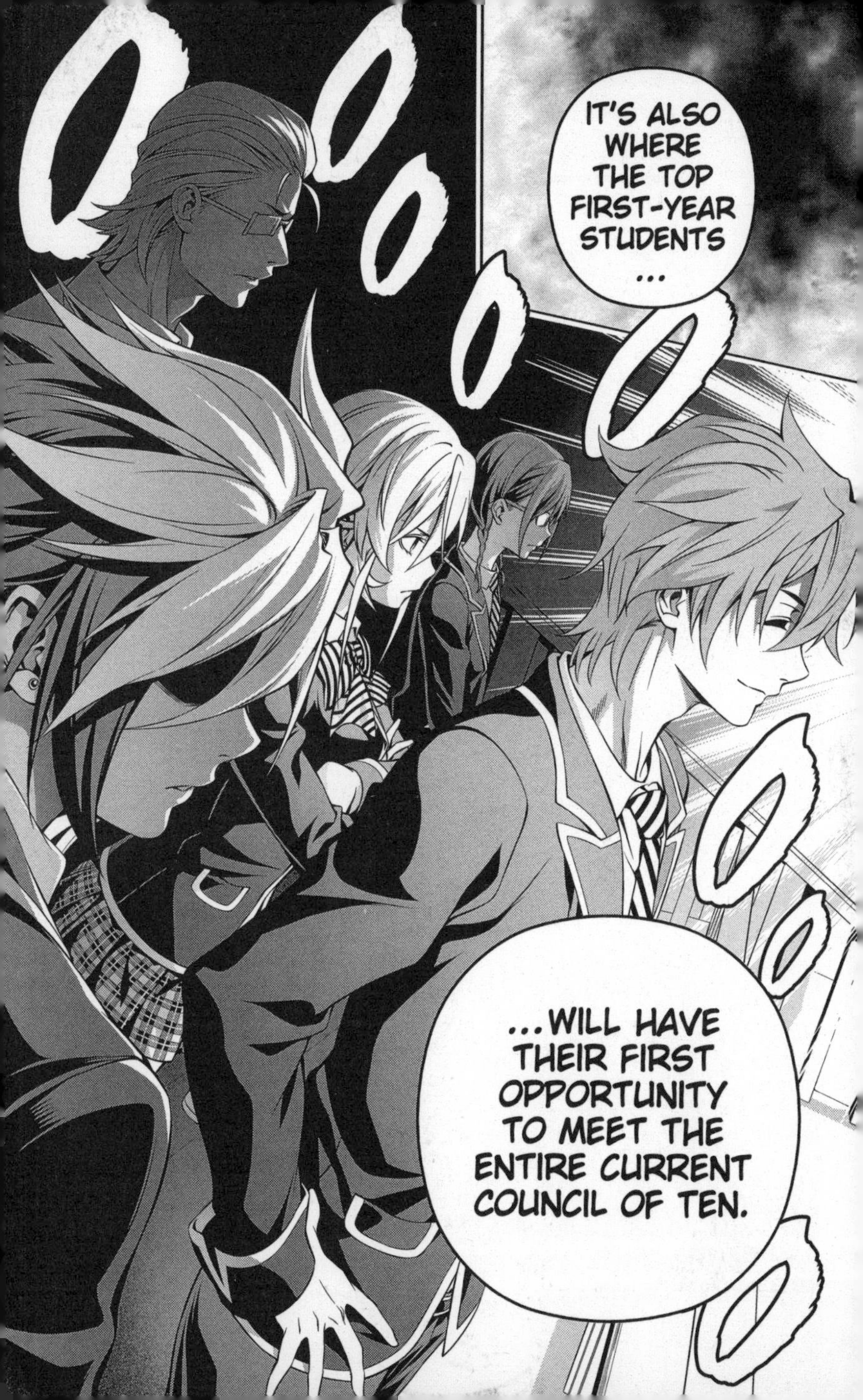
IT'S ALSO WHERE THE TOP FIRST-YEAR STUDENTS ...
...WILL HAVE THEIR FIRST OPPORTUNITY TO MEET THE ENTIRE CURRENT COUNCIL OF TEN.

THE TOTSUKI INSTITUTE
OFFICIAL MASCOTS

MR. CHEF

MR. DOG

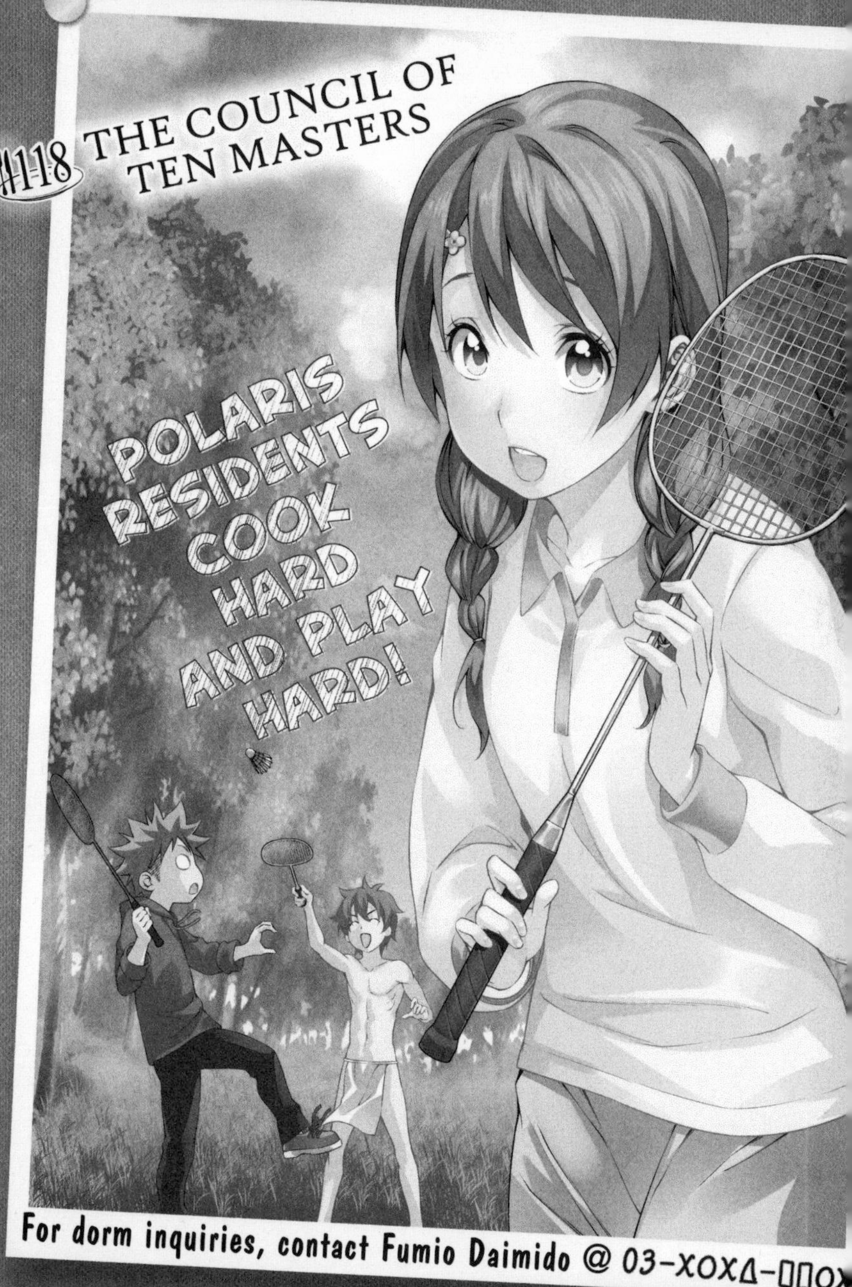
#118 THE COUNCIL OF TEN MASTERS
POLARIS RESIDENTS COOK HARD AND PLAY HARD!
For dorm inquiries, contact Fumio Daimido @ 03-XOXΔ-□□OX

**\*THE MOMIJI MEET AND GREET**

IN THE WEST, THE MOMIJI TREE IS KNOWN AS THE JAPANESE MAPLE. A DECIDUOUS TREE, THE MOMIJI'S LEAVES TURN BEAUTIFUL COLORS IN THE FALL. LIKE CHERRY BLOSSOM VIEWINGS IN SPRING, A POPULAR JAPANESE FALL PASTIME IS THE *MOMIJI-GARI*, OR MAPLE-LEAF VIEWING PARTY. FAMILIES AND FRIENDS VISIT SCENIC AREAS TO HAVE PICNICS AND VIEW THE FALL FOLIAGE. TOTSUKI'S MOMIJI MEET AND GREET IS MODELED AFTER THIS PRACTICE.

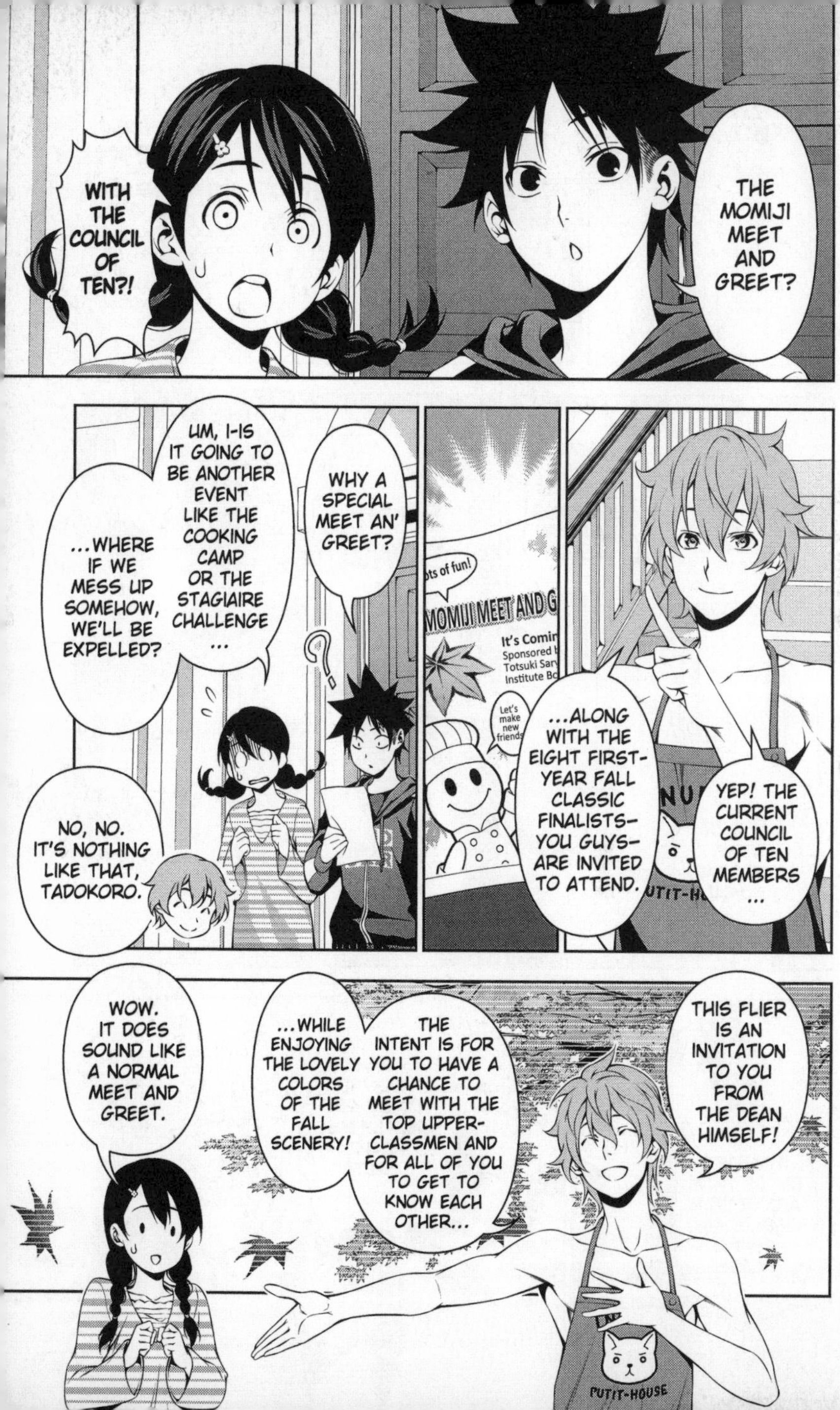
THE MOMIJI MEET AND GREET?
WITH THE COUNCIL OF TEN?!
YEP! THE CURRENT COUNCIL OF TEN MEMBERS ...
...ALONG WITH THE EIGHT FIRST-YEAR FALL CLASSIC FINALISTS—YOU GUYS—ARE INVITED TO ATTEND.
MOMIJI MEET AND G
Let's make new friends
WHY A SPECIAL MEET AN' GREET?
UM, I-IS IT GOING TO BE ANOTHER EVENT LIKE THE COOKING CAMP OR THE STAGIAIRE CHALLENGE ...
...WHERE IF WE MESS UP SOMEHOW, WE'LL BE EXPELLED?
NO, NO. IT'S NOTHING LIKE THAT, TADOKORO.
THIS FLIER IS AN INVITATION TO YOU FROM THE DEAN HIMSELF!
THE INTENT IS FOR YOU TO HAVE A CHANCE TO MEET WITH THE TOP UPPER-CLASSMEN AND FOR ALL OF YOU TO GET TO KNOW EACH OTHER...
...WHILE ENJOYING THE LOVELY COLORS OF THE FALL SCENERY!
WOW. IT DOES SOUND LIKE A NORMAL MEET AND GREET.
PUTIT-HOUSE

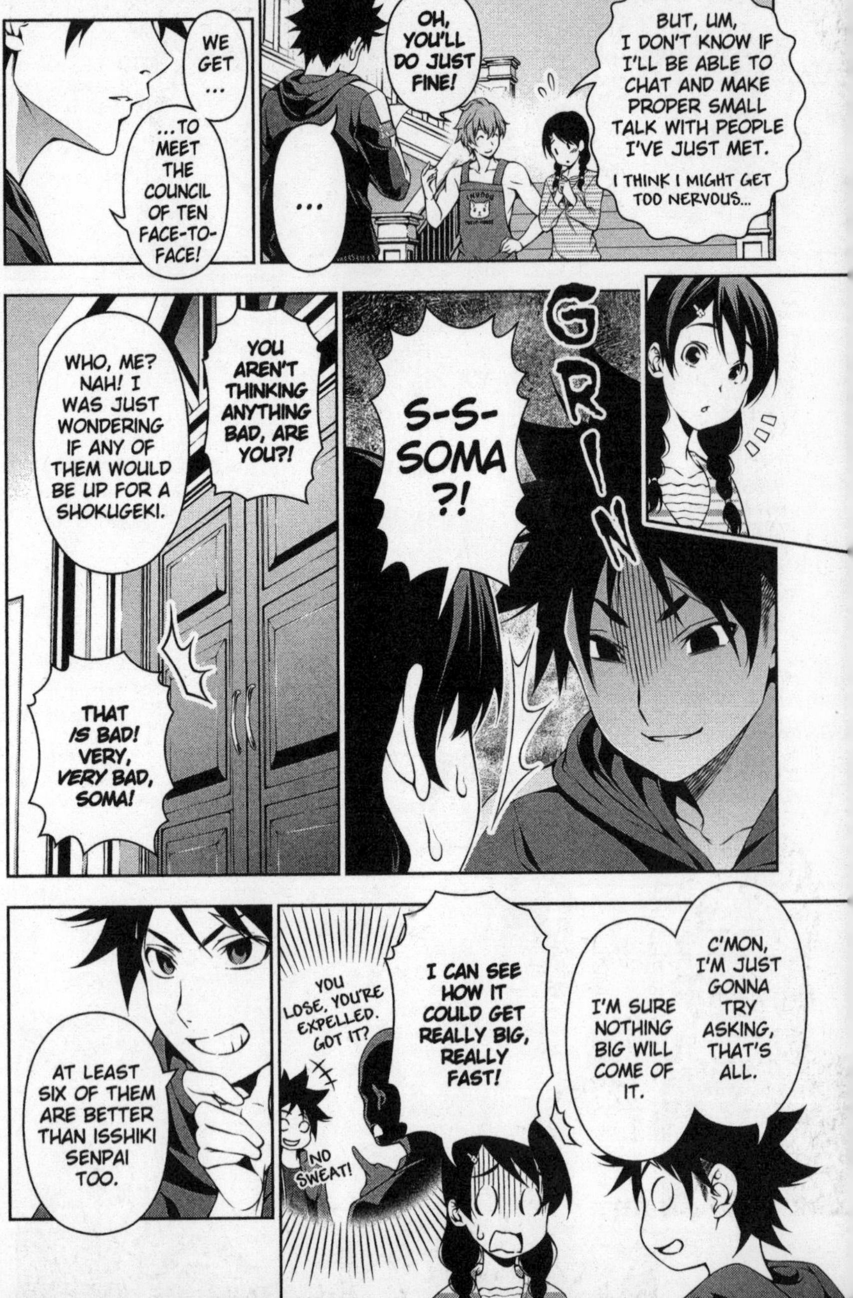
BUT, UM, I DON'T KNOW IF I'LL BE ABLE TO CHAT AND MAKE PROPER SMALL TALK WITH PEOPLE I'VE JUST MET.
I THINK I MIGHT GET TOO NERVOUS...
OH, YOU'LL DO JUST FINE!
...
WE GET ...
...TO MEET THE COUNCIL OF TEN FACE-TO-FACE!
GRIN
S-S-SOMA?!
YOU AREN'T THINKING ANYTHING BAD, ARE YOU?!
WHO, ME? NAH! I WAS JUST WONDERING IF ANY OF THEM WOULD BE UP FOR A SHOKUGEKI.
THAT IS BAD! VERY, VERY BAD, SOMA!
C'MON, I'M JUST GONNA TRY ASKING, THAT'S ALL.
I'M SURE NOTHING BIG WILL COME OF IT.
I CAN SEE HOW IT COULD GET REALLY BIG, REALLY FAST!
YOU LOSE, YOU'RE EXPELLED. GOT IT?
NO SWEAT!
AT LEAST SIX OF THEM ARE BETTER THAN ISSHIKI SENPAI TOO.

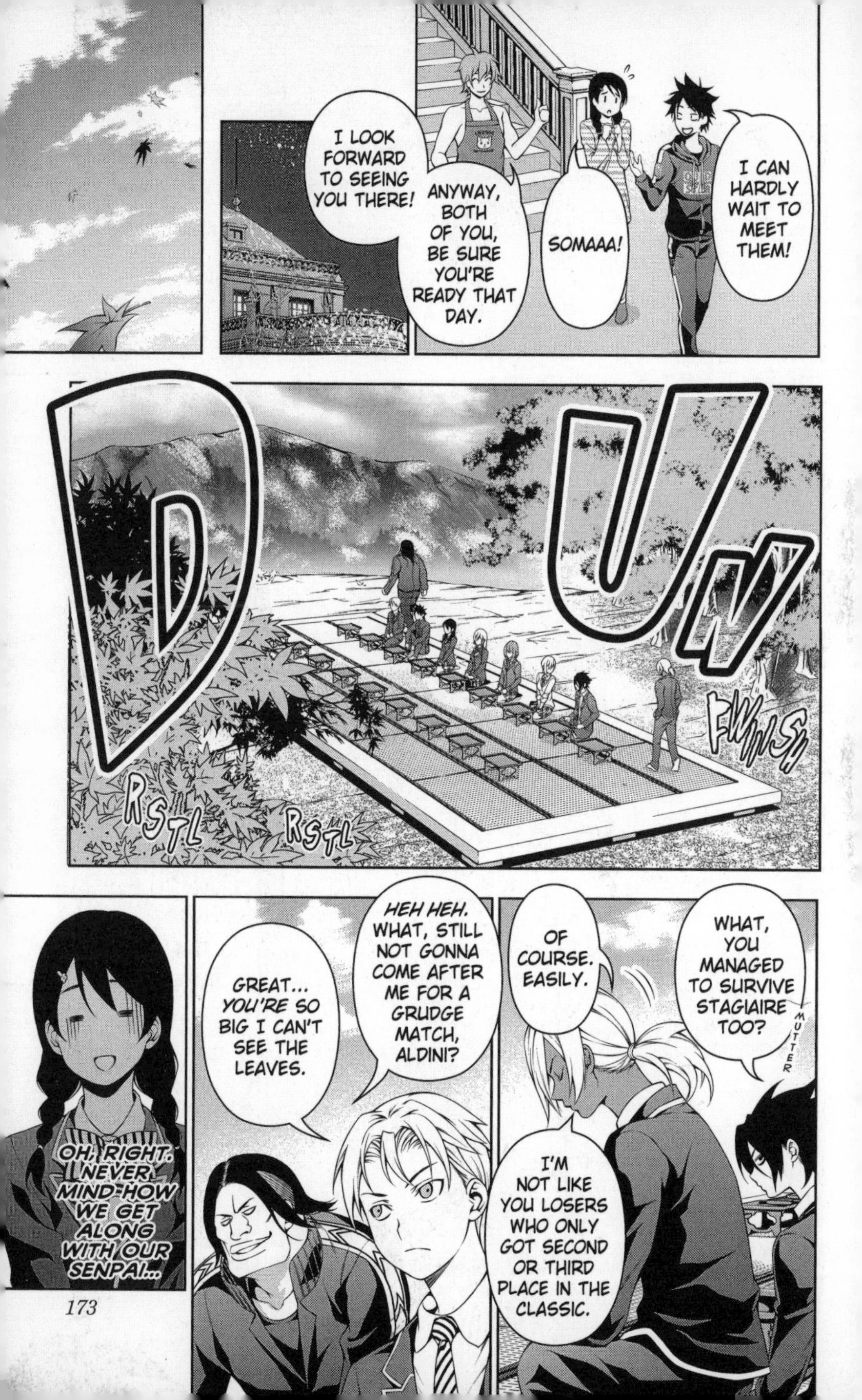
I CAN HARDLY WAIT TO MEET THEM!
SOMAAA!
ANYWAY, BOTH OF YOU, BE SURE YOU'RE READY THAT DAY.
I LOOK FORWARD TO SEEING YOU THERE!
DUN
FWSH
RSTL
RSTL
WHAT, YOU MANAGED TO SURVIVE STAGIAIRE TOO?
MUTTER
OF COURSE. EASILY.
I'M NOT LIKE YOU LOSERS WHO ONLY GOT SECOND OR THIRD PLACE IN THE CLASSIC.
HEH HEH. WHAT, STILL NOT GONNA COME AFTER ME FOR A GRUDGE MATCH, ALDINI?
GREAT... YOU'RE SO BIG I CAN'T SEE THE LEAVES.
OH, RIGHT. NEVER MIND HOW WE GET ALONG WITH OUR SENPAI...

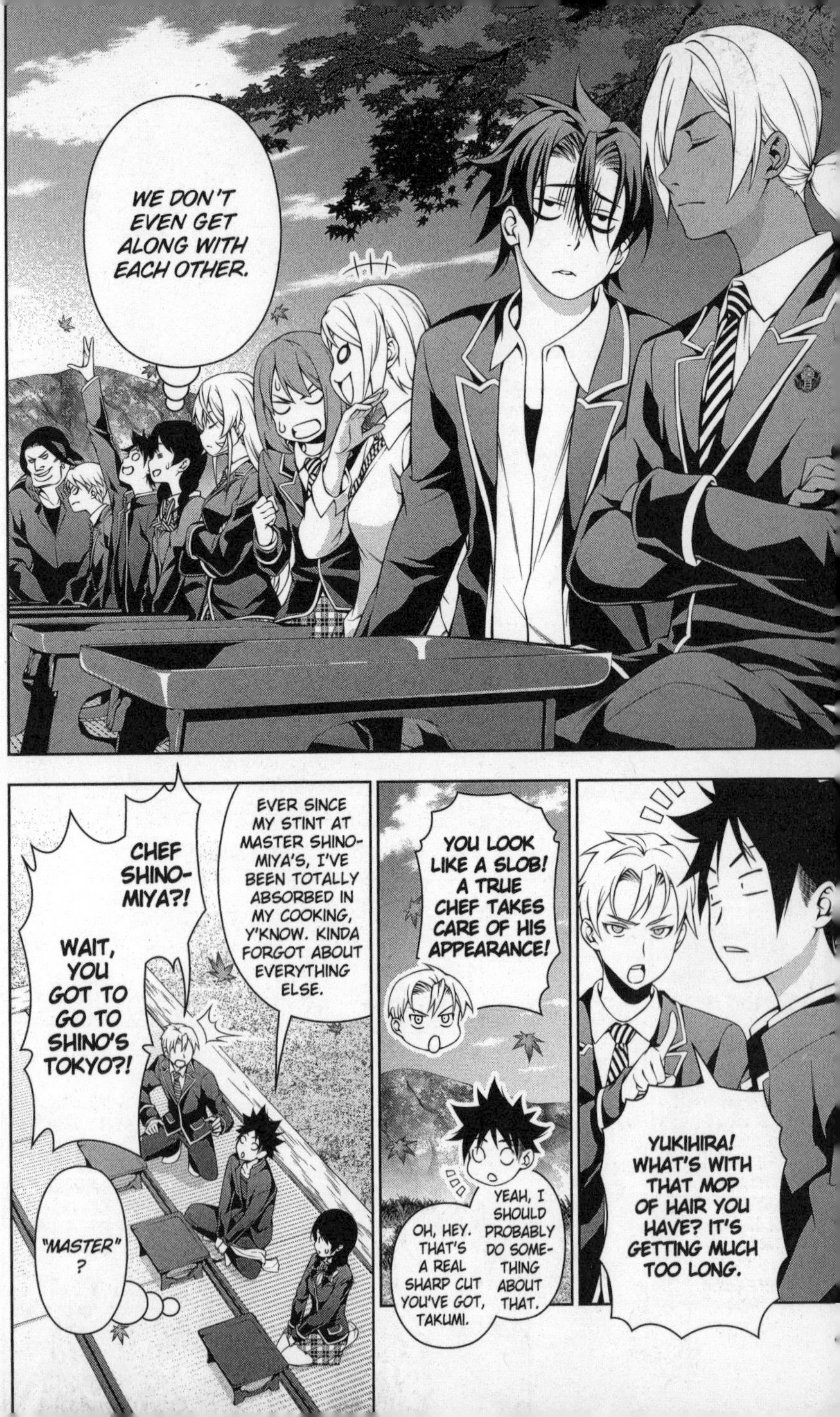
WE DON'T EVEN GET ALONG WITH EACH OTHER.
YUKIHIRA! WHAT'S WITH THAT MOP OF HAIR YOU HAVE? IT'S GETTING MUCH TOO LONG.
YOU LOOK LIKE A SLOB! A TRUE CHEF TAKES CARE OF HIS APPEARANCE!
YEAH, I SHOULD PROBABLY DO SOMETHING ABOUT THAT.
OH, HEY. THAT'S A REAL SHARP CUT YOU'VE GOT, TAKUMI.
EVER SINCE MY STINT AT MASTER SHINOMIYA'S, I'VE BEEN TOTALLY ABSORBED IN MY COOKING, Y'KNOW. KINDA FORGOT ABOUT EVERYTHING ELSE.
CHEF SHINOMIYA?!
WAIT, YOU GOT TO GO TO SHINO'S TOKYO?!
"MASTER"?

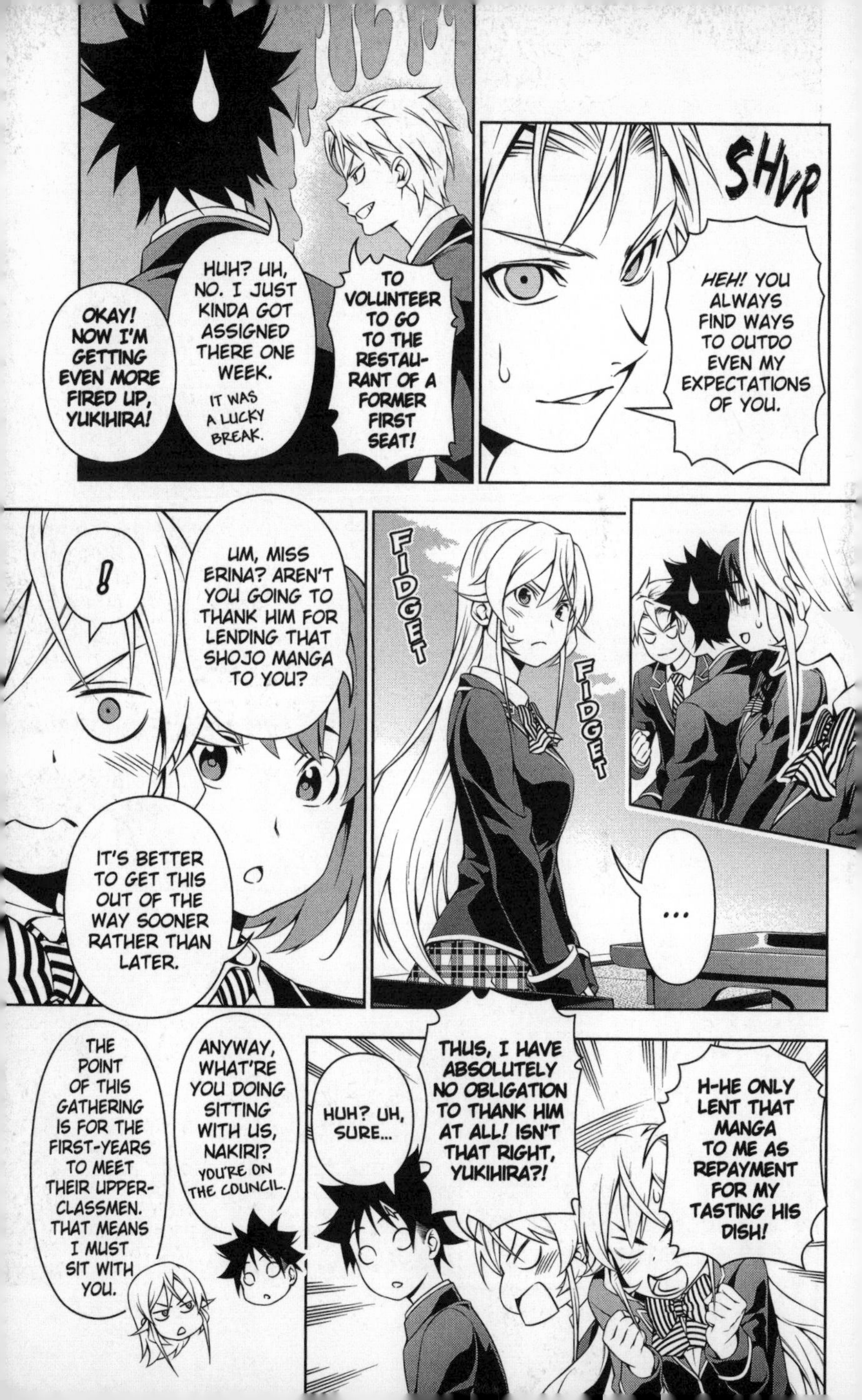
SHVR
HEH! YOU ALWAYS FIND WAYS TO OUTDO EVEN MY EXPECTATIONS OF YOU.
TO VOLUNTEER TO GO TO THE RESTAURANT OF A FORMER FIRST SEAT!
HUH? UH, NO. I JUST KINDA GOT ASSIGNED THERE ONE WEEK.
IT WAS A LUCKY BREAK.
OKAY! NOW I'M GETTING EVEN MORE FIRED UP, YUKIHIRA!
FIDGET
FIDGET
...
UM, MISS ERINA? AREN'T YOU GOING TO THANK HIM FOR LENDING THAT SHOJO MANGA TO YOU?
!
IT'S BETTER TO GET THIS OUT OF THE WAY SOONER RATHER THAN LATER.
H-HE ONLY LENT THAT MANGA TO ME AS REPAYMENT FOR MY TASTING HIS DISH!
THUS, I HAVE ABSOLUTELY NO OBLIGATION TO THANK HIM AT ALL! ISN'T THAT RIGHT, YUKIHIRA?!
HUH? UH, SURE...
ANYWAY, WHAT'RE YOU DOING SITTING WITH US, NAKIRI?
YOU'RE ON THE COUNCIL.
THE POINT OF THIS GATHERING IS FOR THE FIRST-YEARS TO MEET THEIR UPPERCLASSMEN. THAT MEANS I MUST SIT WITH YOU.

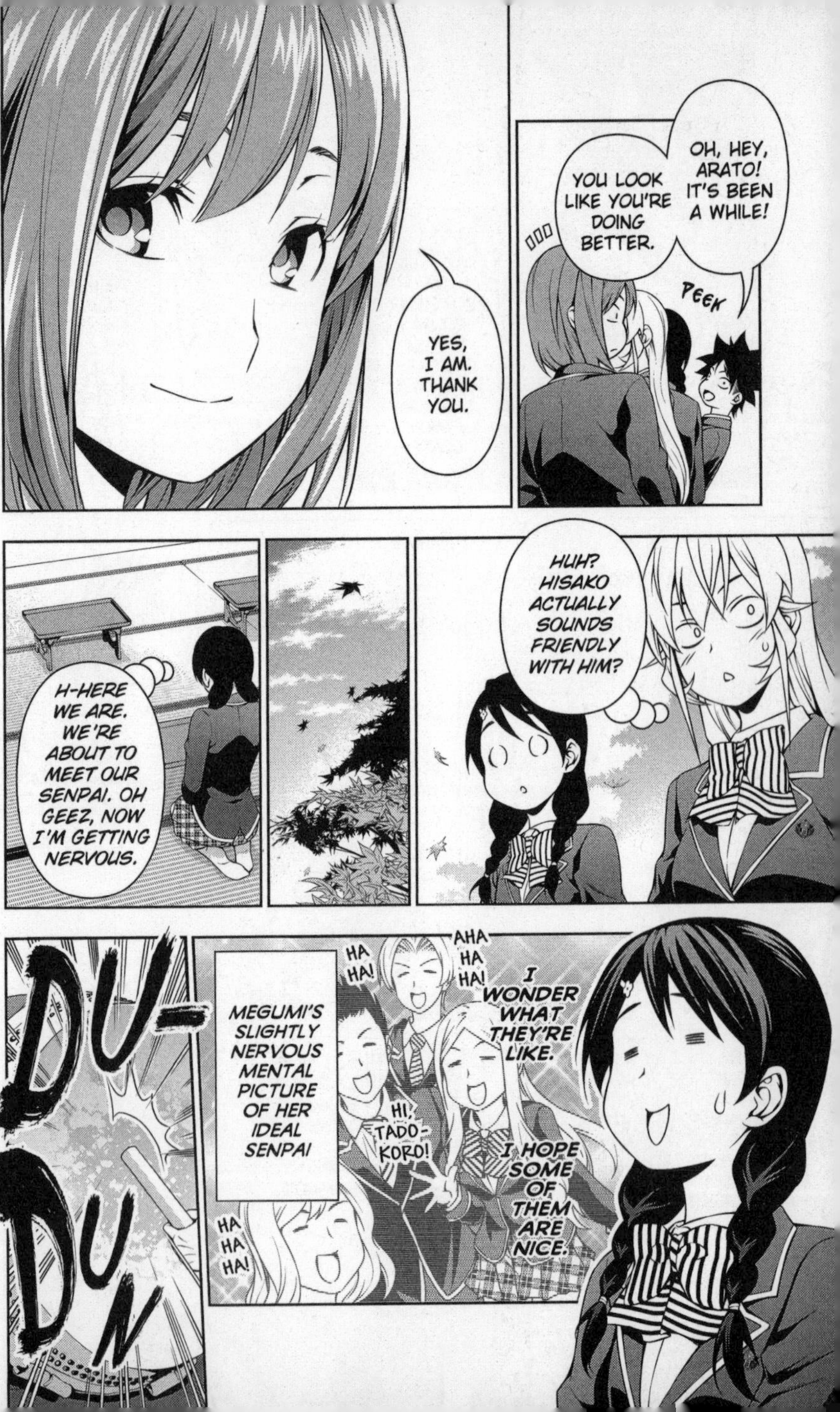
OH, HEY, ARATO! IT'S BEEN A WHILE!
YOU LOOK LIKE YOU'RE DOING BETTER.
PEEK
YES, I AM. THANK YOU.
HUH? HISAKO ACTUALLY SOUNDS FRIENDLY WITH HIM?
H-HERE WE ARE. WE'RE ABOUT TO MEET OUR SENPAI. OH GEEZ, NOW I'M GETTING NERVOUS.
I WONDER WHAT THEY'RE LIKE.
I HOPE SOME OF THEM ARE NICE.
AHA HA HA!
HA HA!
MEGUMI'S SLIGHTLY NERVOUS MENTAL PICTURE OF HER IDEAL SENPAI
HI, TADO-KORO!
HA HA HA!
DU-DUN

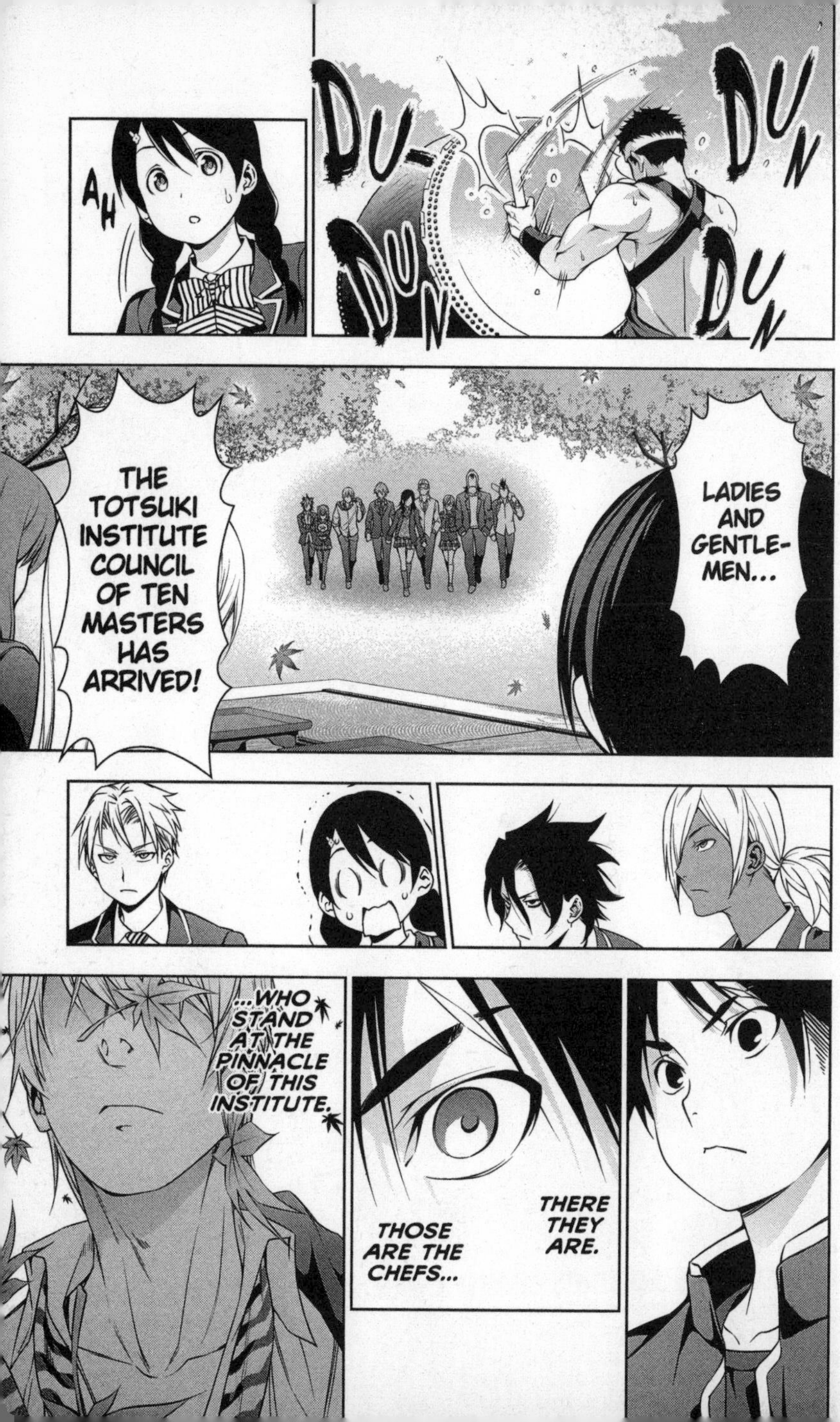
DUN
DUN
DU-DUN
AH
LADIES AND GENTLEMEN...
THE TOTSUKI INSTITUTE COUNCIL OF TEN MASTERS HAS ARRIVED!
THERE THEY ARE.
THOSE ARE THE CHEFS...
...WHO STAND AT THE PINNACLE OF THIS INSTITUTE.

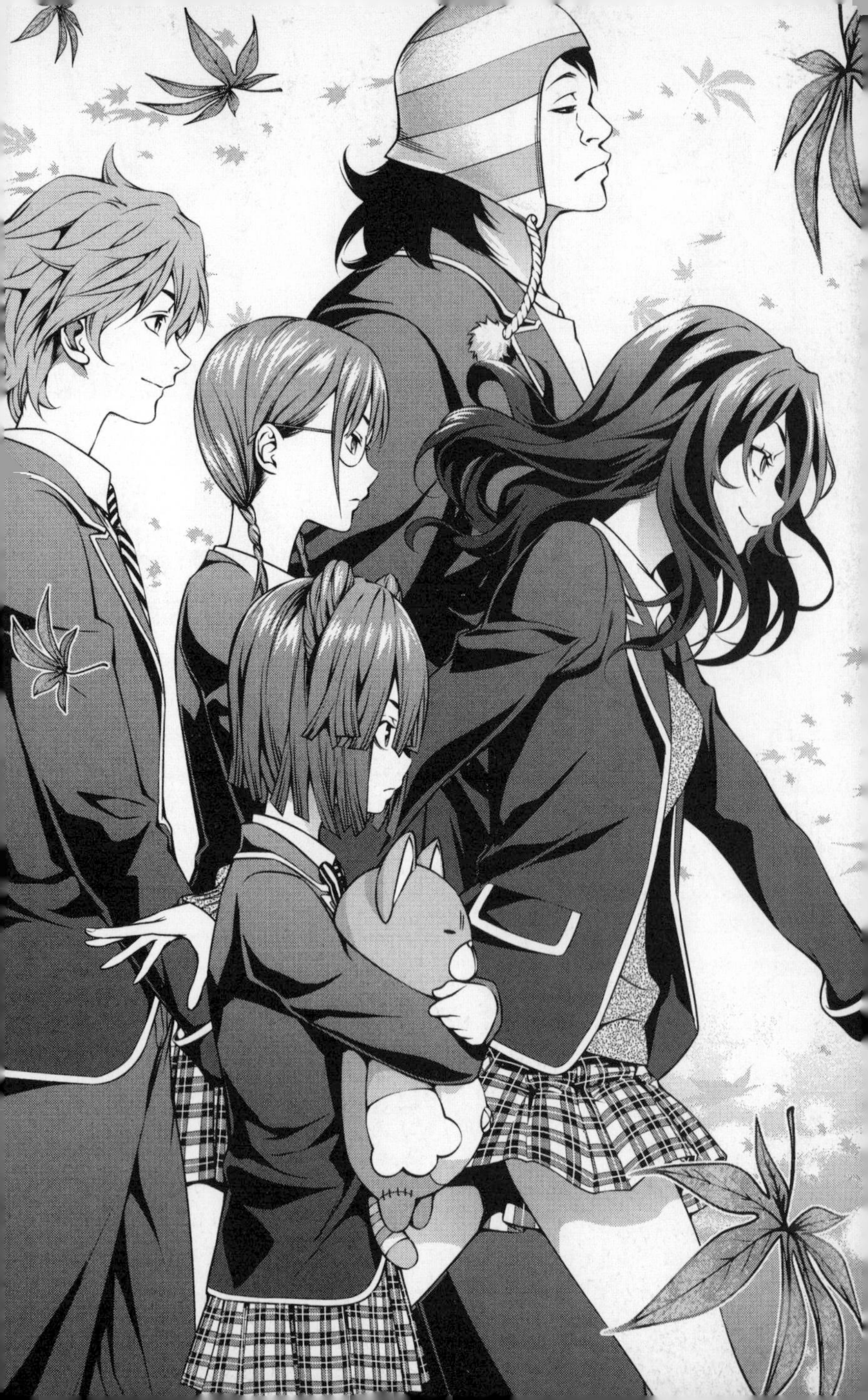

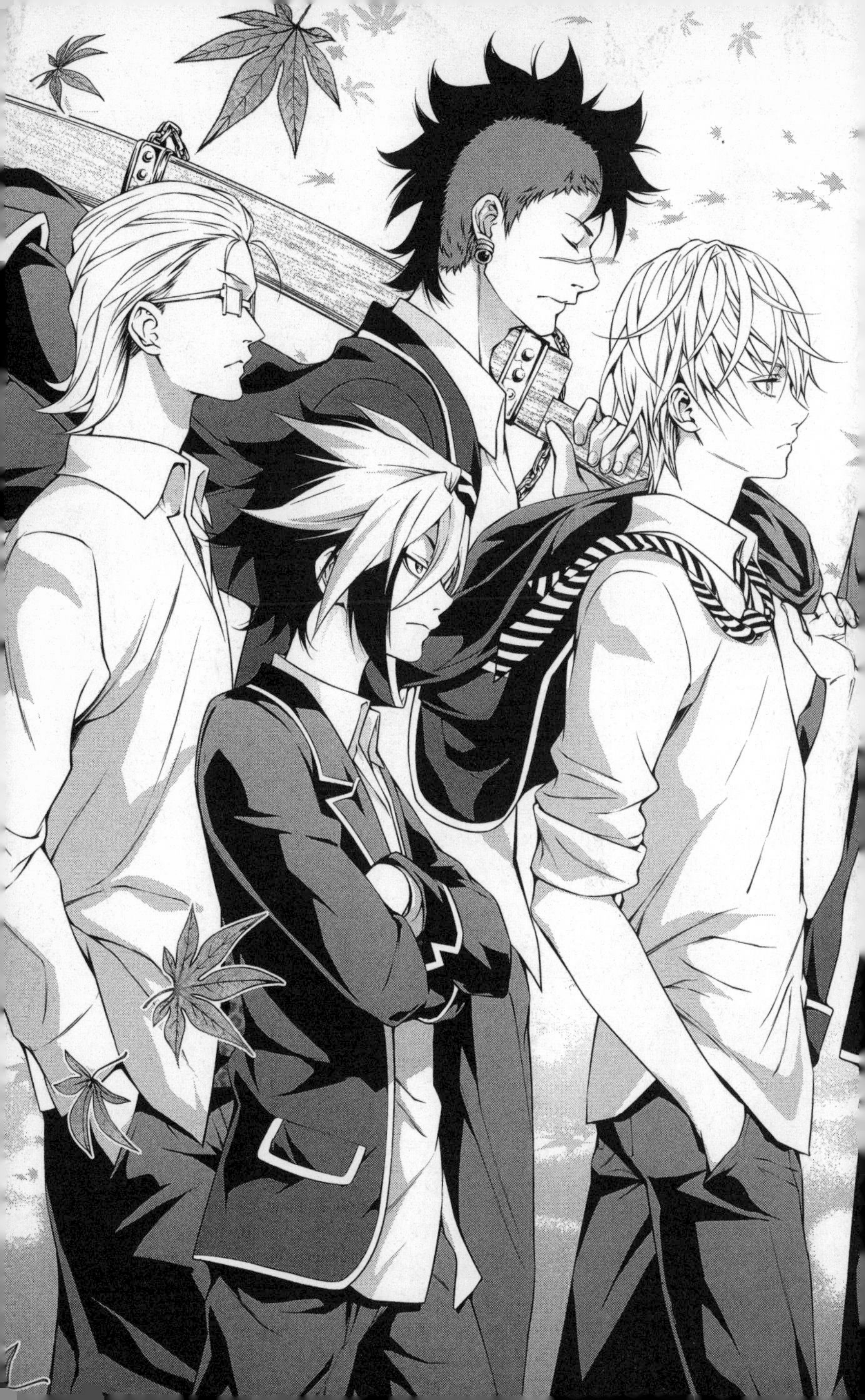

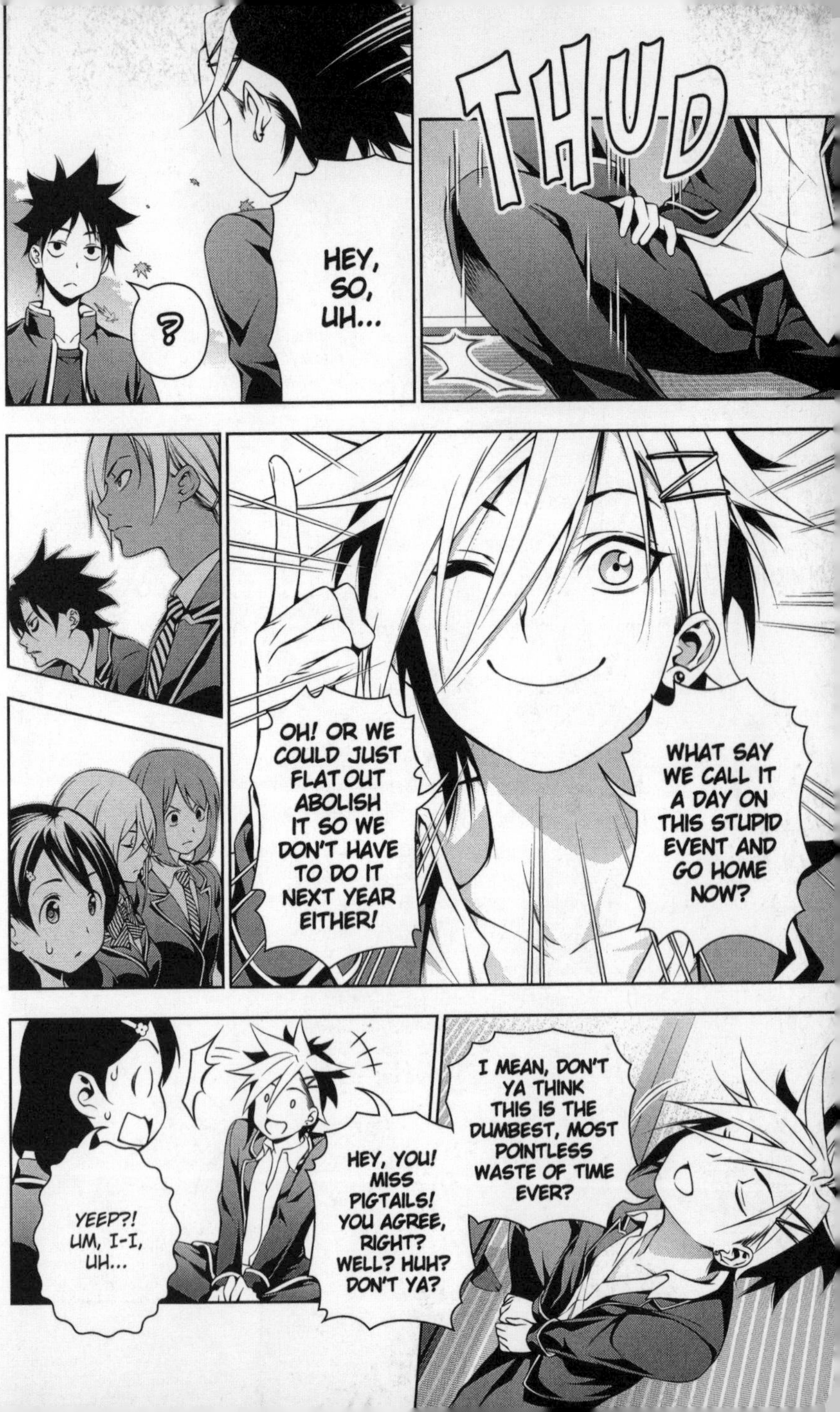
THUD
HEY, SO, UH...
?
WHAT SAY WE CALL IT A DAY ON THIS STUPID EVENT AND GO HOME NOW?
OH! OR WE COULD JUST FLAT OUT ABOLISH IT SO WE DON'T HAVE TO DO IT NEXT YEAR EITHER!
I MEAN, DON'T YA THINK THIS IS THE DUMBEST, MOST POINTLESS WASTE OF TIME EVER?
HEY, YOU! MISS PIGTAILS! YOU AGREE, RIGHT? WELL? HUH? DON'T YA?
YEEP?! UM, I-I, UH...

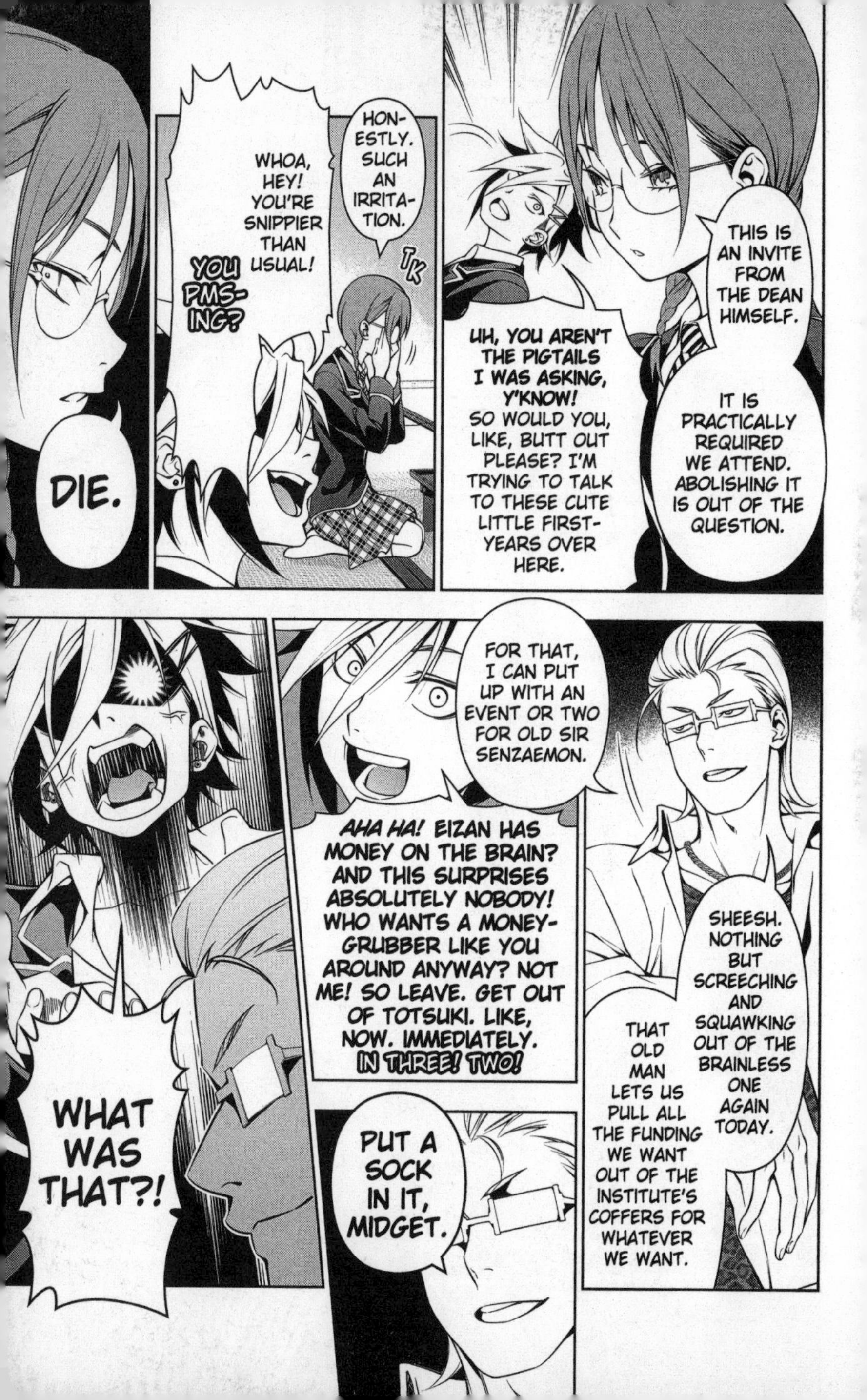
THIS IS AN INVITE FROM THE DEAN HIMSELF.
IT IS PRACTICALLY REQUIRED WE ATTEND. ABOLISHING IT IS OUT OF THE QUESTION.
UH, YOU AREN'T THE PIGTAILS I WAS ASKING, Y'KNOW! SO WOULD YOU, LIKE, BUTT OUT PLEASE? I'M TRYING TO TALK TO THESE CUTE LITTLE FIRST-YEARS OVER HERE.
HON-ESTLY. SUCH AN IRRITA-TION.
TK
WHOA, HEY! YOU'RE SNIPPIER THAN USUAL!
YOU PMS-ING?
DIE.
SHEESH. NOTHING BUT SCREECHING AND SQUAWKING OUT OF THE BRAINLESS ONE AGAIN TODAY.
THAT OLD MAN LETS US PULL ALL THE FUNDING WE WANT OUT OF THE INSTITUTE'S COFFERS FOR WHATEVER WE WANT.
FOR THAT, I CAN PUT UP WITH AN EVENT OR TWO FOR OLD SIR SENZAEMON.
AHA HA! EIZAN HAS MONEY ON THE BRAIN? AND THIS SURPRISES ABSOLUTELY NOBODY! WHO WANTS A MONEY-GRUBBER LIKE YOU AROUND ANYWAY? NOT ME! SO LEAVE. GET OUT OF TOTSUKI. LIKE, NOW. IMMEDIATELY. IN THREE! TWO!
PUT A SOCK IN IT, MIDGET.
WHAT WAS THAT?!

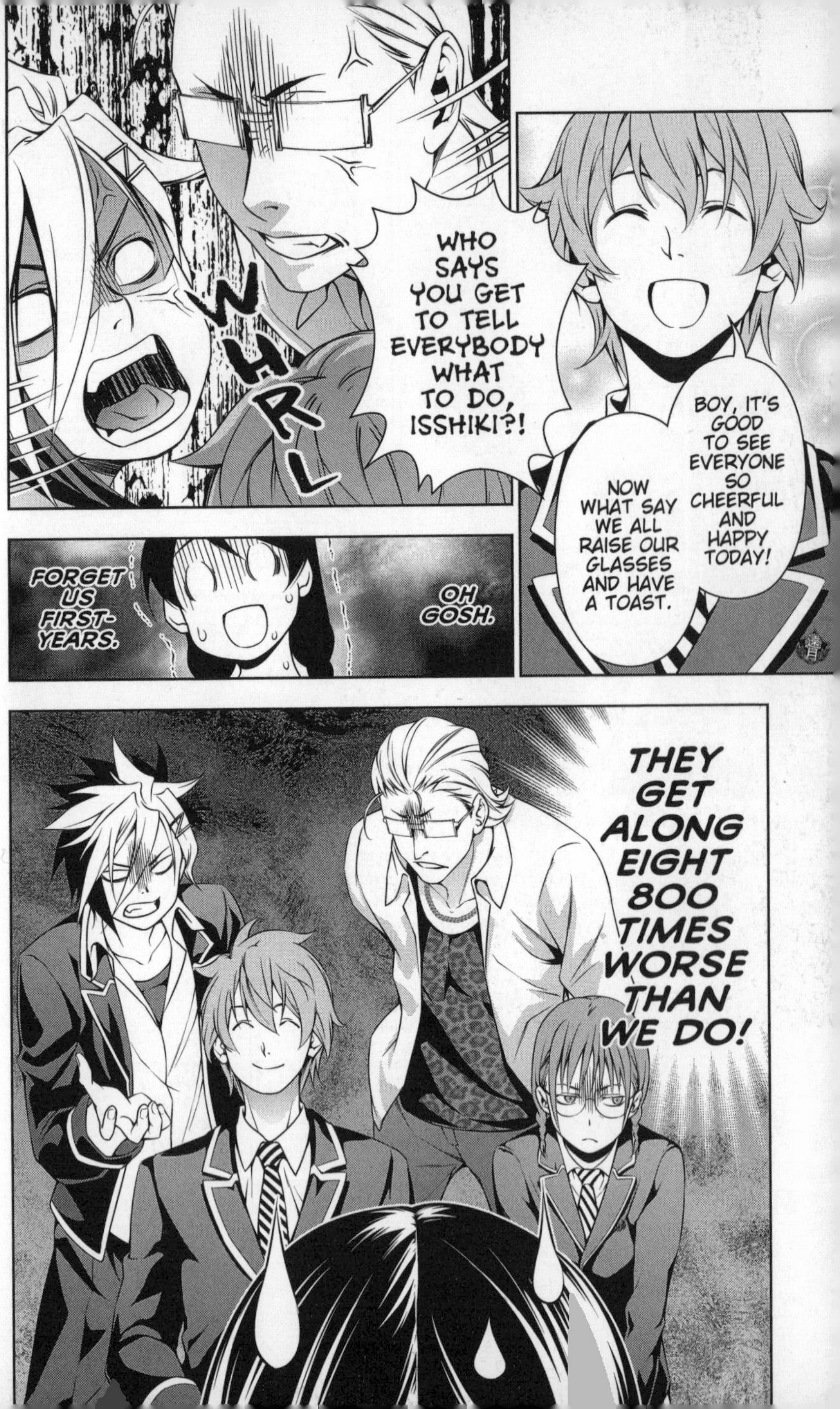
BOY, IT'S GOOD TO SEE EVERYONE SO CHEERFUL AND HAPPY TODAY!
NOW WHAT SAY WE ALL RAISE OUR GLASSES AND HAVE A TOAST.
WHO SAYS YOU GET TO TELL EVERYBODY WHAT TO DO, ISSHIKI?!
WHRL
OH GOSH.
FORGET US FIRST-YEARS.
THEY GET ALONG EIGHT 800 TIMES WORSE THAN WE DO!

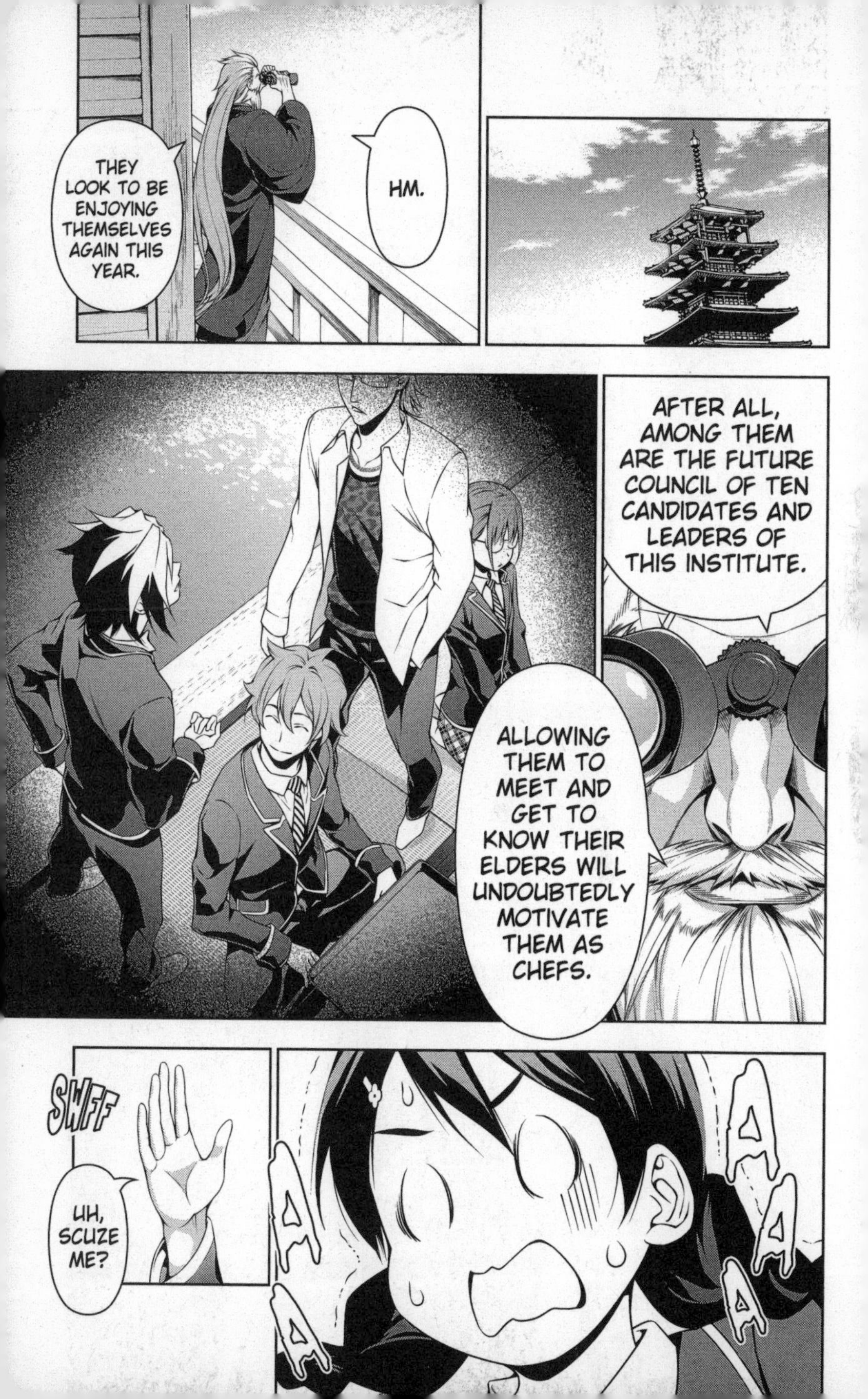
HM.
THEY LOOK TO BE ENJOYING THEMSELVES AGAIN THIS YEAR.
AFTER ALL, AMONG THEM ARE THE FUTURE COUNCIL OF TEN CANDIDATES AND LEADERS OF THIS INSTITUTE.
ALLOWING THEM TO MEET AND GET TO KNOW THEIR ELDERS WILL UNDOUBTEDLY MOTIVATE THEM AS CHEFS.
AAAAAA
SWFF
UH, SCUZE ME?

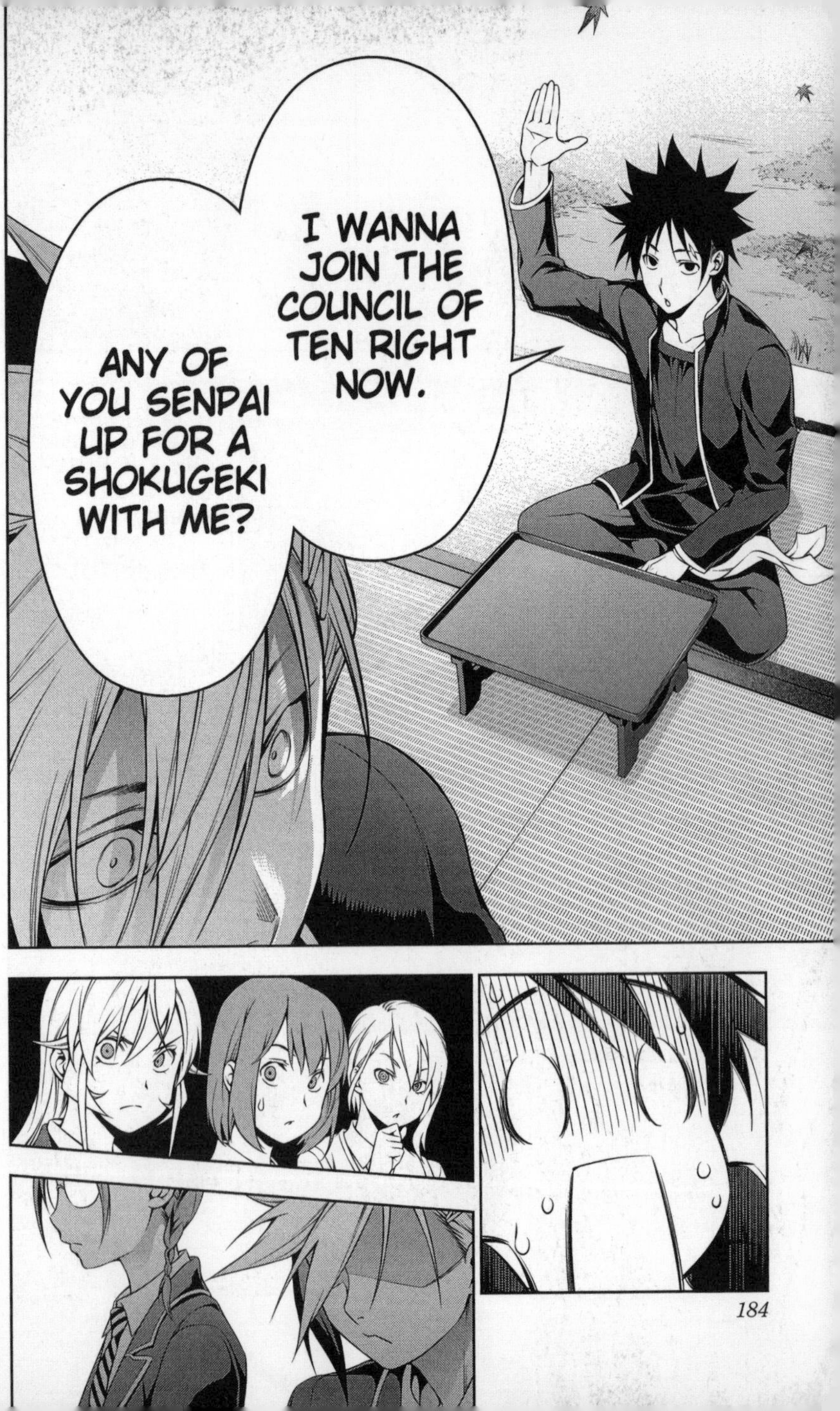
I WANNA JOIN THE COUNCIL OF TEN RIGHT NOW.
ANY OF YOU SENPAI UP FOR A SHOKUGEKI WITH ME?

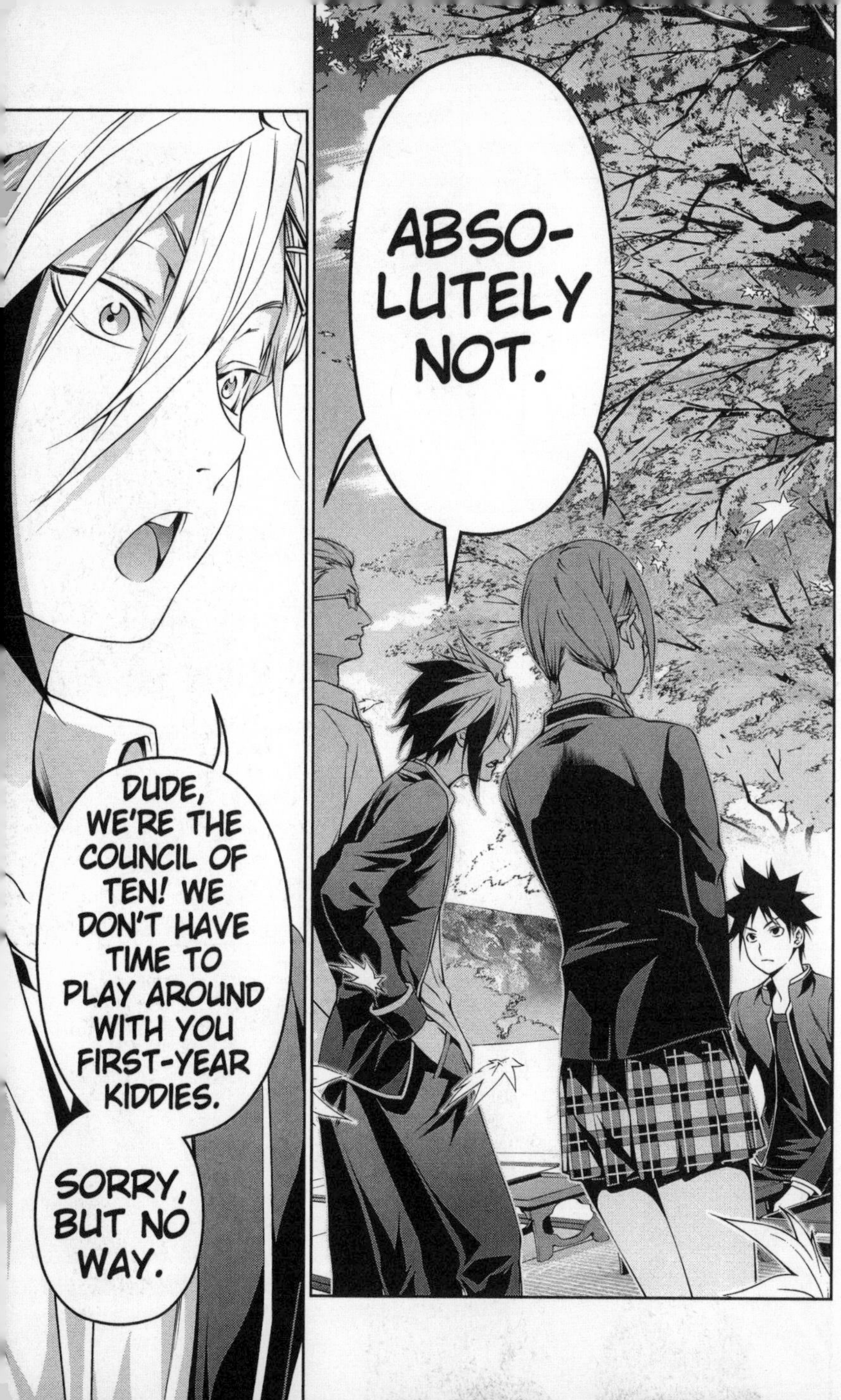
ABSO-LUTELY NOT.
DUDE, WE'RE THE COUNCIL OF TEN! WE DON'T HAVE TIME TO PLAY AROUND WITH YOU FIRST-YEAR KIDDIES.
SORRY, BUT NO WAY.

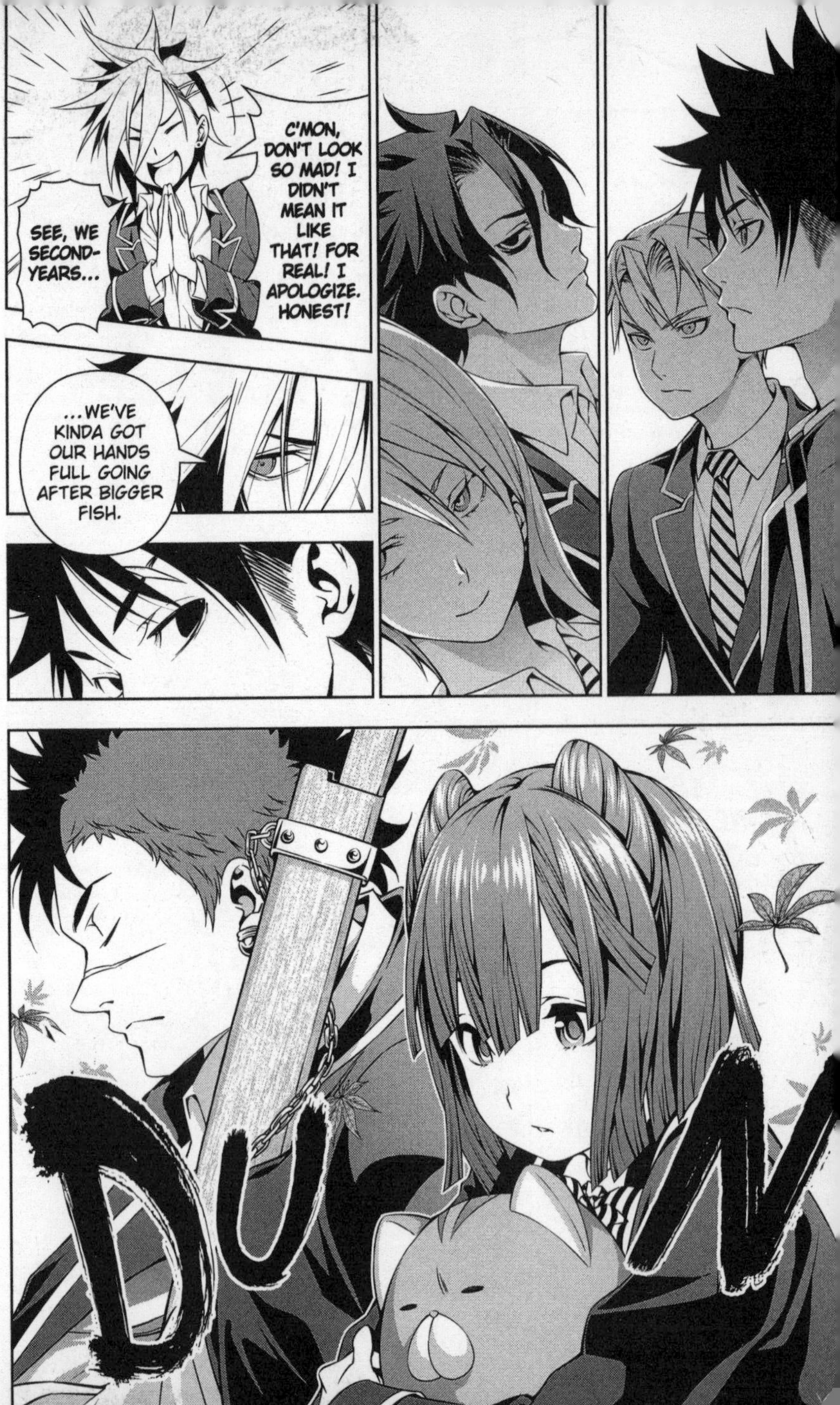
C'MON, DON'T LOOK SO MAD! I DIDN'T MEAN IT LIKE THAT! FOR REAL! I APOLOGIZE. HONEST!
SEE, WE SECOND-YEARS...
...WE'VE KINDA GOT OUR HANDS FULL GOING AFTER BIGGER FISH.
DUN

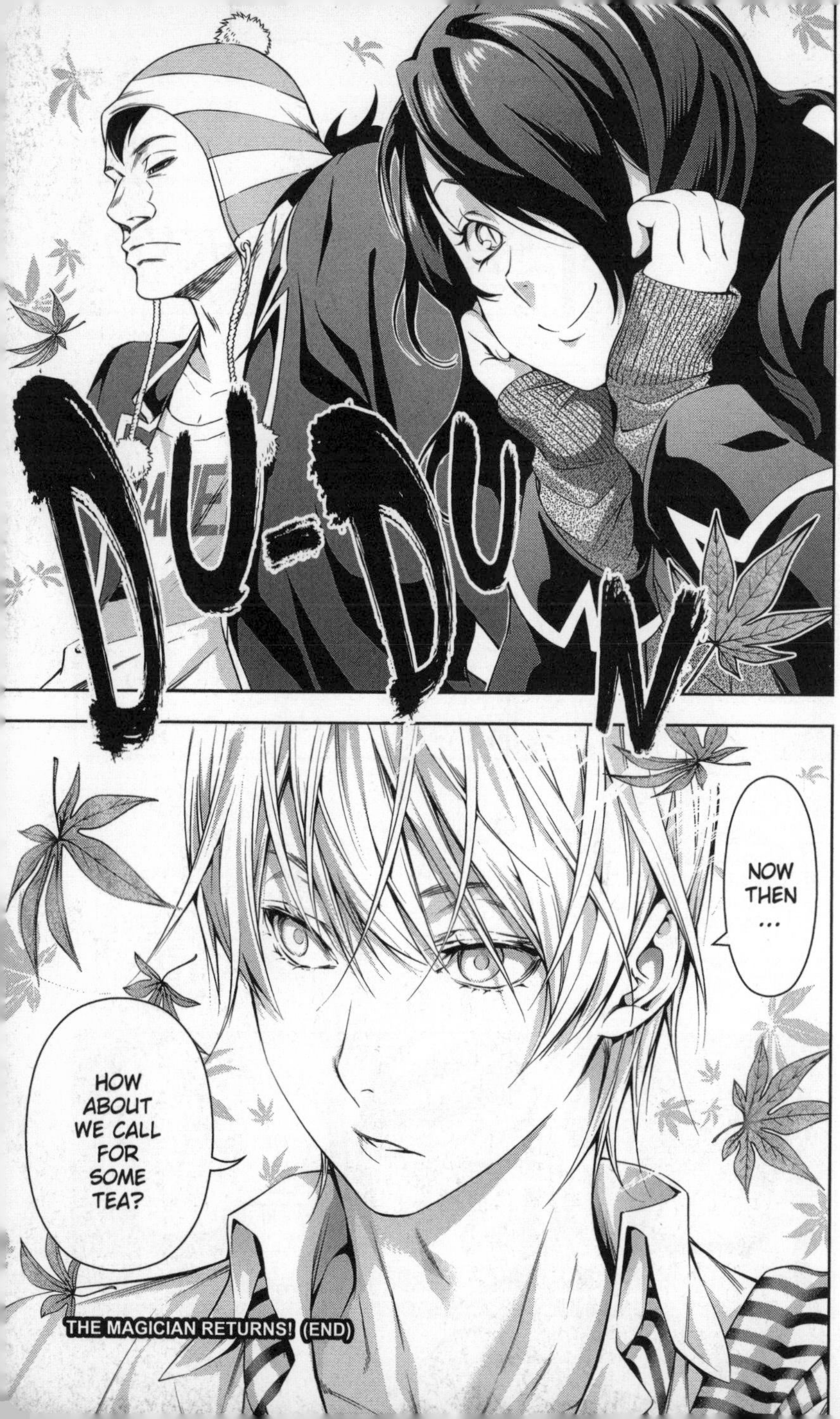
DU-DU-DUN
NOW THEN...
HOW ABOUT WE CALL FOR SOME TEA?
THE MAGICIAN RETURNS! (END)

# SHINO's TOKYO

STAGIAIRE CHALLENGE

BONUS COMIC

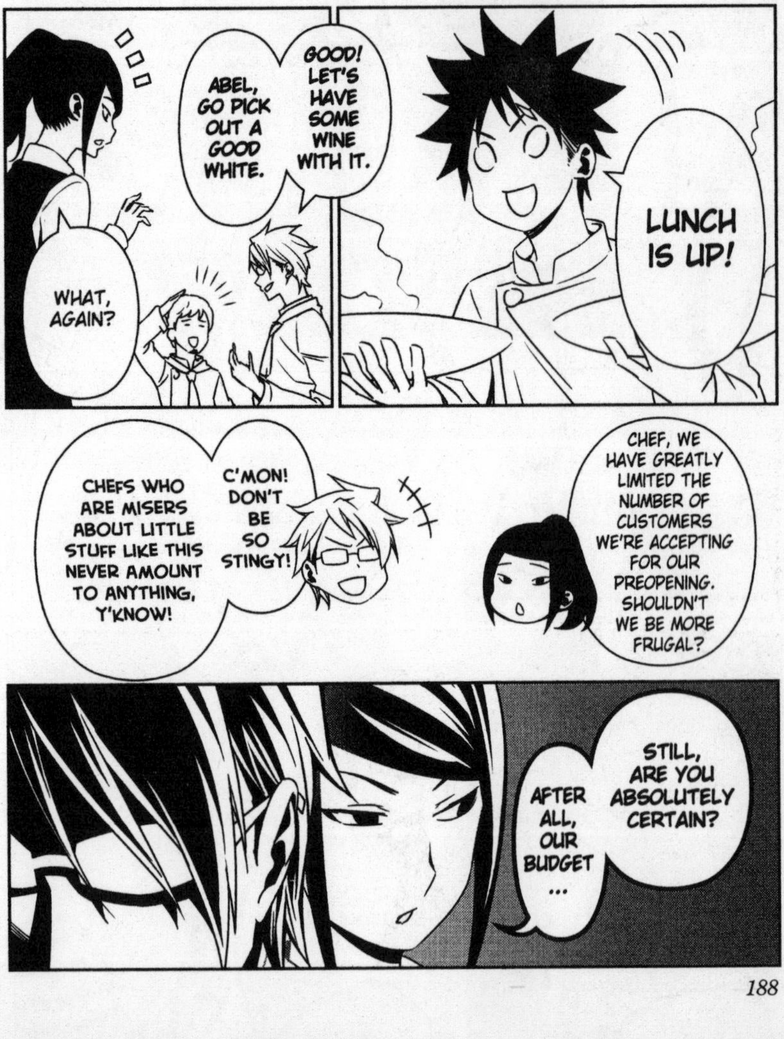
LUNCH IS UP!
GOOD! LET'S HAVE SOME WINE WITH IT.
ABEL, GO PICK OUT A GOOD WHITE.
WHAT, AGAIN?
CHEF, WE HAVE GREATLY LIMITED THE NUMBER OF CUSTOMERS WE'RE ACCEPTING FOR OUR PREOPENING. SHOULDN'T WE BE MORE FRUGAL?
C'MON! DON'T BE SO STINGY!
CHEFS WHO ARE MISERS ABOUT LITTLE STUFF LIKE THIS NEVER AMOUNT TO ANYTHING, Y'KNOW!
STILL, ARE YOU ABSOLUTELY CERTAIN?
AFTER ALL, OUR BUDGET ...

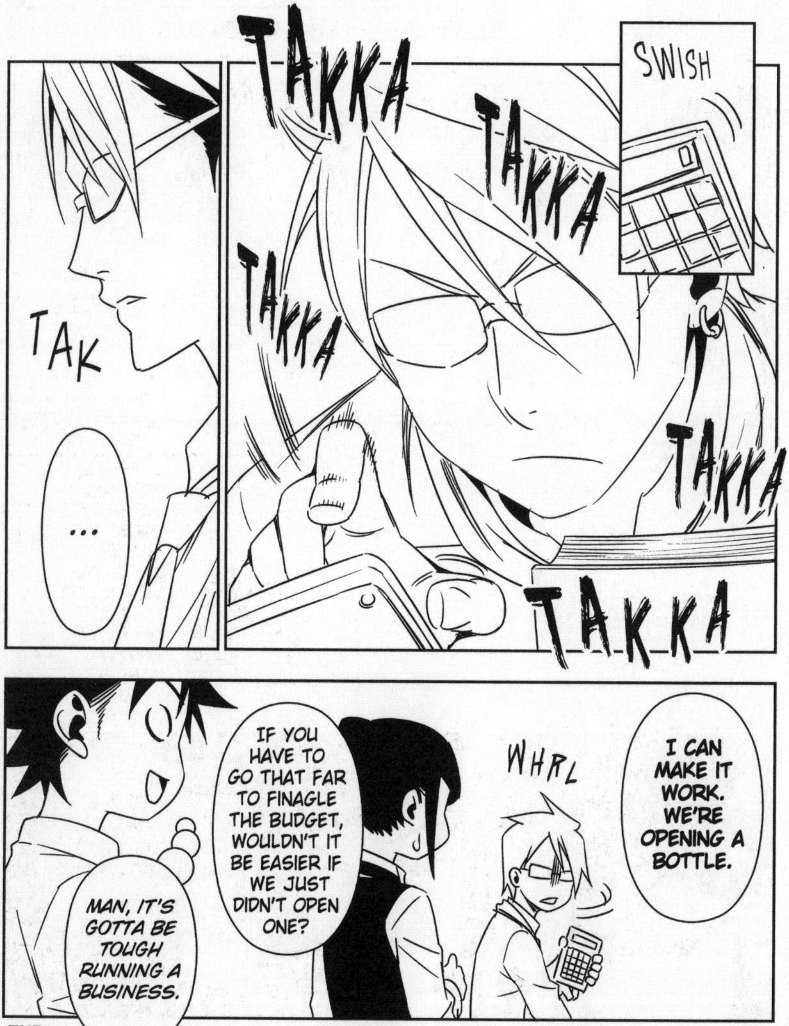
SWISH
TAKKA
TAKKA
TAKKA
TAKKA
TAKKA
TAK
...
I CAN MAKE IT WORK. WE'RE OPENING A BOTTLE.
WHRL
IF YOU HAVE TO GO THAT FAR TO FINAGLE THE BUDGET, WOULDN'T IT BE EASIER IF WE JUST DIDN'T OPEN ONE?
MAN, IT'S GOTTA BE TOUGH RUNNING A BUSINESS.

END